Heroines and Local Girls

Heroines and Local Girls

The Transnational Emergence of Women's Writing
in the Long Eighteenth Century

Pamela L. Cheek

PENN

UNIVERSITY OF PENNSYLVANIA PRESS

PHILADELPHIA

A volume in the Haney Foundation Series, established in 1961 with the generous support of Dr. John Louis Haney.

Published by
University of Pennsylvania Press
Philadelphia, Pennsylvania 19104-4112
www.upenn.edu/pennpress

Printed in the United States of America on acid-free paper
10 9 8 7 6 5 4 3 2 1

Library of Congress Cataloging-in-Publication Data

Names: Cheek, Pamela, author.
Title: Heroines and local girls: the transnational emergence of women's writing in the long eighteenth century / Pamela L. Cheek.
Other titles: Haney Foundation series.
Description: 1st edition. | Philadelphia: University of Pennsylvania Press, [2019] | Series: Haney Foundation series | Includes bibliographical references and index.
Identifiers: LCCN 2018055915| ISBN 9780812251487 (hardcover: alk. paper) | ISBN 0812251482 (hardcover: alk. paper)
Subjects: LCSH: European literature—Women authors—History and criticism. | European literature—18th century—History and criticism. | Women and literature—Europe—History—18th century. | Women—Identity—History—18th century. | Sex crimes in literature. | Sex role in literature.
Classification: LCC PN471 .C48 2019 | DDC 809/.89287—dc23
LC record available at https://lccn.loc.gov/2018055915

For Matthew Shields Ennis

Contents

Preface

Heroines and Local Girls asks a technical question, an affective question, and a historical question. Where does something that many readers identify as "women's writing" fit within world literature? What procedures do texts that count as women's writing follow to procure a sense of attachment among readers? And how did the placement of women's writing in the world literary field build on these procedures to produce a transnational concept of women's identity? The textual devices invented by women writers in the long eighteenth century fostered group affinity across borders of social rank and nation in ways that proved to be enduring and adaptive. Perhaps the most influential of these devices was the focus on the differences in perception between the powerless and the powerful and, commensurately, on the stakes of resisting a hegemonic forcing or overwriting of perception. The transnational category now known as women's writing arose from the possibility of capitalizing on a new supra-national market sector targeting women readers. It solidified with the invention of narrative means for affirming women's versions of women's stories, particularly in the depiction of differential perceptions of sexual violence and of the gender roles associated with European cultures.

Multiple waves of feminism have rightly pointed to the problems with thinking about women as a transnational and unified cadre. Such critiques identify how women's writing may obscure specific intersectional experiences connected to race, class, sexuality, culture, geography, and gender. Yet less investigation has been devoted to how and why the category of women's writing came to be so adept at surviving and multiplying. Why, despite its significant political limitations, has it been able to grow and to absorb different interests as well as to serve as an incubator for new sectors of writing that provide a space of attachment for new identities, including intersectional ones? What might be called an emergent phenomenon of

European women writing in the long eighteenth century provides some answers to this question.

In the following text, translations from French are my own unless otherwise noted. Translations from German, Dutch, and Spanish are drawn from secondary sources. Needless to say, any errors are my own.

Chapter 1

Networks of Women Writers Circa 1785

In 1787, Marie Elisabeth de La Fite (who wrote primarily in French) asked Frances Burney (who wrote primarily in English) for a lock of hair on behalf of Sophie von La Roche (who wrote primarily in German). Burney reported in her journal that she felt that "it would be a species of falsehood" to give someone of whom she thought "so little" a lock of her own hair. She pawned off some needlework instead (*Court Journals* 2:312).[1] The passage about Burney's performance of femininity among women bears comparison with Sophie von La Roche's description, printed in the women's magazine that she edited, of her own performance among men: "For as soon as anyone appears, out comes my needlework, which is as dear to me as my papers and books: especially since I have noticed that men of high birth and intellect show me more respect for the domestic industry of my needle than for the occupation of my quill; the only papers they accept seeing in my hands are the housekeeping accounts."[2] Both writers waved the international female flag of needlework among intellectual contacts, female and male. The gift of needlework allowed Burney to reassert normative female relations and to keep a professional relationship from veering into an intimacy that La Roche perhaps drew from a readerly attachment to Burney's heroines. Through a strategy that she shared in her magazine with women readers and aspiring writers, La Roche's use of needlework served as an alibi of proper industry to screen from view her professional investment in books and letters. That both Burney and La Roche recorded the uses to which they put needlework provides an indication of their savvy and self-awareness in navigating two intersecting worlds of writers and intellectuals: an international world of women writers bound by claims of affinity and the republic of letters more generally, underwritten by national competition for greatness.

At the time of La Roche's request of the lock, the widowed La Fite had recently immigrated to England from the Dutch Republic, where she had collaborated with her husband on a journal of arts and sciences. Burney, already a successful novelist, was cramped by her tedious service at court and was not yet Madame d'Arblay, the wife of a French general. A well-known novelist and *salonnière*, La Roche was writing travel accounts based on her peregrinations across northern Europe to supplement her large family's income. A stubborn historical image of early women writers shows them confined with their needlework at home in the country in which they were born. Yet La Fite, Burney, and La Roche were mobile. They were able to tap into local and international networks of women and of men. Like virtually all of the elite women writers discussed in this book, they registered sometimes as figures within national literary fields and sometimes as members of an international community of women.

Heroines and Local Girls is not an account of the evolution of feminist thought, an argument for a feminine difference, or a project to recover lost women writers. Instead, the book examines how a network of some fifty women writers working in French, English, Dutch, and German staked a transnational position in the European literary field around the capital of virtue. This capital placed affinity and authenticity in tension with aesthetics and authorship. *Heroines and Local Girls* explores how an eighteenth-century transnational network, rather than earlier groups of women writers, set the template for "women's writing" that continues to structure literary production today. It argues that transnationalism produced women's writing, which became a recognizable category in this period because of the mobility across borders of writers and texts. Emily Apter writes of translation alone that it "emerges as a form of creative property that belongs fully to no one. As a model of deowned literature, it stands against the swell of corporate privatization in the arts, with its awards given to individual genius and bias against collective authorship. A translational author—shorn of a singular signature—is the natural complement . . . to World Literature understood as an experiment in national sublation that signs itself as collective, terrestrial property" (15). The emergence of women's writing, through the circulation of transnational practices that hypostatized national gender roles and claimed an ethical value independent of national cultural rivalries, was the *historical* complement to the emergence of world literature, as Apter understands it. Where world literature would collect monumental works representative of distinctive cultural and national qualities and character, women's writing became recognizable as an entity through its set of claims about how exceptional women transcend the gendered destiny of distinctive cultural and national contexts.

National and Transnational Literary Histories

To encapsulate Sophie von La Roche's international request for a lock of Burney's hair, it is necessary to go beyond two older approaches to the place of women in literary networks and to build out a third. One older critical paradigm passes over such figures as Marie Elisabeth de La Fite to consider only "exceptional" women writers. This approach situates notable writers, Helen Fronius explains, as "published through the largesse and patronage of great men" and perhaps as "stifled in their creativity by the strict ideals and high standards of such great men" (234). It also recognizes the cultural practice of depicting exceptional women as muses, which lauded their intellectual and artistic talent by subordinating these to male genius. Born in Hamburg in 1737 to a well-placed family within a community of Huguenot refugees, La Fite made her entrance into the literary world when poet Friedrich Gottlieb Klopstock numbered her among his forty muses and graces. At the age of thirty-one, she married a man who was eighteen years her senior, Jean-Daniel de La Fite, who served as rector of the Walloon church in The Hague and preceptor to the children of Dutch stadtholder William V, prince of Orange (K. van Strien). La Fite began writing by collaborating with her husband and six others on the antideist *Bibliothèque des Sciences et des Beaux Arts* (1754–78).[3] During this period the connection with Pierre Gosse, the publisher of the *Bibliothèque* in the Hague, offered an outlet for La Fite's writing while a fellow contributor to the *Bibliothèque* provided help with her translations.[4] These relationships facilitated her entry into publishing as a translator and, ultimately, as an independent writer.

Sophie von La Roche benefited in publishing her first novel from a friendship that had evolved from the early romantic attachment of the writer Christoph-Martin Wieland. Indeed, readers like La Fite at first believed Wieland to be the author.[5] Later La Roche's literary salon connected her to Goethe, and this connection was strengthened across generations when Goethe extended patronage to La Roche's grandson, the writer Clemens

Brentano. Goethe paid tribute to La Roche, burying in indeterminate hyperbolic praise of her femininity the role her writing and her patronage had played in shaping his own early literary career: "She was the most wonderful woman; and I know no other to compare to her. Slenderly and delicately built, rather tall than short, she had, even to her advanced years, managed to preserve a certain elegance both of form and of conduct, which pleasantly fluctuated between the conduct of a noble lady and that of one of the citizen class" (13:488).

Samuel Johnson grouped together and deftly ranked the British women writers of his age, as Boswell reported: "I dined yesterday at Mrs. Garrick's with Mrs. Carter, Miss Hannah More and Miss Fanny Burney. Three such women are not to be found; I know not where I could find a fourth, except Mrs Lennox, who is superiour to them all" (4:275). Johnson inserted Frances Burney within the literary network of the second half of the eighteenth century on the side of the "ladies" in opposition to the "generation of Amazons of the pen": Aphra Behn, Delarivier Manley, and Eliza Haywood (Todd 125). Burney framed her own position as one of dependence on the professional and personal relationships originally established by her father, the musicologist Dr. Charles Burney, with writers, performers, and patrons, especially Samuel Johnson. Nineteenth- and early twentieth-century literary history did not dissent from her self-appraisal. She squared her public prominence and her interest in professionalized publishing with the ideal of retiring femininity through her self-fashioning as a woman author indebted to men. Thus, as Catherine Gallagher has pointed out, Burney herself contributed to an impression that men were the primary facilitators of women's access to publication, and, by doing so, she created a portrait of herself as one of the rare few to whom favor was granted (203, 228).

In literary histories, a focus on the exceptionalism of a woman who writes and is acknowledged by the male gatekeepers to publishing and literary recognition can reflect a preoccupation with male writers as centers of power and patronage. Or it can register awareness of women writers' presentation of themselves as the chosen few.[6] The exceptionalism in elite women writers' self-fashioning contributed to the position of women's writing in the literary field. Simply put, the argument that a woman in a country has overcome the obstacles that have kept local "girls" silent presents a guarantee of the value of her writing as an achievement in and of itself. Her exceptional achievement is comparable only to the singular achievement of another woman who is the exception to her country's rule.

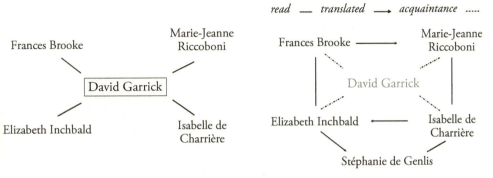

Figure 1. Connections between David Garrick and four women writers.

Different patterns emerge from foregrounding different literary networks imbricating women writers. The London actor, playwright, and theater manager David Garrick—whose wife had hosted the dinner Johnson enjoyed with the celebrity women writers of the age—appears as a prominent cultural power broker for women writers in the British literary field if he is situated as the center, or node, of a set of relations. Garrick enjoyed a correspondence with Marie-Jeanne Riccoboni and gave her advice. He disliked interactions with Frances Brooke in the London theater scene. He briefly met Belle de Zuylen, who was known after her marriage as Isabelle de Charrière, during her visit to London. And he sustained an ongoing connection with Elizabeth Inchbald over performances and publishing projects related to the theater.

With Garrick in the foreground of a network, he appears as a famous mutual acquaintance linking otherwise disconnected women writers from different countries and mediating some of their publishing ventures in Britain. With Garrick in the background, women writers' independent investment in each others' work becomes manifest through their translation relationships. Garrick actively interfered with the connection between Brooke and Riccoboni because of his professional dislike of the former. Brooke had translated Riccoboni's *Lady Juliet Catesby* into English in 1760. Although Riccoboni felt that this translation was superior to any other translations of her work, Garrick insisted that Riccoboni rebuff Brooke (Schellenberg 50). Even so, Brooke went on to translate another novel by Riccoboni without her sanction and acknowledged her as a powerful influence on the formation of her own novelistic style. Moreover, Riccoboni evinced a decided anglophilia in her exploration of protagonists' gender roles, while Brooke played with the attractions of French versions of femininity. For each novelist, translation and narrative impersonation of a foreign voice was understood, as Andrew Piper has described the phenomenon for German women translators more generally, "not as a force for homogenization, but instead as a way of identifying cultural differences" (121).

Viewed via the optic of Garrick's centrality to the life of the theater in mid- to late eighteenth-century England, Elizabeth Inchbald and her work appear strikingly British. Isabelle de Charrière published a translation of Inchbald's novel *Nature and Art* (1796) the year after it appeared, choosing this fairly radical work by a woman over other possibilities as means of encouraging her cotranslator and mentee, the Swiss Isabelle de Gélieu, to develop both her English and her writing style.[7] Inchbald's successful play *The Child of Nature* (1788) was an adaptation of Stéphanie de Genlis's *Zélie, ou l'ingénue* (1781), a response to Molière's comedies about women and an exploration of what happens when a man tries to create the perfect woman by controlling what she reads. The awareness of these translation relationships refocuses attention on the international affinities radiating around Inchbald and her work. It reminds us that she spent three months in France early in her career (Jenkins 27). And it directs attention to how, just as Riccoboni translated and anthologized British theater for the French (with advice from Garrick on what texts to select),[8] Inchbald translated and anthologized continental plays for English readers. Luise Gottsched played a parallel role in translating and anthologizing British and French plays and contributing original German work as she collaborated with her husband to define a German theater and on a broader project of cultural transfer into German.[9] As translators and anthologizers, and as original writers, each of these women defined gendered cultural types in genres that exaggerated language and character—comedy and reported conversation in the novel. This mobile experimentation in framing gender norms within foreign languages and cultures is at work, for example, in Charrière's attempt at an original novel in English. "Letter the First," scribbled by "Emily Fontaine to Harriet Denizet" begins breathlessly: "At last I have heard of my Harriet! God be praised my dear! I know you are well tho' you happened to be at Geneva in one of its worst moments. You health has not sufferd in the least from the fright, witness your complexion as bloomy as bright as ever [*sic*]" (*Œuvres* 8:487).

*   *   *

To foreground the male nodes of literary networks, such as Garrick, is to feature male arbitration of literary recognition as the prime agent in national print cultures. Riccoboni, Brooke, Inchbald, and Charrière operated with an awareness that Garrick was a formidable contact and celebrity within the British literary field and the world of the theater. They all knew Garrick, but they did not know each other's works because of Garrick. Shifting focus enables apprehension of the alternative edges, or links, in networks. In the Riccoboni–Brooke-Inchbald-Charrière cluster, the edges are acts of translation: as a form of entry into writing and into a profession, as a means of exploring gendered experiences in another culture, and as a mode of denoting belonging to an international elite of women writers. These writers participated at once in national literary marketplaces and in a transnational republic of letters. Their relationships across languages, irrespective of Garrick's influence, resulted from a pragmatic engagement in a competitive literary world.

Critics following a second approach to eighteenth-century relationships have shown that women writers benefited from the opportunities opened up by previous generations of women working within a single linguistic or national literary tradition. Betty Schellenberg describes the professional space in Britain from which Frances Burney profited in the late 1770s and onward as comprising

> a complex network, whereby sourcebooks are exchanged, subscriptions promoted, and publishing opportunities watched for, in a spirit of facilitation that was fostered, rather than doled out toward subordinates, by Johnson and Richardson with their valuable trade connections. Similarly, we hesitate to imagine a Sarah Fielding or a Charlotte Lennox or a Frances Sheridan at the center rather than on the margins, as the sought-after literary figure rather than at the periphery of someone else's circle, but in fact, we have contemporary descriptions of each of these three authors using precisely such images. Alicia Lefanu . . . describes both Sheridan and her colleague Sarah Fielding as having been sought-after literary personalities, attracting to themselves not only women writers but also Richardson, Johnson, Ralph Allen, Edward Young, and the like. (11)

Focusing equally on filiations within a single linguistic tradition, Joan Hinde Stewart points out that women writers who wrote in French, including those who lived in France and in the Swiss cantons, were reading and commenting on each other as well as on those who had recently pre-deceased them: Genlis critiqued the manuscript of *Caroline de Lichtfield* for her correspondent Montolieu . . . , admired Le Prince de Beaumont, and, of course, pored painfully over certain novels by Riccoboni and Cottin; Montolieu's friend . . . supplied her with the complete works of Riccoboni; Souza intensely disliked Genlis whom she accused of lies and ingratitude; Cottin alludes . . . to Riccoboni's *Juliette Catesby* and waxes lyrical . . . over Charrière's *Caliste*; Charrière proposed marketing *Trois femmes* the way Souza had promoted *Adèle de Sénange*, while Charrière's protagonists read works by Le Prince de Beaumont, Souza and Genlis. (200)

Stewart suggests, for example, that in 1782, when Stéphanie de Genlis's *Histoire de la duchesse de C****, first appeared as part of *Adèle et Théodore*, all of the novelists she mentions were alive, and, given the stir caused by the work's publication, all of them would have read it within a short time (200).

Equally restricting scope to a single literary language and tradition, Ruth Dawson traces German networking in *The Contested Quill: Literature by Women in Germany, 1770–1800*. Her account of professional influence and shared reading emphasizes the generative quality of the women's monthly *Pomona für Teutschlands Töchter*, which La Roche published in 1783–84:

La Roche from the start structured her journal as a polyvocal place for exchanging ideas not just for women but also by women, and thus, from the start of her work on *Pomona*, she set up the conditions for the emergence of a literary group. She worked to give her readers at least the minimum skills to undertake to write, commented on issues—including literary issues—familiar to them, published contributions virtually exclusively by women, stressed the accomplishments of women, discussed her own experience as a writer, and invited her readers' comments and questions. *Pomona* gave potentially all its readers incentive, latitude, and a place to improve their learning and to practice writing. (134–35)

La Roche served as a node of German women's literary influence by publishing the work of Karoline von Günderrode, Caroline von Wolzogen, Philippine Gatterer Engelhard, Sophie Albrecht, Luise von Göchhausen, and Wilhelmine von Gersdorf and by editing the autobiography of Friderica Baldinger (Paulson 276). In showing that La Roche's journal provided literary access, Dawson, like Schellenberg and Stewart, presents a generation of women writers as opening up a space for subsequent ones by integrating them within professional relationships and practices in a single linguistic or national tradition. Complementing this approach, *Heroines and Local Girls* argues that by the 1780s women readers and writers in local contexts understood themselves in relation to a transnational community rather than entirely in relation to a field circumscribed by domestic literary markets, languages, and practices. Indeed, *Pomona*, graced with the subtitle "for Germany's daughters," devoted space to women writers in France, England, Italy, and Germany, connecting readers of the periodical to women readers and writers at home and abroad (Griffiths 142–43).

La Fite's negotiations over the lock of hair depended on her awareness and leverage of an international network. For Frances Burney, well established as a novelist by the public reception of her first two novels, the request by "Poor Mc La Fite" for a lock of hair offered the opportunity for satire in her journal: "Then she begged *anything, a bit of paper I had twisted, a morsel of an old Gown, the impression of a seal from a Letter,—Two pins out of my Dress,* in short, any thing; & with an urgency so vehement I could not laugh it off" (*Court Journals* 2:312). Yet for La Fite, who had greased the wheel by praising Burney for her "fame, youth, and modesty" in her book *Eugénie et ses élèves*,[10] transmission of Burney's needlework had the potential to further anchor her relationship with Sophie von La Roche, following La Fite's publication of a French translation of La Roche's first novel in the Dutch Republic. La Roche would, indeed, subsequently introduce a German translation of one of La Fite's works in 1791 and sanction La Fite's French translation of *Miss Lony* in 1792. It is hard to imagine that La Fite's earlier introduction of Stéphanie de Genlis to Frances Burney in 1785 had nothing to do with Genlis's eventual help in getting La Fite's *Eugénie* into print in 1787 with Genlis's Parisian publisher. That edition opened with a preface written by Genlis herself who fussed self-deprecatingly about La Fite's citation in the text of a flattering English review of Genlis's work: "It will prove at least that a woman Author can praise another with pleasure," Genlis wrote of La Fite's leveraging of the review, "and this example is infinitely more common than is imagined. It even seems to me that no rivalry exists between women who write, and that they all receive the testimony of trust and friendship from each other, or at least benevolence and esteem."[11] Subsequently, La Fite introduced and translated into French Hannah More's *Thoughts on the Importance of Manners in the Great* (*Pensées sur les mœurs des grands*, 1790). In her preface, she

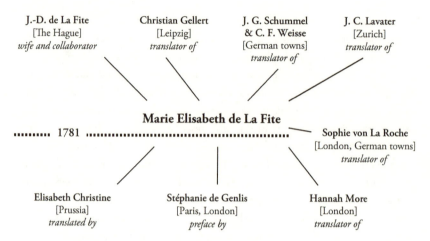

Figure 2. Marie Elisabeth de La Fite's network—with 1781 marking beginning of widowhood and employment by Queen Charlotte.

shrewdly inserted herself into the circle of the bluestockings before the public eye as she recalled being a "witness last year" to high praise of More's essay in the company of Elizabeth Montagu and Elizabeth Carter (vi). La Fite herself was the target of More's own vigorous use of praise for networking. "Pray say something handsome of me to Madame de la Fite," More wrote to her friend Mary Hamilton, author of *Munster Village*, "I can truly say I am always pleased with what she does, . . . I admire Mme de la Fite and hope to cultivate her friendship. . . . Her *Entretiens* I have bought many sets of, and recommend to young people, for whom I think they are well calculated and judicious."[12] Although Burney pointedly termed her fellow member of Queen Charlotte's household a *Sventurata* (*Court Journals* 2:27), or a hapless wretch, with a mixture of pity and annoyance at La Fite's frequent attempts to seek her out, La Fite's networking borders on the heroic. La Fite managed to have her name appear in print alongside those of three of the most notable women writers in three different languages: Stéphanie de Genlis, Sophie von La Roche, and, with Frances Burney continuing to elude her, Hannah More.

Scholars have long noted such specific international connections or influences among women writers across borders and literary languages, sometimes attributing these to a special receptivity based in gender. One of the most prominent researchers to organize systematic collection of data about links, Suzan van Dijk described the quest for a "lecture féminine" in a study of Isabelle de Charrière's readers: "It will perhaps be possible to verify whether women can in effect be considered as more open to a message coming from another woman—and, more generally, how they read and received their reading" ("Lecture" 89–90).[13] Isabelle Brouard-Arends proposes in *Lectrices d'ancien régime* that "women's books have often first been written for other women in an affective complicity and in a pooling of private concerns" (10). Without pretending to explore innate affinities among women readers and writers living two centuries ago, it is nonetheless possible to investigate the cultural practices that encouraged women to see, or allow themselves to see, the writing of other women as having special authority for them, as speaking to them. How did women's writing come into being as a category and acquire a literary value as such? How did this supranational category form in a period of transition toward the nationalization of literary markets and of literature? It seems important to question the appealing notion that women's writing was simply waiting in the wings fully formed for the historical period when women at last acquired the freedom, literacy, and time to write. Questioning is the more urgent since this brand of feminist common sense has the potential to blind readers to the ways that new global candidates for the status of "woman writer" must enter the literary field of European and North American readers and literary arbiters by subscribing to criteria developed when women's writing emerged in the European eighteenth century.

Numerous literary historians have identified important groups or circles of women writers and intellectuals working within and across languages and nations. In *The Republic of Women: Rethinking the Republic of Letters in the Seventeenth Century*, Carol Pal explored the small network of women intellectuals that coalesced through correspondence with Anna Maria van Schurman. In the essay collection *Early Modern Women and Transnational Communities of Letters*, edited by Julie D. Campbell and Anne R. Larsen, contributors took up Kate Chedgzoy's challenge to attend to "the full complexities of the locations" that early modern women's writing comes from, as well as "why that locatedness matters" (893). As Diana Robin notes in the foreword to the volume, these essays on sixteenth- and seventeenth-century relationships "argue for nothing short of a new formulation of the intellectual history of women: a history focused not on one national culture but on the connections among women and men across the Continent and Britain" (xvii). Scholarship on the late eighteenth and early nineteenth centuries points to "the growing internationalism of writing and authorial identity during this same period and the important role that women played in this process" (121), as Andrew

Piper argues in his work on German women translators. Many scholars of translation agree with Piper that textual evidence is indicative of a "larger project by women writers to establish their own international republic of letters" (133). *Translators, Interpreters, Mediators: Women Writers 1700–1900*, edited by Gillian Dow, identifies, through Dow's introduction and contributor's essays, many of the major themes to be explored in examining relations among women writers, including women's "refusal to be confined within national boundaries when it comes to their own creativity" (20). In prefatory remarks to the essay collection *Women Writing Back/Writing Women Back: Transnational Perspectives from the Late Middle Ages to the Dawn of the Modern Era*, Anke Gilleir and Alicia C. Montoya move "Toward a New Conception of Women's Literary History." "It was through international contacts," they write, "by creating new female networks, that early modern women authors . . . created something we would call today 'women's writing'—by definition not bound by any national or geographic limitation" (18). Margaret Cohen and Susan Dever argue in an introduction to the essay collection *The Literary Channel: The Inter-National Invention of the Novel* that "in the process of searching for organizing cultural paradigms beyond the novel-nation homology, feminist literary historians observed the implication of patriarchy and fatherland and found in narratives and subgenres pioneered and consumed by women readers (notably the Gothic, historical romance, and sentimental fiction) imagined communities and literary codes that worked across the enclosing boundaries of the nation" (9). All of these essay collections provide crucial scholarship that sketches relationships among women writers across languages and national boundaries as well as the cultural constraints that shaped these relationships. The working group Women Writers in History is making available digital tools and resources related to the study of women authors and their "dialogue" with one another.[14] This working group was preceded by the NEWW Women Writers project and joins other databases of women writers, including Sophie: A Digital Library of Works by German-Speaking Women, Orlando: Women's Writing in the British Isles from the Beginnings to the Present, The Women Writers Project at Northeastern University, and SIEFAR: Société internationale pour l'étude des femmes de l'ancien régime. (In Chapter 2, I trace the deep history to the biographical and anthologizing drive behind databases that collect information about women writers.) The approach in essay collections, anthologies, and digital projects is generally to identify pairs or small clusters of women and to explain the terms of their relationships. These ambitious research programs and collaborations are laying the groundwork for understanding the emergence, mechanisms, and costs of the transnationalism of women's writing. In their introduction to the essay collection *Women's Writing, 1660–1830,* Jennie Batchelor and Gillian Dow go further. They urge scholars to remember "that the future of women's literary history must depend not only upon a sustained and critical interrogation of the imperatives that drove its historic obfuscation, but also upon those that have structured the logic of its recent resurgence" (Batchelor and Dow, 15–16). This book takes that enjoinder seriously. In support of a broad account of how women's writing became a recognizable and enduring international category, I offer an initial synthesis that describes the emergence of set codes from forces related to history, habitus, market, community, and the world of letters.

Developing a broad account is risky for all the usual reasons attending projects of comparative literature: linguistic barriers; the inability to cover in depth or in breadth the scholarship and primary texts in multiple national literary areas; genre bias favoring the novel over poetry or journalism; the likelihood of making a major error of omission and interpretation; and the inevitability of a scholar's "home" literary field exerting a centrifugal force on any reading resulting in a reassertion, as a recent call for participation in a Spanish working group warned, of problematic "approaches based either on the 'national context' or the centre-periphery dichotomy" (Bolufer, *Expression*). To incurring these risks, I plead guilty. I hope, however, that even my blunders, particularly with respect to the Dutch and German literary traditions where I have had to rely most heavily on secondary literature, may lead to greater understanding of why women's writing in the eighteenth century bears the marks of an emergent phenomenon. In particular, the poor fit between scholarship identifying early modern links among women and accounts of world literature begs an explanation of how the category of women's writing developed in relation to the formation of an autonomous literary field.

To try my hand at this entails identifying relationships among writers and their texts across borders rather than meditating on the important differences in their feminism and politics. In Chapter 5, for example, at the significant expense of a discussion of comparative political reactions to the Terror, I emphasize the similarities in the ways that Burney and Germaine de Staël navigate the problem of women's deterritorialization through formal experimentation. Each chapter in this book revisits influential arguments by theorists and feminist literary historians. Each also sketches and links into the whole a different sector of the network of European women writers. And each explores the eighteenth-century consolidation of a modern trope—the city of women, herstory and writing back, coming to writing, in a different voice, and women's writing as resistance. By weaving stories of the lives of women writers and the relationships among them into and across the chapters, I have tried to heighten readability while reinforcing awareness that reception (including feminist literary history) of women's fiction is historically bound to interest in women writers' lives—and for cause. Taken as a whole, *Heroines and Local Girls* provides a historicist explanation for the particular angle at which women's writing intersects with world literature.

Chapter 2, "Two Quarrels," moves the start of the timeline for the textual incorporation of feminine virtue through moral reasoning back to the late seventeenth century, earlier than the mid-eighteenth-century gender and sensibility shift associated with the rise of a composite elite. Responding to Joan Kelly's "Early Feminist Theory and the 'Querelle des femmes,' 1400–1789," the chapter sets up two debates at the gateway to modernity as intersecting axes: the battle of the Ancients and Moderns and the quarrel of women. In early modern contestation around national literary greatness in battles of Ancients and Moderns, authors were implicated in a linear intellectual structure in which modern national achievements purportedly derived from or could be compared to the greatness of the past. The signal genre of the quarrel of women, catalogs of exceptional women, represented women as belonging to the timeless transnational space of the conversational circle outside of nation and history: a city of women. Surveying the network of Italian women Renaissance poets, the humanist network around Anna Maria van Schurman, and connection among early modern English women poets, I argue that Madeleine de Scudéry and her extended network, including Marie-Madeleine Pioche de la Vergne, comtesse de La Fayette, and Marie-Catherine Le Jumel de Barneville, baronesse d'Aulnoy, novelized the form of the catalog of women.[15] Reinforcing the structure of the catalog, they embedded an ever-expanding compendium of stories of women into framing conversations focused on the evaluation of lives. Unlike women's poetry and scholarship, these "romances" of women's and girls' lives could easily be translated, annexed, excerpted, appended, and marketed within the early modern print environment. Indeed, Aphra Behn and Delarivier Manley successfully introduced plebeian women with extraordinary lives, sometimes presented autobiographically, into the continental form. Ease of translation favored dissemination of stories of exemplary women across national borders rather than women's poetry or scholarship. The textual embedding of stories of women within conversations among women, in texts as varied as La Fayette's *La princesse de Clèves* and Manley's *The New Atalantis*, for example, communicated that women's interpretation of lives among themselves differed significantly from public histories.

Responding to arguments by Frances Ferguson and Joan DeJean on the rise of the novel, Chapter 3, "Ravishing and Romance Language," examines two novels published by women in 1752 seeking means of addressing sexual harassment and assault in the wake of Samuel Richardson's *Clarissa*: Charlotte Lennox's *The Female Quixote* and the revised edition of Françoise de Graffigny's *Lettres d'une Péruvienne*. These widely read and translated novels melancholically situate as lost the imaginary Scudérian world in which women's own stories of ravishing are believed. The novels highlight the rift between, on the one hand, belief in a woman's story based on a sense of affinity among the powerless and, on the other, what we might now call gaslighting—forcing a woman to believe a narrative supplied by the powerful through control of available evidence. Translations and rewritings of these novels suggest that for women readers and writers, a literary language other than their own, French, served as the screen onto which to project a nostalgic fantasy of female authority over the interpretation of personal experience and feeling. Moreover, Lennox and Graffigny introduced a lasting theme that demanded formal innovation in the novel: the contest between a woman's internal wishes (and her description of it) and external attempts to shape and force her consent (and worldly accounts of her desires).

Chapter 4, "The Repertoire of the School for Girls," looks at continuities between pedagogical texts and novels across Britain and Western Europe, literary repetition in a chain of over a dozen women writers, from Madame de Maintenon to Mary Wollstonecraft, and concrete practices of networking. Revisiting issues raised by Nancy Armstrong's study of the British novel and of conduct manuals in *Desire and Domestic Fiction*, the chapter contrasts the group conversations among girls in pedagogical texts by and for girls and women, with the one-on-one generational mentor-to-pupil structure of pedagogical texts for boys, most famously Rousseau's *Emile, or on Education* (*Émile, ou de l'éducation*, 1762). Representations of and by educated women emphasized collective female group identity and collective moral reasoning on women's lives rather than the generational passing of the torch of genius from man to man. This informed how women writers entered into print and established literary relationships in the second half of the eighteenth century. For women writers, as theorist Étienne Wenger proposes of "communities of practice" more generally, repertoire provided "the styles by which they express[ed] their forms of membership and their identities as members" (*Communities* 83). Rather than denoting a lack of creativity, repetition among women writers constitutes evidence of the emergence of a transnational "community of practice" identified with moral utility rather than aesthetic achievement.

Against an older criticism proposing an association between nation, novel, and domestic heroine on the basis of novels written by men, Chapter 5, "Heroines and Local Girls," examines the transnationalism of the heroines created by women writers. The first half of the chapter focuses on the self-proclaimed first novelists to write in Dutch, Elizabeth Bekker-Wolff and Agatha Deken, and on the Dutch-born Isabelle de Charrière (with short discussions of works by Marie-Jeanne Riccoboni, Frances Brooke, Isabelle de Montolieu, Sophie von La Roche, and Frances Burney). Contrasting the production of transnational affinity in these writers' works with the national community imagined via the novel, as Benedict Anderson and others have described it,[16] the chapter argues that prerevolutionary women's fiction relied on mobile and culturally hybrid heroines to invent a new novelistic code: development of broad affinities around the condition of woman within the context of description of local rites of gender. Examining turn-of-the-century and proto-Romantic fiction, the second half of the chapter argues that after the French Revolution women writers reinscribed this code of culturally transcendent heroines and culturally trapped local girls. Yet they deliberately disconnected the imagined literary community of exceptional women from affinity with the French language and a feminized French culture, opening the way for English to become the imaginary home of women's writing in the next century.

Chapter 6, "Heroines in the World," evaluates the costs of the transnational position for women's writing that emerged in the eighteenth century. It considers relationships between the works of Isabelle de Charrière, Elizabeth Inchbald, Thérèse Heyne Forster Huber, and Germaine de Staël as they respond to Kant's idea of cosmopolitanism and to a crisis in the legitimacy of women's fiction after 1794. The chapter exposes the legacy of the eighteenth-century construction of women's position in the literary field for postcolonial and global women writers into the twenty-first century: the vexed extension of the code of heroines and local girls outside of Europe to colonial heroines, the ambivalent power of story validation based on affinity, the limitations of the capital of virtue but also its continuing role in publicizing suffering and need.

Women's Writing and the Republic of Letters

Pascale Casanova goes perhaps further than other theorists in internationalizing Pierre Bourdieu's account of the literary field. She argues that a "world republic of letters," operating according to rules of value that are separate from the rise and fall of the economic and political power of nations, emerged through endowment of literary languages with authority by virtue of their age and longevity. For Casanova, newcomers to the literary field may not necessarily proceed "in the same way, but all writers attempt to enter the same race, and all of them struggle, albeit with unequal advantages, to attain the same goal: literary legitimacy" (40). Casanova identifies the contestation for literary legitimacy funneled through the aesthetic capital attending the rival European literary languages that successively acquired literariness after the domination of Latin: Italian, French, Spanish, English, German, Russian. She then examines how this linguistic-aesthetic capital governs the entry of postcolonial writers into the world literary field. Jane Austen is the single woman writer Casanova mentions to have published before the 1880s. In *The World Republic of Letters*, the expansion of women's writing and reading in the eighteenth century is presumably to be subsumed into the broad pattern of the rise and rivalries of discrete national literatures and European languages in the formation of world literature, with French as its dominant language and Paris, as Casanova controversially claims, as its capital.[17]

With every early modern bid to politico-cultural power came the accompanying claim of a state's possession of a woman who, for her extraordinary writing and intellect, stood out as an exception. In seventeenth-century European contests, the singular phenomena of Anna Maria van Schurman, Katherine Phillips, and Anne Le Fèvre Dacier, for example, indicated the degree of greatness that the Dutch, the English, and the French had attained. Certainly too, by the late seventeenth and early eighteenth centuries, not only did French dominate as the European language of letters and civility, but, dovetailing with Casanova's chronology of bids for literary legitimacy, France was known for "uncommon genius among the ladies" (Thicknesse ix). Why then carve out a separate story for "women's writing"?

The first part of the answer begs the question: women's writing does not belong to a single language or nation, even if two golden ages dominate the imaginary genealogy from which literary history has begun the process of digging out. First, according to this tale, there was a French age of conversation and letters beginning with Scudéry's "romances" and posthumously described in the volumes of letters by Marie de Rabutin-Chantal, marquise de Sévigné, published into the 1750s. Then came an English very long nineteenth century of the novel starting with Jane Austen or perhaps Maria Edgeworth or even Frances Burney, passing through the Brontës, and closing with Virginia Woolf. This book charts the actual interregnum between these conceptual golden ages, from conversation to novel, emphasizing that the practices of women from a composite elite shaped their transnational position in the literary field, in particular their speculative exploration of the gender roles associated with different national characters. The image of a French golden age of conversation was textually produced as a heritage by European writers as they forged the market category of women's writing.[18] *Heroines and Local Girls* follows an evolution. Conversations among women appeared in texts as the medium for evaluating life stories of exceptional heroines from many nations who rose above the ordinary. Letters offered the context for subjecting a heroine's conduct to the scrutiny of her friends. Finally, the consolidated category of women's writing unified the story of the writer with the story of her protagonist by identifying writer and protagonist as exceptional figures in a national landscape and by placing them within a constellation of transcendent and nationally representative types. The progress from one golden age to another is thus the evolution from texts that represented the conversation group to texts that were able to assume and virtualize the conversation group as an imagined community of readers of women's writing.

It is also a progression from French as the imagined home language of literary affinity for exceptional women to English as that language. While these languages equally serve as loci of aesthetic literary distinction in the terms laid out by Casanova, an overlapping role is that of an imaginative home for women's voice. Where French and English may exert a literary dominance owing to "the prestige of the texts written in them" (Casanova 17), they also exert a pull due to their investment with an idea that women have "found their voices" or "come to writing" within them. Linguist Bonnie Norton argues that "language learners who struggle to speak from one identity position may be able to reframe their relationship with others and claim alternative, more powerful identities from which to speak, read or write" within a target language (3). This is a different linguistic credential than the endowment of a language with literary capital or "literariness" that Casanova describes. Since the eighteenth century, women writers have worked in a world literary field configured by the force of claims about the challenge of finding a place "from which to speak, read or write" *and* by the force of "literariness." Casanova, Bourdieu, and others ascribe value to the circulation of literary capital, and they connect literariness with national languages. The capital that organizes the position of affinity groups—what I am calling here the capital of virtue—may equally be described as a force in the literary field, one that, for women readers and writers, created affinity with target feminized languages.

This approach involves identifying how a language becomes invested with a myth of providing liberatory voice for an identity group. It explores how a set of learnable codes function as access points to literary production. The approach is not the same as a center-periphery model of cultural influence. One of the key claims in *Heroines and Local Girls* is that women's writing, in its emergence as a market category, was comparative from the beginning. Even as successive languages and cultures became invested with associated gender roles, they also became arrayed within an increasingly inclusive imagined trans-European comparative geography. The novel by and for women annexed new cultural contexts in a simultaneous demonstration of the thesis of women's shared condition and of the supporting evidence of specific wrongs endured by "local girls." The novel's comparative geography of gender was a structure initially produced in the core of world literary space that could be mastered by "semiperipheral cultural transmitters" but that was also contingent on semiperipheral replication.[19]

My approach is compatible with recent revisions to the idea of cultural transfer, a methodology developed to describe the evolution of French and German cultures as interdependent, plural, and affected by enclaves of influence and transference zones rather than as configured by unilateral, targeted, and intentional cultural influence (Espagne). Acknowledging the mobility of cultures also entails recognizing how claims about the fixed character of a culture serve as touchstones and barriers.[20] In *Bluestocking Feminism and British-German Cultural Transfer, 1750–1837*, Alessa Johns demonstrates how, in a period opening with French domination of continental literary culture, women's cultural mediation of increasingly intense British-German links during the Personal Union—the period between 1714 and 1837 when the kings of England were, at the same time, electors of Hanover—produced alternate accounts of liberty and social reform. Johns rightly argues that "*both* nationalism and internationalism characterize" the late eighteenth century, and she suggests that "women, exactly because of their ill-defined political identities, were well positioned to promote what Kwame Anthony Appiah calls 'patriotic cosmopolitanism'" (6).[21] The process of British-German cultural transfer yielded political discourses that were affected but not wholly determined by French Revolutionary and Napoleonic cultural forms. Johns's work joins Adriana Craciun's in *British Women Writers and the French Revolution: Citizens of the World* in clarifying how women's implication in identifiable activities of cultural transfer, such as, for example, Helen Maria Williams's eyewitness letters recounting the French Revolution for British readers, produced the sentiment that "it required but the common feelings of humanity to become . . . a citizen of the world" (69).

The vision of culture as both mobile and ostensibly fixed that informs cultural transfer studies certainly undergirds *Heroines and Local Girls* but from a distinct angle. The book explores how eighteenth-century Europeans came to feel through their engagement with an increasingly recognizable repertoire of texts that the international domain covered by women writers was analogous to a culture with its own conditions or rules for inclusion or exclusion. The focus then is not on the production of cosmopolitanism through processes of European cultural transfer but on the textual production of a non-national but nation-like literary identity: virtuous womanhood. This nation-like literary identity operated in interplay with the aesthetic capital that helped consolidate the boundaries between national literatures and between nations.

*   *   *

Pascale Casanova's account of a "world republic of letters" cannot entirely explain women's writing because the category emerged through ethical claims about the experience of an identity group, defined both beyond and in connection with the boundaries of the nation. The broad account that I piece together here situates transnationalism as a cause rather than a feature of the emergence of the category of women's writing. On the one hand, it locates women's writing as the first transnational literary category to be niche-marketed as a recognizable commercial identity to a composite European elite. On the other, it argues, albeit critically, for the value of the capital of virtue promoted and traded upon in eighteenth-century women's writing and minted in alignment with the Enlightenment project. This argument is perhaps encapsulated by a fictional exchange between women staged by Dorothea Schlegel's review of Germaine de Staël's *Delphine* in 1803. In the review, the three female interlocutors speculate about the validity of French models by simultaneously exploring ideals of femininity and the possibilities for women's writing and reading in German:

> Currently in France the only interesting novels are written by women, and what is more, one is always seduced in some way in Paris. Who can resist the cute little volumes lying out by the hundreds along every street and tempting us with the vignettes displayed?—Very true, said Constanze, I can hear the name of a book or its author ten times without being especially drawn to it; but if I see a sweet little figure in the prints as I pass by I am at once curious. Why is she so unhappy? Why is it that the old man is prostrating himself at her feet? Who is having this beauty abducted? The booksellers are doing well by this feminine curiosity, they have surely sold some bad books by this means.[22]

The women in Dorothea Schlegel's scenario articulate how "cute little volumes" and the image of a "sweet little figure" draws them—when they are in Paris—to a distinct market targeting women. They are traveling agents of cultural transfer and conversationalists engaged by books to consider stories of female virtue.

"What acquirement exalts one being above another?" Mary Wollstonecraft asked rhetorically to validate penning *The Vindication of the Rights of Woman* (1792) at the end of the period in which women's writing became a category: "Virtue, we spontaneously reply" (28). The capital of virtue privileges texts for their cultivation of the care, education, and preservation of the self as that self is challenged by cultural institutions, beliefs, and practices and as that self negotiates belonging to groups or identities. Its ethical kernel lies in the question of whether a person is truly virtuous or whether conditions of adversity and a dominant climate of opposing indications about the right path to follow can force her to part from virtue. As such, the question generates probing, providing for three kinds of narrative situations in which a heroine is tested. Conditions of adversity test whether she can remain virtuous when, for example, she is starving or unprotected. Conditions of a lack of practical wisdom test whether her virtue, for instance, her inability to tell a lie or her generosity, leads her to adhere to her virtue in a way that places herself or others at risk (or humiliates her—a favorite outcome in Burney's fiction). Conditions of differential perception offer the most narratively dramatic test and the one that lays the groundwork for group affinity. In this test, authorities (a father, a husband, a guardian, a judge, or society at large) present as virtuous a path that serves their interests. They use their power to array evidence in support of their picture of the virtuous path. They limit the heroine's access to information and to other people who might corroborate her perceptions. They constrain and try to force her will.

Sexual virtue served as the fatal and fundamental feminine virtue to be tested in eighteenth-century narratives through infinite variation on these three conditions. The problem of a woman's sexual virtue could be enlisted to stage contests between the arranged marriage and the love match, the rake and the man of sensibility, the woman who succumbed and suffered and the woman who resisted, city and country, nobles and gentry, gentry and plebeian, court and country house, educated and uneducated, patriarchy and fraternity, legitimate heredity and illegitimacy, state mercantilism and market capitalism, metropole and colony, French and not French, castle and garden, civilized and wild. Katherine Binhammer concludes of British fiction that even "before women dominate the field of fiction writing in the last decades of the century, women's lives prevail as the novel's central concern" (184). If the number of novels focused on women multiplied across the eighteenth century, this is partly due to the many uses of trials to women's virtue.

For the formation of women's writing, as distinct from the broad range of narratives of seduction, the condition of differential perception around sexual virtue and challenges to it offered the most provocative and important contest. It pitted a hegemonic version of the real against a powerless woman's struggle to trust her own perception of events. Seduction, sexual harassment, sexual assault, forced marriage, domestic abuse, breast-feeding, female friendship, widowhood, property control, appearing in public, childbirth outside of wedlock, and sex outside of marriage, these crucial moments of the heroine's story constituted junctures where different versions of the real came into question. Since the 1980s, critics have explored these moments in eighteenth-century fiction through a Foucauldian lens by understanding them as novelistic sites for constitution of a modern bourgeois female subject. Nancy Armstrong explained influentially in *Desire and Domestic Fiction* that eighteenth- and early nineteenth-century British novels and conduct manuals defined for women "the whole domain over which our culture grants women authority:

the use of leisure time, the ordinary care of the body, courtship practices, the operations of desire, the forms of pleasure, gender differences and family relations" (26–27). The leisure and pedagogical writing by women that *Heroines and Local Girls* explores certainly provided "an education of desire," to use Ann Laura Stoler's phrase, building shared interests and investments for women readers in the service of emerging class behaviors and values.

At the same time, the focus on crises of sexual virtue in women's writing revolved around a struggle over representation of the real. This focus extended beyond the drama of attempts to control language or stipulate states of consciousness in Samuel Richardson's transformative *Clarissa*, which critics have variously explored.[23] In focusing on virtue, women writers after Richardson depicted battles between alternate perceptions and histories. They relied on claims of affinity among women to legitimate alternate heroines' stories, the "she said" in the face of a powerful version of the real that sought to make women complicit with hegemonic explanations of experience. The capital of virtue, as both conservative and liberal women writers deployed it, involved founding critique of hegemonic representation in the experience and perceptions of an identity group, as represented and authenticated within the transnational category of women's writing. Sheldon Pollock has written that "the practices of literary culture" are "practices of attachment." Literature, he writes, "constitutes an especially sensitive gauge of sentiments of belonging: creating or consuming literature meant for large worlds or small places is a declaration of affiliation with that world or place" (18). *Heroines and Local Girls* explores the practices of attachment, the sticky glue of women's writing that, for better and for worse, connected women in small places to a notion of being a woman in the world through the nascent idea of herstory in a different voice.

Networking

La Fite's failed brokerage of the lock of hair originated with a tea party that she hosted at Windsor to introduce La Roche to Burney. In one of her three published travel journals,[24] La Roche described the gathering:

> The ladies speak perfect French. This little friendliness made it a really delightful evening for me, as my English is none too good, so that I should have missed a great deal of the talk over their embroidery. Here

was a picture, too, of a first-class English tea-party. The tone was intimate and refined: the hostess busies herself delightfully and just enough to allow of grace and deftness. While Mme. La Fite prepared tea, the ladies continued their fancywork, sewing bands of fine muslin. While we sipped at our tea, pretty and practical discussions took place, in the course of which I was asked a number of questions about France and the Countess Genlis. (*Sophie* 180)

The tea party was hardly as innocuously domestic or as representatively British as the sewn bands of fine muslin might suggest. For one thing, as La Roche points out, it was conducted in French. For another, La Roche was not simply a foreign tea-party guest. She understood herself as above all "eine femme de lettres," as she wrote in a telling mixture of German and French in a letter to a cultivated female friend.[25] Burney was at the time second keeper of the robes to the (German) queen of England, Queen Charlotte, who maintained a staff of educators for her extensive family. La Roche gushed that Burney was "famous as authoress of *Miss Evelina* and *Cecilia* . . . a true ideal in figure, culture, expression, dress and bearing" (*Sophie* 179). Avoiding La Roche as much as possible during her visit, the thirty-five-year-old Burney sketched her cuttingly: "Could I have conceived her character to be unaffected, her manners have a softness that would render her excessively engaging. She is now *bien passé*—no doubt fifty. . . . I can suppose she has thought herself all her life the model of the favourite heroine of her own favourite romance, and I can readily believe that she had attractions in her youth nothing short of fascinating" (*Court Journals* 1:167). Another tea-party guest was Lady Sophia Fielding, woman of the bedchamber to the queen. La Roche described her, relying on contemporary cultural touchstones, as "vivacious, and with more fire in her large blue eyes than I imagined possible in an English woman" (*Sophie* 179). Lady Sophia Fielding was the daughter of Lady Charlotte Finch, the impressive head governess to the fifteen British royal children of George III and Queen Charlotte. Finch had published a music-teaching manual and employed enlightened teaching techniques, including dissected maps, or jigsaw puzzles, with her charges.[26] She was a friend and educational collaborator with a Frenchwoman who had run a school in Cavendish Square for the daughters of noble families, Jeanne Marie Leprince de Beaumont; La Roche thought that Finch was "the original" for one of Leprince de Beaumont's governess characters (*Sophie* 179). Leprince de Beaumont authored numerous works, including the influential first magazines for children and adolescents, which met with success across Europe and fostered a common European childhood culture for a composite elite (Kaltz). The woman all of the guests discussed over their tea was Stéphanie-Félicité Ducrest de Saint-Aubin, comtesse Bruslart de Genlis, and marquise de Sillery, who visited England in 1785 where she was recognized for her books by Oxford University. The first woman educator of princes of royal blood, she served as the "governor" to the five children of the Duc de Chartres, including Louis-Philippe, future king of France. As was rumored at the time, she was the duke's mistress and perhaps also the mother of one or two illegitimate children with him (Naudin 179). Counted by sheer number of pages, Genlis proved to be perhaps the most prolific author of her age (Diaconoff 78). Her 140 published volumes included the famous educational epistolary novel *Adèle et Théodore* (1782). Intercalated within the novel was a sensational story of domestic abuse based on the life of the Italian Duchess of Cerifalco (Genlis, *Histoire*). The first-person story of the duchess's psychology and perceptions during a nine-year underground imprisonment by her husband helped inspire Ann Radcliffe's Gothic *Romance of the Forest*, with its two central characters Adeline and Theodore (Clark Schaneman). Sophie von La Roche had just met Stéphanie de Genlis during her stop in France. Burney had become acquainted with Genlis the year before when La Fite introduced her to Queen Charlotte's household.

Not present at this particular tea party was the young Germaine de Staël, who would dominate discussion at the turn of the century. Novelist, *salonnière*, and author in 1799 of the first work of comparative literature, she was also the first woman to be widely recognized as a political exile. La Roche had dined with Staël's parents while passing through their Swiss home in Coppet on her way to England. Burney would write with naked admiration on meeting Staël six years later that "she is a woman of the first abilities, I think, I have ever seen. . . . She has suffered us to hear some of her works in manuscript which are truly wonderful, for powers both of thinking and expression" (*Journals and Letters* 358). Allowing her to craft simultaneously her famous novel *Corinne, ou l'Italie* and a major piece of criticism *De l'Allemagne*, Staël's travels in Germany in 1803–04 and 1808 brought her into contact with Sophie von La Roche; Dorothea Schlegel, the writer largely responsible for translating *Corinne* into German; and an emerging generation of women writers and intellectuals. When she hosted Germaine de Staël at her cottage in 1803, La Roche felt herself separated "by my advanced age and our divergent viewpoints" and admitted to lacking the courage to speak before "this stream of eloquence—whose golden content I appreciated." For her part, Staël commented that La Roche cried too much.[27]

The same year that Staël silenced La Roche with a flood of "golden content," Maria Edgeworth would take a nostalgic tour of women writers' network of the previous generation, crossing the Channel in the opposite direction from La Roche. On a trip to Paris, she visited a shabby apartment in the Arsenal where, just as a "great puff of smoke came from the huge fireplace," she met a person "very thin and melancholy" with "altogether an appearance of fallen fortunes, worn-out health, and excessive, but guarded irritability" (Edgeworth 1:137).[28] It was Stéphanie de Genlis, who grudgingly admitted to having read Edgeworth's *Belinda* (1:139). A decade later, in 1813, Edgeworth casually mentioned missing Frances Burney d'Arblay and Germaine de Staël in London (1:226). In 1820, traveling in Switzerland, she paid homage to Staël with a posthumous visit to her home in Coppet. Edgeworth gushed, "We came here yesterday, and here we are in the very apartments . . . opening into what is now the library, but was once that theatre on which Madame de Staël used to act her own 'Corinne'" (2:355). Only a few days earlier, Edgeworth had chatted with the septuagenarian Isabelle de Montolieu, author of *Caroline de Litchfeld*, translator into French of Jane Austen's novels, and contact of Stéphanie de Genlis. "She must have been a beautiful woman: she told me she is seventy," Edgeworth wrote to provide a rapid celebrity sketch of Montolieu for her readers: "fine, dark, enthusiastic eyes, a quickly varying countenance, full of life, and with all the warmth of heart and imagination which is thought to belong only to youth" (2:351).

This multigenerational tea-party network bespeaks the eighteenth-century cult of female writerly celebrity that Dierdre Lynch has noted in her discussion of La Roche's "crush" on Burney (*Economy* 207). One edge to this network is the perception of shared exceptionalism, involving competition, admiration, gossip, snide remarks. Another edge is the imagined relationship of female affinity that La Roche thought should be fostered ("I love everything that comes from the pen of a person of my sex"[29]), that Burney rejected, that La Fite tried to leverage, and that Genlis celebrated in her preface to La Fite's work. Still another is the practice of translating, imitating, emulating, or reworking the text of another woman writer. Taken as a whole, the tea-party network collects together women who recognized themselves as members, or as would-be members, of a group characterized at once by national differences and by transnational connections. In the tea party assembled by La Fite, the colonial imports of tea, china, muslin, and perhaps even the

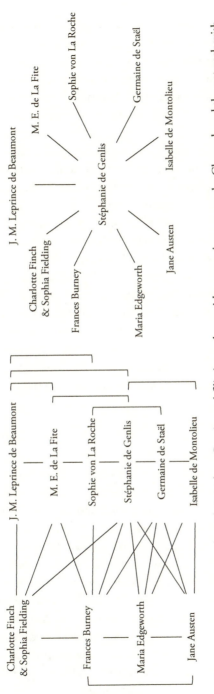

Figure 3. A tea party network, with British or Continental filiations, along with connections across the Channel, and the network with Stéphanie de Genlis as node.

wood for tea-table marquetry served as props supporting a shared performance of elite European femininity.[30] In the travel account description of the
tea party, La Roche proffers women's communal practice of conversing over
needlework to communicate the virtue and utility of an international assembly of prominent women writers and educators. Circa 1785, one leg of the tea
table was planted in patronage by an enlightened European aristocracy
invested in the education of its children. One leg rested on the international
prestige of French as the language for polite and intellectual expression. One
leg stood in national literary marketplaces expanding to address women readers. And one leg was poised on a transnational network, a group of women
readers and writers who understood themselves as such. The Terror, the Revolutionary Wars, and the rise of Napoleon made inroads on the French
empire over female literary affinity. Sophie von La Roche confessed to a
friend that she would only read English books. She was disturbed by the way
"Prostrated Germany" was "kicked around" and, as one of her characters
opined, distressed that the "unfortunate spirit of proud self-love had transformed half of the otherwise charming inhabitants of France into unfeeling
tigers" (H. Watt 46). The comments imply a kind of literary exile from the
imagined space of female affinity in French as well as from a German nation.
By 1815, women writers' tea table balanced on three legs: national literary
capital, national market capital, and the transnational capital of virtue.

Habitus

Clara Reeve's *Progress of Romance* is a peculiar eighteenth-century literary
history to have been published in 1785 because it devotes little energy to such
prestigious national forms as tragedy, epic, and satire or to relating these to
classical antecedents. Nor does it separate out a distinct form of the novel as
British, as did many of Reeve's contemporaries. Instead, Reeve traces the
novel's coalescence from a brew of trans-European romances and, in the
process, accords women writers and readers pride of place in the development
of an important literary genre. Reeve set her universal history of romance
against the British national literary histories that had excluded it: "The
learned men of our own country, have in general affected a contempt for this
kind of writing and looked upon Romances, as proper furniture only for a
lady's Library" (xi).[31] In two evocative gestures, Reeve appended the story of
an illustrious woman, "Charoba, Queen of Aegypt," to her work and constructed the body of *The Progress of Romance* in the form of a series of polite

weekly conversations between her mouthpiece Euphrasia, a female friend Sophronia, and a doubting male Hortensius. Reeve's female interlocutors provide their own history of female conversational affinity, neatly consigning enjoyment of such romances as Scudéry's *Artamène, ou Le Grand Cyrus* and *Clélie, Histoire romaine* to "our grandmothers, whose patience in wading thro' such tremendous volumes, may raise our surprize." Reeve's mouthpiece, the exceptional Euphrasia, nonetheless argues that if romance "taught young women to deport themselves too much like Queens and Princesses, it taught them at the same time that virtue only could give lustre to every rank and degree." Sophronia responds, "You remind me of what my good Aunt have often told me, that they, my Mother, and a select party of relations and friends, used to meet once a week at each others houses, to hear these stories;—one used to read, while the rest ply'd their needles" (68–69). Through the female friends' account of literary heritage, Reeve sets up an analogy between women's collective enjoyment of romance in the past over their needlework and the contemporary members of literary côteries. Both generations are invested in the capacity of collective conversational moral reasoning to breed virtue.

Why was the form of the conversation the best way to communicate the progress of romance? As Reeve explains in the introduction, "While I was collecting materials for this work, I held many conversations with some ingenious friends upon the various subjects, which it offered to be investigated and explained. This circumstance naturally suggested to me the Idea of the dialogue form. . . . In this Idea I was confirmed by the great success of some late writers in this way, particularly of *Madame de Genlis,* in her excellent work called the *Theatre of Education*" (xv). To write about romance as a woman and to imagine its universal history sprang organically for Reeve and her contemporaries from the fabric of early modern experience among educated women: the female conversation group as a pastime and medium for learning, emulation of models of female virtue, and conversancy with and translation of modern foreign languages. Reeve's written conversation demonstrates the difficulty of unraveling from lived oral practice either the inherited textuality of female conversation or its discursive connection to a literature of female improvement.

This same conversational frame for criticism and the parsing of female virtue structured Dorothea Schlegel's review, "Conversation About the Newest Novels by French Women Writers" ("Gespräch über die neusten Romane der Französinnen") in the first volume of *Europa* in 1803 at a moment in which Germaine de Staël's works were prompting linked discussion of national literary character and the woman writer across Europe. Schlegel developed her review through a conversation including a male interlocutor but dominated by three women who represent three critical positions: sentimental, Enlightenment, and Romantic viewpoints (J. Martin 40). Each woman's voice in the conversation offers the reader an entry point, the letter framing the conversation encourages the female addressee to judge for herself, and all agree that *Delphine* is "one of the most interesting women's novels of our time."[32]

Looking back over more than a half-century of literary struggle, Stéphanie de Genlis declared that "it is more glorious than one might think to elevate oneself to the first place among literators of the second order, for one would never obtain this without purity of moral principles. . . . Through work and meditation a sort of merit is acquired that the great men rarely have had. Finally, intelligence, persistence, good sense and happy arrangements allow one to flatter oneself for making eminently useful, and consequently durable works" (Genlis, *Dictionnaire critique* 325). Such declarations have been dismissed as the profession of modesty required of a woman endeavoring to make headway in the world of publishing—a profession required especially of aristocratic women when they ventured into "going public" by owning up to authorship.[33]

Yet as Pierre Bourdieu points out in his description of literary fields, "Every position, even the dominant one, depends for its very existence, and for the determinations it imposes on its occupants, on the other positions constituting the field." He clarifies that "the structure of the field, i.e. the space of positions, is nothing other than the structure of the distribution of the capital of specific properties which governs success in the field and the winning of the external or specific profits (such as literary prestige) which are at stake in the field" (*Field* 30). What did it mean for Genlis, whose work was read from Scotland to Russia, to identify herself with "literators of the second order"? What was at stake in aligning her chosen order with virtue and in contrasting it with the one occupied by "the great men"?

Despite critical revisions to Bourdieu's timeline and geography in his *Rules of Art* for the structure and genesis of the literary field, his division of literary lines of force into two axes, aesthetic capital (Casanova's literariness) and market capital, remains paradigmatic in literary studies. Proposing that the "first" literary field emerged in the nineteenth century, Bourdieu argued that it was an "economic world turned upside down" in which the aesthetic value of a work registered as the inverse of the market value of a work (*Rules*

81). The symbolic index of literary greatness was not whether a book sold well, to the contrary. Contestation among players in what was essentially a social field entailed occupation of conflicting zones. Bourdieu reads Gustave Flaubert's *Sentimental Education* (*L'éducation sentimentale*, 1869) as both a description of the structure of the nineteenth-century literary field and as an exemplar of a literary work bidding for aesthetic rather than for market value. Genre fictions that were successful in the marketplace occupied a different literary space than the magisterial realist novel by the literary giant that Gustave Flaubert embodied and that his character Frédéric Moreau failed to become.

Alain Viala and Geoffrey Turnovsky push back the timeline for the formation of the first literary field by emphasizing that a nascent literary marketplace existed in late seventeenth-century France, facilitating development of a notion of autonomous literary value, as distinguished from the idea of honorable cultural service to a patron. Viala explains that "the main agents of this space, the writers, are caught up in this interplay of specific logics and of struggles. In keeping with their own social and cultural capital, inherited from their family background and incorporated into their *habitus*, they adopt attitudes, genres and themes, and, if the occasion arises, attach themselves to literary schools, all of which affords them a position that is more or less conspicuous, more or less rewarding, whether in symbolic or financial terms, within these practices" (81). Describing Boileau's defense of a high literature not debased by market forces, Viala clarifies that the existence of a literary marketplace is a precondition for the development of claims about autonomous and elevated literary value. Like Bourdieu, moreover, Viala assumes the coextensiveness of a literary field with a literary language (here, French) and with a bounded national identity, borders, and market (France). A case such as transnational success of the multivolume "novels" of Madeleine de Scudéry, written with the collaboration of her circle, falls outside of this kind of account of the literary field. Clearly, a focus on a tightly bounded national literary field determined by language needs to be adjusted to accommodate the complex organization of the late seventeenth- and eighteenth-century book trade. As historians of the book from Robert Darnton to Jeffrey Freedman have shown, an array of printers, booksellers, reviewers and book fairs across Europe produced, distributed, and sold a vast number of French books, translations from the French, as well as books in other European vernaculars. Moreover, an army of translators (some of whom were entry-level practitioners, some of whom were unacknowledged laborers contracted to translation brokers, and some of whom, such as Antoine LaPlace, were highly professionalized) facilitated cultural transfer.[34]

Women's writing became an identifiable category *across* national literary fields within this climate. "In keeping with their own social and cultural capital, inherited from their family background and incorporated into their *habitus*," women writers triangulated their position in relation to national aesthetic value and the purported crassness of the local literary marketplace. Their habitus included the cultivation of personal chastity and stoicism despite the experience of, but possession of limited language for, describing either coerced or desired sex. It incorporated conversational sociability, condensed in the image of a woman reading aloud to a sewing circle, as the default means of girls' education and as the template for polite female association. It involved exposure to modern European languages, especially French, particularly in the first two thirds of the century when it remained the language of civility and letters and when translation was both an acceptable leisure activity and modest trade for women of the middling ranks. This contrasted with a male writerly habitus in which the cultivation of personal chastity played a lesser role, although, as Jean-Jacques Rousseau's detailed description of the man who tried to "force" him to "indecent familiarities" in Turin makes clear, unwanted sexual experience and sexual violence sometimes played a role in male writers' lives (*Confessions* 1:113).

The male writerly habitus was more oriented toward civic virtue; formal training in classical Greek and Latin, including hallowed genres and models of individual oratory; learning structured by a tutor or instructor; and national aesthetic emulation and rivalry in privileged genres such as tragedy and satire. The habitus shared by many educated women across Western Europe, although it was shaped by regional cultural and class differences, translated into a position in the literary field: the emphasis on the higher moral educational worth of telling exemplary women's histories, comparing them across societies, and modeling virtue-focused reasoning within the text. Among elite women writers, habitus also involved living away from their country of birth for considerable periods and an experience of nationality not as direct personal membership but as contingent on the status of their fathers or husbands. While participating in national and linguistically bound literary fields complete with their cultural prejudices and evolving national gender roles, women writers laid claim to a position across national literary fields through investment in the symbolic capital of virtue.

In *The Sentimental Education of the Novel*, Margaret Cohen offers a feminist corrective to Bourdieu's account of the French literary field. Considering the conditions leading to Flaubert's realist apotheosis, she analyzes the positions of writers in the early nineteenth-century French literary marketplace. She shows that male writers challenged the dominance of sentimental writing in the French literary field and women writers' dominance of the successful form of the novel by emphasizing a masculine aesthetic superiority. The new realism claimed aesthetic detachment and symbolic ascendancy through male writers' presentation of sentimental writing as low and feminine marketplace pandering. As Cohen explains in a section of her work entitled "Reconstructing the Literary Field," "gender turns out to be a powerful symbolic weapon in Balzac and Stendhal's campaigns to assert the importance of their new practices. Both Balzac and Stendhal associated the invention of realist codes with the masculinization of a previously feminine form in their polemic and their poetics. Their strategy exploited the fact that the prestigious sentimental works in the first thirty years of the nineteenth century were written by women and that women were prominent sentimental social novelists, as integral to the cultural life of the July Monarchy as the form they employed" (13). After the July Monarchy, "realism" ascended through claims of superior literariness dependent on an association of women writers and their work with the marketplace.

In Britain, a century earlier, "gender turns out to be a powerful symbolic weapon" in a parallel negotiation of positions in the literary field surrounding the emerging market commodity of the novel. Catherine Ingrassia explains that in early eighteenth-century Grub Street, "The participation of women, while seemingly peripheral, actually fueled the gendered characterization placed on the commercialization of the literary marketplace, the proliferation of speculative investment, and the readers and writers of the novel" (3). Aphra Behn, Delarivier Manley, and Eliza Haywood functioned as symbols of crass commercialism for their age. They collected, as lightning rods, the energy and anxiety attending the explosion of a commercial book trade in England. Their "amatory fiction," as Ros Ballaster has dubbed their work, often drew on French styles and sources (C. Turner 51) and were fluidly classed by pundits with the French imports sold in translation or in the original in the British marketplace. In *Licensing Entertainment: The Elevation of Novel Reading in Britain, 1684–1750*, William Warner describes the enduring gendered nationalist rhetoric attending accounts of the novel in Britain:

Repeatedly it is claimed that England is to France as the (elevated) novel is to the romance, as fact is to fantasy, as morality is to sensuality, as men are to women. (Terms can be added to this series: genuine and counterfeit, simple and frothy, substantial and sophisticated.) Grounded in a caricature of France as effeminate and England as manly, this loaded set of oppositions is simultaneously nationalist and sexist. Proliferating inexhaustibly, these oppositions seem to touch every region of culture, and weave themselves like a gaudy thread through all the literary histories of the novel's rise. (21)

Claims about the aesthetic superiority of an eighteenth-century and masculine brand of realism powered consolidation of a British national literary field. Histories of women's writing in Britain point to a gap in the 1730s, when, under pressure from attacks associating their writing with a morally low and foreign influence and in response to changing behavioral norms, women renegotiated the terms of their participation in the British national literary field. By mid-century, they had abandoned racy and partly continentally inspired fictions for writing in the "service of virtue," as Clara Reeve would describe Eliza Haywood's reformed return to novel writing in 1751 with *The History of Miss Betsy Thoughtless* (*Progress of Romance* 121).

Repertoire

Benedict Anderson has argued influentially that "the convergence of capitalism and print technology on the fatal diversity of human language created the possibility of a new form of imagined community, which in its basic morphology set the stage for the modern nation" (46). Even so, the European early modern print industry identified and capitalized on new audiences of girls and women from the middling and upper ranks across languages and borders, setting the stage for a new form of imagined community constituted by and through the practices of consuming and producing women's writing. Since women from the composite elite learned modern European languages, especially French, as part of their induction in the polite forms of femininity and sociability, they constituted a multilingual market. The first magazine for Danish women, Laurent Angliviel de la Beaumelle's *The Danish Spectatress, or the Modern Aspasia* (*La Spectatrice danoise, ou l'Aspasie moderne*, 1749–50), for instance, was published in French. At the same time, translation provided women with a modest entry into the literary marketplace, since it obviated any pretense to the self-important and public stance of authorship. Translation also numbered among the few respectable means available to a middling rank or well-born woman to make or supplement income.[35] The capacity to read in a second language and the capacity to translate allowed literate eighteenth-century women to coalesce into a multilingual market sector and "community of practice" for and within a transnational print culture.

The idea of a community of practice was first developed by Étienne Wenger and Jean Lave in the 1990s to describe the ways that individuals become members of a profession or share a craft by negotiating meaning and identity in social contexts. As Wenger explains in a 2010 essay:

> Engaging in social contexts involves a dual process of meaning making. On the one hand, we engage directly in activities, conversations, reflections, and other forms of personal *participation* in social life. On the other hand, we produce physical and conceptual artifacts—words, tools, concepts, methods, stories, documents, links to resources, and other forms of *reification*—that reflect our shared experience and around which we organize our participation. . . . Meaningful learning in social contexts requires both participation and reification to be in interplay. Artifacts without participation do not carry their own meaning; and participation without artifacts is fleeting, unanchored, and uncoordinated. But participation and reification are not locked into each other. At each moment of engagement in the world, we bring them together anew to negotiate and renegotiate the meaning of our experience. The process is dynamic and active. ("Communities" 180)

Learning occurs socially rather than being bounded by an individual's own cognition. Incorporation into a social learning system may happen virtually, that is, without the physical presence of other members of the group or network.

Wenger emphasizes that the "social world is a resource for constituting an identity" and negotiating meaning, hence the satisfaction of social learning systems that admit individuals to practice, to a community's "regime of competence," and to contributing to renegotiation of that regime. For eighteenth-century women readers and writers, participation involved becoming familiar with a "repertoire" of artifacts. Numerous texts were important for male and female audiences, such as Samuel Richardson's *Pamela* and *Clarissa* or Jean-Jacques Rousseau's *Julie, or The New Heloise,* as well as *Emile, or on Education.* Yet certain texts had special importance as reified objects particular to the repertoire for women readers and writers. As Isabelle de Charrière reported in 1788, "For forty years, the letters of Madame de Sévigné have been in the hands of all German women, all Dutch women, all the women in Switzerland who are reasonably well-bred, and the reign of Louis XIV is better known to them than any part of the history of their own countries" (*Œuvres* 10:79). Women readers might practice by experimenting with a translation, much as did the adolescent Maria Edgeworth when she took on the challenge of rendering Genlis's *Adèle et Théodore* into English. Readers and writers might rely on "links to resources," such as the reading list "of books deserving public honors on the score of utility" that Clara Reeve provided at the end of *The Progress of Romance* (102–4); the numerous early modern catalogues of illustrious women or of women writers, including Genlis's *On the Influence of Women on French Literature* (*De l'influence des femmes sur la littérature française,* 1811) or Sophie von La Roche's *My Desk* (*Mein Schreibetisch,* 1799), which "functioned at least in part as a reading list for women" (J. Martin 52). And they might move beyond reading as practice to writing as practice by translating, rewriting, reworking, extending, making new contributions to the repertoire in the process of negotiating new meanings. Through the frequently repeated image of girls and women engaged in conversation or in reading letters and absorbed in discussing or learning the story of a virtuous or nonvirtuous woman, eighteenth-century writing by women provides a refracted depiction and also a beckoning model of a distinctive international community of practice. The young woman's life story served as a touchstone of practice (Dow, "Biographical Impulse").

For this community, French had a heightened importance as a shared language of practice and as an imaginative locus of identity until the 1790s, when cultural horror over the Terror and changing patterns of language learning and travel due to British-German cultural transfer during the Personal Union, the French Revolution, and the Napoleonic blockade shifted the organizing language of practice for the community away from French and eventually toward English. The very Frenchness of this network functioned, paradoxically, not as a Gallocentric literary anthem but as a site of transnational affinity. From the textual image of women or girls gathered in conversation to measure a female life developed the capital of virtue on which women's writing traded. When women read, this trope suggested, they entered a virtual circle to judge the virtue of the literary heroine. Reading women's writing amounted to an exercise in evaluation and in affinity.

The Capital of Virtue

For women writers across Western Europe, the shift to the "service of virtue" in the second half of the eighteenth century did not entail a wholesale divestiture from French, France, and foreign fictions. Nor did it demand sequestration within and a full embrace of national literary life and an eighteenth-century brand of protorealism. Writing by women in German and Dutch in the 1770s, 1780s, and 1790s joined the well-developed British and French chorus of attacks on French court life, French fashions, and French frivolity and finesse, all viewed as particularly pernicious for the health of women and of nations. Women writers embraced the late eighteenth-century critique of French corruption. Yet they counterbalanced this with subscription to the idea that France owed its cultural distinction to the participation of women in cultural life—to the mixing of the sexes. Again, Wollstonecraft in *A Vindication* is adept at describing a theme, despite a feverish Francophobia inspired by the events of the French Revolution: "In France, there is undoubtedly a more general diffusion of knowledge than in any part of the European world, and I attribute it, in a great measure, to the social intercourse which has long subsisted between the sexes" (13). Wollstonecraft drew on threads in Enlightenment natural philosophy. One thread wound through the works of writers from Montesquieu to John Millar to Rousseau and linked the progress of nations with the role and treatment of women in private and public life.[36] Montesquieu's *Persian Letters* (*Lettres persanes,* 1721) popularized an idea that he would turn into system in *Spirit of the Laws* (1748). Climate shaped the nature of relations between the sexes and these, in turn, explained the level of development of arts and sciences; "the society of women spoils morals [mœurs] and forms taste" (*Œuvres* 7; sec. 11). John Millar's *Origin of the Distinction of Ranks* (1771) argued that prosperous nations were characterized by the mingling of women in public and social contexts. Yet, while modest women in domestic contexts anchored the conditions for prosperity, too bold a presence in society yielded degradation and decline. As Harriet Guest summarizes Millar's position, "The degenerate condition of women indicated the perversion of those passions that, in their moralised and contained form, had been the motors of commercial progress" (Guest, *Empire* 57). The quality and character of a culture correlated with the status of women in a society. Influenced by this discourse as it wound through natural philosophy, travel accounts, and fiction, Wollstonecraft's comparative measure of the treatment of women in particular cultures supported identification of the wrongs of women as members of a transnational class.

Adding the capital of virtue as a third line of force to Bourdieu's portrait of the literary field makes it possible to describe a literature that accrues value for a group as an expression of that group's identity and as a codification of the pathways to group membership and self-realization beyond the nation. Women's writing emerged as a literary category in counterpoint with the rise of national aesthetics and the expansion of literary markets. Neither simply a reaction to nor collusion with patriarchal and national literary forms, but rather both, it offered an invitation to group membership through a literary project of self-transformation grounded in recognition of the primacy of gender and of perfectibility via embrace of gender. Exceptional literary heroines provided emulatory models. More important, the stories of their transcendence in practicing virtue and telling their stories unfurled alongside the tales of local girls subjected to culturally specific rites of gender. Through the heroine's exceptional overcoming in the telling of her story, women's writing orchestrated a readerly attachment to learning about the local wrongs experienced by local women and an investment in a generalized notion of women's experience.

Sharper description of how Enlightenment and post-Enlightenment literatures facilitate the recognition of identity groups involves accounting for the interplay of the capital of virtue with aesthetic and commercial capital. Such a three-dimensional description offers several advantages. It identifies subject formation in relation to group affinity as a visible pull (rather than as covert operations) on literary works in modern marketplaces. It provides a means for discussing the production of text-based affinity across languages. In other words, an idea of affinity in translation complements Benedict Anderson's monolingual opposition between sacred languages/sacred texts and national print-languages. As in Gilles Deleuze and Félix Guattari's idea of a minor literature, attention to the capital of virtue allows exploration of the shapes that resistance may take in literature. Yet it moves away from implying a one-to-one correspondence between resistance and aesthetic innovation or between resistance and aesthetic conservatism. And it opens a discussion of how transnational literatures and literary forms may respond to multiple cultures and languages. It encourages reflection on the Enlightenment project—

the description and construction of humans as they should be—in its interplay with aesthetic and market lines of force. It stimulates contemplation of that project as an enduring literary value, or form of capital, vexed by the potential for yoking literature into the service of tribalism.

Finally, suiting my purposes here, it explains the power of women's writing as a transnational category intersecting with national literary fields without resorting to the temptations Catherine Ingrassia cautions against: "the tendency to place women writers in an exclusively female literary tradition or to add uncritically another woman to the canon." A study of eighteenth-century women writers should not, Ingrassia argues, "read these women discretely or as part of an alternative literary history" (12). Nor should it fall into the historical trap of measuring literary value through, as Betty Schellenberg writes, "the theory of genius which reinforced arguments for the ontological uniqueness of literary works, and therefore, the rights of proprietary authorship." This theory, Schellenberg continues,

> appears to have worked ultimately, in its longevity as the dominant, "Romantic" model of the author, to subordinate those authors whose work authorized itself by its relation to a tradition, to a contemporary community, or to a social good. Thus much of what the women writers [in Schellenberg's study of women in Britain] and their readers articulated as the signs of their success—placement in a male-defined tradition, substantial subscription lists headed by prestigious names, the satisfaction of a loyal group of readers, recognition for their expert craftsmanship or for their modeling of valued social qualities—came to be devalued or deemed irrelevant as measures of literary achievement. (14)

Identification of the capital of virtue at work in women's occupation of a position in the literary field has a revisionist quality in resetting the romantic scale of literary value. Crucially, it decouples literary value from monolingualism and from the marketplace, while providing a means of acknowledging texts that are recognizable not solely in relation to an author function but in relation to the work they perform for a group of readers and writers. The interest in tying the capital of virtue to the emergence of women's writing lies precisely in identifying how literary affinity groups beyond language and love of country complemented—and complement—national literatures in the formation of an autonomous world literary field.

Seen in this way, the capital of virtue provides means of describing not only women's writing but of establishing a contrast with the ideal of (manly) cosmopolitanism. Enlightenment cosmopolitanism finds expression in such signal texts as Marana's *The Turkish Spy* (*L'espion du grand seigneur*, 1684–), Montesquieu's *Persian Letters* (*Lettres persanes*, 1721), Oliver Goldsmith's *The Citizen of the World* (1760), and Immanuel Kant's "Idea for a Universal History with a Cosmopolitan Purpose" ("Idee zu einer allgemeinen Geschichte in weltbürgerlicher Absicht," 1784). It was partially practiced in such institutions as Masonic lodges and stock exchanges in the seventeenth and eighteenth centuries. "Historical evidence suggests," Margaret Jacob writes, "that in the eighteenth century the cosmopolitan became a viable ideal because, even amid wars and national rivalries, select places existed where another, more benign experience became occasionally possible. Small enclaves flourished where social, religious, and national boundaries were routinely crossed and seeds of an expansive social experience took root. The cosmopolitan ideal proclaimed by Enlightenment writers matured partly because of the fecundity of those experiences" (11). What was different about transnational networks of women readers and writers was the interplay of participation and reification (Wenger, "Communities" 180). Where cosmopolitanism remained an "ideal" with some basis in practice, women's writing—constituted through a generative repertoire that was used and expanded by a virtual community—emerged from women's habitus and a reification of codes supported by the eighteenth-century marketplace.

The most profoundly disruptive code was the claim of differential perception that emerged in women's novelistic rewritings of sexual assault, seduction, and abuse scenarios. The radical notion that both perception and desire are subject to hegemonic coercion became paired with the claim that knowledge of the self can only surface when one compares one's own story with the stories of people "like" oneself. A second code involved the identification of the woman writer with her heroine to performative effect; "coming to writing" demonstrated that the woman writer, like her heroine, was superior to the rest of her sex in having overcome silencing to register differential experience. The third code, yielding a literary catalog of the international wrongs of woman, featured the heroine who transcended the fate of her sex owing to superior education and reason and who stood in contrast with local girls who were fully subjected to the rites of gender characteristic of their cultures. These three codes formed the currency of the capital of virtue in eighteenth-century women's writing.

The choice of the word *virtue* in the phrase "the capital of virtue" invokes the eighteenth-century endowment of physiology and experience with value independent of an inherited or putatively divinely arranged role. Often registered in the physiologized discourse of gendered sensibility, virtue functioned as a lever for the Western European transition from a society of ranks, undergirded by an international aristocracy, to a class system, strengthened by bourgeois ideals of gender complementarity, within the modern nation state.[37] The idea of virtue threaded through Enlightenment debates about whether to found rights in the individual, in national citizenship, or, to use Kant's language, in "a right of citizens of the world to try to establish community with all."[38] To link virtue with capital makes visible the nascent prestige of identity categories and the claim for acknowledgment of the experience and perception associated with these categories in the eighteenth-century literary marketplace.

The capital of virtue functioned (and functions) through a transnational literary invitation to writers and readers to participate in innovation on a shared repertoire. The capital of virtue privileges a supposedly translatable fidelity to supranational identity above an untranslatable fidelity to national aesthetics. While works laying claim to the capital of virtue may or may not enjoy market success or receive aesthetic acclaim, or both, the assertion of the connection between a specific differentiating experience and an underrepresented or falsely represented voice is their primary currency. *Heroines and Local Girls* suggests that women's writing was the first modern literary category to capitalize transnationally on the virtue of identity. By building replicable codes and disseminating distinctive practices, women's writing showed the way to subsequent media-constituted affinity groups based in virtues of sexuality, class, race, subculture, intersectionality, even psychological type. The capital of virtue constitutive of women's writing in the eighteenth-century European literary field anticipated the global literary marketplace's segmentation of affinity-based reading publics in terms of differential experiences, voices, and desires. The benefits of the capital of virtue manifest in the acknowledgment of an identity group's history—including subordination, abuse, silencing, and denial of rights, as well as its contemporary experience of finding collective voice. The costs accrue when readers may only count a story true if the marketplace has identified its author as a member of the reader's own discrete circle, city, or tribe.

Chapter 2

Two Quarrels

In 1803, the feminist writer Mary Hays compiled a six-volume *Female Biography: Or Memoirs of Illustrious and Celebrated Women, of All Ages and Countries.* Hays's catalog retained some "femmes fortes," or warrior women, of the Middle Ages and Renaissance, women who had waded into the civil arena in full armor, but it listed numerous women writers and artists as well. In Hays's alphabetically organized catalog, the entries under S, for instance, were heavily devoted to a transnational group of women of letters. These included the ancient Greeks Sappho and Sophronia, the Dutch-German Anna Maria van Schurman, the Italian Isabella Sforza, the French Madeleine de Scudéry, and the Anglo-Irish novelist and playwright Frances Sheridan (3:441–82).[1] The irresistible Semiramis—whom Dante after Virgil had called the "empress" of "many languages" (75)—appeared in Hays's roll call as an atavistic reminder of duplicitous warrior queens from the first centuries of the *querelle des femmes* but perhaps also as a sign of how "distinguished ladies" were a cipher. As a whole, Hays's work reiterated a centuries-old form that assembled exemplary women into a transnational, detemporalized city of ladies. It was a compilation of classical, Italian, French, and English lives that had been discussed many times, although Hays, unlike many of her predecessors, had the grace to note her sources, from Bayle's *Historical Dictionary* (trans. 1709; *Dictionnaire historique et critique*, 1697), to the *Biographium Faemineum: The Female Worthies or, Memoirs of the Most Illustrious Ladies, of All Ages and Nations* (1766), to Anne Thicknesse's *Sketches of the Lives and Writings of the Ladies of France* (1778), to Stephen Jones's *New Biographical Dictionary; or Pocket Compendium* (1794).

In an essay on the *querelle des femmes* written in 1982, Joan Kelly argued that the "four-century-long debate" "sparked" by Christine de Pizan in *The*

Book of the City of Ladies became "the vehicle through which most early feminist thinking evolved." Kelly was invested in demonstrating the "richness, coherence, and continuity of early feminist thought" (5). Scholarship since that essay was written has revealed early feminist thought to be as diverse as it was rich.[2] Its coherence is as much a matter of form as of content. The form of the *querelle* imparted an imprint on the field of British and European women writers as it emerged over the course of the eighteenth century. This was something Kelly intimated when she noted the tendency of feminist writers to respond to misogynist intertexts through recourse to Christine de Pizan's figure of the city of women. "Formal patterns," Franco Moretti has written, "are what literature uses in order to master historical reality and to reshape its materials in the chosen ideological key." "If form is disregarded," Moretti cautions, "not only do we lose the complexity (and therefore the interest) of the whole process—we miss the strictly political significance too" (*Way of the World* xiii). The *querelle des femmes* arrayed literary works by women in a different, albeit intersecting, pattern from the quarrel of Ancients and Moderns—the early modern quarrel configuring ideas about national literary aesthetic value.

The mode of literary history that became dominant in Britain and Europe by the second half of the eighteenth century emphasized continuities, a national heritage passed from one male writer to the next. Goethe congratulated himself on having been born German since it gave him a relative liberty he might not have enjoyed had he been forced to write in English as an Englishman: "But had I been born an Englishman, and had those manifold masterworks pressed in upon me with all their power from my first youthful awakening, it would have overwhelmed me, and I would not have known what I wanted to do!"[3] Notwithstanding his role in coining the term *Weltliteratur*, or "world literature," Goethe's awareness of great works written in English did not interfere with his ability to write. He contextualized his authorship within an emerging German national literary tradition, one that he was playing a key role in crafting and that stood in relation to other national literatures. In "On German Literature," Frederick II of Prussia put the problem in the stark language of national cultural rivalry:

I am dismayed not to be able to lay out for you a more ample Catalog of our good productions: I do not accuse the Nation: it lacks neither spirit nor genius, but it has been delayed by causes that have prevented it from growing up at the same time as its neighbors. . . . We are ashamed that in certain genres we cannot equal our neighbors, [and so] we desire through tireless efforts to make up for the time that our calamities have caused us to lose. . . . Let us therefore not imitate the poor who wish to pass for the rich, let us acknowledge our destitution in good faith; that this may encourage us instead to obtain by our own efforts the treasures of Literature, whose possession will raise national glory to its full height.[4]

Like other literate men of their age, Goethe and Frederick II viewed modern literary achievement in relation to the model of literary greatness set by antiquity and by more recent contestation for preeminence among European nations. The aesthetics of German literature had to be forged not solely in relation to European "neighbors" but also in reaction to the Laocoöns of the past. Modern national literary canons formed through dual processes of cultural transfer. Meditating on and importing the classics, each European national literature looked, as Hassan Melehy has argued, "to another time and another place in order to produce itself as something in the present and in a certain geographical location" (11). The topos of *translatio studii*, of the transfer of knowledge and culture from Greece to Rome to medieval and Renaissance Europe, informed rivalry for authorial and national literary greatness. Each national literature in formation also incorporated the means employed by other national literatures to "produce" themselves via an interpretation of and reaction to literary antiquity.

The turn of the eighteenth-century quarrel of Ancients and Moderns lastingly configured intellectual filiation as a problem of inheritance and reaction within national and linguistically unified fields. Since the early Renaissance, these fields had used antiquity, and works written in Latin and Greek, as a reference point for constructing long and deep literary genealogies to legitimate national literatures. As Pascale Casanova declares in *The World Republic of Letters*, "The temporal law of the world of letters may be stated thus: *it is necessary to be old in order to have any chance of being modern or of decreeing what is modern.* In other words, having a long national past is the condition of being able to claim a literary existence that is fully recognized in the present." Moreover, as Casanova points out, to be a literary "modern" requires a certain knowledge of preceding and immediate literary trends so as to lay claim, effectively, to novelty (91). National literatures have a vertical structure, where claims about the past must be made in order to make claims about the present. Goethe and Frederick II's over-the-shoulder glances at classical, French, and English literature were hardly original with them. The early modern literary field coalesced around a principle of literary aesthetic capital with prestige accruing to the age of a (national) language's literariness. If, following the dominance of Latin, Italian was an early leader, French, Spanish, and English entered into concurrence in the sixteenth century. Dutch claimed a stake in the seventeenth century, yet French monopolized the center of the literary field by the seventeenth and eighteenth centuries with important rivalries emerging between French, British, and by the end of the century, German literatures. In Casanova's model, German entered the field in the eighteenth century ready to do battle with the French "capital" of world literature, while Russian followed suit in the nineteenth century, and so on.

Casanova's omission of early modern women writers from her discussion is less indicative of oversight than of the inadequacy of her model to describe their case. The eighteenth century marked the moment at which large numbers of women began to enter and participate in national literary markets alongside men, both benefiting from their help and competing with them. Across Western Europe, literacy rates for women rose significantly between 1690 and 1750 (Melton 82). In Britain, 201 women novelists published over the course of the long eighteenth century, while, as Judith Stanton as shown, the total number of English women in print rose steadily over the second half of the century, from 28 between 1750 and 1759 to 191 between 1790 and 1799 (251). By the mid-eighteenth century, 35 percent to 40 percent of adult women in England could sign their names, as opposed to 60 percent of men (Melton 82).[5] In France, the number of French women in print stayed fairly consistent before 1789, with 73 in print between 1754 and 1765. As Carla Hesse has demonstrated, the number rose dramatically after the fall of the *ancien régime*, with 329 women in print in the period from 1789 to 1800 (37). French literacy rates for women remained low throughout the century; 27 percent of women could sign their names by 1786 to 1790 as compared to 48 percent of men (Melton 82). In the last third of the eighteenth century, a large German female reading public was sufficient to support publication and increasing female contributions to moral weeklies (Tautz 329). Already active in translation and playwriting at mid-century, women wrote "some of the best-selling titles" as the German literary market expanded (Fronius 2). As in the rest of Western Europe, German literacy rates for women varied broadly depending on whether a woman was rural or urban or a member of a social or religious group. German Pietists, who valued reading, showed high literacy rates for women, and among English Quakers, literacy was almost universal

(Melton 83–84). Region affected literacy rates for women in the Dutch Republic as well; 64 percent of brides in Amsterdam could sign their names at marriage in 1780 (de Vries and van der Woude 314). Active as poets in the seventeenth century, women writers became increasingly visible in polemic political writing, novel writing, and pedagogical writing in the last two decades of the eighteenth century. Suzan van Dijk's preliminary inventory identifies 55 eighteenth-century women writers in the Netherlands, with the majority producing occasional and secular verse and religious writing and verse ("Early Historiography" 88).[6]

The eighteenth century was also the period in which the forms of women's writing, already partly shaped by centuries of debate on the woman question in manuscript and in print, acquired solidity. On the one hand, as women writers entered the European literary world in the eighteenth century, their relationship with its "fields of force" was governed by the same principles of national prestige, determinations of the qualities associated with aesthetic capital based in reactions to classical aesthetics, and institutional supports to and assessments of literariness as their male counterparts. In particular, pundits sounding the horn of national greatness ritually presented the unusual or exceptional achievement of one woman or of a coterie of women as an index of the advanced cultural state of the nation. Although more likely to be perceived as emblems than as inheritors of national literary traditions, women writers did participate alongside men in the making of them. On the other hand, fields of force within an ongoing *querelle des femmes* presented female authorship and intellectual filiation in ahistorical, denationalized terms mediated by translation between modern languages. When Sophie von La Roche contributed to an emerging German literature by publishing a periodical for women, *Pomona für Teutschlands Töchter* (1782–84), she inserted her fictional correspondence with a young girl named Lina, who imbibed virtue as she learned to write elegant letters in German, next to articles containing brief histories of illustrious French, English, Italian, and German women (Strauss Sotiropoulos and Griffiths). The implication was that Lina and the reader might fashion themselves through contemplation and discussion of the lives of women from all times and countries. An international and atemporal, all but rote, collection of women, as materialized in hundreds of catalogs, biographies, anthologies, magazines, and miscellanies expanded to accommodate new women writers and new lives. Within the expansive terms set by the *querelle des femmes*, women's writing always necessarily intervened in the international and timeless woman question, since the fact of it appeared to constitute positive and negative evidence of women's worth, virtue, and educability. Far more than for male writers, the exemplarity or interest of women writers' lives counted in the assessment of their work, not coincidentally, since gendered literary codes associated the virtue displayed within the text with the virtue displayed outside of it—including the modesty women demonstrated in publishing their writing in the market-place.

The form of the quarrel of women wove together the international eighteenth-century literary field of women writers, which transected national literary traditions and rivalries. The political significance of the quarrel of women form resided in its distribution of women's writing through a symbolic capital of virtue rather than through a symbolic capital of aesthetics—the capital at issue in the quarrel of Ancients and Moderns and in the consolidation of national literary fields. The form's significance lay too in its suspension of the national identity of women and of genealogies of national literary and monolingual inheritance in favor of an assimilation of the life of the woman to a transnational pantheon. While discussion of the quarrel of women and its iconic characters is by now a well-trodden path, reviewing it sheds light on how women were inserted into literary "history" up until around 1750. Significantly, the transnationalism of the woman question as it had developed since the Middle Ages persisted in conceptualizations of affinities among exceptional women or of the character of the exceptional woman.

My assumption in this chapter is that literary history looks different when it is not systematically constructed as a national genealogy. The intention here is not to recover a lost history of women writers in each national literature—to add Frances Burney, Sophie von La Roche, and Germaine de Staël to Casanova's Jane Austen, a project that numerous literary historians have already achieved. Instead, the purpose is to elucidate the transnational "fields of force" pulling on women writers in the eighteenth century—to explore how a powerful discourse of conversational affinity and timeless exceptionalism functioned as a counterweight to women writers' membership in national literary heritages. If the quarrel of the Ancients and Moderns interpolated male writers through a figure of vertical textual inheritance and reaction, the quarrel of women interpolated women writers via a spatial figure of horizontal conversational affinity—through the conceit of a familiar recounting of lives.

SAPPHO, so celebrated for her impassioned and elegant poetry, was a native of Mitylene, in the isle of Lesbos. She lived in the forty-second Olympiad, six hundred and ten years before the Christian era. She composed a great number of odes, elegies, epigrams, epithalamiums, &c. and received from her contemporaries the title of the tenth muse. But few of her numerous productions have descended to posterity; yet those few justify the panegyrics which have been bestowed upon her. (Hays 3:459)

Lack of access was one obvious reason that women's writing was less directly influenced than men's by the comparison with antiquity and a text-based encounter with the past. Women offered an immense new market for print capitalism from the late seventeenth century on, when literacy and books insinuated themselves into women's lives at an exponential rate. If unsupervised reading in general was construed as compromising women's innocence, classical texts in particular appeared to present threatening sexual and non-Christian content. "Latin and Greek marked an important rite of passage forced upon (and jealously reserved for) boys," across early modern Europe (C. Turner 56). As Janet Todd writes, "Latin was regarded as a male preserve, a code that separated the sexes and which enshrined the masculine civic and heroic virtues unattainable by any woman. Even though women often learned it, they still felt a painful inferiority because they had not received it within formal education" (120). Greek and Latin, were, in any case, viewed as too difficult for all but the most unusual of women. When eighteenth-century British and European girls and women did master a second language, they did not for the most part learn the text-based classical languages but rather contemporary European languages associated with conversational sociability. Hilary Brown explains that in the loosely grouped principalities where German was spoken, for example, daughters of the aristocracy or

> in rare cases girls from bourgeois families in which learning was valued—might be given private instruction in foreign languages. Indeed, it was common for daughters of the nobility to spend time studying languages alongside other subjects such as religion and music, so that they would have the necessary accomplishments should they one day find themselves at the head of a court. But the focus was likely to be on modern European languages rather than the Latin or Greek that would have been a fundamental part of many boys' education. . . . Daughters of the nobility who were taught the ancient languages were usually expected to acquire only a passive understanding sufficient for reading select theological works; among the bourgeoisie, girls were exposed to Latin or Greek only in the rarest of cases, such as in the families of humanists. (20)

As Isabelle de Havelange has shown, the consensus in pedagogical fiction published between 1750 and 1830 was that Latin should be reserved for boys and French for girls (578).

At the very end of the seventeenth century, François Fénelon noted that Spanish and Italian were considered court languages for girls who might be married into or attached as companions or ladies in waiting to Spanish and Italian noble families. Yet he argued in his *On the Education of Girls* (*De l'éducation des filles*, 1687) that Spanish and Italian books were "dangerous and capable of heightening the flaws of women" (244). For much of the eighteenth century, French served as the primary language of choice for young women across Europe who did learn a foreign tongue. With a cultural veneer applied by the linguistic politics of Louis XIV and polished in the formal and informal institutions of the Republic of Letters, French was the fashionable international language prized as a political and diplomatic medium in European courts and as a polite vehicle of sociability.[7] Establishing themselves in Protestant countries after fleeing France following the Revocation of the Edict of Nantes, French Huguenots, among them the literate daughters of humanists, often became the governesses, tutors, readers, and teachers who spread literate French across the continent and Britain. At least "88 different grammars, dictionaries and manners for teaching the French language" were published in England alone between 1694 and 1800.[8] As Michèle Cohen argues, French was often seen as the opposite of classical Greek and Latin, as a language best taught through conversation (73). In his influential *Some Thoughts Concerning Education* (1693), John Locke insisted that the "right way" for the French language to be taught "is by talking it into children in constant conversation, and not by grammatical rules" (125). Since conversation was also deemed the most prudent method for the education of girls (and since girls were deemed to be predisposed to prattling), learning French through conversation resonated as especially suitable for women. In the second half of the century, attacks on the artifice, effeminacy, and degeneracy of French culture multiplied, often within French texts themselves. The claim that Fénelon had made about books in Spanish and Italian was transferred onto French. English culture opened to German influence and German culture to English influence during the Personal Union. Yet as English and, once again, Italian by the 1790s became increasingly favored as possible languages for women, French maintained a feminized cultural ascendancy and continued to mediate female literary affinity, albeit in an increasingly nostalgic and often polarizing form.

Classical genres—satire, epic, elegy, ode, epigram, epithalamia, maxim, tragedy, and history—served as the preserve of male writers engaged in making a name for themselves either through a translation from Greek or Latin or through a transfer of the genre into their own national vernacular, as in Milton's writing of English epic in *Paradise Lost*. The minor genres in which women could more readily publish in the late seventeenth-and eighteenth-centuries—romances and novels, translation, magazines, compilation, letters, and travel accounts—did not boast recognized classical precursors (G. Kelly, "Women's Provi(d)ence" 176). Hence their minor status.

When women scholars did overcome significant barriers to learn and translate the classics, their achievements registered chiefly as noteworthy exceptions to the rule. The famous Hellenist Anne Dacier, for instance, would be classed throughout the eighteenth century within the ever-evolving pantheon of exceptional women. Subsequently, Elizabeth Carter's translation of Epictetus in 1758, as Susan Staves writes, "made English people feel that they had finally produced a female scholar to rival the famous French Anne Dacier" (*Literary History* 23). Dacier's translations of Homer remained a standard well into the nineteenth century. She became a vocal proponent of the Ancients in the second phase of the quarrel of Ancients and Moderns, arguing that classical texts, in the original language, preserved ideal models of virtue, heroism, love, and honor unequaled in modern writing (Moore): "In working to justify Homer, I also work to justify my translation: for I haven't translated it to draw towards myself the vain praise of having put into our language the first and the greatest of poets, I translated it to make, if I could, a useful work, and I know of useful works only those that in instructing the mind, form the heart" (Dacier, *L'Iliade d'Homère* ix). Dacier's translations of Homer were addressed to all modern readers and took the form of prose rather than verse in a recognition that Homer's Greek could not be rivaled. Her parallel edition of *The Poetry of Anacreon and Sapho* (*Les poésies d'Anacréon et de Sapho*, 1716) was, however, addressed to women: "In translating Anacreon into our language I wanted to give to Ladies the pleasure of reading the most polite and the most gallant Greek poet that we have" (235). Despite her training, skill, the accolades for her work, and her direct leadership of the Ancients in the quarrel of the Ancients and the Moderns, she steered clear of presenting herself as a scholar among scholars. Commentators often depicted her either as an exception or simply as a translator, a term that eclipsed her vast classical erudition.

The writings of actual classical women were not available to serve as independent models for literary imitation by early modern women writers since they were entirely lost, as in the case of Corinna, or fragmentary and quoted in the writing of men, as in the case of Sappho. Witness Dacier's indication in the preface to her own translation that Sappho had written a large body of work and had invented poetic forms, subsequently lost: "She had composed nine Books of Odes, several Books of Epigrams, Elegies, Epithalamia, and many other Poems. She even invented two types of verse, which were called Eolics and Saphics. I find also that she had invented a musical instrument, and a kind of harmony of which we have no knowledge. Almost all of her Works were made in praise of her female friends; but one thing surprises me, that these female friends were almost all foreigners and that she couldn't make herself be liked by the Women of her country" (*Les poesies* 240). Where Anacreon, Ovid, Virgil, Homer, Juvenal, and Horace functioned for early modern European male writers as the authors of distinguished works from a golden age with a form and content to be emulated and bested, Corinna and Sappho appeared instead, framed within the writings of male writers, as figures whose intriguing lives stood in the place of irretrievably lost or fragmentary bodies of work. Dacier reiterated Sappho's monicker as the "tenth muse" and introduced her translation of Sappho's surviving poetry with a cautionary biography. Tellingly, Dacier herself would appear alongside Sappho in the abundant eighteenth-century contributions to the quarrel of women that lumped exceptional women all together, regardless of their country of origin or the period in which they lived, and that implied affinity among them as if they were, like Sappho, drawn to foreign female friends.[9]

The quarrel of women developed a characteristic form from its origins in the Middle Ages, receiving name only retrospectively from early twentieth-century literary historians (Dubois-Nayt, Dufournaud, and Paupert 8). It presented relationships among women through a figure of ahistorical conversational affinity rather than through the figure of historical national and textual inheritance. Through the staple trope of virtual conversation, it removed women writers from history and place and unified them across national borders on the basis of their exceptionalism. It relied on a constant retelling of the lives of exceptional women, walking the line between gossip and hagiography. As an international and vernacular form, the quarrel depended on continual translation and annexation of new material, new lives, into catalogs and anthologies. Over time, it underwent permutations to accommodate changing ideas about the education of women, social class, and national identity. Before the second half of the seventeenth century, the debate had identified exceptional women as gender anomalies capable of leaping over the boundaries segregating their sex to excel in the male civic domain. As Boccaccio put it in his compendium of extraordinary women, "What can we think except that it was an error of nature to give female sex to a body which had been endowed by God with a magnificent virile spirit?" (87). Classical erudition in a woman, for example, constituted an anomaly as well as an aristocratic privilege. The classical scholar Anne Dacier worked at the very end of the period in which gender anomaly, what Thomas Laqueur has called the "one sex model," could explain female achievement. In the key period at which the quarrel of the Ancients and Moderns erupted at the end of the seventeenth century, the quarrel of women was just beginning to incorporate an essentially modern debate about the necessity of educating women as women for the larger social good. The argument was based in social hygiene; education could ensure that young women would be virtuous and that mothers would conduct themselves in a way that would ensure the health of their children. Despite the permutation opening the woman question to broader arguments about education for women of all ranks, the horizontal transnational form of the quarrel of women continued to structure women's writing and its reception as a conversation among women into the early nineteenth century.

CHRISTINE DE PIZAN. (No entry in Hays, *Female Biography*)

The humanist assembly of famous or exceptional women from different times and places into a catalog, single virtual space, or collectivity dated from the fourteenth century when Plutarch's *Mulierum Virtutes* (first century CE) was reinvented by Giovanni Boccaccio in his influential and frequently translated and imitated *De claris mulieribus* (*Concerning Famous Women,* c. 1362–75) and, a decade later, by Geoffrey Chaucer in *The Legend of Good Women,* 1385/6) (V. Brown xx–xxi). Both of these works stand as instances of cultural transfer from antiquity into modern national vernaculars. The quarrel of women was neoclassical; it drew on a genre revived from antiquity—the catalog of famous women—and built its argument for or against the virtue of women through the accretion of classical references that then served as the substrate for modern additions. Boccaccio's catalog of famous men, *De casibus virorum illustrium,* was "more ordered, more unified, more conventional, and more linked to universal verities than the *De claris mulieribus*" (McLeod 77). His inclusion of artists, writers and scholars in both works constituted a major innovation in the humanistic catalog. In *Concerning Famous Women,* Boccaccio evaluated the virtue and deeds of one hundred women from

Greco-Roman antiquity and an additional six postclassical women. This incitement to evaluate the virtue of the women whose lives were represented would constitute a powerful dynamic within the *querelle* carried forward into the eighteenth century. Famous women in Boccaccio's catalog ranged from the apocryphal learned Pope Joan, who gave birth to an illegitimate child in the streets of Rome, to the prostitute Leena who bit out her own tongue rather than betray fellow Christians, to Amazons who rode to battle, to wives like Lucretia whose suicides in the face of rape protected family honor. The numerous men and handful of women in *De casibus* served as historical models of civic contributions. In contrast, the model women in *Concerning Famous Women* owed fame to their positions as virtuous wives, mothers, and daughters. They were the collateral victims of historical civil conflict, but within an intimate and dehistoricized realm. Boccaccio presented women leaders, writers, and orators as notorious interlopers who were severely punished for their incursions in the male civic domain (Jordan). Boccaccio's famous women were loosely grouped together without regard for chronology or geography, becoming largely detached from temporality by the moral conclusions that he drew from each biography (King and Rabil xvii).

In *The Book of the City of Ladies* (*Le livre de la cité des dames,* first published in 1405, with a Dutch translation commissioned in 1475,[10] and printings in French in 1497 and in English in 1521), Christine de Pizan borrowed the device of the dream from Boccaccio's *De casibus*. Born in Venice, de Pizan was well integrated into a French court culture fascinated by Italian cultural achievement. Between 1399 and 1402, she stimulated the *querelle des femmes* in a series of works. Most famously in *The Book of the City of Ladies*, she wrote a counter-dream to the one framing Jean de Meun's misogynist addition to *The Romance of the Rose* (*Roman de la rose,* c. 1265). To the original *Romance* by Guillaume de Lorris, written around 1230 and widely read thereafter, Jean de Meun had added an account of the impossibility of finding a chaste woman, along with new erotic content and sexual wordplay that transformed the work into a literary tour de force in the French language. De Pizan "wrote back" to de Meun and argued directly with the Latin screed against marriage and women in Mathéolus's *Lamentations*. In *The Book of the City of Ladies*, the character Christine dreams of conversations between herself and three ladies. Providing a template for later writing, these familiar conversations incite the telling of the histories of virtuous women. As the title implies, the frame of the dream encourages the female reader to imagine exemplary women from different periods and countries united by "principles of Christian virtue, nobility and female collectivism," within the single atemporal and allegorical space of a city (Pohl, *Women* 1). When "Christine" addresses the "ladies" at "the end of the book," she explains that the "substance with which" the city "is made is entirely of virtue, so resplendent that you may see yourselves mirrored in it." She expostulates, "My most honored ladies, may God be praised, for now our city is entirely finished and completed, where all of you who love glory, virtue, and praise, may be lodged in great honor, ladies from the past as well as from the present and future, for it has been built and established for every honorable lady" (254). Christine de Pizan's interwoven forms of spatialized community, catalog, testimonial biography, familiar conversation, and "writing back" to a misogynist and, in the case of de Meun's additions to the *Roman de la rose*, eroticized, pretext migrated across Europe alongside Boccaccio's revival of the catalog form. The resulting *querelle des femmes* was, as Margaret L. King and Albert Rabil write, "a literary explosion consisting of works by both men and women, in Latin and in vernacular languages . . . involving probably several thousand titles" written and circulated in medieval manuscript and Renaissance print culture (xvii). The catalog or list of notable women emerged as the signal genre of the *querelle*. Cornelius Agrippa of Nettesheim, a German humanist, developed the "most exhaustive and frequently pirated list of illustrious women in his *De nobilitate et praecellentia foeminei sexus . . . declamatio* (1529)," which was translated into many European languages (Erdmann xiv). As the publishing history of Agrippa of Nettesheim's volume testifies, the catalog became a quintessentially modern and transnational genre easily adapted to a variety of vernaculars. Lists of women along with capsule descriptions of their lives could be copied, translated, emended, and augmented. Catalogs of women defied the ethics of *fidelio*. Inherently hybrid, supranational, and dependent on plagiarism and translation, they gathered women from all times and places together. They fed the appetite of a growing publishing industry and, with the constant annexation of new lives, subordinated or erased national literary history in the process of marking timeless female exceptionalism and scandal. Moreover, the catalog's characteristic formula—the name of a woman as an entry title followed by a capsule life story, with an emphasis on the correlation between romantic/sexual experience or virtue and notoriety—could, with the arrival of print, easily be transferred to other genres: lyric, scandalous chronicle, novel, magazine, and so on.

Medieval and Renaissance catalogs virtually assembled exceptional women (or "worthies," as they were called in the English literature), into a city, knave, fort, gallery, or, following a mid-sixteenth-century Italian fashion, a palace or garden.[11] The catalogs' ritual marshaling of women's lives amounted to a "roll-call of women," as Ina Schabert aptly terms it. "As the deceitfulness of animals is again and again illustrated by the cockatrice, the serpent, the crocodile, the basilisk and the hyena, so the intellectual capacity of women is mechanically exemplified by Aspasia, Corinna, Deborah, Lady Jane Grey, Elizabeth I and others" (73). Lists of women served as the standard evidence for rhetorical displays on both sides of the *querelle des femmes*.[12] Martine Vasselin argues that the sixteenth-century catalog "abolish[ed] established frontiers between historical, biblical, and pagan figures, literary characters, and mythological figues; it confer[red] upon them all the same ontological value. . . . This indifference to sources, times, and places, this equality in abstraction, in terms of contemporary Christian moral values projected indiscriminately and anachronistically into a cloudy past, brands texts and figurative works with the same seal" (32–33). The "seal" implied connection among notable women from different times and places. Contemporary women, presented in partially hagiographic "lives," were evaluated within the same framework as the historical and allegorical women whose lives could be found alongside theirs (Dunn-Lardeau 33, 39). Discussing the first English printing of the manuscript *Book of the City of Ladies*, Bryan Ainsley's 1521 *Boke of the Cyte of Ladyes*, Mary Beth Long points out that the account of saints' lives in the third section of *Boke* would have jibed nicely with "the number of female saints' *vitae* printed in the period from 1485 to 1525" and would have appealed to women readers, "the primary consumers" of hagiographic texts. Without a frame of reference for the quarrel of women or knowledge of Christine de Pizan, readers may well have understood *Boke* as male authored and belonging to the devotional category of legendaries. Long cites Alain Boureau's explanation of hagiography's "appeal to book buyers" from the thirteenth through the sixteenth centuries:

> The dual nature, theological and magical, of the hagiographic book made it a sacred object that one could manipulate. Like a cult object, it could be possessed in common and be endowed with sacred power, but like devotional materials, it was an individual continuation of cultic activities and the mark of a religious practice. It took its place among medals, pious images, and pilgrimage tokens. It signalled, recalled, evoked a vow or ongoing practice. When it was read, leafed through, or put on display

it became a spiritual guide, along with breviaries, missals, and books of hours. (19)

While catalogs in the late medieval and early modern world laid claim to authority by building on humanist practices of culling from established references, the list of illustrious women, repeated and expanded, may have had a devotional character for some readers as well. It may have encouraged readers to leaf through lives in search of models and in search of the self-transformation and inclusion in the city that the cult object offered.

ISABELLA SFORZA, who deserves a place in the catalog of learned women, lived in the sixteenth century. Some of her letters are inserted in a collection published at Venice, by Hortensio Lando, 1549. Among these is a letter of consolation, written to Bonna Sforza, widow of the king of Poland, lately deceased. Also one to Margaret Bobbia, in vindication of poetry. This collection of letters is referred to by Christofano Bronzini, in a dialogue, in which one of the speakers is represented as denying the capacity of women to put together in writing two words, *i.e.* sentences more probably was meant by this man of straw). His adversary, in reply, quotes the collection of female letters, published by Hortensio Lando, the propriety, ingenuity, elegance, and elocution of which he praises, distinguishing more particularly those of Isabella Sforza. (Hays, *Female Biography* 3:476)

ALOYSIA SIGEA OF TOLEDO, CELEBRATED for her learning, who wrote a letter to Paul III. In five different languages, Latin, Greek, Hebrew, Arabic, and Syriac: she was afterwards called to the court of Portugal, where she composed several works, and died young. (Hays, *Female Biography* 1:131; under "Aloysia")

Virginia Cox notes, "In a lecture on the modern Italian literary tradition delivered before a prestigious Roman academy in 1563, the Mantuan poet Curzio Gonzaga (1536–99) identified as one of that tradition's great claims to distinction the presence of women as writers within its ranks. If antiquity gloried so greatly in the single figure of Sappho, how much more so should present-day Italy, equipped with a plethora of female literary luminaries, 'the splendor and marvel of the age.'" Gonzaga cited seventeen women who wrote in Italian, from Veronica Gambara (1485–1550) to Vittoria Colonna (c. 1490–

1547), although at least 150 Italian women published single-authored works between 1540 and 1659 (Cox, *Lyric* 1–2). Moderata Fonte's *The Worth of Women* (*Il merito delle donne*, 1600) printed posthumously, went further in reclaiming the architecture of the community of women through recourse to the *locus amoenus*; the garden offered an ungoverned recess where women might meet and talk. Fonte gathered a group of seven women in a Venetian palazzo garden where, guided by Fonte's mouthpiece Corinna, they vindicated their sex in an informal conversation that included medical remedies, fables, poems, and parody of male privilege in learning Latin and classical rhetoric (Cox, *Prodigious Muse* 237). To the traditional "examples of women's excellence," Marinella's *Le nobiltà et eccellenze delle donne et I difetti, et mancamenti de gli huomini* (1600 and 1601) added "examples of men's defects." (Cox, *Lyric* 239). Cox points out that early anthologies of Italian women's lyric, notably Lodovico Domenichi's 1559 anthology *Rime diverse d'alcune nobilissime et virtuosissime donne*, heavily favor representation of "social relations among women, whether of friendship or patronage," over love poetry; Domenichi "showcased" several poetic correspondences between women, including a sonnet exchange between Veronica Gambara and Vittoria Colonna, in his volume (*Lyric* 26). Sixteenth-century Italian women scholars and Italian women lyric poets published extensively. The far greater availability of printing presses in Italian city states than elsewhere in Europe proved conducive to a higher frequency of publishing works by women. Yet these sixteenth-century Italian women writers and the anthologies that collected their poetry remained largely untranslated,[13] although they participated in the "very public emergence of women writers as a group for the first time in Italy, during the years 1530–70," as Diana Robin has written (xvii). Isabella Sforza's *Della vera tranquillità dell'animo*, an essay on seeking repose of the soul through retirement from the world, prose not poetry, was one of the rare works to be translated into French (1549) and Spanish (1568). Tullia d'Aragona's prose philosophical dialogues in *Dialogue on the Infinity of Love* (*Della infinità d'amore*, 1547), with their intricate questioning of Platonic ideals of love and direct discussion of sex, were never translated.

When information about Italian women migrated across Europe, it was not through dissemination of their poetry but rather through integration of their "lives" (particularly the lives of women who, like the Mancini sisters, married from and into powerful political families) into catalogs and other texts purporting to demonstrate the true nature of women. At best, they were the subject of catalog biographies. At worst, they were transfigured into the

female "academies," "schools," or "universities" of early modern pornography, where experienced bawds or courtesans taught female pupils the intrica-
cies of sex work by telling the stories of their own sex lives. Early modern
erotica transformed the idea of an Italian female collectivity engaged in philosophical conversation into an aggressive and enduring pornographic counter-
trope. The Latin grammar, that exclusively male preserve, provided the form
for Ferrante Pallavicino's *The Whore's Rhetoric* (*La retorica delle puttane*,
1642), which, like Aretino's earlier education-themed erotica, *was* translated
and reprinted in multiple editions. Tullia d'Aragona became transmuted into
"Tullia," the courtesan sex teacher in Nicolas Chorier's highly popular pornographic dialogues *Aloisiae Sigae toletanae satyra sotadica de arcanis amoris et
veneris* (1660). Chorier fictionally ascribed the dialogues to the female classical
scholar Aloisia Sigea of Toledo, thereby eclipsing her actual historical existence and work as a teacher in the Portuguese court. Predictably, Chorier's
version of the "life and work" of Aloisia Sigea and of Tullia d'Aragona was
translated, republished, reedited, and excerpted numerous times. As James
Turner writes, "Small in number but highly visible, intellectual women
formed a strong irritant that explains the enduring popularity of the erotic
'Female Academy' trope, which culminates but does not conclude in Pallavicino's dedication of *La retorica delle puttane* to 'the University of the Most
Celebrated Courtesans'" (52). The satire or attack on women's learning and
friendship through the figure of the school gathering women in intimate
conversation about their sexual experiences and initiations shadowed the
trope of female conversational affinity well into the eighteenth century.

> KATHERINE PHILLIPS. KATHERINE, celebrated under the poetical name of
> Orinda. . . . During her retirement at Cardigan, she cultivated poetry as
> an amusement, to beguile her solitary hours. Copies of her poems being
> dispersed among her friends, they were collected and published anony-
> mously, in 8vo, 1663, without the knowledge or consent of the author.
> Mrs. Phillips's vexation at this circumstance, which she appears acutely
> to feel . . . occasioned her a severe fit of illness. (Hays, *Female Biography*
> 3:281)

Utopian female friendship, often in a *locus amoenus*, functioned as an
important topos in women's writing in Britain from the beginning of the
seventeenth century on, as Nicole Pohl has shown. City, castle, garden, college . . . the space of female retreat, according to this discourse, amplified

exemplariness through virtuous friendship and emulation. As early as 1611, Aemilia Lanyer, in her preface to *Salve Deus Rex Judaeorum*, "invited" a list of "worthy" ladies to "grace this little book" and envisioned the English country house of Cookham as a place of female respite.[14] Responding to Sir Philip Sydney's patriarchal *Arcadia*, which sought to fashion a new English-verse romance out of the Hellenistic model provided by Heliodorus and influenced by early French pastoral romances and romans à clef, Lady Mary Wroth imagined a pastoral and aristocratic women's community in *The Countess of Montmorency's Urania*.[15] At the turn of the eighteenth century, Mary Astell famously relied on the trope of the dedicated space to propose a women's college in *A Serious Proposal for the Ladies*. In it, the concept of "virtuous friendship" played a crucial role. Eschewing a political and activist path for achieving female liberty, Astell developed a Cartesian-inspired philosophy privileging the soul and virtuous emulation between female friends. She argued that carefully chosen female friendships fostered in a protected female space elevated women morally. As Jacqueline Broad explains, "The resemblance of the friend's soul to our own is important: Astell says that such friendship can contribute toward a woman's self-improvement because virtuous friends will be as devoted to 'bettering the beloved Person' as they are to bettering themselves. There can be no envy amongst such friends, for 'how can she repine at anothers wel-fare, who reckons it the greatest part of her own?' Virtuous friendship has a special power to deliver us from 'vicious selfishness'" (72).[16] Radical in her proposal and in the Cartesianism at its basis, Astell nonetheless played a familiar chord in arguing that female virtue depended on conversation, in the contemporary sense of social "intimacy," between women.[17]

The print market produced odd pirated amalgams, indifferent to "sources, times, and places," such as *De preclaris mulieribus, that is to say in Englyshe, of the ryght renoumyde ladyes,* a volume published in 1789 containing a sixteenth-century translation of a small portion of Boccaccio's work to which was annexed an unattributed selection of Mary Astell's late seventeenth-century "An Essay in Defense of the Female Sex." Although the catalogs, like Boccaccio's, and pornography, like Chorier's, jumped from language to language and from one pirated edition to the next, philosophical prose by women on the woman question was rarely translated.

Verse by women encountered formidable barriers to migration. The majority of sixteenth-century Italian women writers and large numbers of seventeenth- and early eighteenth-century English women writers wrote in verse. Any translation, of course, invites questions about whether to counterfeit the supposed national character of the source language or whether to suppress linguistic difference and national conventions. Yet the linguistic specificity of meter, rhyme, and figure rendered poetry relatively intractable unless the emphasis was precisely on national aesthetic rivalries. The translation of poetry suited self-conscious literary exercises in which the aesthetic riches of a modern or national language contested the pretenses of the Ancients or a peer European nation. As a proponent of the superiority of the Ancients, Anne Le Fèvre Dacier deliberately rendered Homer in prose to demonstrate, as she explained, "the grandeur, nobility and harmony of the diction, which no one has approached, and which is not only above my strength, but perhaps even above that of our language."[18] In contrast, but relying heavily on Dacier's scholarship, Alexander Pope magisterially translated the dactylic hexameter of Homer's *Iliad* and *Odyssey* in a way that demonstrated the English heroic couplet's ascendancy. Culture wars might be distilled into arguments about the sublimities of dactylic hexameter, terza rima, iambic pentameter, and alexandrines and varieties of figurative language. A poem by a woman was significantly less likely than a poem by a man to serve as representative of a national aesthetic achievement to be rivaled or bested in a translation, although the biography of a woman poet might stand as an index of national achievement and could easily be inserted into a collection of transnational lives. Katherine Phillips became the most celebrated woman poet writing in English, yet the two editions of Phillips's collected poems (1664, 1667) were, as far as I can determine, never translated. Nonetheless, her life became available to compilers of catalogs in English and in European languages.

In England, by the turn of the eighteenth century, women were publishing large numbers of volumes of poetry (Hampsten 21). As Paula McDowell has proposed, the active political and religious dissent in this poetry and in other writings would be edited out in the process of compiling anthologies, miscellanies, and catalogs to satisfy growing demand in the marketplace for women's writing. Domestic anthologies, McDowell writes, "saw the carving-up of 'volumes of poetry by a politically and socially diverse group of women into anthologies that foregrounded generalized 'female' experience' highlighting private or personal issues, and excluding or marginalizing women's oppositional religious and political expression."[19] Collections privileged certain authors over others (Katherine Phillips, for example, over Delarivier Manley) and decontextualized authors' works. A partisan political poem might be traduced, for instance, into an innocuous paean to loyalty and friendship. Entries in English-language catalogs, anthologies, and miscellanies stripped away material networks in favor of idealized relationships. Influenced, in part, by the French culture in which she was steeped (she produced a verse translation of Corneille's *Pompée*), Katherine Phillips styled herself the "Matchless Orinda" bound by friendship to other Royalist women poets in a Society of Friendship. Members of the Society, as Janet Todd writes, "gave each other names of romantic heroines like Rosania and Lucasia" based on neo-Platonic continental models (42). Laura Mandell explains that "women poets do not appear in the volumes presenting British poetic history" (112), although the claim is perhaps too categorical.[20] Nonetheless, like poetry by women published in Italian, the poetry women published in English remained essentially untranslated even as some women, such as the matchless Orinda, became emblems of national distinction and migrated into the variable international corpus drawn on by catalog compilers.

MARY QUEEN OF THE SCOTS. (154 page-long entry)
(Hays, *Female Biography* 3:1–154)

As a transnational, multivernacular form, catalog accounts reproduced disputed facts, sometimes presenting these as merely hearsay, and entertaining a double discourse that was half scandalous secret chronicle and half encomium. The odd assortment of figures from antiquity and the Bible— alongside European nobility, such saintly commoners as Jeanne d'Arc, and royal mistresses of recent centuries—left the question of female exceptionalism infinitely interpretable, infinitely fascinating, and infinitely open to new cases. At the same time, the lack of temporal specificity and the contiguity within catalogs and lists among ostensibly fabled and historical women promoted an allegorical mode of reading. The catalog form encouraged speculation on what a specific exemplar indicated about women in general. The seventeenth-century fascination with the *femme forte* brought allegorical thinking to a head. The *femme forte* was an exemplary woman pressed by necessitous circumstance into becoming a military or political leader. In Pierre Le Moyne's *La gallerie des femmes fortes* (1647), dedicated to Queen Anne of Austria at the apex of her power as regent during her son Louis XIV's minority, the *femmes fortes* ranged from the classical Judith, who took Holofernes's head in order to save her people, to Zenobia, queen of the Palmyrians, to Margaret More (daughter of Thomas More), Mary Stuart, and Blanche of Castille. Le Moyne's *Gallerie* introduced each individual *femme forte* with an engraved emblem of the scene in which she had demonstrated her greatness.

In the section devoted to "Judith," the narrator enjoined, "Look at how she has prepared herself to strike the fatal and important blow that will remove the Head of one hundred and fifty thousand men and restore heart and spirit to twelve fallen Provinces" (41). The opening emblem and "eye witness" account of the heroic woman in her moment of glory was followed by a celebratory sonnet, an encomium, and a moral question. The case of Judith, a woman whose seductive beauty and virtue made her God's perfect instrument, prompted reflection "on the choice that God has made of women for the Salvation of States reduced to extremity" (47). In one of the final cases of the *Gallerie*, in which an anonymous "Victorious Captive" immolates herself to avoid rape and uses her flaming body to set fire to Turkish galleys attacking Cyprus, Le Moyne posed the question animating the entire collection: "whether heroic transport is necessary to the perfection of the chastity of women" (334). The sequencing of elements in Le Moyne's *Gallerie* drew the reader toward reflection on women in general based on the case of the exceptional woman's life. Such a structure allowed the reader to travel the continuum between gossip and moral reasoning.

Following the same pattern half a century after Le Moyne, catalogs would cast into doubt the seemingly invulnerable reputation of early modern classicist Anne Dacier with the hearsay that she had married a second time despite the validity of a first marriage.[21] Until the end of the seventeenth century, exemplary women such as the famed scholar Anna Maria van Schurman were still treated as wonders or errors of nature, as creatures "beyond" the normal bounds of what nature produced while also illustrating its principles.

> Anna Maria Schurman, . . . The powers of her understanding were not inferior to her ingenuity. At eleven years of age, being occasionally present at the lessons of her brothers, she frequently set them right by a whisper, when examined in their Latin exercises. (Hays, *Female Biography*, 3:462)

It was the life of the accomplished classicist Anna Maria van Schurman (1607–78) that would be most widely annexed to the *querelle des femmes* in the early modern period, both to address Le Moyne's question and to serve as an index of national Dutch achievement. A German-born Dutch woman equipped with the intellectual "portfolio of a Humanist scholar" (Pal 54), Schurman participated directly in cultural transfer from antiquity and in the quarrel of the Ancients and Moderns just as would Anne Dacier a generation later. She corresponded actively with male scholars and served as the node of an international network of women scholars that included Bathsua Makin, Marie du Moulin, Marie de Gournay, Princess Elisabeth of Bohemia, Katharine Jones, Lady Ranelagh, and Dorothy Moore (Pal 54). In her own time and today, Schurman has received an outpouring of scholarly attention. Recognized from a young age for her talent in writing, engraving, calligraphy, *découpage*, and playing the lute, Schurman became an unofficial student at the University of Utrecht and the first woman to attend a university, albeit modestly seated in a special loge "that concealed her from the male students." "There," as Joyce Irwin explains in her introduction to Schurman's writing, "she learned the ancient languages that gave her perhaps her greatest intellectual distinction: she knew Greek and Hebrew well enough to write letters in the languages; she wrote an Ethiopic grammar; and she also learned Chaldean, Arabic, and Syriac well enough to utilize them in biblical exegesis" (Schurman, *Anna Maria van Schurman* 5). Dutch male scholars discussed Schurman's achievements in their correspondence with their European peers, transforming her into a tourist attraction for intellectuals. Descartes visited her in Utrecht (Pal 250).

Schurman's position as an example of female achievement and her moral treatise "Whether a Christian Woman Should Be Educated?" made her into a desirable contact for women seeking leverage into the literary or scholarly Republic of Letters. Written first in Latin in 1637, the treatise was then published in 1641 with a postface comprising letters on the woman question that Schurman had exchanged with Calvinist theologian André Rivet. The letters were subsequently translated into French, and the treatise and the letters went into editions in French, English, Dutch, and German. In the treatise, Schurman argued that Christian daughters of the aristocracy should be able to apply themselves to solitary scholarly study. Such study posed no menace to their virtue. Relieved of domestic tasks because of their rank and living in virtuous retirement from the civic realm, they were entitled to "the right to interiority" (Schurman, *Anna Maria van Schurman* 269).

Although Schurman was a partisan of the Ancients (Pal 60), as a token in the quarrel of the Ancients and Moderns, she was adduced as proof of modern national Dutch achievement. Ironically, it was her skill in classical languages that distinguished her as a denotation of modern national greatness. Latinist Jean Louis Guez de Balzac wrote of Schurman, "I do not think that this Sulpitia who was so highly praised by Martial ever produced more beautiful or more perfect Latin: but how she possesses modesty and decency in addition to the grace and beauty of her poetry! How the virtue of her soul mingles pleasantly with the productions of her mind!" (Pal 64). Schurman became a central figure in a bid for national cultural preeminence in the Dutch Republic patterned after a classical model. As Riet Schenkeveld-van der Dussen explains, "Intellectual men with experience beyond the Netherlands saw other countries starting to follow the classical example of assigning an important cultural role to women." She continues, "This was held to be a sign of cultural maturity and worth, and it was felt that the Dutch Republic's cultural status would be well served with such women poets. From that perspective, the few women who did take up the pen were greeted with enthusiasm. Just as Greece had its Sappho and Italy its Vittoria Colonna, so the Netherlands should have its own major women poets" (40).

Within a competitive early modern European system that engaged culture as a measure of national greatness, for the Dutch to mention Schurman was to indicate that their own country had achieved a state of civility comparable to the cultivation in ancient Greece (39–64). In a similar vein, Luise Gottsched, the writer, translator, and editor who in the middle of the eighteenth century contributed to the invention of a specifically German theater, was labeled a "Sappho" (Kord 10).[22] George Ballard prefaced his *Memoirs of Several Ladies of Great Britain* with an expression of surprise that foreign biographies of illustrious women had neglected England, "more especially, as it is pretty certain, that England hath produced more women famous for literary accomplishments, than any other nation in Europe" (vi). In a bid to revive the national literary greatness of Spain's golden age, the *Memorial literario de Madrid* as late as 1785 enlisted the same rhetoric: "There is no cultivated nation which cannot present a considerable number of learned or studious women" (Peruga 17). The claim was that Spain was as "cultivated" as other countries as evidenced by its literate ladies, but not, however, that Spanish women writers were inserted in a deep Spanish national literary history of evolution from Cervantes through to the present age.[23]

Yet the selection and elevation of exceptional women within national contexts and the description of their lives had the cumulative effect of placing all exceptional women within the same imaginative space. It created a denationalized (horizontal) conception of connections among women writers and intellectuals rather than independent (vertical) national female traditions or national traditions in which women were integrated. In a collection of poems, *In Praise of Women* (*Het lof der vrouwen*), the poet Johanna Hoobius (1614–c.1642) depicted Schurman as exceptional, timeless, and not particularly Dutch:

> The world, as long as it has stood on its foundations,
> Has seen no wiser woman, none more perspicacious.
> A mind in which such wit and wisdom are displayed?
> However rare the language, she can speak it well—
> This truly is a maiden without parallel. (Schenkeveld-van der Dussen 44)

Schurman was a "maiden without parallel" among other such maidens from all eras and nations. In his catalog of 1639, Jan van Beverwyck "placed her at the pinnacle of learned women both ancient and modern" (Schurman, *Anna Maria van Schurman* 5–6). Schurman's purported fondness for eating spiders[24] correlated with her odd exceptionalism.

In 1722, Giuseppa Eleonora Barbapiccola introduced her own translation into Italian (from the French not the Latin version) of René Descartes's *Principles of Philosophy* by assimilating herself to the "example" of "famous women": learned classical women, including Aspasia and Zenobia; and Italian women "closer to our own age," such as "Constanza, wife of Alessandro Sforza" and "Venetian Cassandra Fedele," of whom "Poliziano said that [she] treated a book as her wool, a pen as her spindle, and a stylus as her needle." Last, she cited Anna Maria van Schurman and Anne Dacier out of historical order, implying that Dacier was Schurman's predecessor in achieving renown, when, in fact, the opposite was the case: "In more recent times, among those of the female sex who cultivate learning, there is no one who appears more splendid than Anna Maria Schurman of Maastricht. . . . She has made herself as famous as Madame Dacier. . . . Let us leave aside for further study the many other ancient women, as well as those modern ones still living, because the list of their names alone would be enough to make quite a fine volume about them" (52–55). Barbapiccola's flawed chronology and rapid movement across borders proved symptomatic of the way the textual architecture of the city of women suppressed history in favor of timeless space and demanded comparisons and affinities with the most splendid figures of the pantheon such as Schurman.

Always perceived as a model of female achievement, even withdrawing from the public eye to care for two aging aunts, Schurman drew a final spate of attacks for her controversial embrace of the religious doctrine of mystic Jean de Labadie. Charges of apostasy, lack of chastity, and derogation from her social rank attended her choice to live in a mixed-sex Labadist community in Amsterdam, as the aristocratic Paula to Labadie's St. Jerome. She became an advocate in the Labadist movement to repudiate both the institutionalized church and rational approaches to faith—a movement that would ultimately contribute to the birth of Pietism (Pal 243–44). At this phase in her career, she sought to free herself of the celebrity she had gained for her scholarly exploits and of the uses to which that had been put, including advocacy for Dutch cultural ascendance within the Republic of Letters. Her book *Eukleria, or Choosing the Better Part* (1673) both affirmed Labadism and criticized her own past hubris or lack of modesty. *Eukleria* simultaneously relied on the conventions of spiritual autobiography, which, as Patricia Meyer Spacks writes, "explicitly declares that lives have plots arranged by God"[25] and employed the *querelle* framework of inviting the reader to reflect on the virtue of woman through encounter with an exceptional woman's life story. It offered a spiritual bookend to her earlier "Whether a Christian Woman Should be Educated?" by arguing on the basis of her own fall into pride that heroinism in scholarship eroded female virtue.

The 1659 preface to *The Learned Maid*, the English translation of Schurman's treatise on women, figured the book as a foreign woman invited to join the "Closet" of the "Honourable Lady" to whom the edition was dedicated: "This *strange maid* . . . drest up in her *English Habit*, cometh to kiss your hand. She hopes you will admit her to your *Closet*, and speak a good word for her to your worthy *Friends*, and endear her to *Them* also. Her *Company* will be the more *delightfull*, because her *discourse* is very *rational*, and much attending to the *perfection* of that *Sexe*, whereof you, *excellent Lady*, by your *Noble Virtues* are so great an *Ornament* and *Example*" (preface). The preface played every note of the discourse on female exceptionalism, friendship, and transnationalism and lingered on the invitation to join the city.

Carol Pal explains that "the difficulty" in understanding reception of Schurman "lies in the fact that Anna Maria van Schurman figured so prominently in two contradictory currents of seventeenth-century scholarship":

The first was the actual functioning of the republic of letters, that letter-based web of working relationships in the service of scholarship and faith. In that process, van Schurman was a colleague both to male scholars in the republic of letters and to the intellectual women who would form her female epistolary network. The second current, however, was the ongoing discourses on female excellence that had attracted the pens of learned men since the fourteenth century. In that polemical process, van Schurman's renown made her an instantly recognizable name, a scholarly celebrity whose reputation was often deployed in rhetorical displays whose real focus lay elsewhere. (75)

The record of this first current, the connections among the women thinkers who corresponded with each other in the international network around Anna Maria van Schurman and the subjects of their debates in a larger republic of letters, remained largely restricted to manuscript culture and often to Latin. The second current, an exemplary structure prizing the story of female virtue as an object for moral reasoning and that assimilated modern exceptional women to classical exceptional women, redounded in international print in the vernacular catalog form that was accessible to many women readers.

In a letter, Schurman herself drew on the second current rhetorically in advising Princess Elisabeth of Bohemia about what to read: "Justus Lipsius outlined this method [of comparing great lives] more completely in his book entitled *Admonitions and Political Examples*, demonstrating to certain people, and to public figures, how they could make use of both ancient and modern examples. And in fact it seems to me that the latter are in no way inferior to the former, if we consider less the force and eloquence of the Historians than their subject matter. I would dare to compare a single Elizabeth, who in her lifetime was Queen of England, or a single Jane Grey, to all the illustrious women of ancient Greece and Rome."[26] "If we consider less the force and eloquence of Historians than their subject matter": this is the important point. The aesthetics of writing about or by women held less weight in the discourse of the quarrel of women than the exemplarity of women's lives and the comparison or juxtaposition of them across time and space.

Framed with respect to the powerful discursive figure of the women's circle, actual Renaissance and early modern networks of women intellectuals and writers, like the network around Anna Maria van Schurman, tended to disappear and be replaced by figurative renderings.[27] Early in her career, the French writer Madeleine de Scudéry unsuccessfully sought out an epistolary relationship with Schurman through a correspondence about the virtue of Joan of Arc so as to leverage her own position as a woman writer. When perennial secretary to the Académie Française Valentin Conrart put Madeleine de Scudéry into correspondence with the intellectual Marie du Moulin (niece of André Rivet and along with him a correspondent with Schurman), he fantasized about the possibility of uniting Marie du Moulin, Schurman, and Scudéry as "the three Graces who were separated" on the question of the honor of Joan of Arc. He hoped to see their "hearts united by the divine bond of a virtuous friendship."[28] When women writers corresponded, their connection was often mediated by invocation of a famous female life and by allegorization of their own relationship.

> MADELEINE DE SCUDÉRY, descended from an ancient and honourable house, was born at Havre de Grace, 1607. Educated with care under a sensible mother, she was distinguished while in her childhood for intellectual acuteness, for a lively imagination, and a just and delicate taste. In the endowments of her person, nature had been less liberal. By her wit, and the disadvantages of her figure, she obtained the name of Sappho, whose genius she emulated, with greater purity of manners. She came early to Paris, where her talents excited attention, and procured her admittance into the first literary circles. (Hays, *Female Biography* 3:464)

Nowhere was the formal procedure of the juxtaposition of lives, the concomitant elision of lines between historical and fictive women and the evacuation of historical time through allegory and analogy more evident or more influential than in the work of Madeleine de Scudéry (1607–1701). Scudéry was born the same year as Schurman but outlived her by twenty-three years to see the dawn of the eighteenth century.

It was through recourse to the figure of Sappho that Scudéry answered, if only for a few generations, both Schurman's question about whether an aristocratic woman might remain virtuous and exercise the "right to interiority" as a private scholar and Le Moyne's question about "whether heroic transport is necessary to the perfection of the chastity of women" (334). Scudéry did this in a way that was responsive to a growing female readership from a composite elite largely limited to reading in a national vernacular or sometimes in French, the international language of the Republic of Letters. Bereft of the benefits of a formal education in Latin and Greek and probably unable to read classical languages, Scudéry nonetheless drew extensively on classical sources for the stories and characters with which she populated her historical romances. She probably relied on her brother Georges and, later, members of her salon to help with translation and compilation from classical texts as well as with writing (DeJean, *Tender Geographies* 71–78). By incorporating characters and plots from antiquity and classical sources in her "modern" fiction, Scudéry created an end-run for her readership on the problem Schurman had posed—of whether a Christian woman might be permitted private study of classical texts and languages. In and through Scudéry's fictions, women encountered classical stories *as told by* characters in a collectivity. The collectivity then capped each story with a "conversation" about its moral implications. Scudéry's work staged a polite sociability that facilitated reception of stories drawn from the classics through a contemporary interpretation of female virtue and heroism in vernacular conversation.

Writing collaboratively, Madeleine de Scudéry developed an influential model of women's intelligent and polite, yet unstudied and worldly conversation in social gatherings. The model was roughed out at first in a reinvention of the centuries-old catalog. *Les femmes illustres, ou les harangues héroïques,* first published in French under the name of Georges de Scudéry in 1642 and 1644, would also appear in six English editions between 1681 and 1768 as *The Female Orators; or the Courage and Constancy of Divers Famous Queens, and Illustrious Women, Set Forth in Their Eloquent Orations, and Noble Resolutions: Worthy the Perusal and Imitation of the Female Sex,* as well as in German in 1654 and 1659. Scudéry gathered a "bouquet" of famous women from antiquity. The illustrious women spoke their "harangues" in first-person conversations and drew conclusions about their own lives instead of being evaluated or subjected to innuendo in third-person catalogs like Le Moyne's.[29] In the final speech of the first volume, for example, Sapho abandons the civil arena of military exploits to men, exhorting her friend Erinna to earn fame by writing and to relinquish notoriety based on ephemeral corporeal beauty. By claiming natural eloquence as a uniquely female talent and associating this female gift with virtue, the dialogue between Sapho and Erinna cemented the celebration of women for the exceptionalism of their cultural achievements as opposed to their Amazonian exploits at war or their martyrdom for family or religion (DeJean, *Tender Geographies* 82). The dialogues as a whole reinforced the architecture of the horizontal sociability of women when Cleopatra, Octavia, Sapho, and Lucretia all appeared in the same arena.

The widely read *Artamène, ou le Grand Cyrus* (1649–53) by the Scudérys and their circle returned to the figure of Sappho, presenting the scene in which the life story of an ancient Greek woman named Sapho is narrated as an experience that creates a bond of affinity among a group of princesses. Sapho is to be "compared" to "that learned young girl so beloved of the Muses" known as Sappho and is also comparable to Mademoiselle de Scudéry herself, who was often identified in her group by that name, as her contemporaries certainly knew (*Story of Sapho* 15). "Sapho" codified the exceptional woman, incorporating the form of the city of ladies into a single lady whose very virtue was to generate a circle of polite and virtuous yet also cosmopolitan conversation. Generations of literary heroines doubtless owe their fine eyes to a genealogy descended from Scudéry's Sapho, "who possesses above all else . . . eyes so beautiful and lively, so full of spirit, that one can neither brave the brilliance of her regard nor turn away from it" (14). The eager princesses assembled in *Artamène* learn that Sapho knows

> how to write and speak of all things so perfectly that nothing whatsoever falls outside her understanding. Don't imagine that her knowledge is simply intuitive—Sapho has seen all that is worth seeing and has taken pains to learn all that merits her curiosity. She also plays the lyre, sings, and dances gracefully. She has even sought to know all those works with which so-called learned ladies entertain themselves. But what is admirable in her, this person who knows so many varied things, is that she knows them without pedantry, without conceit and without disdain for those who are unlearned. Her conversation is so natural and easy, so charming, that in general conversation she is never heard to say anything but what someone untutored, but of large understanding, might say. Knowledgeable people know perfectly well that Nature alone cannot have opened her mind without study, but Sapho so desires to behave as befits her sex that she almost never speaks of anything that is not deemed suitable for ladies. (15–16)

Taking advantage of the seventeenth-century fashion for literary portraits[30] while rejecting Schurman's model of (aristocratic and Christian classical) scholarship through reference to the "so-called learned lady," *Artamène* staged scenes of polite and fashionable conversation. The story of Sapho appears within *Artamène* as a subject for entertainment, emulation, and reasoning about character and virtue—as a woman's biography that creates a bond among the women who have heard it.

At ten volumes, 13,095 pages, and 2,100,000 words, *Artamène* continues to hold the record for the longest novel ever written.[31] Engaging with it was more a social practice than a linear read, much like the medieval legendaries of saints' lives. The cost of a full set of tomes intended for leisure rather than scholarship and published serially would have been more easily borne by a group of readers connected through their sharing of the text than by an individual. Faced with such a huge book, impossible to remember in its entirety and filled with myriad divergences from a nominal primary narrative thread, readers doubtless dipped regularly into sections, using them to illustrate or spark conversation or to seek models for decision-making and behavior, much as do the characters in the text. Questions about behavior and character may well have motivated readers to jump from selection to selection rather than reading sequentially. Indeed, this is the way that the character Arabella in Charlotte Lennox's satiric *The Female Quixote* (1752) uses the great historical romances written by the Scudérys and their contemporaries when she seeks moral guides for her own behavior, although she makes the mistake of interpreting stories on her own rather than in the company of friends. "As a work elaborated in the heart of a salon," the editors of the modern online edition of *Artamène* ask, "is not this novel, in its conception, a function of the mode of consumption of worldly genres, reading out loud in an interactive social context?" Mary Pendarves (later Mary Delany) would describe precisely that mode of reading in a letter to her friend Ann Granville (later Ann Dewes). At a house party in Killala, Ireland, in the summer of 1732, the guests entertained themselves by reading Scudéry's second romance aloud in the French original: "We have begun Clelia, she is a much better French lady than an English one."[32]

"Clelia," or Scudéry's *Clélie, histoire romaine* (1654–60), sustained *Artamène*'s promotion of slippage between actual conversation and virtual conversation, between readers and historical figures or conversing characters. Another long read, at ten volumes, it met with an eager public in French and in English, German, Italian, and Dutch translations.[33] The frame narrative is a "transposition of Scudéry's salon," where a mixed conversational grouping uses stories of lives from antiquity to stimulate discussions about how one should act in questions of love, taste, and honor (Paige 81). Scudéry offset her recourse to classical models of female virtue by associating them with recognizable contemporary figures. Readers absorbed *Clélie* as a roman à clef offering clues as to Scudéry's famous and sometimes notorious contemporaries: Ninon de l'Enclos (famous as a literary courtesan); Madeleine de Souvré, marquise de Sablé; Marie-Madeleine Pioche de la Vergne, comtesse de La Fayette; Marie de Rabutin-Chantal, marquise de Sévigné (a welcome figure at court); Madame de Montespan (Louis XIV's mistress); and Madame Scarron—Françoise d'Aubigné, the young wife of the writer Paul Scarron, later known as Madame de Maintenon. The roman à clef form identified the interlocutors of Scudéry's salon (including the men Jean-François Sarasin, Gilles Ménage, Jean Chapelain, and Antoine Gombaud, chevalier de Méré, who are less well-known today) and other contemporaries simultaneously with both France and French and with Greco-Roman antiquity and classical languages.[34] The characters figured on an idealized, transhistorical map of civility and exemplarity. The famous *carte de Tendre* in *Clélie* codified the behaviors associated with the allegorical group and presented a feminized model of neo-Platonic love spread across a timeless allegorical space. *Clélie* celebrated women's exceptional ability to foster elevating conversations and narratives and idealized the conversation group over the actual literary and social network.

Predictably, Scudéry's circle became the butt of misogynist satire and was attacked for an Amazonian separatism. Notably, Molière helped to make his own name as an author with his send-ups of the language of the circle, whom he termed *Les précieuses ridicules* (1659). In this play and in *Les femmes savantes* (1672), he suggested that behind an elaborate veil of overly ornate language, the *précieuses* around Scudéry disguised a basic ambition for intellectual domination and circulated "pernicious amusements of idle minds, novels, verse, songs, sonnets."[35] Reacting to claims that her long novels were outmoded fantasies and contained scandalous stories, between 1680 and 1692 Scudéry stripped the classically based adventures from her writing and published five volumes of conversations. There, she provided a model of the mixed gender conversational ideal that placed women, such as the "character" Plotine in the position of arbiter of politeness and taste. These model philosophical conversations celebrated Méré's idea of *honnêteté*, an ideal of sociability involving fairness, tolerance, politeness, and the suppression of personal desires for the sake of meeting a collective goal (Conley, "Scudéry"). Appearing at first in French, the prestige language of aristocratic courtly sociability and of the Republic of Letters, Scudéry's novels and conversations were translated rapidly into multiple European languages. Barbara Helena Kopsch, the educated daughter of a German merchant, took up Scudéry's virtual invitation to conversation by producing an illustrated "creative translation" of the *Conversations* headed by an emblem and motto and followed by a verse or prose commentary (Kopsch). Kopsch developed a parallel rendering of Madeleine de l'Aubéspine's discourses, *Cabinet des saines affections*, as well. Hilary

Brown points out that Kopsch's works "interact with the *discours* or *conversation* in question. . . . Through her pattern of alternating translated and emblematic sections, she aligned herself with the respective French author and gave the impression of being in dialogue with her" (28).

The constant extension of conversation to include more interaction, more alignment, more stories of exemplary women and the incitement through these stories to more reflection about the self help explain the conversational structure in the comtesse de La Fayette's most important and most frequently read, translated, and anthologized novel. *La princesse de Clèves* (1678) is often described as the first modern novel in the French tradition because of its psychological intensity and brevity relative to works like *Artamène* and *Clélie*. Both the princesse de Clèves and the reader encounter stories of the lives of notable women related to the court of Henri II, including Elizabeth I, Anne Boleyn, Mary Stuart, the Duchess of Valentinois, and Catherine de Medici[36]—all of whom had become staples in the ambivalent catalogs of worthies that graced early modern libraries. La Fayette adapted Scudéry's conversational frame for assessing the lives of exceptional women and for drawing personal lessons about heroinism, politics, and virtue. Often in the company of her young friend Mary Stuart, who recounts most of the stories of other women in conversation, the princesse de Clèves interprets other female lives, internalizes them, and devises her own model of virtuous conduct. She is the ideal listener to the catalog. Through exposure to conversations relaying positive and negative exempla, she reasons her way to stoic conclusions. She learns to resist her passion for an accomplished and handsome lover, the duc de Nemours, and to protect herself from sexual commodification within a web of court intrigue. The stories of notable and notorious women become a collection of portraits hanging in the gallery of the princesse de Clèves's mind. They provide her with the examples and counterexamples that, implicitly, lead her to conclude that the only path available for preserving her own virtue is to avow her passion for the duc de Nemours (first, famously, to her husband and then to the duc de Nemours himself) and to seek *repos*, a place of ethical repose, by withdrawing entirely from the world of the court. The protagonist's growing understanding of how secret amours and intrigues produce political results—for example, Nemours's passion for the princesse de Clèves destroys his own chances for marriage to Elizabeth I and, consequently, weakens alliances across the Channel—leads her to withdraw from the world so that she will no longer be an unwilling pawn in European court politics.

In a sense, the princesse de Clèves's story is but the frame narrative that allows the other intercalated and politically implicated stories of women to be told. The innovation lies in how the narrator makes implicit the causality of listening to exemplary stories in conversation. Because of their presence, the stories appear to make the princess measure her own possible choices against the lives of the women she hears about and who are, in two cases, her intimate friends. Because of sequencing in the frame narrative, the conversational recounting of women's lives seems to incite the heroine's moral reflection and decision-making. *La princesse de Clèves* fictionally models the use of stories of women's loves and lives as the basis for reasoning about personal behavior. It makes reasoning about virtue through examination of the lives of others into a reading- and conversation-based practice that demonstrates natural nobility of mind. Such a gendered nobility of character can be fostered; it is no accident that the princesse de Clèves's mother, Madame de Chartres, has given her an unusual education in which, from the very beginning, she has been exposed to the ambivalent lives of women. Yet *La princesse de Clèves* oscillates between the spicy anecdote and secret history (*histoire secrète, histoire gallante, chronique scandaleuse*) of the court of Henri II, via reported conversations about the amours of the women of the court, on the one hand, and the use, on the other hand, of these anecdotes as exemplars of loss of virtue and therefore as objects for the protagonist's evolving moral reflection and understanding of worldliness. The text allowed readers to have their cake and eat it too since the ethical reflections and avowals of the princess compensate for the notorious anecdotes she hears. The young German Luise Gottsched "cut her teeth as a translator" on *La princesse de Clèves*, having learned French from her mother, who encouraged her to copy French texts and read literary works aloud (H. Brown 29).

The extended Scudéry network, including writers into the 1690s and turn of the century, functioned as a fashionable celebrity circle epitomizing the acme, and for some, the moral turpitude, that French national culture appeared to have reached during the reign of Louis XIV. Lives and writings of members of the circle became fodder in the eighteenth century for publishing built around precisely the oscillation between the satisfying secret history of the court of Louis XIV and the gratifying moral reflection. Not only were the prose "novels" and "histories" written by Scudéry and her collaborators and by La Fayette quickly printed in multiple languages in the late seventeenth century, the letter form became especially popular, moving from the sensational expression of lovelorn abandonment in *Lettres portugaises* (1669), to the inclusion of letters in novels, to the publication of letter-writing manuals, to the flourishing of a full-blown epistolary genre. Editions of the letters of Madame de Sévigné containing anecdotes about the court and the illustrious circle served as model letter manuals for readers of French, English, Italian, and Spanish and for those who sought to learn French, beginning in 1725.[37] Editors chose selected letters to emphasize Sévigné's maternal virtue in her correspondence with her daughter, Madame de Grignan, and to model a "refinement that was central to a new merit-based notion of nobility" (Goodman 198). They culled revelatory anecdotes about the court of Louis XIV and the cultivated world of the salon that were frequently captured in conversations reported in the letters.

A publishing boom from the 1750s to the 1770s presented to the public all over again the extended network around and beyond Scudéry, in the form of memoirs, histories and letters, translations and biographies, some of which were excerpted in magazines for women. The memoirs of the "Aspasia of France," as Hays called her (352), literary courtesan Ninon de l'Enclos, written by Douxménil, combined with an equally fictitious correspondence between her and the marquis de Sévigné and Monsieur de Saint-Évremond, virtually wallpapered Europe between 1750 and 1778. Multiple French editions were published in Amsterdam, Paris, Liège, and Rouen; a German translation came out in 1752 in Leipzig; and Elizabeth Griffith's extremely popular English translation appeared at least six times between 1761 and 1806. Laurent Angliviel de la Beaumelle's *Memoirs of Madame de Maintenon* (1755) provided mid-eighteenth-century readers with a portrait of the famous figure and her educational project at Saint-Cyr. La Beaumelle (who would go on to found a French-language women's magazine in Denmark) presented Maintenon's life as swinging between the sensational, the literary, the political, and the spiritual. By 1757, Charlotte Lennox, editor of her own women's magazine in England who satirized Scuderian romances in more than one work, had translated Angliviel de la Beaumelle's voluminous work into English. That same year, Madame de Maintenon's pedagogical conversations appeared in English translation in London and in a Dutch-published French-language edition, while Luise Gottsched, her friend Dorothea Runckel, and her husband Johann Christoph Gottsched each translated a volume of the *Memoirs* into German (H. Brown 214). An extract from Lennox's translation of the *Memoirs* appeared in the *Critical Review* in April 1757 and then reappeared under the title "Striking Instances of the Charitable Character of Madame de Maintenon" in the *Lady's Magazine* in December 1778.[38] Another burst of publishing interest recreated the circle for the nineteenth century beginning about 1805. Madame de Genlis, who was, like Madame de Maintenon, a French royal educator and mistress, would write a historical novel about her in 1806, following her *La duchesse de la Vallière* (1804) and followed by *Mademoiselle de La Fayette ou le siècle de Louis XIII* (1813). The letters of La Fayette and Ninon de l'Enclos were repurposed in 1805 and 1806 with new additions of letters purportedly written by the novelist and *salonnière* Tencin and by Charlotte-Élisabeth Aïcha, known as Mademoiselle Aïssé, who had been purchased by Tencin's brother-in-law in Constantinople as a child and subsequently educated in Paris (Auger *Lettres de Mmes. de Villars*). Mademoiselle Aïssé was already known to the reading public through a novelistic avatar as the perhaps virtuous, perhaps vicious, mysterious woman at the center of Abbé Prevost's *Story of a Modern Greek Woman* (*Histoire d'une Grecque moderne*, 1740).

The networked relationships, the literariness, and the aristocratic pedigrees of the women who all knew Scudéry or followed immediately after her generation of writers gave their romans à clef and their histories an "insider" or "eye-witness" narratorial privilege with respect to recounting the backstory to political intrigue. For non-French readers, narratives produced by women in the extended Scudéry network had the advantage of being the secret history of women from their own nation too. What were Madame de La Fayette's story of Mary Stuart in *La princesse de Clèves* or her history of Princess Henrietta but the secret histories of women from Britain transposed by politically motivated marriages and international court politics to France? What were histories of such royal mistresses as Madame de Valentinois and Madame de Maintenon but stories of how marriage to the kings of France tried the virtue of princesses from elsewhere, princesses such as Marie de Medici of Italy, Anne of Austria, Maria Theresa of Spain, and Marie Leszczyńska of Poland? What were the histories of the great courts of Europe but the international stories of how a princess raised in one country was traded in marriage and fared abroad? For example, the *Mémoires de la cour d'Espagne*, written by Marie-Catherine Le Jumel de Barneville, baronne (comtesse) d'Aulnoy, opened with a racy presage of international Hapsburg incest followed by an account of Maria Anna of Austria's journey from Vienna to marry her uncle Philip IV (their daughter would later marry Maria Anna's brother, Leopold I, Holy Roman Emperor). A portentious translation error on Maria Anna's entry into Spain led her to believe, according to the *Mémoires,* that it was the custom of Spaniards to cut off the legs of their queens and that it was this fate that awaited her (3). Princesses figured as the victims of an international trade for reasons of statecraft but also as the secret cause of international events. Aulnoy, who is better known today for her fairy tales, opened the *Mémoires de la cour d'Espagne* in a conversational voice that explained recent history as a function of Leopold I's passion for his sister Maria Anna. When he sends her off to marry Philip IV, he enjoins her to produce a litte "infanta" in Spain he can marry (2). In her *Nouvelles d'Elisabeth Reyne d'Angleterre* (1674), Aulnoy relied on the device of the mixed-gender conversational circle of courtiers to frame reprised stories of women from the catalog and to present a picture of European countries linked together by the sexual and political intrigue of the great European royal and aristocratic families. The *Nouvelles*—or, in one English translation, *The Novels of Elizabeth, Queen of England Containing the History of Queen Ann of Bullen* (1680–81)—pretexted that conversations were what most touched the heart of Queen Elizabeth I in order to present the story of her mother as told by Northumberland. The standard catalog entry on Anne Boleyn expanded in this text into an entire volume-length "novel." In volume 2, Elizabeth I herself becomes the storyteller to assembled lords and ladies of the court. She recounts the Turkish story of "Bassa Soliman and the Princess Ermina," which, through juxtaposition, manifests as a parallel to the story of England. Aulnoy's histories became popular from the 1680s to the 1720s and were printed in multiple editions in French and in English, as well as in one German edition. They relied on the conversation format, but they also integrated first-person narration of memoirs and, building on the *Lettres portugaises*, love letters purportedly written by famous noble lovers. Most significantly, while moving away from the polite *bienséance* of the "novels" of Scudéry and La Fayette, Aulnoy's works echoed their indeterminate assignment of national origins to heroines. In the secret histories of the French, Spanish, English, and Turkish courts, love, sex, progeny, succession, and politics sent exceptional princesses and ladies traveling across the borders of Europe.

Acquiring reference status as *the* women's literary circle, the extended network around "Sapho" reiterated, narrativized, and performed an inherited formal pattern of female conversational sociability drawn from the quarrel of women. The writings and literary example of Scudéry and the women with whom she overlapped in her long life proposed a model of discussion and debate—a right not to interiority and not to classical scholarship à la Schurman but to affinity-based reasoning about female behavior. The network drew on romance rewritings of classical sources and on retellings of secret histories in which the narrators appeared directly implicated due to their aristocratic lineages. The network's literary model acknowledged and amplified the correspondence between female writer and literary-biographical character. It also provided a means for women writers and readers to insert themselves into the idealized conversational group by debating the virtue of characters-writers on the basis of their stories and by selecting certain stories and certain biographies of women writers as objects for their own readerly and writerly collection, translation, and commentary. J. Watts, the English editor of a collection of French romances containing two novels by the comtesse de La Fayette, predicted in his 1729 dedication of the volume to Princess Anne that she too would join the city of ladies: "If new Discoveries of Virtue, opening Scenes of Wit, and fresh Instances of the best Temper, flowing from a Young Lady of consummate Beauty; can surprise and delight in Romance; what must they do in a true History; such as your HIGHNESS will furnish out to after ages?" (*Select Collection*, unnumbered page). The comtesse de La Fayette prefaced the *History of Henrietta of England* (*Histoire de Madame Henriette d'Angleterre*, published posthumously in 1720) by recalling how a conversation in 1664 between herself and the cloistered Princess Henrietta, exceptional for her mind and merit, led to the writing of her history. Ann Floyd, the 1722 English translator, rendered it in the following way: "'Do you not believe,' said she, 'that if those Things which have happen'd to me, and many other Affairs relating to 'em, were well writ, they would compile a diverting History? You have a good Pen,' said she, 'take the Pains to write, and I will furnish you with Memoirs'" (x). Elizabeth Griffith, the English translator of the memoirs of Ninon de l'Enclos, gushily acknowledged that despite her poor French, she had caught on and translated "in such a free manner as one tells a story or repeats a conversation" (Douxménil xii).

The relative ease of transferring life to prose and prose text to translation, suggested in the passages above, proved contagious. Translators and rewriters, as much as the original circle figured allegorically in *Clélie*, functioned fluidly as protagonists and conversational storytellers in each others' letters, novels, memoirs, and prefaces to translations. They figured female interlocutors within frame narratives as interpreters and intelligencers, thus providing an alibi for retellings of dangerous stories about less-than-virtuous lives. They became a virtual city of women, recounters in and of the secret stories behind politics in the recent and current age. They grafted off of the narrative procedures dominated by aristocratic women in France in the late seventeenth and early eighteenth centuries. Delarivier Manley's *Lady's Pacquet of Letters* appeared in 1707 spliced with a translation of Aulnoy's *Mémoires de la cour d'Angleterre* (1695).[39] Her *Secret Memoirs and Manners of Several Persons of Quality, of Both Sexes: From the New Atalantis, an Island of the Mediterranean* was published in 1709 with a frontispiece claim on the second volume of having been "written originally in *Italian*, and Translated from the Third Edition of the *French.*" In large part an alibi providing the author with unsuccessful cover from charges of libel, the feint of double translation also connected the work to the scandalous chronicles of the courts of Europe written across the channel. (*The New Atalantis* would actually be translated; it came out in at least four French editions beginning in 1713 and in German editions in 1712 and 1740). These histories were French and they were not. They traveled, they were adapted, they were translated, or they claimed to have been translated. They drew readers in a way that was unprecedented—with the exception of the catalogs that they mimicked and expanded—for writing by or about women.

> FRANCES SHERIDAN. . . . with superior talents and engaging manners, was exemplary in every relative duty. Her admirable Domestic Tale of Sydney Biddulph is well known, and justly esteemed by the public.
> (Hays, *Female Biography* 3:476–77)

Looking backward as they sought to transform the novel into a polite, aesthetically and nationally distinguished form, mid- to late eighteenth-century British commentators would associate the most notable features of late seventeenth- and early eighteenth-century prose by women in Britain with an outmoded and unwanted French influence (Warner, *Licensing* 21). Aphra Behn, Delarivier Manley, and Eliza Haywood were all tarred for their immodest cultivation of "French" tastes. The continental and global settings of their fictions and their creative reworkings of the scandalous chronicle, the *nouvelle*, and the epistolary or letter novel associated them with women writers in France whose works had been translated for an avid market of male and female readers into English (Ballaster 42). As many critics have noted, the sexual scandal of this "French" writing overshadowed the role that Behn, Manley, and Haywood played in inventing the novel in Britain as well as their work of cultural transfer. This included translation of French works into English, from Behn's translation of Bernard le Bovier de Fontenelle's highly successful *Entretiens sur la pluralité des mondes* (1688) to Haywood's versions of Marivaux and Prevost and her unattributed translations of works by Madeleine-Angélique de Gomez (Dow, "Stéphanie-Félicité de Genlis"

275). But it also included, for the first time, the significant transfer of prose by British women writers to the continent with multiple editions of their major works appearing in French, German, and, in the case of Behn's famous *Oroonoko*, by the end of the eighteenth century even in Russian.[40]

To Katherine Phillips's Matchless Orinda surrounded by her pastoral society of female friends, playwright and novelist Aphra Behn became the roving "Astrea"—the personification of commercial grit, bawdy, scandal, and foreign influence ("Astrée" was, indeed, the protagonist of Honoré d'Urfé's long French romance) (Ballaster 43). The "poles" of Orinda and Astrea then served as useful third terms for defining Restoration and Augustan women writers. Delarivier Manley presented Catherine Trotter as an amalgam of both, while Trotter's patron wrote that she was "like the morning star Orinda" (Todd 41–42). In the *New Atalantis,* Delarivier Manley ambivalently satirized contemporary Whig court ladies and lumped them with Phillips's idyllic society of friends by painting them as a lesbian separatist "Cabal": "They have no reserve; mutual love bestows all things in common, 'twould be against the dignity of the passion and unworthy of such exalted, abstracted notions as theirs."[41] In turn, the phrase "Amazons of the pen" would be used rhetorically to gather Behn, Manley, and Haywood into a foreign collectivity dominating the marketplace through anti-male aggression and sexual excess.[42] At mid-century, women writers such as Frances Sheridan had to disavow any connection with the political and popular fictions of Behn, Manley, and Haywood; erase a British female literary genealogy; and break with French women's writing, now critically termed "romance," if they were to gain traction "in the newly respectable form of the novel" (Ballaster 3).

What had decidedly differentiated Behn, Manley, and Haywood from the extended network around Scudéry and reaching beyond her to Aulnoy was their plebeian origins. To claim privileged knowledge of or connection to the exceptional lives worthy of chronicle, they needed to transform their narratorial personae as well as the definition of female exceptionalism. This also entailed transformation of the nested allegorical and emulative relationship between the lives of female reader, female narrator, and female protagonist. The reading Paula McDowell has provided of Delarivier Manley's self-fashioning is instructive here. Manley drew together "the largely aristocratic French tradition of 'feminocentric' fiction used as a tool of social and political satire, and the long-standing tradition of middling women's political activism through print." She positioned herself as a spy or provider of political intelligence, patterned after the secret intelligencer narrative positions that her immediate predecessors Aulnoy and Behn had derived, in part, from their employment as spies for France and England respectively (*Women of Grub Street* 263). In her most well-known work, *The New Atalantis*, Manley offers a cutting "Tory-motivated exposé of the supposed secret lives of rich and powerful Whig peers and politicians of the reigns of the Stuart kings and queens from Charles II to Anne I," Ros Ballaster explains (Manley, *New Atalantis* v).

Significantly, *The New Atalantis* unfolds through a conversation among three female figures: the deity Astrea, her long-lost and abandoned mother Virtue, and Intelligence, who guides Astrea in her travels across the island of Atalantis, helping to uncover and explain its iniquity. If, in the *Book of the City of Ladies,* three female deities help Christine uncover and chronicle the hidden histories of virtuous women, in *The New Atalantis*, Astrea, Virtue, and Intelligence expose stories of women's sexual downfall and erotic adventure, illustrating the corruption of the age. "Intelligence" is neither an elevated and noble divinity like Astrea and Virtue, nor low like the gossipy scandal-monger and midwife "Mrs. Nightwork" whom the trio of conversationalists encounter. As McDowell argues, "If Mrs. Nightwork's methods are similar to Lady Intelligence's, the ends to which she puts her news are different. The traditional gossip's stories are malicious and told merely to entertain. The female 'intelligencer,' by way of contrast, does not circulate titillating stories for their own sake, but rather deploys them for worthy political ends" (*Women of Grub Street* 256). The line drawn here is consistent with Manley's distancing of herself and her own sexually explicit prose from Aphra Behn (*Women of Grub Street* 226). Manley distinguishes the worthy intelligence she offers from Aphra Behn's supposed profiteering in writing *Love-Letters Between a Nobleman and His Sister* (1684). (The novel had capitalized on the scandalous elopement of Lord Grey of Werke with his sister-in-law Lady Berkeley and the subsequent disclosure of Grey's involvement in the Rye House Plot to assassinate King Charles).

Instead of connecting herself to her immediate British predecessor, Manley presented herself as *the* exceptional English woman through comparison to an acknowledged illustrious French woman. In the opening frame narrative to Manley's autobiographical *The Adventures of Rivella*, the chevalier d'Aumont confesses to Lord Lovemore his curiosity about "the ingenious women of your nation": "Wit and Sense is so powerful a Charm, that I am not ashamed to tell you my Heart was insensible to all the fine Ladies of the Court of *France*, and had perhaps still remain'd so, if I had not been softned [*sic*] by the Charms of Madam *Dacier's* Conversation; a Woman without either Youth or Beauty, yet who makes a Thousand Conquests, and preserves them too." When Lovemore protests against the idea that a scholar like Dacier may possess charm, d'Aumont calls him a "novice" in the ways of love: "I must agree with you that her [Dacier's] Perfections are not of the Sort that immediate delight, and warm the Blood with Pleasure, as those do who treat well of Love: I have not known any of the Moderns in that Point come up to your famous Author of the Atalantis. She has carried the Passion farther than could be readily conceiv'd." He then names a series of Manley's "Inchanting Descriptions" "that must warm the coldest Reader" (2–3).

Delarivier Manley's situation of herself as first among "the ingenious women" of her nation and her seriocomic comparison with classical scholar Anne Le Fèvre Dacier were of a rhetorical piece. Rather than place herself within a British genealogy of women writers, she laid claim to a transnational charm, appearing as a Sapho, albeit an admittedly overweight one, with sparkling eyes in the *Artamène* tradition and with the knowledge of both an intelligencer and *salonnière*. The comparison with Dacier then incites Lord Lovemore to recount the life of the exceptional Rivella/Manley. Catherine Gallagher has pointed out that at the five different stages of participation in the British literary marketplace of the long eighteenth century, from Behn, to Manley, to Charlotte Lennox, to Frances Burney, to Maria Edgeworth, women writers in Britain positioned themselves as having "*nothing* in common" (xv). They disassociated themselves from an internal national filiation. In the process, they created the "nobody" who was the ambivalent referent, the character of fiction both connected to and disconnected from the female author. Manley connects herself to the great French translator of Homer and Anacreon rather than with women of Britain. Subsequent women writers in Britain would disavow Manley entirely.

> SEMIRAMIS. . . . Semiramis was said to have been changed into a dove, because she was under that form depicted and worshipped. Hence it appears that Semiramis was merely an emblem. (Hays, *Female Biography* 3:468)

Perhaps because they adapted the catalog form, the first literary histories written by women in the second half of the eighteenth century simultaneously acknowledged the significance of France as possessed of a female literary genealogy *and* situated the "ladies of France" within the ahistorical space of the city of women. Fortunée Briquet managed the problem by simply annexing women authors of interest to France in her *Historical, Literary and Bibliographical Dictionary of French Women and of Foreign Women Naturalized in France* (*Dictionnaire historique, littéraire et bibliographique des Françaises et des étrangères naturalisées en France*, 1804). In 1778, when Ann Forde Thicknesse wrote *Sketches of the Lives and Writings of the Ladies of France*, she acknowledged the important contemporary British literary coterie of women grouped around Elizabeth Montagu—the Bluestockings. Indeed, *Sketches* was dedicated to "Bluestocking" Elizabeth Carter; "while I am holding forth specimens of the literary talents of the women of another nation," Thicknesse wrote in praise, "I would not be thought unacquainted with the superior excellence of the first writer in our own."[43] Notwithstanding, Thicknesse exclaimed that "it is in France that we must look for such uncommon genius among the Ladies" (iv). She offered lives up to her readers as "well worthy of the imitation of such who have abilities or inclination to follow their example" (ix). Echoing the terms of Manley's comparison between "Rivella" and Dacier, Thicknesse wrote that of female "literary talents,"

> England has hitherto produced but very few; among the most distinguished of whom, we are happy to name a Carter, an Aikin, and a Montague. . . . One would have thought, the great reputation these Ladies have gained by their justly-admired talents, were sufficient to have inspired more English women with an emulation to excell, and a desire of being ranked among the learned, as well as the most beautiful of their sex.—When I say, the most beautiful, let it be observed, however, that I mean *natural* beauty *only,* in which, it must be confessed, the English women surpass all other nations. But the *art* of *captivating*, they must give up to the French Ladies, who, in spite of bad complexions, and the neglect of that exquisite neatness which is the first and most essential superiority the English Ladies have to boast of, are irresistibly charming:—their high breeding, their easy address, their natural gaiety, and the advantages which their language afford them of expressing themselves in the most polite and insinuating terms, cannot fail making a very favorable impression on the mind of strangers.—In short, there is no nation under the sun where women are so perfectly skilled, *dans l'art de plaire,* as are the Ladies of France. But it will appear, by the following account, that they are not entirely indebted to the toilet for the conquests

they make, but are ambitious of possessing those charms, which can *never fade.* (v–vi)

The "ladies of France" dominated the imaginative space of writing by women in the eighteenth century, poor complexions and all.

Reading Thicknesse's discussion of French women's charms "which can never fade" might lead one to conclude that Pascale Casanova's chronology in *The World Republic of Letters* of the entrance of nations into the literary field easily encompasses writing by women as well. And to a certain extent this is true. The same cultural forces conducive to the flourishing of publishing in Italian city-states in the sixteenth century allowed women poets and scholars to write, albeit subject to different constraints and pressures. As a generation of scholarship devoted to recovering lost writers has demonstrated, women wrote and were published during the Dutch and Spanish golden ages. The same French language that dominated intellectual and literary life in Europe in the late seventeenth and early eighteenth centuries provided a language of expression for aristocratic women writers. The same English literary marketplace and relaxation of press control that fostered male jockeying on Grub Street in the late seventeenth and early eighteenth centuries fostered women writers, albeit at first in genres considered to be inferior. And the same German publishing industry that encouraged translation, cultural transfer, and then an original German literature and a *Weltliteratur* toward the end of the eighteenth century and into the early nineteenth century allowed intermittent and then more frequent interventions by women translators, poets, playwrights, and, ultimately, novelists. Writing about British collections of writing and "lives" of women writers, Margaret Ezell has pointed out that anthologies were "the flagships of the drive to establish a working, workable body of literature which represents women's writing in English throughout history" (40). Yet anthologies and catalogs added women into the record at a cost. Women entered and participated in the construction of a transhistorical, non-national circle of women—a separate discursive space that announced itself in terms of relations of singular exceptionalism rather than of aesthetic value.

Unlike women's poetry and scholarship, "romances" or "histories" of women's and girls' lives could easily be translated, annexed, excerpted, appended, and marketed within the early modern print environment. Indeed, Aphra Behn and Delarivier Manley successfully introduced plebeian women with extraordinary lives into the imported and largely aristocratic Continental form when they published in English. The interplay between the "fatality of human linguistic diversity," printing technology and capitalism may have enabled the rise of distinctive national vernaculars, as Benedict Anderson explains it, when the drive for new markets (and new readers) assembled idiolects into larger print-languages. These, then, "laid the bases for national consciousnesses," Anderson argues, in part by creating "unified fields of exchange and communication" and awareness of fellow readers "connected through print" (45). By the late seventeenth century and throughout the eighteenth century, however, the fatality of ease of translation favored dissemination of stories of girls across national borders precisely to feed national markets in the larger print-languages of French, English, Dutch, and German. Translation of these stories capitalized on the emerging sector of girl and women readers in different print-languages. Translation produced a transnational readership (reading in French, English, Dutch, and German) for fictions of exemplary womanhood. The ease of translating prose stories of women's lives helped make the network around Scudéry, rather than Italian or English women poets or scholars, into the archetype for women writers. And it produced "women's writing" as a transnational category connecting a woman writer with her personal story, across national literary fields.

In 1811, Stéphanie de Genlis wrote what might have appeared to be a national literary history of French women. "French women" included those who had become so "by adoption, on marrying French princes," since "it was necessary to place them in this class [of French] so as to speak of the most illustrious patronesses of writers, for almost all the queens of France were foreign princesses" (De l'influence 1). Genlis's very title—On the Influence of Women on French Literature, as Patronesses of Letters and as Authors, or, a Summary of the History of the Most Famous French Women (De l'influence des femmes sur la littérature française, comme protectrices des lettres et comme auteurs, ou précis de l'histoire des femmes françaises les plus célèbres)—identified female fame with literariness, hesitating before the possibility of allowing the words "French" and "woman" to modify "author" directly. Constructing a filiation from Queen Radegonde to Sophie Cottin, Genlis's catalog modernized Le Moyne's tactics in the Gallerie des femmes fortes by transposing the assessment of a famous woman's honor onto her literary style. The female author's delicacy in her treatment of scenes, character, and language became a proxy for her personal virtue.

Genlis's introductory essay explained the status of literature by women by placing it within the context of the rise of national literatures across Europe. If the Swedes, Danes, Russians, Poles, and Dutch had not yet achieved the literary greatness of the French, English, Italians, Spanish, and Germans, this was not because they, as peoples, were endowed with inferior capacities. Rather, she wrote, "We can excel in an art only when this art is generally cultivated in our nation and in the class where heaven has placed us" (vi). So too, Genlis argued, woman had not reached the literary pinnacle of authoring great tragedies and epics—that generalized measure in the quarrel of the ancients and moderns of national aesthetic distinction. Women as a group were analogous to a less cultivated nation.

Reiterating the "equality in abstraction" and "anachronism" of the medieval catalogs of women, the English radical Mary Hays in 1803 and the French moderate Genlis in 1811 strategically endowed a cult of imagined affinity. Their revised roll call allowed women to invite themselves through a new hagiography to the city or the garden of exceptional ladies. The juxtaposition of women within a textualized collectivity permitted trafficking in the transnational timeless currency of female lives—of their virtue or lack of virtue. The celebration of distinctive *aesthetic* capital belonged, in contrast, to the vertical consolidation of national literary cultures and fields—to the rivalry among nations that had—or, according to Genlis's construction of women as a nation—had yet to achieve literary greatness.

Chapter 3

Ravishing and Romance Language

This chapter explores the fate of the city of ladies at the point in the middle of the eighteenth century when a protorealist insistence on likelihood as the proper measure of fiction elevated the novel and eclipsed the illustrious women of romance. The widespread popularity in and after 1752 of Charlotte Lennox's *The Female Quixote* and Françoise de Graffigny's *Lettres d'une Péruvienne* (*Letters of a Peruvian Woman*) indicates the nostalgic appeal of the city of ladies in the new world of the protorealist novel. Both novels responded to the centrality of sexual-psychological siege in the works that crucially defined the French and the British modern national novel. They did so by offering an escape clause to the contract of an emerging realism: romance becomes a woman's interior resource for defending herself against external cultural claims, including new realist codes equating female adventure with sexual ruin and virtue with passive stoicism (even suicide) in the face of sexual harassment and assault. Both novels, too, suggested that a heroine's story of coercion or assault might appear valid or invalid depending on whether, on the one hand, it was assessed in terms of a perceived affinity or "similitude" of destiny between a female audience and the heroine or, on the other, judged according to the emerging evidentiary norms of realist fiction and empirical history. Moreover, they presented an epistemological rupture between the world of the city of ladies, cast as the heroine's interior mental landscape, and an external world seeking to force the heroine's consent to its alternate reality. To borrow critic Emily Nussbaum's description of a spate of television shows and films focused on rape survivors, Lennox and Graffigny are "less obsessed with pure-cut violent misogyny than with the queasy intersection of seduction and mind control, with fantasies about overriding consent and the excuses that abusers make for their worst acts" ("Graphic, Novel").

Variant definitions of *ravish*, now uncommon but still in current usage in the mid-eighteenth century, capture these novels' depiction of "a person, the mind" being drawn "forcibly *into* or *to* some condition, action, etc.," of a person being "driven or carried away *from* a belief, state, etc.," (*OED*)[1] or of the "mind or heart of someone" being charmed (*Dictionnaire de l'Académie française*, 1694). Psychological struggle is played out under threat of that other form of "ravishing": to "drag off or carry away (a woman) by force or with violence" and/or "to rape, violate (a woman)." With a nostalgic glance toward romance, Lennox and Graffigny tap these meanings of ravishing to depict what we now call gaslighting, thanks to George Cukor's 1944 film *Gaslight* featuring a young woman (played by Ingrid Bergman) whose always charming but murderous husband manipulates the environment in which he imprisons her and convinces her that she cannot trust the evidence of her own senses. In 1752, by marking a rupture between romance and some graver epistemology of "likelihood," Lennox and Graffigny hesitantly suggested that ravishing was not the work of a single malevolent man but of a culture as a whole.

Landmark feminist scholarship in the late 1980s and early 1990s explored the centrality of sexual-psychological siege to national inventions of the (modern) psychological novel in France and in Britain with, respectively, the publication of Madame de La Fayette's *La princesse de Clèves* in 1678 and Samuel Richardson's *Clarissa, or the History of a Young Lady* in 1748. In *Tender Geographies: Women and the Origins of the Novel in France*, Joan DeJean builds her reading of La Fayette's novel around a discussion of seventeenth-century definitions of the word *aveu* (avowal). When the eponymous heroine of *La princesse de Clèves* realizes that she is struggling with a passion for the duc de Nemours, she famously "avows" this love for another man to her husband, attempting to enlist his support in her struggle to remain virtuous. The duc de Nemours secretly observes the scene of avowal from a place in hiding but shares the story as a novelty with a friend who then circulates it among members of the court. DeJean points out that in seventeenth-century legal and penal language, an *aveu* corresponded to a forced confession. The *aveu* was the criminal's ratification of a story of his crime that was elicited by any means, including torture, and composed and given order by the accuser. DeJean writes that "the princesse's use of *aveu* does not, however, correspond to this contemporary neologism. No one forces her to speak; her *prise de parole* is freely elected. Nor is the text of her avowal prearranged; it is because her husband and Nemours know only what she chooses to reveal that their curiosity drives them to try to learn more. Finally, the princesse does not speak as a criminal: she stresses that 'the innocence of my conduct and my intentions gives me the courage [to do this].'" DeJean explains that in presenting the avowal, "Lafayette imagined a new function in the novel for the first person and for conversation. She has every character acknowledge this formal innovation: the princesse announces 'an *aveu* that no one has ever made to her husband'; the prince refers to 'the greatest mark of fidelity that a woman has ever given to her husband'; Nemours pronounces the scene 'extraordinary'" (122–24). DeJean goes on to suggest that through the princesse's *aveu*, the novel presents "a kind of first-person self-revelation still an innovation in 1678" and that it situates this "sincerity" at the basis of friendship and of an emerging model of companionate or sympathetic marriage (119). For DeJean, the *aveu* "is the equivalent" for La Fayette's generation of the famous *carte de Tendre* in Scudéry's *Clélie*, which had charted the road to a perfected private relationship of inclination and tenderness between lovers as an alternative to an arranged marriage contract protecting patriarchal investments in rank, family, and property (120). DeJean argues that the *aveu* is the first step in the princesse de Clèves's multiple attempts to secure permission from her husband to seek *repos*. The princess tries repeatedly to retire to her own property and, ultimately on her husband's death, withdraws from the world of the court, its sexual intrigues, and its arranged marriages. For all that the novel announces the exceptionalism of the avowal, the princesse de Clèves resorts to the extraordinary *aveu* because she is pressed from all sides. The court's constant circulation of stories about illustrious women who succumb to sexual intrigue and Nemours's incessant strategizing to elicit a sign of her internal state constitute a psychological siege. Thus, while the *aveu* is extraordinary and is made at a time of the princesse de Clèves's choosing, it is hardly made freely and without coercion. When, after her avowal, the princesse goes on to ask her husband to allow her to flee the court and retire to her own property, she fantasizes about removing herself from a world in which each of her actions is construed as a sign betraying her inner state and is interpreted according to a court logic.

Writing about the British invention of the psychological novel, Frances Ferguson argued in "Rape and the Rise of the Novel" that Samuel Richardson's *Clarissa, or the Misfortunes of a Young Lady* (1748) "declares itself to be inaugurating a new genre" (23) by depicting through rape the attempt to coerce an internal state. In relying on the depiction of rape to frame the new British psychological novel, Richardson, in effect, reiterated and outdistanced the classical origin myth for poetry, told through the story of the rape of Philomela.[2] At the outset of "Rape and the Rise of the Novel," Ferguson writes that "any crime raises questions of the credibility of perpetrators, victims and witnesses. The crime of rape raises these questions in the way that any crime might. As crimes go, however, it is remarkable for focusing attention on mental states and their apprehension" (88). Ferguson goes on to argue that "in fact, the law of rape continually draws and redraws its terms, as if to underscore the desire to identify the crime as a project of stipulating formal criteria ever more precisely, ever more thoroughly in an effort to minimize the problems that can arise in the effort to identify psychological states" (94). Attention focuses on definitions of consent, such as the legal age and mental state of the survivor. Ferguson continues, "Consent or nonconsent as mental states may be unspecifiable but defining legal infancy as the necessary inability to consent makes the determination of any mental state irrelevant. If psychological states like intention and consent frequently look inaccessible, the statutory definition of them solves the problem created by their inaccessibility by making them irrelevant. The law enables itself to identify rape, then, by denying the possibility that a very young woman could ever have the psychological state that would count as consent" (94).

In *Clarissa*, the crucial plot element of rape encourages scrutiny of the female protagonist's psychological state. Indeed, the text situates the search for an answer to the question of whether Clarissa is culpable of consent as a red thread through the reading experience. While some have read the novel's vindication of Clarissa's virtue as entailing respect for her capacity to say "no," Ferguson argues that Clarissa's unconsciousness during the rape "ensures that her nonconsent will be inescapable" (100). Clarissa's subsequent period of madness and wasting away, marked textually by interruptions to her letter writing and by her mad papers, fulfills the demands of a formal stipulation that a rape victim be *incapable of having consented* at the time of the rape in order for a finding of nonconsent to be validated.

DeJean's account of the *aveu* and Ferguson's account of the formal stipulation of Clarissa's incapacity to consent make two moves. First, both critics rely on legal definitions to clarify the restricted conditions under which individual (private) voices were understood in the past to have validity. They foreground how each novel responds to legal stipulations so as to create an opportunity for the sexual virtue of heroines to be communicated unambiguously. The princesse de Clèves anticipates and eschews the forced confession of adulterous guilt scripted by others when she avows her secret passion and enlists her husband's help in resisting it. Clarissa's unconsciousness and subsequent madness preclude charges of sexual complicity and guilt. Second, DeJean and Ferguson argue that each novel heralds its own innovation. Seduction—the scene of attack on a woman's sexual virtue—creates the necessity for revealing a woman's interior thought. Her revelation serves as the foundation for a structure of feeling, sympathy, allowing readers to assess the relationship between her interior and exterior. The female protagonist wanted sex outside of marriage and consented. Or she felt adulterous desire and did not consent. Or she neither wanted sex outside of marriage nor consented to it. Such a brief, DeJean and Ferguson point out, allowed *La princesse de Clèves* and *Clarissa* to proclaim as singular and new their techniques for depicting interiority: first-person speech and letter writing, respectively, about the female self. The scene of sexual harassment and assault and a woman's resistance to it provides in each novel the opportunity to proclaim the invention of a national psychological novel.

Novels have the advantage over other forms of being able to depict the correspondence or absence of correspondence between an individual's internal and external state. They may jump from focalization privileging interiority to an external depiction of a cultural landscape in which a character interacts with others. Sentimental and psychological fiction specialize in depicting the siege waged on an external state in an attempt to coerce an internal state—to force a declaration of something hidden inside or to force a declaration that conforms with the interests of those engaged in eliciting it. Nonjuridical definitions of "consent" in the eighteenth century, those to be found in dictionaries and encyclopedias, interestingly concede the impossibility of understanding it as an individual and independent act of free will removed from an external, even overdetermining, context. Within these definitions, sex and marriage recur as illustrative cases. Chambers's *Cyclopedia* (1728) confines *consent* to nervous physiology within the system of a body: "CONSENT *of Parts*, in the Animal Oeconomy, a certain Agreement, or Sympathy, by means whereof, when one Part is immediately affected, another, at a distance, becomes affected in like manner, See SYMPATHY" (308). In what the *Oxford English Dictionary* would later term an obsolete noun definition involving "a relation of sympathy between one organ or part of the body and another,"[3] Chambers's prime example of *consent* is the "Pleasure of Kissing" and "its Effects" in exciting "Love, and even Lechery, to this Pair of Nerves": "Dr. *Sachs* judges it to be from the Consent of the *Labia Uteri* with the *Labia Oris,* that a breeding Lady, frighted with the sight of scabby Lips, had

Pustules of the like kind broke out in the *Labia Uteri*" (308). Here, the idea appears to be that the "breeding Lady" experiences negative external lip-to-lip "sympathy" between herself and the possessor of scabby lips, which is then involuntarily expressed in the manifestation of scabbiness in her own body via internal lip-to-labia sympathy. Consent, which slips into sympathy, is an involuntary expression of an externally coerced sexual state.

Definitions of the verb *consent* in Samuel Johnson's *Dictionary of the English Language* (1755) covered a span: "to be of the same mind," "to co-operate to the same end," and, last, "to yield; to give consent; to allow; to admit." Beginning in 1694, successive editions of the *Dictionnaire de l'Académie française* defined the verb *consentir* as "to acquiesce to something. To adhere to the will of someone." And, in a phrase that fares poorly in trans-lation, the *Dictionnaire* offered the ambiguous *"vouloir bien trouver bon"* (literally, "to be willing to find good"; roughly, "to be okay with"). The *Dictionnaire* example of marriage provided little clarification as to the rela-tionship between consent and independent will: "*The family has consented to this marriage. As for me, I cannot consent to it. I will never consent to it. I consent to everything you wish. I consent that you do, etc.* Commonly, it is said, *The one who remains silent, consents [Qui se tait, consent].*" These phrases, italicized in the *Dictionnaire*—in the typographical mode that corresponded in novels both to reported speech and to reported letters—certainly may be read as independent examples of usage, while also functioning as the familiar family drama of the age in miniature. "It" serves as the pronoun replacing "this marriage" in a way that communicates a struggle between family and child over an arranged marriage. The imposition of external will ("I consent to everything you wish") concludes with the communal silencing of the child through the ratification of received wisdom encapsulated in the idiom, "Qui se tait, consent." The definition finishes with a legal, soon to be archaic, transitive usage: consent "is sometimes active; and as such is hardly a usage except in Law. *To consent to the sale, adjudication of land.*" Had the dictionary examples of usage been a narrative, one additional element in the story might well have been featured: the link between securing consent to marriage and adjudicating transfer or consolidation of land and property.

The *Encyclopédie* (1751–72) paraphrased Chambers for its third entry on "consentement des parties" but opted in its first definition for a noun string as headword: "consentement, agrément, permission (*Gramm.*)." This "gram-matical" definition admitted to the ambiguity around coercion: "terms rela-tive to the conduct that we have to maintain in most of the actions of life, where we are not entirely free, and where the event depends in part on us, in part on the will of others." The second "logic and moral" definition of the noun *consent* highlighted correspondences between the interior and external states of an individual and those of another individual: "It is an act of understanding, by which all of the terms of a proposition being well conceived, a man perceives internally and sometimes designates to the outside, that there is an absolute identity between the thought and will of the author of the proposition and his [the man's] own thought and will." This definition admits of formidable barriers to consent: *all of the terms* of a proposition must be understood by the person who consents, yet the structure of "designation" is such that one might consent to a portion of a proposition but be understood as consenting to "all of the terms." Consent or lack of consent may ("sometimes") exist independently of the external expression of consent. The interior and exterior states of two individuals must "have absolute identity," and there must be a correspondence between the "thought" and "will" of each. Diderot, the author of this *Encyclopédie* definition, amplified the barriers:

> Negation and affirmation are, according to the occasion, signs of *consent*. The mind gives only a single consent to a proposition, however composite it might be; it is thus necessary to distinguish well the sign of consent from consent: the sign of consent may be forced; it is not the same with consent. . . . The *consent* of childhood, of insanity, of fury, of drunkenness, of invincible ignorance, is reputed null; the same for that which is exacted by fear or surprised by skill; in every other circumstance, consent founds the appearance of fault and the right of punishment and reprisal. *See* PACT. (*Encyclopédie* 4:32).

The sign of consent was not the same as actual consent and could be coerced from an individual. Under these constraints, the cases in which an individual might be justly found at "fault" for consent appear limited indeed. In fact, demonstrating the psychological and social murkiness of consent formed the basis for Diderot's *La religieuse*, a novel exploring a woman's (voluntary or involuntary?) adoption of the religious veil, that alternate destiny to marriage for women in Catholic Europe. In eighteenth-century dictionary definitions of *consent*, relations between a man and a woman or among members of a family serve as the theater for defining the word, and consent is an intelligible, unambiguous correspondence or sign. In the *Encyclopédie*'s more complex excavation of the term, Diderot highlights the "nightmare scenario" of consent, as Emily Nussbaum sketches it: "Say yes to anything and you've signed away your right to ever say no" ("Graphic, Novel"). Moreover, he stages consent as a drama of identity between an individual's thoughts and her avowal of them, on the one hand, and of coerced elicitation and interpretation of signs, on the other. It is this double couple of coerceable sympathies that Lennox and Graffigny explore around 1752.

Toni Bowers points out that in rape and seduction narratives "when it is one person's unquestioned right to pursue and the other's job to resist or consent, the answering voice will remain secondary and subordinate, her 'choice' preemptively limited to the narrow option 'yes' or 'no.' Under the sign of liberal (that is, patriarchal) consent theory, every sexual act becomes an instance of seduction, and seduction in turn signifies in the shadow of rape. Indeed, the category 'rape' might well be understood as a kind of scapegoat for 'the violence within seduction.'" Bowers emphasizes that as "the reserved location of violence, 'rape' allows for the pretense that seduction/courtship is *not* a power play, that the gendered partners really are equal unless (or until) the man uses direct physical force" (21). Graffigny and Lennox use the discursive slipperiness of ravishing to expose the power play of cultural gaslighting. Rather than proclaiming the invention of a new form from the scene of rape, and rather than championing avowal as the means for a woman to declare innocence, they highlight the failures of a new form by suturing it awkwardly to romance.

The Likelihood of Ravishing

In Charlotte Lennox's *The Female Quixote*, dreams of joining the city of ladies animate Arabella who believes the "great Store of Romances" she has read in "bad Translations" from the "original French" to be accurate accounts of the world (7). Arabella thinks it probable that she will someday be carried into a country "far distant" from her own. When her uncle Sir Charles insists that "it is not very likely you should be forcibly carried away into *Turky*," Arabella interrupts. "'And why do you think it unlikely, that I should be carried thither?" She continues with a train of questions drawn in equal measure from Medieval and Renaissance catalogs and mid-eighteenth-century natural philosophy: "Do not the same Things happen now, that did formerly? And is any thing more common, than Ladies being carried by their Ravishers, into Countries far distant from their own? May not the same

Accidents happen to me, that have happened to so many illustrious Ladies before me? And may I not be carried into *Macedonia* by a Similitude of Destiny with that of a great many beautiful Princesses, who, though born in the most distant Quarters of the World, chanced to meet at one time in the City of *Alexandria*, and related their miraculous Adventures to each other?"

At this point in the conversation, Mr. Glanville, Sir Charles's son and the cousin to whom Arabella's father has promised her so as to unite estates, smiles at Arabella's construction of cause and effect. He asks, "And it was for that very Purpose they met, Madam?" Arabella responds without missing a beat: "Why, truly . . . it happened very luckily for each of them, that they were brought into a Place where they found so many illustrious Companions in Misfortune, to whom they might freely communicate their Adventures, which otherwise might, haply, have been concealed, or, at least, have been imperfectly delivered down to us" (261). Sir Charles doubts Arabella's measure of probability: women traveling, women being taken by a "ravisher," women being illustrious, women sharing their adventures—all are equally improbable. Glanville questions Arabella's construal of the relationship between women's lives and women's storytelling. He teases her with the suggestion that she is arguing, illogically, that women traveled from all over the world just so that they could tell their stories to each other.

Arabella, haply, eludes their skepticism. Her argument is that illustrious women did not meet in Macedonia for the "very Purpose" of telling their adventures; they simply made the best of both chance and their destiny as "Companions in Misfortune." The claim that "otherwise" illustrious women's histories might "have been imperfectly delivered down to us" functions as a sort of liar's (or ravished woman's) paradox. To say that Arabella is wrong entails admitting that women's histories have been handed down "*imperfectly.*" In this view, since the history of women has been "concealed" or is at best imperfect, doubt falls on Sir Charles's argument that women are "unlikely" to be ravished (and carried to Turkey). Without adequate histories of women as reference, how can he know for sure? On the other hand, to say that Arabella is right entails the claim that women's histories have been handed down correctly, implying that illustrious women did find "companions in misfortune to whom they might freely communicate their adventures," and suggesting more generally that Arabella, who has read what has been handed down, is probably more accurate about women's adventures than Sir Charles, who has not done his reading. If, for example, Sir Charles seems unaware of the history of Lady Mary Wortley Montagu, who was still alive in 1752, readers at least knew that she had traveled to Turkey, accompanying her husband on his diplomatic mission, between 1716 and 1718 and had circulated stories of her adventure, although her letters were not yet in print.[4] (True, Lady Mary Wortley Montagu had not been carried to Turkey by "Ravishers"; marriage led to displacement).

Arabella's question, "Do not the same Things happen now, that did formerly?" is the real poser. To acknowledge that the same things did not happen across time was to open the door to the familiar quarrel about whether the classical age was superior to the modern. On a more challenging level, it also admitted an anthropological awareness that values and beliefs—what counts as true and what appears probable—are contingent on the time and place in which one lives as well as on the interests of the people surrounding one. In concert with the emerging natural philosophy of the age, from the works of Scottish Enlightenment thinkers to the Continental arguments of Montesquieu and Rousseau, Arabella's conundrum about cultural and historical difference is framed within the context of gender. She poses the seventeenth-century question: what does the likelihood that a woman might prove to be illustrious indicate about the greatness of the society in which she lived? But in the course of the novel, she lives the eighteenth-century question: what is the relationship between national character and the role of women in a society? Fundamentally, Arabella's conundrum offers up the question of how likely it was that a woman would be "ravished" as a baseline for evaluating the condition of women. Was a woman in the past or in other countries more likely than a woman in the Britain of 1752 to be dragged off, carried away by force or with violence, or raped or violated? What qualities in a woman's story of being ravished made it credible? When no evidence was offered to support the argument that a woman's story of rape or attempted rape is unlikely—as none is offered to Arabella after she escapes from the two men following her in a dodgy part of London—what were the conditions that made discounting a woman's story acceptable? Could the way in which a society credited or discredited a woman's story also be a measure of that society's relative worth, and did the capacity of a woman to communicate her version of events stand as a measure of her merit?

Appearing four years after *Clarissa*, the story in *The Female Quixote* of whether Arabella's fears of ravishing can be credited declares itself to be split between genres, the old genre of French romance and the new genre of the psychological novel. *The Female Quixote* rehearses the age-old problem of whether a woman's story of rape can be believed by examining the social and epistemological conditions that might make it possible or impossible for a woman to appear credible.

The threat of rape hovers constantly over Arabella. The novel provides no reliable resources to help the reader determine how "real" is the threat of ravishing. All of the characters around Arabella scoff at her fears of being ravished. Yet Arabella's fears seem likely when the reader considers narrative cues about her status and vulnerability. Imprisoned in a castle from birth by a tyrannical aristocratic father in political exile, Arabella has become, at the time of the beginning of the story, a young, beautiful, and unprotected orphan and heiress who can only conserve all of her fortune if she marries her cousin Glanville. With no frame of reference other than French romances, Arabella lives surrounded by Glanville, his sister Miss Glanville and, eventually, their father Sir Charles Glanville, as well as a fortune hunter who tries to entrap her into a tryst and forced marriage by styling himself as a new Artamène or Oroondates to her Clelia. The third-person satiric voice of the narrator along with all of the characters except Arabella herself present her marriage to her cousin as expected and reasonable behavior in a mid-eighteenth-century England that values conservation of family property. Arabella's refusal of consent to marry Glanville and her initial interest in the fortune hunter, who seduces her with the language of romance—in other words, by manipulatively playing to her understanding of cultural order—suggest that the reader subscribe to emerging mid-eighteenth-century novelistic norms and cast her as deluded. Since her speech, self-presentation, and behavior are all patterned on the historical romances that have constituted her sole education, casting her as deluded appears to make perfect sense.

Yet in *The Female Quixote*, it can never be stipulated conclusively that Arabella is incapable of consent owing to insanity. Much of the case for exploring whether or not her consent is "null" revolves around her expression of fears of ravishing. Early in the novel, Arabella's refusal to consent to marrying her cousin Glanville in conformity with her father's and uncle's legal entailment for conservation of property among male family members is explained as a fantasy derived from her insane addiction to romances. She is, in a certain sense, irremediably ignorant because of a childhood spent in confinement with access only to books communicating an anachronistic set of values. The stipulation made by Arabella's male family members that romances have clouded her reason automatically invalidates her recurring perception that she is about to be ravished. At the same time, the stipulation itself appears invalid because the characters who judge the validity of her fears are not disinterested. All of the characters around Arabella have something to gain—property—by eliciting the sign of her consent and by proving that her fears of ravishing are unfounded and are merely the product of her reading. Although romance addiction appears to invalidate Arabella's judgment, it has endowed Arabella with the education that makes her capable (in Diderot's sense) of consent to marriage—a capacity that her father enshrines in his will when he gives her the liberty to consent or not to marriage with her cousin while also shrinking her inheritance if she chooses to marry outside of the family. Reading has taught Arabella to evaluate propositions and to avoid errors in logic (it was not *for the very purpose* of communicating their histories that illustrious ladies convened in Macedonia) even when they are willfully attributed to her. It has given her the sense of virtue embedded in a world-view that allows her to resist coercion. Romance reading equips her with an alternative to bowing to her relatives' will and to their terms. It enables her to submit Glanville to a series of heroic tests so that she can determine whether he loves her. Romance qualities set Arabella apart from other women, notably, her dull, vain, and conformist female cousin Miss Glanville. Unschooled by romance, Miss Glanville demonstrates the harvest of a poor education when she becomes enamored of the duplicitous fortune hunter and compromises herself in a tryst designed to entrap Arabella.

Over the course of the novel, Arabella's romance exemplarity both validates and invalidates her psychological state as one that might "count" for consent. It provides her with the reason and awareness of alternatives to the marriage of convenience necessary for independent judgment. Yet this same independent judgment in a young woman of marriageable age makes Arabella incapable of consenting to the only proposition—marriage to her cousin—that is reasonable in the society in which she lives.

The novel as a whole focuses attention on the contrast between the fictive world of romance, where Arabella could have adventures and tell the story of them to a believing audience and where her consent would have validity, and the mid-eighteenth-century world in which her stories of ravishing appear unlikely and in which her consent can never be independent of cultural coercion. *The Female Quixote* relies, of course, on the highly popular device of quixotism. Cervantes's *Don Quixote* (1608) afforded many European writers a means of ridiculing new groups of supposedly credulous readers—servants and women—as well as their favorite genres.[5] A decade before Lennox published her novel, her friend and contact Henry Fielding mocked the reading-inflated ideas of a manservant in *The Adventures of Joseph Andrews*, "written in

Imitation of the Manner of Cervantes, Author of Don Quixote." In William Warner's words, Fielding inserts a critical author-narrator as ironic guide to the reader, so that *Joseph Andrews* "displays many forms of naïve reading, tests them by experience and finds them wanting." ("Novels" 102). A habitual translator of works from the French, Lennox had also likely encountered Adrien Perdou Thomas de Subligny's quixotic "send-up" of the female readers of Madeleine de Scudéry's *Clélie*. Subligny's *The Mock-Clelia* (*La fausse Clélie*) appeared in French in 1672 and again in 1718 as well as in an English translation in 1678.[6] Scenes and characters in *The Female Quixote,* such as the climactic moment when, inspired by Clelia's leap into the Tiber, Arabella throws herself into the Thames when she fears that the unknown men walking behind her plan to rape her, appear to have been taken directly from Subligny (Marshall 167).

Yet while Subligny mocks the "mock-Clelia" for being so credulous as to believe that she really is Scudéry's Clelia and provides her with completely illusory adventures (confirmed as such by the narrator), Lennox takes care to point out that Arabella does not believe she *is* Clelia; she is not that kind of insane. Further, although the doctor who cures Arabella of her romance addiction argues that it was unlikely that the men walking behind her were going to rape her and that there was no need for her to throw herself into the Thames, the narrator offers no certain proof that Arabella's apprehensions of rape were unfounded. Arabella simply does not have enough information to realize that the world in which she finds herself is not the one she has encountered in her cloistered education, but she does know enough to reason that she is subject to coercion. Her fears of rape are both a distraction from the central issue of coercion of her consent to marriage and analogous to it. Lennox argues that women's failings, particularly their moral faults, are owed to their inadequate educations. But, unlike Fielding in *Joseph Andrews*, Lennox proposes that in comparing her reading with the world, a heroine might well find the latter wanting since, within it, her story can never be credited. Proving to Arabella, once and for all, that her fear of ravishing is unreasonable becomes the mechanism for severing her adherence to a romance epistemology (where the proposition that a woman may be ravished is true and where a woman's story of being ravished is true). It serves as the means of inserting her into a modern epistemology, where her consent to marriage with Granville would be part of a composite proposition involving consolidation of family property. Through the vagueness in the proofs surrounding the likelihood of Arabella being ravished, a reluctance to stipulate that Arabella is incurably ignorant or insane, and a story of a group closing in around Arabella to extract her consent to marry, *The Female Quixote* underlines Arabella's question: is a woman less likely to be ravished now than in the past? And the novel underscores Arabella's argument: it is only when a woman tells her story to her companions in misfortune that the assertion of having been ravished will have validity. Beyond that circle of affinity, her story will only be a story and an unread or ridiculed one at that.

Likelihood, probability, commonality, validity . . . these are the terms of the eighteenth-century debate about the potential danger or utility of fiction. As early as the 1670s, responses to Madame de La Fayette's *La princesse de Clèves* debated the verisimilitude (*vraisemblance*) of the princess's famous decision to avow her love for another man to her husband so that he might support her in her struggle to remain virtuous (Judovitz 1037). How likely it was that a character might take a particular action, like the princess's *aveu*, or become subject to particular circumstances, like being ravished, was the realist question. While in the late seventeenth century French romances had "seemed to offer a literary world common to men and women," as Margaret Doody writes, by the middle of the eighteenth-century, romance was conceived as idle entertainment purveying dangerous chimeras about illustrious adventures that lay outside the ordinary person's reach ("Introduction" xvi). It was both feminized and consigned to the past. Yet, as William Hazlitt later insisted in the oft-quoted mature vindication of the novel, fiction could be of another kind. If the actions and circumstances it portrayed were probable, then fiction could provide "a close imitation of men and manners" and the opportunity to learn from seeing "the very web and texture of society as it really exists, and as we meet with it when we come into the world." Fiction could be legitimated if, through its imitation of life, readers became "acquainted with the motives and characters of mankind," could "imbibe" "notions of vice and virtue from examples," and were "taught knowledge of the world" (106). This great divide, so difficult to assess in practice, between an improper and improbable and a proper and probable kind of fiction was pressed into service in forging national literary distinctions. The "realist" view that solidified over the second half of the eighteenth century divided fiction into two. One kind of fiction—an "older" kind, or a commercially successful kind, or a kind that was especially beguiling to women and servants, or a "French" kind—was improbable. Ravishing of the sort that companions in misfortune might discuss fell firmly within this category. The French man who translated *The Female Quixote* into French subscribed to these very and increasingly commonplace oppositions in the preface he wrote in 1773: "English Novels are so continuously in fashion that this title alone suffices to give them a reputation. . . . They generally paint less delicately than we do, but their tableaux are more simple, more varied, more truthful and more interesting, albeit frequently burdened with minute details." Yet, the translator continued, *The Female Quixote* was no work of "Fielding or Richardson." It "is in a bizarre genre; I dare to hope that it will please at least for its Singularity." "For the rest," the translator continued, "it is about a young English woman born in a retired location, far from all species of society, without a mother, without a guide, and having, to bring charm to her *ennui*, only the ridiculously heroic Works of Madame DE SCUDERI" (iii–iv).

Lennox registers the consignment of the adventures of illustrious women to an outmoded and foreign past by having Arabella's conventional cousin Miss Glanville think that "adventures" refers to sexual escapades, whereas Arabella uses the word in the romance sense to refer to histories of virtuous and exemplary female lives (87–88).[7] Indeed, Lennox presents a non-romance model of proper womanhood, as critic Margaret Doody points out ("Introduction" xi), in the form of a "virtuous and nameless Countess" who begins to teach Arabella that good women do not have adventures. Unlike the princesses gathered in Macedonia, the Countess's history is short and collapses the difference between coercion and consent: "And when I tell you, pursued she with a Smile, that I was born and christen'd, had a useful and proper Education, receiv'd the Addresses of my Lord—through the Recommendation of my Parents, and marry'd him with their Consents and my own Inclination, and that since we have liv'd in great Harmony together, I have told you all the material Passages of my Life" (Lennox, *Female Quixote* 357).

What recourse, then, if one were to write a fiction about a heroine after the mid-century divide marking the decline of romance, than to tell the story of a "young . . . woman born in a retired location, far from all species of society, without a mother, without a guide"? In such a fiction, dramas of perception produced by isolation and narratives of psychological-sexual siege took the place of the adventures foreclosed by female retirement. From mid-century on, women writers acknowledged the banishment of illustrious women's adventures from proper literature, but they did so through accounts of a gendered epistemological dysphoria experienced by an ill-at-ease heroine caught between cultures. French romance remained within their repertoire as a lost model of illustrious existence—as a psychological territory. For, if romance "taught young women to deport themselves too much like Queens and Princesses," as Clara Reeve would write in *The Progress of Romance,* her 1785 treatise that privileged a feminized and transnational romance heritage over the legacy of antiquity and that placed *The Female Quixote* at the top of the list of recommended modern novels for female readers, "it taught them at the same time that virtue only could give lustre to every rank and degree" (67). Or, as Margaret Doody puts it, "For the powerless to imagine a route to power is indeed 'romancing' on their part" ("Introduction" xviii).

In posing a question about epistemology—who sets the terms of what counts as true or untrue, likely or unlikely—the theme of ravishing without rape opens a weak imaginative escape clause in the emerging contract of formal realism and verisimilitude in the novel: the fantasy of a lost place filled with illustrious companions in misfortune whose "shared destiny" equips them with an alternate principle for authenticating a woman's story. *The Female Quixote* arrives at an uneasy pact with realism by presenting Arabella's consent to marry Granville as inseparable from consent to Granville's world of property and of mediocre (adventureless) destinies for nameless women. The escape clause, however, offers the conditional proposition that if you are an illustrious woman, you will consent to Arabella's story. You will be in sympathy with it through something akin to a consent of parts. The story is true, according to this clause, because of a "shared destiny." The novel proposes that illustrious women resided only in the realm of romance and of readers who retained romance as a resource for negotiating, as Diderot put it in the *Encyclopédie,* "the conduct that we have to maintain in most of the actions of life, where we are not entirely free, and where the event depends in part on us, in part on the will of others" (4:32).

Ravishing Without Rape

While bemoaning the dangerous effects of reading fiction as a transnational pastime, critics of *The Female Quixote* expressed doubt that completely outmoded French romances could really have had a powerful effect on a young woman. *The Female Quixote*'s "principle fault," the French translator wrote in his preface, "is that of being a Critique of several Novels that it is no longer dangerous to read" (*Donquichotte femelle* iv). Apparently, mid- to late seventeenth-century French romances were so completely out of style that even to critique them whiffed of anachronism. Nonetheless, as far as plotlines went, mid-eighteenth-century readers were as credulous as Arabella. Françoise de Graffigny's *Lettres d'une Péruvienne* told precisely the story Arabella outlined of an illustrious woman carried away by ravishers to a country far distant from her own. On the day of her wedding to her ultimately faithless cousin Aza, the protagonist Zilia is taken by Spanish "ravishers" (*ravisseurs*) (18) from the Incan Temple of the Sun where she has grown up with other noble virgins and governesses for company. Zilia is saved from the Spanish at sea by a French knight of Malta named Déterville who falls in love with her and transports her to Paris. There she is exposed to the French consignment of women to superficial social activities. When Déterville interns her in a convent for safekeeping while he returns to war, Zilia becomes enchanted by reading French books and learning to read, write, and think in French. By the end of the novel, she tells her story by translating and collecting her own letters recording her experience of ravishing. First published in 1747 (*before* Richardson's *Clarissa* declared itself the inauguration of the genre of the psychological novel) and then expanded in 1752, the year that *The Female Quixote* was published, Graffigny's work became a must-read, one of the most popular novels across Great Britain and Europe in the second half of the century. *Lettres d'une Péruvienne* was reprinted in French forty-six times in the three decades after its first publication in 1747.[8] It was quickly translated into English (1748), going into at least twenty English editions before 1800, Italian (1754), and German (1792), Russian (1791), and Spanish (1792), Portuguese (1802), and Swedish (1828). French-Italian and French-English parallel editions appeared perennially from 1759 on, with one edition bearing the title *Cours de langue italienne,* suggesting that the book's conceit as a text written half in "Peruvian" (translated into French by the protagonist Zilia) and half directly in French gave it the feel of a perfect medium for learning another language and for entering into another linguistically bound culture (D. Smith 5).[9] Frances Burney and her friend Mrs. Rishton used one such edition to practice reading Italian out loud in 1773.[10] At least five continuations of the novel were written in French, English, and Spanish.[11]

The Female Quixote also numbered among the most popular novels of the period (Paulsen 168n7). It too was translated, as "Don Quixote in Petticoats" in German in 1754, as "Donna Quichote" in Dutch in 1762, and under a direct translation of the original title in French in 1773 and 1801, and in Spanish in 1808 (Lorenzo-Modia). German translator and playwright Luise Gottsched possessed an English copy sent to her personally by Charlotte Lennox (H. Brown 31). While the anachronism of Lennox's presentation of a romance-bewitched heroine was duly noted in eighteenth-century commentary, critics were hardly concerned with what appears now as the most improbable feature of Graffigny's novel: the stunning anachronism involved in the heroine being ravished from sixteenth-century Peru under the Spanish conquest only to find herself in eighteenth-century Paris (Kaplan xiii). Instead, commentators devoted a great deal of debate to the ending of the novel in which the heroine Zilia does not consent to marry the Frenchman Déterville. *Cinq années littéraires* opined of the ending, "Someone has to be killed here. . . . It is Zilia, the only person in whom you are truly interested. She has to be killed so that she will interest you even more."[12] So engaging was the problem of the ending that writers in France, England, and Spain wrote their own continuations to Graffigny's novel. Without touching the anachronistic premise, these continuations engineered Zilia's consent to marry Déterville through her total assimilation to French culture. Or they transformed her choice of virginity into Christian resignation to the incest taboo—in this version, Zilia's refusal to marry her cousin, Incan crown prince Aza, even though both she and he have converted to Christianity, correlates with her abandonment of Peru and embrace of European civility (Mallinson, "Introduction" 84). Probability was evidently a matter of perspective and of investments.

Identifying a cultural pattern as old as Christine de Pizan's *Book of the City of Ladies*, feminist literary historians have labeled one of the major strategies Graffigny and Lennox use in their novels "writing back."[13] Writing back to texts written by men communicates that a woman is taking an opposing side in an argument or that male and female perspectives share no overlap. Writing back may also stake the claim that the male author has willfully misrepresented a single reality out of self-interest or that experience is substantively different for men and women. In the most audacious forms of writing back, standpoint matters as a marker of how disparities in power produce divergent perspectives and experiences among different actors.

Writing back—for example, Lennox's writing back to Cervantes, Subligny, and Fielding—contrasts with the strategy of deriving a work in a contemporary vernacular from an earlier form or pre-text. The strategy of derivation, used by early modern male writers to connect their own tragedies, epics, and satires with the greatness of the past, draws a line of both distinction and continuity between literary heritage and contemporary literature. Graffigny and Lennox "write back" to highlight how disparities in power produce divergent perspectives, but they combine with this the strategy of establishing continuity between their works and the standpoint of historical romances.

In *Lettres d'une Péruvienne*, Graffigny notably employed the defamiliarizing technique of the stranger from elsewhere who observes and critiques the culture of the reader. The technique had been inaugurated in the previous century by Marana's *L'espion du grand seigneur*, a novel in letters supposedly written by a single foreign observer, the spy of the title, and translated by a third person who plays no role in the story. Embroidering themes from *L'sspion du grand seigneur* (1684; *Letters Writ by a Turkish Spy*, 1687) while borrowing its technique, Montesquieu's famous *Les lettres persanes* (*Persian Letters*, 1721) highlighted religious differences and parallels in political forms between France and the Orient. Yet diverging from *L'espion*'s heavy focus on religious differences between cultures,[14] Montesquieu tagged his sketch of cultural difference heavily to the organization of gender roles. The letters in *Persian Letters*, written by multiple fictional correspondents, portray Parisian women as pretty, vivacious, and not rigorously virtuous social beings. The relative participation in public life by women in France correlated for Montesquieu with the country's intellectual liveliness and the contention for honor characteristic of monarchies. Looking back on the world created during Louis XIV's reign and trying to label the character of the emergent modernity of the 1720s, Montesquieu associates French cultivation with the country's peculiar brand of femininity.

Using the device of the stranger from elsewhere, Graffigny would write back to *Les lettres persanes*, arguing that if Parisian women were excessively artificial and worldly, wholly occupied by amorous intrigue, and overly concerned with their own appearance and seductive influence, it was due to a failure in education. Significantly, Graffigny exposes the peril of Zilia's position as a woman ravished from Peru and taken to Paris where she must adapt as a foreigner.[15] Montesquieu's Usbek and Rica deliberately set out from Persia as cosmopolitan aristocrats aware that it is only one country among many. They appear to have no financial worries, no intimate relationships with people in Paris, no difficulties communicating in French, and no physical jeopardy due to misunderstanding, poverty, vulnerability, or miscommunication as they travel from home. Usbek suffers from personal rather than cultural myopia; he understands and describes France in broad strokes without being able to perceive his own despotism in his control of the women and eunuchs of his Persian harem.

Graffigny's Zilia, on the other hand, has grown up believing that the Incan empire covers the entire world. She must not only learn a foreign language but grapple with the strange idea that the world is composed of more than one culture. In contrast with Montesquieu's detached and affluent Persian observers in Paris, who are puzzled by French customs without intimately feeling their weight, Zilia the captive depends for survival on treatment by European men. Her vulnerability as a foreign woman is emphasized by two ruptures in the text that remain unnarrated and that correspond to Zilia's utter loss of the ability to communicate as well as the absence of control over her own body. Zilia does not write during a long illness on shipboard after her kidnapping by Spanish ravishers, and, on arriving in Paris, she stops recording her thoughts for half a year until she learns to write in French. Only when an enamored Déterville uses the Incan fortune stolen by the Spanish and taken as booty by the French to buy Zilia a house and to present her with the deed is she partially freed from being a hostage in a foreign land. This financial independence, as many critics have noted, allows Zilia to "translate" her letters and share them, according to the conceit of the novel, on her own terms.

At the same time that Graffigny wrote back to Montesquieu on the question of women's education, she incorporated and modernized the techniques for writing the heroine's history developed in historical romances. Like Scudéry, who plundered histories of antiquity to populate her voluminous novels, Graffigny lifted from Garcilaso de la Vega's early seventeenth-century chronicles of the Incan empire and the Spanish conquest, the French translation of which had most recently been published in 1744 (DeJean and Miller xviii). Scudéry had presented the first-person heroine's history as recounted to others, enfolding it within a third-person narrative frame. To accommodate new tastes in reading, Graffigny eliminated the conversational frame and trimmed the novel's length to something closer to Madame de La Fayette's *nouvelles*, and she offered her first-person heroine's history entirely through the single voice of Zilia in Zilia's letters. Graffigny's Peruvian conceit is that Zilia "writes" the first half of her story in Incan *quipu*, or knotted threads, addressed to her betrothed Aza, and that subsequently, after learning her second language, she continues in French, only to go on to translate the *quipu* letters sometime after the time of the story. Periphrasis, the poetic circumlocution so admired and so satirized as emblematic of Scuderian *préciosioté*, is Graffigny's staple figure for depicting the style of Zilia's writing in Peruvian *quipus* (as translated by Zilia). "In untying the secrets of your heart," Zilia exclaims, referring to the only return "letter" in *quipu* that she receives from Aza, "my own bathes in a perfumed sea. You live and the chains that were to unite us are not broken!" (22). The detail taken from Garcilaso de la Vega of the *quipu*—the knots Zilia ties to write to Aza and unties to read his *quipu* "letter"—anchors the figure (but the figure might as well be that of an asp or lyre) and makes this text "Peruvian" rather than something out of Scudéry's Aegypt or Greece. The *quipu* serve as a figure for two hearts tied together in perfect consent and sympathy consistent with the feminized model of Platonic love celebrated by the *précieuses*. As Zilia discovers, this complete consent is impossible in France given the mediated nature of French writing and language.[16] Graffigny's original ending to the novel, in which Zilia proposes intimate friendship with Déterville and refuses sex and marriage, situates complete consent and sympathy as a desired and irremediably lost state.

The conceit of translation from the Peruvian, underwritten by the device of the outsider looking in, provides an exotic alibi for the antiquated language of passion and periphrasis that Zilia uses. Zilia's acquisition of the fluency and cross-cultural awareness to translate her *quipu* letters into a polished French offsets the Scudérian/Peruvian sentiments in the writing. Graffigny employs the proto-Romantic currency of portraying Zilia as the last member of a dying Indian race and the last person who can speak and translate the Indian language. The representation of "Peruvian" as a dead language excuses or compensates for recourse to a Scudérian language and imaginary. Zilia's Peruvian ideas offer the vehicle for the reader to weigh Graffigny's most explicit points about the present. The French are beguiled by artifice, while Peruvian, although a lost language, is always a truthful one. Because of their poor educations, French women are hostages in their own country, bereft of the reason that would allow them to live virtuously and resist family and marital coercion.

Letters XVI and XVII recall the celebration of emblems of illustrious figures in early modern catalogs, on the one hand, and anticipate Jean-Jacques Rousseau's critique of the artifice of the theater and praise for the transparency of village celebrations, on the other.[17] In these letters, Zilia compares the treachery of French theater unfavorably with Incan performances that inspire virtue and greatness through historical example of exemplary figures. Within this context, Zilia herself becomes an exemplary figure whose personal story offers a modernized model of the *femme forte* for readers. Zilia's refusal to marry Déterville and her preservation of her chastity constitute the last stand of Peru. She commemorates these, like the members of the Scudéry network, in her letter writing after the moment. Graffigny's most Scuderian flourish is perhaps the place of publication listed on the frontispiece of the nine editions published in 1747; written at "Peine" (Trouble or Sorrow) substitutes for written at Paris (Kaplan 28; D. Smith 10–11), in an echo of the famous *carte de Tendre* in Scudéry's *Clélie*, which provided a geography of emotional experience on a physical map.

Graffigny praised Madame de La Fayette's well-received *Zaïde* (1669) in her personal correspondance and evidently drew on it as a source text for *Lettres d'une Péruvienne*. In *Zaïde*, the Spanish-speaking hero Consalve discovers Greek-speaking Zaïde shipwrecked on the seashore. Recognizing that she cannot understand him, he declares his love for her in his own language, "je vous aime" ("I love you"), and he reminds himself that "je ne puis la retenir sans injustice et avec bienséance" ("I cannot hold her here without injustice and with decency") (*Zaïde* 182). Early in *Lettres d'une Péruvienne,* when Zilia is trapped on his ship, Déterville teaches her to repeat "oui, je vous aime" ("yes, I love you") and "je vous promets d'être à vous" ("I promise to be yours") to him in French (*Péruvienne* 48). Thus, Déterville forces her to abjure Peruvian culture's central tenet of only speaking the truth and, literally, extracts the sign of consent from her with a trick of confidence when she is at her most vulnerable. He gets her to give herself away by asking her to utter words she does not understand. In contrast with the source scene in *Zaïde*, in which, in the neutral space of a beach, Consalve expresses his own feelings with awareness that he cannot be understood and, all the while, abjures control over Zaïde, Graffigny's scene of entrapment on a foreign ship casts a spotlight on how the perfect consent described by Diderot breaks down and becomes coerced consent. An individual who does not know the language in which a proposition is made cannot be determined insane or "incurably ignorant" *and* cannot be held responsible for a sign of consent made in incomprehensible words. Graffigny points out that psychological (internal) states are stipulated externally by those who control language. Sensitive to this, on shipboard, Zilia "me fais une étude gênante d'arranger mes pensées comme s'ils pouvaient les pénétrer malgré moi" ("makes an uncomfortable study of arranging [her] thoughts as if they could penetrate them despite [me]") (38). The rest of the novel may be seen as Zilia's effort to regain control over the meaning of the parroted sentence, "yes, I love you," by showing that she does not consent to the states of feeling Déterville willfully ascribes to her and by insisting that Déterville understand that the love she consents to with him is one of intimate friendship not passion and marriage. Her Peruvianness, corresponding especially to her love for Aza, even after Aza converts to Catholicism and marries a Spanish woman, constitutes the illustrious difference, the alternate epistemology, enabling Zilia to control her own consent.

Graffigny deepens her exploration of consent when she reworks the most famous scene from *Zaïde* to describe Déterville's return from war at a moment when Zilia can at last talk to him in French. At the siege of Talavera, La Fayette's lovers are reunited by chance: "They advanced towards each other, and, each speaking at the same time, Consalve used the Greek language to beg her forgiveness for appearing before her in the guise of an enemy, in the same moment that Zaïde told him in Spanish that she no longer feared the misfortunes of which she had been apprehensive and that this would not be the first danger from which he would have protected her" (257).[18] The protagonists in *Zaïde* understand immediately why each has learned the other's language, and this shared understanding and sentiment makes them blush and casts them into a long, shared silence. In contrast, in *Lettres d'une Péruvienne*, when Zilia speaks French on Déterville's return from battle, Déterville angrily exploits the ambiguity in the French word *aimer*, insisting over and over that she loves him ("You love me, Zilia . . . , you love me and you are telling me that you do"; "Vous m'aimez, Zilia . . . , vous m'aimez et vous me le dites!"). Zilia tries to limit the meaning of the word to Platonic friendship, as she explains in her writing (94). The chasm between the two novels could not be greater. *Zaïde* depicts two-way language learning as inspired by and demonstrative of a perfect sympathy between lovers that erases cultural difference and the need for language altogether. *Lettres d'une Péruvienne* depicts Zilia's learning of French as necessary for her survival in a radically foreign culture and argues that her meanings continue to be subject to coercion even after she has learned the language. In leaving Déterville insistently monolingual, unlike his predecessor Consalve who learns Greek to speak to the woman he loves, Graffigny underscores the idea that Zilia's meanings are subject to coercive external stipulation everywhere except within the story she tells and translates herself. This story retains and translates the epistemological conditions of the lost world of a Scudérian Peru that confirms the truthfulness of Zilia's account of ravishing without rape.

Like Graffigny, Lennox created a heroine who owes her education to Scudéry's world. Critics have been quick to point out that were it not for her "substituting the reality of French romances for that of eighteenth-century

English society" (Mack 193), Arabella would neither have the power nor the conviction to tell her own story. Arabella's Scuderian language offers the vehicle for the reader to weigh Lennox's most explicit points about the present: the English are mercenary and superficial. Their conversation, reading, and entertainment serve only for the idle destruction of reputations. Forced to rely on gossip for information, literally incapable of controlling language when gossip leads and misleads them, English women are too poorly educated to be capable of reason and virtue. Recourse to the popular conversational staple of "raillery," as Arabella points out in one of her admired speeches (which subscribe to Scudéry's model of polite female discourse in the *Conversations* and in her speeches of illustrious women) is the very opposite of instilling virtue through portraits of exemplary people. Zilia and Arabella are these exemplary people, distinguished as exotic beings in a foreign land. In each novel, contemporary (non-romance) female characters placed in parallel with the heroine, Déterville's sister Céline and Glanville's sister Miss Glanville, exemplify the narrow-minded conventionality—the national mediocrity—of women who have not benefited from the heroine's education in the lost world's epistemology.

Unlike the later bildungsroman, which would chart the male protagonist's progress over time from a state of innocence to broader worldliness and self-knowledge,[19] *Lettres d'une Péruvienne* and *The Female Quixote* are novels of dislocation.[20] The heroine does not so much lose youth and gain maturity as she becomes bicultural. She shifts from one country and its language to another. In the bildungsroman, the male protagonist undergoes "*Bildung* [education, development, formation]" to emerge on the basis of private experience as a "productive member of society" (Kontje 9). The hero sees behind the curtain. Rules that have always been in operation become visible. Disenchantment follows but so too does a dawning awareness of a world illuminated either by its decipherable codes or, after Flaubert's *L'éducation sentimentale*, its poverty of meaning. The hero, who once could only babble, transitions from youth to adulthood and becomes the fluent and witty, if disillusioned, master of the language to which he was born.

In Graffigny's and Lennox's novels, the young heroine is fully fluent in a first language at the time that the story begins. Zilia and Arabella do not enter the world, *le grand monde*, by choice. They are "ravished" from their first world and transported into a demanding modernity, only to find that their first language does not signify to those around them—no matter how much they insist on its validity. The heroines are not provincial bumpkins uninitiated to the ways of *the* world; they are foreigners unversed in the ways of the country in which they find themselves "without a mother, without a guide." At first, they are even unaware that other countries and cultural norms exist. It does not occur to Zilia that there is any place outside of Peru. Similarly, Arabella cannot conceive of the idea that romance does not signify to others.

Anachronism—the telling detail in Graffigny's and Lennox's novels—was probable or improbable depending on how it staged a nostalgic revival of a seemingly past epistemology, style, and idea of exemplary femininity. *Lettres d'une Péruvienne* established a neat split down its center between a *translated* romance (Peruvian) half and a mid-eighteenth-century second half composed of letters written in French by Zilia after she has experienced the enlightenment of a French education. The letters communicate Zilia's thoughts and emotions; the move to expression in French thus appears as an overlay onto an underlying foreign and Peruvian interiority. Zilia's refusal of consent to marry, while troubling, nonetheless appears consistent with an interior thought and will. *The Female Quixote*, on the other hand, relied heavily on third-person narratorial report of conversations, or exteriority, so that social reception is always at the fore. Arabella's romance speech, which contains an ethical core despite stylistic anachronism, appears alongside the alternately absurd and sensible claims made in modern-day speech by those around Arabella, as well as alongside the pastiche of romance in the mouths of those who seek to entrap or appease her. In *The Female Quixote,* the status of romance as a touchstone for female virtue and identity is unstable; it is the psychic precondition for Arabella's heroism, but it is also, when external-ized, evidence of madness. Arabella's ultimate consent to marry her cousin and thereby consolidate the family fortune indicates that her internal thought and will have been adjusted to the will of others.

Where the bildungsroman hero of the end of the eighteenth century and the nineteenth century advances from one phase of life to the next along a single broadening epistemological continuum, the heroine in these mid-eighteenth-century novels confronts acculturation and translation from one epistemology to another. She balances ravishing from home against the possi-bility of retaining that home's organization of meaning and values within her mental landscape. Each novel safely consigns the heroine's Scuderian home epistemology to the exotic past (Graffigny) or to antiquated fiction (Lennox) and uses the marriage plot to preclude the heroine from returning home. Zilia does not marry the crown prince Aza and so the Incan empire plundered by the Spanish becomes effectually extinct. Arabella vows to give up her reading and does marry Glanville, effectively an assent to the new world order.

Even so, the devices of the stranger from elsewhere and of quixotism converge to orchestrate a cosmopolitan insight that does not appear in the works by Montesquieu and Fielding (along with their predecessors) to which Graffigny and Lennox write back. Montesquieu had offered up an early form of relativism, suggesting that the horizon of an observer is inherently limited by what he counts as significant phenomena. Responding with irony to Samuel Richardson's popular novel *Pamela*, Fielding had suggested that fiction offers misleading moral models and that experience in the world is a better pathway to common sense. Montesquieu and Fielding both update late seventeenth- and early eighteenth-century empirical skepticism and moral satire by giving them play in the relatively new universe of the novel. They offer readers opportunities to experiment with different guides for interpreting the world while leading them toward a resolution in which the failures of each guide are recognized and acknowledged. The satisfaction of this strategy lies in the sense of intellectual superiority it engenders: I see the flaws; I identify the failings of the characters in the novel. In contrast, Graffigny and Lennox dramatize through their return to the theme of "ravishing" how violent is the process that instantiates one epistemology as superior to (as more true than) another. They focus on how differently ravishing may be interpreted, depending on standpoint, and on how standpoint invalidates the capacity of women to consent "freely" or have their stories be interpreted as "likely." This instantiation leaves behind a melancholic longing for the old, displaced, disproven, but somehow, for the heroine and those sharing a "similitude of destiny," true epistemology of romance.

Graffigny and Lennox sustain the slippage in the meanings of "ravishing": rape, kidnap, mental alienation, charm, and wonder. Arabella and Zilia are ravished from their proper Scuderian worlds but never experience rape. Neither *Lettres d'une Péruvienne* nor *The Female Quixote* can present a rape since, in a post-romance world, rape correlates either with the heroine's lack of virtue or mental incompetence. Still, rape haunts the stories. The Spanish kidnap Zilia by force—the engraving of the scene accompanying the 1797 edition depicts a half-naked (and oddly light-haired) Zilia being carried forcibly out of the temple by two men while armed soldiers stand in the background.[21] Déterville, "agitated" and with a "face enflamed" just barely restrains himself from taking hold of Zilia, muttering to himself, "No . . .

respect . . . her virtue" (56), and another Frenchman puts his hand on her breast, emboldened by the familiarity of others (68). Arabella is the victim of elaborate strategies to force her consent, and threats, including a kidnapping plot, hover around every corner. Both protagonists are confined in closed spaces. Both must rely for knowledge of events that directly affect them on unreliable informants with vested interests. Perhaps most important, both experience long illnesses corresponding to textual gaps that are reminiscent of Clarissa's post-rape illness in Richardson's novel and both find their way of communicating significantly altered afterward. In the semiotics of post-Richardsonian fiction by women, the long illness is the sign of ravishing, and the cure marks the moment at which the female protagonist becomes aware of the rupture between the world to which she owes her sense of self (akin to a Lacanian mirror-stage, in which she appeared to control her own meanings and image) and the world in which her meanings are construed for her (akin to a Lacanian symbolic).

Ravishing without rape makes it possible for the heroine to remain virtuous, and it makes it possible to avoid stipulations that the heroine is insane or incapable of consent. Rape provides the opportunity for Richardson's novel to engage with psychological states. Ravishing provides the terrain in *Lettres d'une Péruvienne* and *The Female Quixote* for describing the external conditions that coerce psychological states, such as control over information, constraining consent to the point that it cannot be conceived as having been given freely, or presenting multiple propositions for consent as if they were a single one.

At the same time, ravishing without rape conjures the foreign, fictive, interior, or past world that has provided the heroine with the moral and rational education she uses to negotiate the contemporary world into which she has been swept with her virtue intact. Ravishing, as romance sign, marks the divide between a present world in which the heroine's story cannot be credited and the education received in the lost world that has provided her with the mental capacity necessary for consent. It also serves as a portal for imagining alternate but irretrievable epistemological and cultural conditions under which a woman's consent might be valid and her story credited. Nostalgia for the lost Scuderian world is a nostalgia for a world of perfect sympathy, where female virtue, female reason, and female adventures are not oxymorons. Affiliation with the Scuderian world both qualifies and disqualifies the heroine for survival in the present. Privileged as the very essence of the heroine, the lost Scuderian world provides the standpoint empowering her to give or refuse consent independently of external stipulation as to her mental state. The Scuderian world becomes the locus of female exceptionalism, a fantasy site of melancholic longing, coded as French, that is productive of female affinity around the idea of a "shared destiny" as "illustrious companions in misfortune." These novels broadcast the message that the heroine is on her own, cast adrift, carrying the lost Scuderian world within her as she travels abroad. She, and we the readers, cannot go back.

Investment in Romance Language

Even today, it is difficult to identify many fictional depictions of women's interiority and consciousness that are not narratively triggered by and that do not unfurl within the context of psychosexual as well as epistemological and cultural siege. The siege on consent—ravishing—is a powerful topos in modern narrative, binding together as it does psychology, power, sex, desire, and interpretation with contracts, education, property, will, and cultural hegemony. The ravishing narrative oscillates between validation of sympathy and a spectacle of successful and violent coercion. It slides along the slope from partial consent to complete loss of control over the interpretation of one's will. It dabbles in a discourse of educational determinism and reform by exploring the consequences of limited access to information on the formation of mind and behavior. It depicts and manipulates alignment and misalignment of the internal wishes of a powerless person, her external signs of will, the internal wishes of a powerful person, and his external signs of will. It explores the permeability, indeed the interdependence or lack of autonomy of this double couple of "sympathies." And it hypothesizes the absolute alterity of women versus men. Investment in a separate literary world—a city of women where companions in misfortunes may share their stories and have them credited—emerged in the eighteenth century in connection with the new use of *ravishing* as a means for relishing depiction of an interiority under siege. This literary world, the story of girls, became a way of claiming fortification.

Written from a place named "Peine," *The Female Quixote* and *Lettres d'une Péruvienne* nostalgically embrace a protective and prescriptive literary territory. They declare affiliation with a fortifyingly feminine world of romance heritage associated with the French language. Affiliation with this imaginary literary world involved investment in claims about the heroine's psychological capacity to resist by demonstrating sexual virtue and by controlling the personal story of sexual virtue. The eighteenth-century emergence of the story of exceptional girls involved a supranational avowal of affiliation, even as it was initially coded as French.

Among the eighteenth-century translations of *Lettres d'une Péruvienne,* two were by women, Miss Roberts and Maria Romero Masegosa y Cancelada. The English translator, Miss Roberts, explained in the preface to her translation that she began working on it as an "exercise in the French language." Writer John Hawkesworth had "recommended" it "as a Novel of that delicate kind which was peculiarly adapted to a Female Writer; abounding with moral and religious truths; and being originally written by a Woman justly celebrated among the French Authors, was the more suitable to a Translator of the same Sex."[22] While serving as a portal to other work— Roberts would go on to translate Jeanne-Marie Leprince de Beaumont's *The Triumph of Truth* in 1775—Roberts's version of Graffigny allowed her to develop original material as a writer. She annexed a new story about an original character to Graffigny's work and through this advanced an argument for female Christian resignation in the face of impossible (textually presented as incestuous) love (Kaplan x). Similarly, Maria Romero Masegosa y Cancelada, one of perhaps two women who translated Graffigny's novel into Spanish at the end of the eighteenth century, also took liberties, adding "*algunas correcciones.*"[23] In inserted letters and editorial changes, she corrected French anti-Spanish sentiment by softening the picture of the conquest and by converting Zilia to Catholicism. Her emendations, as Theresa Ann Smith has suggested, allowed her to bring Spanish Enlightenment discourses into alignment with the softened moral Enlightenment popularized in works by Genlis and others (116–43). Romero's preface included a self-portrait where she presented herself as precisely the sort of frivolous young woman that Graffigny critiqued. She narrated her own salvation through finding the right target identity and investment as a story parallel to Zilia's coming-to-writing-through-translation narrative of negotiating a compromise between Incan truthfulness and French Enlightenment knowledge. Romero addresses the city of ladies directly in her preface:

> Ladies, women colleagues and friends, I speak from experience. There was the time when, in spite of the wish and teachings with which my father endeavored to inculcate in me the pleasure of rational diversions, my sole amusements were going for a stroll, conversing with friends, and

outward adornment, never taking thought of how I might be employing my mind. I believed to have in my head a library of the most distinguished works ever written because I had the read the comedies of Calderón, the novels of Doña María de Zayas, and other works of this sort: I was very keen on reading, but my choices were so poor and my father's duties left him so little time to instruct me, that it came to pass that anything that wasn't pure nonsense became hateful to me. But my brother, who was as keen or even more so than I on reading; who had chosen better; who felt sorry seeing me lose my time and my eyesight reading so much and such idle foolishness; and finally who had more leisure to devote to my reform, began to tempt me with books suited to my station, which little by little allowed me to emerge from that partial stupor in which I found myself submerged; and lastly, he not only managed to get me to read worthwhile and pleasant things, but also to despise and abandon all that claptrap and the worthless hodgepodge of books that had enthralled me to such an extent. . . . He was so capable of eliciting my emulation, that envying the knowledge he had of the French language, and not contenting myself with reading good books in Spanish, and some Italian works, of which language we had a certain familiarity, I devoted myself to translating it, which I succeeded in doing, in spite of his help, with a great deal of trouble, since I had to run my household and also, because of the many responsibilities that beset me (the village where I live is a reliable witness to this), I was unable to dedicate myself freely to its study. Finally, having succeeded in this endeavor, I translated this fine work that I presented to the public.[24]
(12–15)

Translation of a best-selling mid-century novel allowed Romero to insert herself from Spain imaginatively into a literary world of female affinity. Notably, her translation was not so much a simple apprenticeship in writing as it was a means of claiming as the basis for her independent production both shared values and participation in a shared culture. Sherry Simon writes that translation is "an intensely relational act, one which establishes connections between text and culture, between author and reader" (*Gender* 83). Romero's autobiographical preface rehearsed her entry into a community as well as the procedures—reading the right books, translating, writing—for entering it. These were the very procedures that were narrated sympathetically in Graffigny's novel and satirically in Lennox's.

Male translators and editors of *Lettres d'une Péruvienne* prefaced the work with a biographical note on the author Françoise de Graffigny, reinscribing a homology between a woman's life and her text.[25] In Roberts's and Romero's prefaces, the translation and rewriting of a signal text (one which was itself a rewriting of Scudéry's and La Fayette's contributions to an emerging repertoire) figured as the means of their own entry through French into a community of women readers and writers, as well as the opportunity to renegotiate that community's values. Working in and through a second language, I am arguing, correlated with "investment" in an identity. Linguist Bonnie Norton has coined the term *investment* to signal "the socially and historically constructed relationship of learners to the target language and their often ambivalent desire to learn and practice it. If learners 'invest' in the target language, they do so with the understanding that they will acquire a wider range of symbolic resources (language, education, friendship) and material resources (capital goods, real estate, money), which will in turn increase the value of their cultural capital and social power" (6). When women writers staged scenes like Maria Romero's autobiographical account of her improving encounter with the *Lettres d'une Péruvienne* or Lennox's descriptions of Arabella's moral consultation of *Artamène* and *Clélie,* the reading of key works from a foreign land was figured textually as a resource. This text-based home or lost world allowed protagonists to display virtue in contrast with their more conventional friends. Romero models for the reader her own transformation and entry into the city of ladies on reading Graffigny, replaying a process that Graffigny herself recorded in her letters when she described her own experience on reading La Fayette's *Zaïde* (Kulessa 63).

Investment describes the way that individuals assume identities and values associated with a target language and, consequently, learn a second language more or less successfully. "Language learners who struggle to speak from one identity position," Norton argues in *Identity and Language Learning*, "may be able to reframe their relationship with others and claim alternative, more powerful identities from which to speak, read or write, thereby enhancing language acquisition" (3). The poststructuralist insight that "identity is constituted in and through language" informs Norton's notion that "every time language learners speak, read, or write the target language, they are not only exchanging information with members of the target language community, they are also organizing and reorganizing a sense of who they are and how they relate to the social world. As such, they are engaged in identity construction and negotiation" (4).

Norton's argument helps explain the significance of a French language incorporating a spectrum from romance, to politeness, to sensibility for emerging women writers and readers. Beyond being the language of the Republic of Letters, of courts, and of polite society, French was the language of romance writing, practiced and personified by the illustrious extended Scudéry network of women writers and its inheritors. Reading and writing women's novels and memoirs in French, translating these from the French, or even reading and writing on the basis of a translation from the French all involved investment in a fantasy of specifically women's values and identity—in a city of women. Moreover, affinity with the French and feminized literary world of the city of women seems to have involved assumption of a "more powerful identity from which to speak, read or write." The fashionable cultural ascendancy of French and the early eighteenth-century French domination of the literary market partially explain the proliferation of eighteenth-century women who relied on French in their writing and who created female characters educated in France, versed in French literature, or born of a French mother or grandmother.

Yet French appears, in addition, to have resonated as a linguistic investment in a feminized form of cultural capital. The linguistic coding of a separate women's literary world invested with cultural capital shifted to British English by the nineteenth century, to American English in the twentieth century, and to the English, French, and Spanish of postcolonial women's writing more recently. Yet the terms of investment governing practices of attachment to this world, regardless of linguistic coding, have remained much the same as they were when they emerged. First, a linguistically marked small literary world promises itself as a site of investment and as a resource against ravishing. Second, those who invest in this world are drawn to it through its lingua franca. They shuttle between the fantasy of a lost supranational female power that the language appears to represent and the competing lure of subscription to national gender roles and to the aesthetic norms of national literary fields. Put more simply, a literary language other than their own may serve as the screen onto which readers and writers project a fantasy of female power and linguistic control over the telling and reception of their own story as part of a collective woman's story.

*   *   *

By what process did (illustrious) women become storytellers? Arabella in *The Female Quixote* suggests that ravishing has something to do with it, but she also proposes that her own knowledge of "a great Store of Romances, and, what was still more unfortunate, not in the original *French*, but very bad Translations" (7) leads directly to a "similitude of destiny" in which she will become a storyteller. Indeed, her fantasy alternatives to the dismal plot of a marriage of family convenience are pulled from the vast store of women's stories that she has read. *The Female Quixote* advances through a selection and combination of stories of illustrious women as Arabella makes their stories her own. Arabella's story unfolds through a repetition and renegotiation of the meaning of the earlier "miraculous" adventures of women who "shared a similitude of destiny." It is, indeed, a pastiche of stories of ravishing. Providing her protagonist with anachronistic reading habits to comic effect, the author Charlotte Lennox nonetheless describes sardonically the process by which women readers in the eighteenth century became storytellers by building, drawing from and improvising on a shared repertoire. The very repetition of elements in the repertoire allowed the work of these writers to become reified as "writing by women" while contributing to a picture of women's writing as a discourse that was always autobiographical in its recounting of women's "similitude of destiny." It is worth remembering that Lennox herself was a perpetual reader, translator, and redactor from the French. When Lennox's Arabella is finally cured of her investment in romance, *The Female Quixote* is freed to become a heralded work by a proper *British* woman writer rather than an improbable fiction written by a woman who had spent too much time investing in promises made in a foreign language.

At the end of the century, Charlotte Smith, like Charlotte Lennox a practiced translator from the French and like Lennox dependent on writing for her livelihood, would draw on the familiar trope of unfortunate ladies sharing their stories in her third novel *Celestina* (1791). As Celestina de Mornay travels in a coach, her fellow passenger, Sophy Elphinstone shares her personal history, which begins with a ravishing.[26] Sophy explains that she and Celestina are "something like the personages with whom we are presented in old romances, and who meet in forests and among rocks and recount their adventures; but do you know, my dear Miss de Mornay, that I feel very much disposed to enact such a personage, and though it is but a painful subject, to relate to you my past life?" Celestina replies reassuringly, " 'And do you know, my dear Madam, . . . that no wandering lady in romance had ever more inclination to lose her own reflections in listening to the history of some friend who had by chance met her, lost in the thorny labyrinth of uneasy thoughts, than I have to listen to you" (255). Lorraine Fletcher notes in her introduction that Smith deliberately represented herself in a way that readers (including Mary Wollstonecraft and a reviewer for the *Critical Review*) recognized in the story of Sophy Elphinstone's suffering as mother of many children and wife to an irresponsible city merchant and West India trader. Fletcher writes that "by reference to an earlier form of fiction, Smith keeps us conscious that this too is 'story,' that women's painful lives which are the subject of such stories change little from one generation to another, that Celestina, Sophy, the author and the reader will find much in common" (C. Smith 29). If Sophy and Celestina meet by chance, their conversational sharing of personal stories of gendered calamity is an inherited and constitutive code of women's writing or, as Arabella tartly advises her future father-in-law, not merely a means of finding solace but a comparative measure of the "Accidents" that happen to women, past and present, at home and in "Turky" or beyond. When Richardson (re)invented the psychological novel in English with the publication of *Clarissa*, how to forestall the external stipulation of a woman's internal state became a conundrum. After 1752, a recognizable category of writing focused on a woman's struggle to stipulate her own mental state. It privileged affinity with "companions in misfortune"—"I feel it to be true because it resonates with my experience"—as the basis for validation independent from but running in parallel with realist empirical claims.

Chapter 4

The Repertoire of the School for Girls

Why is there so much repetition in fiction written by women in Britain and across Western Europe after the middle of the eighteenth century? One traditional answer to this question is that Samuel Richardson's *Clarissa* "functioned as a lodestone, exerting its enormous force on the themes and structures of women's writing and reorienting their narratives" (Perry, "Clarissa's Daughters" 5). Ruth Perry associates at least thirteen English epistolary novels by women with a Richardson effect, such as Sophia Briscoe's *Miss Melmouth: or the New Clarissa* (1771), yet she argues against an earlier dismissal of such novels as pale imitations by uninventive women writers. Leaning on Nancy Armstrong's work in *Desire and Domestic Fiction*, Perry offers one explanation for the rewriting and repetition. What was "at stake," she suggests, was a "question that was increasingly pivotal to changes in English culture in the eighteenth century, namely,—what was the nature and place of female sexuality?" (14). Perry proposes that women novelists' ruminations about female sexuality were elicited by the emergence of a new national bourgeois model of gendered domesticity that social historians place in the middle of the eighteenth century. In concert with conduct manuals, the national novel after mid-century allowed women to imagine themselves as reigning over private life, as Armstrong defines it, "the whole domain over which our culture grants women authority: the use of leisure time, the ordinary care of the body, courtship practices, the operations of desire, the forms of pleasure, gender differences and family relations" (26–27). In other words, exploration of British gender roles and the lodestone of desire, not of *Clarissa* per se, offer explanations of repetition among British women writers.

The repetition phenomenon, however, appears in novels, periodicals, plays, and pedagogical works or conduct manuals written by women in languages other than English. In support of a Rousseau-lodestone hypothesis for the novel, Margaretmary Daley counts sixteen German novels written by women between 1771 and 1819 as responses to Jean-Jacques Rousseau's *Julie, ou la nouvelle Héloïse* (1761), including one novel that another critic has interpreted as a response to *Clarissa*.[1] Like Abbé Prevost's translation of *Clarissa* in France, Johann David Michaelis's translation in German between 1748 and 1753 "spawned literary imitations, popularized sensibility, and inspired new understandings of feminine expression and female agency" (Johns, *Bluestocking* 40). In French, women novelists returned to the rape, sex out of wedlock, and loveless marriage elements appearing in both Richardson's and Rousseau's novels, as, for instance, when Jeanne-Marie Leprince de Beaumont presented her own "new" Clarissa Harlowe in *La nouvelle Clarisse* (1767) or when Marie-Jeanne Riccoboni variously developed these elements across her entire œuvre.[2] In the first novels written in German and in Dutch by women, repetition took the form of using epistolary exchanges to address the theme of ravishing as well as questions about education and exemplarity derived from a corpus of works addressing women readers.

What was going on? Were British and European women writers simply uninventive imitators of Richardson and Rousseau? Was "writing back" to male writers the only stimulus for writing as a woman? Were all women writers across Europe engaged in rehearsing the same (British) national exploration of "the nature and place of female sexuality"? None of these extensions of the lodestone hypothesis seems particularly satisfying. Rehearsal of the same themes, plots, and codes did occur alongside confirmation of competing stereotypes of national gender models. Yet what becomes evident if we move away from an analysis built primarily around male influence on women writers is that repetition was not merely the symptom of what Ann Laura Stoler calls an "education of desire" or of the powerful attraction (and repulsion) of Richardson and Rousseau. Derived from and constitutive of a repertoire, repetition was a function of the emergence of a women's position in the transnational literary field of the eighteenth century—of the accretion of productive steps and moves giving women's writing its identity and offering a choreography drawing in and guiding new performers as they slipped onstage. After *Clarissa* opened a rift between how a woman might tell her own history to sympathetic listeners and how a woman's mental state might be judged according to external social norms, the topos of a woman's version of a woman's story became clearer.[3] In alignment with this topos, the project of educating girls so that they might make independent judgments based on reason and virtue became the basis for an emerging repertoire of women's reading and writing.

Theorist Étienne Wenger has proposed that a shared repertoire allows people to "create meaningful statements about the world" and provides "the styles by which they express their forms of membership and their identities as members" (*Communities* 83). Variations on the themes of ravishing, of the punitive arranged marriage, and of the closeted education permitted exploration and development of a gendered style. Repetition and rehearsal in texts by women writers offer a historical record of a repertoire that allowed international women readers to coalesce through their experiments in writing over the second half of the eighteenth century into what Wenger calls a "community of practice." By identifying, by circulating, but also by changing a shared repertoire of tropes and texts, women readers and writers formed a group of practitioners bound by the affinity that the repertoire imparted. The shared repertoire of women readers-writers allowed what Wenger calls "further engagement in practice" (83). Women explored the themes of ravishing, loveless marriage, and restrictive educations often by piggybacking on translations of writing by women abroad or by referring to key scenes or characters in writings by other women. They also piggybacked on the market success of Richardson's and Rousseau's novels by incorporating reference to their characters into their titles. Margareta Geertruid van der Werken (also known as Madame Cambon), for example, wrote two highly popular Dutch epistolary novels for children, *De kleine Grandisson* (1782) and *De kleine Klarissa* (1790). Miss Roberts's and Maria Romero's translations of Françoise de Graffigny's *Letters of a Peruvian Woman* (discussed in Chapter 3) which annexed new material to the novel, constituted, like Graffigny's rewriting of La Fayette's *Zaïde*, "further engagement in practice." Roberts and Romero registered membership in the evolving field of women writers through use of the field's repertoire. The very relatedness of themes, plotlines, and heroines, along with both repetition of internal intertextual references and explicit claims of difference to writing by men, constitutes evidence of how a repertoire permitted formation of a community of practicing women readers and writers in an emerging zone of the eighteenth-century literary field. The internationalism of the community of practice that women readers and writers constituted and that their repertoire registered, along with that community's constant use of tropes of national gender identity to "create meaningful statements about the world," stamped a lasting imprint on the category of literary expression that we know as "women's writing."

Pierre Bourdieu proposes that the habitus of writers informs the position they stake in a literary field. As Loic Wacquant neatly summarizes the idea, habitus is "the way society becomes deposited in persons in the form of lasting dispositions, or trained capacities and structured propensities to think, feel and act in determinant ways, which then guide them" (316). The eighteenth-century habitus of women writers included the conversation circle as a medium for transmission of a gendered education and the learning of modern languages, especially French. The emerging position of women as a distinct category in the literary field drew on the relative prestige and femini-zation of the French conversational model[4] as well as the practice in middling and upper-rank households of integrating girls and women in listening to instructive conversation or reading aloud as they completed handiwork. It also derived from the opening for entering the literary field that translation work provided to women. As a subordinated literary practice, through which the translator could claim to be useful but not original, translation supplied women writers with modestly rewarded work as well as boundless source material throughout their careers while also encouraging a veritable straddling of national literary fields. The development of a transnational position for women writers in the literary field thus drew on an inherited transnational discourse and textual tradition comparing the lives of illustrious women and associating virtuous female access to knowledge with communal feminized space, as well as women's modern educational habitus as conversationalists, translators, and, ultimately, educators.

The position of women writers took on definition through emerging debates about the importance of educating girls for the sake of social, moral, and physical hygiene. A century of writing culminated in Mary Wollstone-craft's position that a woman's virtue arose from "the exercise" of her "own reason" (76). Such female virtue was socially transformative. As Mary Woll-stonecraft put it,

> But it is vain to expect the present race of weak mothers either to take that reasonable care of a child's body, which is necessary to lay the foun-dation of a good constitution, supposing that it do not suffer for the sins of its fathers; or to manage its temper so judiciously that the child will not have, as it grows up, to throw off all that its mother, its first instruc-tor, directly or indirectly taught, and unless the mind have uncommon vigour, womanish follies will stick to the character throughout life. The weakness of the mother will be visited on the children! (315)

Debates on the social value of the education of girls were fueled by the practices of women educators, including, in Catholic Europe, convent traditions embracing Christian withdrawal from worldliness and deliberate cultivation of a reasoned virtue and, in Protestant Europe, both memories of Protestant nunneries and an idealization of withdrawal into a plain and ordered life in the country house.[5] The family networks and prestige of European royal families, endowed with children in need of the most up-to-date educations, contributed to dissemination of new educational models for the teaching of girls (Orr, "Aristocratic"). These models, in turn, fed the repertoire of the community of practice, with their familiarized or softened version of Enlightenment and their formal reliance on a structure of assessing female exemplarity—the selection of the most virtuous life from among a catalog of female lives. Focusing on the crucial Enlightenment project of the education of women, this chapter examines the expansion of a mid-eighteenth-century repertoire for the evolving international community of practice constituted by women readers and writers. It explores the way that the familiar conversation built around the examination of exemplary female lives structured women writers' claims of a position—disseminating the capital of virtue—in the literary field. And it considers how the habitus of conversation and the habitus of translation generated the internationalism and reified national gender roles organizing that position.[6]

Learning Through Conversation

What education most girls did receive in the late seventeenth and early eighteenth centuries revolved around practical skills and social attributes, such as needlework and politeness, developed in an oral context and represented as belonging to oral group culture. Reading itself was molded to fit the sanctified form of the women's circle. Conduct literature, novels, paintings, and engravings contrasted the potential dangers of silent solitary reading for women with the benefits of coming into contact with print in collective oral contexts. In the ideal, girls "kept their hands busy" with practical tasks while a girl or woman from the group read a useful work aloud (Constant 232). Girls were encouraged to learn in and through the presence of others. Education consisted of seizing the ideas arising in conversations and acquiring associated traits of politeness, reasoning, and virtue that had been, in essence, vetted by the group. Adélaïde Gillette Billet Dufrénoy (1765–1825), who published her first work at the age of twenty-two in 1787, provided a fictional portrait of this model for the heroine of her 1812 novel *The Woman Writer* (*La femme auteur, ou les inconvénients de la célébrité*), who listens to conversation in her parents' home: "The conversation there almost always turned on interesting subjects. While these were discussed with more or less warmth, Anaïs learned in silence, next to her mother, to embroider or to do needlepoint. This amiable child was not so captivated by this work that she could not lend her attention to the conversations held around her; they partially engraved themselves in her young memory; she learned without studying and her mind and reason formed, so to speak, without her knowing" (6).

The portrayal of female intellectual activity as more easily condoned when it occurred in a collective and conversational context, free of the deleterious health consequences, asocial demeanor, and mental delusion that hard study could bring down on the weaker sex, wove through inherited written and visual codes.[7] Nadine Béringuier has shown that "to replicate the familiar setting perceived as most appropriate for girls' education, [French] conduct-book authors favored narrative forms that privileged direct (written and oral) forms of communication between individuals, the epistolary and dialogic forms. These forms simulated the 'immediacy' of relationships between mothers and girls in need of guidance and minimized the 'disruption' that the mediation of writing could cause to such a bond" (21).

Visual images inscribed and confirmed gendered versions of the access to ideas. Images of a man absorbed in solitary study, writing, or artistic production, often derived from depictions of St. Gerome or Erasmus, fueled developing ideas of independent male literary genius. In contrast, images of a solitary adolescent young woman or royal mistress carelessly grasping a small open book, such as François Boucher's 1757 portrait of a semirecumbent Madame de Pompadour, suggested abandon to fantasy at a minimum or loss of virtue and erotic opportunity at most. When pages covered with writing slipped into the hands of the notable women who had their portraits taken in the second half of the century, a book's closed covers, the page's large unsecretive format (especially in the representation of musical scores), or the presence of a writing desk, along with the female subject's age, carefully covered colletage, and focused gaze, proposed a socially redeeming purpose. Group portraits of intellectual or artistic men, such as Zoffany's *Portrait of the Academicians of the Royal Society* (1771–72), communicated a formal institutional membership as well as the manly camaraderie necessary for accomplishing great and complex projects. The classical sculpture assembled on shelves in Zoffany's background set the measure of aesthetic excellence that the academicians must rival. Richard Samuels's famous *Portraits in the Characters of the Muses in the Temple of Apollo* (1779) subscribed to the convention of introducing musical instruments and other signs of application to social arts into the group portrait of women. In transforming the women writers and artists in Elizabeth Montagu's coterie into classical muses, Samuels made the circle known as the Bluestockings a symbol of Britain's cultural achievement by suggesting an analogy with a Greek golden age. The portrait offered a picture of a redeeming female collectivity that was neither dangerously private, nor ostentatiously public, nor bound to a private communion with the printed word.

Historian Carla Hesse points out that "in the eighteenth century, the improvised spoken word—especially its eloquent excess—was coded as a feminine cultural trait, while the written word and its power to discipline speech was viewed as the masculine rhetorical domain" (30). At the same time, the association of women's learning and knowledge with oral culture has, somewhat paradoxically, a textual history. To a certain extent, women's conversational habitus was a textual product, as the medieval and Renaissance convention of gathering illustrious ladies in conversation in a single volume suggests. The number of published conversations that emerged from members of Scudéry's côterie, in a variety of forms—whether conversations, memoirs, or letters—contributed directly to the European image of a French golden age of conversation. The purported capacity of elegant conversation to instill an elevating and graceful politeness, as well as a socially responsible and reasoned but not pedantic personal style, became a pedagogical model for emulation.[8] In the universe of the *Précieuses*, as critics dubbed the cultural movement for which Scudéry functioned as both a prized and mocked figurehead, exemplary women directed conversation among men and women toward polite and reasoned goals, arriving at moral conclusions and elevated norms for speech and civilized group behavior. As a feminized cultural model, *préciosité* came in for praise and full-on attack. In Molière's account of *préciosité,* the vanity, pride, and lust of women who were improperly managed by weak husbands and fathers led them to excesses of pedantry and self-regard that were fully paraded in their worldly conversational excesses. Summing up over a century of attacks on clever female conversationalists in her play *What Should We Call Her?* (*Comment la nommera-t-on?* 1788), Isabelle de Charrière gave the wary bachelor Verteuil the following lines: "Ah, do you know what a clever woman [*femme d'esprit*] is? Have you paid attention to what this title means? An almost complete extinction of everything natural for which a perpetual attempt to judge well and speak well is substituted—to merit being quoted for finesse, for taste, for knowledge of things of the mind. A clever man is the opposite of an idiot, but a clever woman is the opposite of a woman who is natural, innocent and simple" (*Œuvres* 7:131). The influential legacy of late seventeenth- and early eighteenth-century French women conversationalists, recorded and disseminated in print, produced these two irreconcilable opposites in the Enlightenment discourse on women: the innocent and natural woman and the *femme d'esprit* possessed of lively conversational skills.

The famous project of Françoise d'Aubigné, marquise de Maintenon at Saint-Cyr, offers an early example of the role of textual conversation modeling in the education of girls. The Saint-Cyr project circulated through the teaching practices of early eighteenth-century women educators and, in a second wave, through mid-eighteenth-century publications focused on the exemplary and cautionary figure of Françoise d'Aubigné herself. With the Saint-Cyr project as one point of entry, a picture begins to emerge of how women's habitus informed the repertoire of women's writing and of how repertoire contributed to a "woman's" position in the literary field.

Maintenon elicited debates about female virtue both as a notorious celebrity in the French worlds of letters and of court politics and as a patroness-educator who undertook an early Enlightenment experiment in the education of girls that relied heavily on conversational sociability. For subsequent generations, Françoise d'Aubigné's romanesque life would furnish an irresistible arena for reflection on the careers and fate of exceptionally talented women. The granddaughter of Protestant general and poet Agrippa d'Aubigné and godchild of the parents of maxim writer François de la Rochefoucauld, Françoise d'Aubigné grew up as an impoverished member of the aristocracy. Her father, Constant d'Aubigné was imprisoned for counterfeiting after prior criminal convictions for abduction, treason, and the murder of his first wife. He married the daughter of the prison warden, Jeanne de Cardilhac. Their daughter Françoise was born at the prison of Niort in 1635. Abandoned by Constant d'Aubigné, and fought over by relatives who sought to control her religion, Françoise begged in the streets as a child and was treated as a servant by a Catholic relative. Still in her teens, the impoverished Françoise d'Aubigné married the disabled writer Paul Scarron, twenty-five years her senior, and through him gained access to privileged literary and worldly circles. Madeleine de Scudéry became an important friend. After Scarron's death, Françoise d'Aubigné became the enlightened and discreet governess of the numerous illegitimate children borne by her friend Madame de Montespan to Louis XIV. The king conferred on her the title of marquise de Maintenon, drawing on the name of the estate she purchased with a royal pension. In part owing to a successful styling of herself as a highly devout woman and practicing Catholic from a famously Protestant family, she replaced Montespan in the aging king's favor, serving as confidante and counselor and, after the death of Queen Maria Theresa, his morganatic wife. In the early 1680s, she established schools for working girls at Montmorency and at Rueil. In 1686, Madame de Maintenon established a secular educational community at Saint-Cyr for the daughters of the impoverished nobility, among whom she had once numbered, and secured dowries sufficient to marry them. She developed an extensive educational program, which was memorialized in the *Memoirs and Letters of Madame de Maintenon* that were published in 1755, thirty-six years after her death (Conley 2–9).

For eighteenth-century readers, the question of whether Madame de Maintenon had sex with Louis XIV before or after her morganatic marriage to him oriented response to her legacy as an educator and a philanthropist. The question of the marriage was one of the two controversial points that made the *Memoirs and Letters of Madame de Maintenon* an international publishing sensation in the middle of the eighteenth century. The second was the question of the extent of Maintenon's religious manipulation of Louis XIV. Anxiety about dangerous female influence on affairs of state and pointed national religious prejudices coalesced in the fabricated charge that Madame de Maintenon was responsible for Louis XIV's decision to revoke the Edict of Nantes, a century-old law of religious toleration (Lauriol; H. Brown 170). Laurent Angliviel de la Beaumelle wrote and published *The Memoirs and Letters of Madame de Maintenon* in 1755–56 at the behest of the nuns of Saint-Cyr who sought a thoroughgoing defense of their patron, including documentation of her marriage to Louis XIV and exoneration against the charge of responsibility for the Revocation of the Edict of Nantes, which had resulted in the exile of hundreds of thousands of Huguenot families from France and their dispersal across Northern Europe. English and German versions of La Beaumelle's work quickly followed; Charlotte Lennox's English translation came out in 1757, while notable translator Luise Gottsched worked with her husband and her friend Dorothea Henriette von Runckel to translate three volumes into German in quick succession. The publication and translations of the *Memoirs* were a major event, since they promised an alternate and more intimate version of the age of Louis XIV than the one provided by Voltaire, controversial evidence that the royal line had been adulterated by marriage to an impoverished woman who was not a peer and whose male ancestors were prominent Protestants, and fodder for negative and positive arguments about the influential role of women in French public life.[9] Imprisoned for a pro-Protestant essay while he was working on the *Memoirs*, La Beaumelle acceded to the wishes of the Catholic nuns of Saint-Cyr and sought to make his own career by painting Maintenon as a saint-like heroine, a disinterested and intelligent woman sincerely committed to faith and virtue.

Readers of the *Memoirs* were treated to a portrait of a charismatic woman and, not surprisingly, given the inception of the book, to extensive discussion of Madame de Maintenon's charitable educational project for girls at Saint-Cyr. Paralleling the modeling of polite sociability through conversation in the works of Scudéry's circle, Maintenon situated conversational sociability as something to be learned by girls from printed conversations. Convinced of the potential pedagogical value of theater[10] for staging conversations about moral dilemmas, Madame de Maintenon experimented first at Saint-Cyr with plays inspired by scenes from the Old Testament commissioned from the great tragedian Racine. Her ability to draft the most famous playwright of the age to write plays for her school was a measure of her power. The choice makes sense in the context of the primacy of tragedy as an instrument for communicating French exceptionalism and for ritually reaffirming noble distinction, and given Racine's endowment of tragic heroines such as Phèdre with extraordinary speeches on the necessity of subordinating passion to duty. The students of Saint-Cyr performed to the admiration of the circle around Louis XIV. When, purportedly, the success of the performances led to the girls fighting over applause and drew unwonted (sexual) attention from members of the court, Madame de Maintenon concluded that even Racine's devout plays were too worldly for girls' education (Birberick). She sequestered the school. After a series of conversations produced by her friend Madeleine de Scudéry and the school headmistress Madame de Brinon also proved too worldly for her taste, Madame de Maintenon wrote her own model conversations for the students at Saint-Cyr; these were subsequently published as *Les loisirs de Madame de Maintenon* in 1757, following on the success of the *Memoirs*. The conversations could be read silently or aloud by a reader or by a group. As a pedagogical tool and literary form, they thus bridged the divide between theater and text, group audience and individual reader, collective response and private contemplation, even as they conjured an atmosphere of protected female intimacy among girls on the verge of entering the world through marriage, sexual activity, and childbearing. The initial conversations occur among a group of girls speculating from the shelter of Saint-Cyr on the question of what is "society" and what equips one to enter it well.

Maintenon sought to develop girls' moral reasoning and to direct their thought in a way that was responsive to the educational ideas of her contemporaries. Writing in the 1690s, John Locke in England and Fénelon in France had adopted the classical idea from Horace that learning was best accomplished through pleasure. Both Locke and Fénelon argued that the child was capable of active reasoning, moral education, and self-control. As the preferred intellectual training for boys, dialogue with an intelligent and worldly tutor should supplant the traditional rote repetition and formal disputation in Latin and Greek taught in colleges. Locke insisted in *Some Thoughts Concerning Education* (1693) that the tutor should draw the boy into using his reason: "All of their time together should not be spent in Reading of Lectures, and magisterially dictating to him, what he is to observe and follow: Hearing him in his turn and using him to reason about what is propos'd, makes the Rules go down the easier, and sink the deeper, and gives him a liking to Study and Instruction" (147). Locke was critical of the idea of schools for girls; the home was the best environment for fostering the "Retirement and Bashfulness" best suited to their sex (129). Like Locke, Fénelon influentially touted the advantages of one-on-one dialogue for educating boys. The fictional conversations between Odysseus's son Telemachus and the tutor Mentor in Fénelon's *Télémaque* (1699)—a text revising and renewing Homer's *Odyssey* for the early Enlightenment—continued to be among the most widely read works in the Atlantic world well into the early nineteenth century. Fénélon employed the long-standing educational genre of the *miroir des princes* (to which Christine de Pizan had contributed) by penning *Télémaque* on behalf of his pupil the young duc de Bourgogne, grandson of Louis XIV. The *miroir des princes* presented advice to young scions by placing them within allegorical settings; Odysseus's son Telemachus guided by the sage Mentor yielded a classical avatar for the young duc de Bourgogne guided by Fénelon. Within the frame of travels in search of Odysseus, education occurred through one-on-one dialogues between Télémaque and Mentor. As a complement to *Télémaque*, Fénelon's *Dialog of the Dead* (*Dialogues des morts*, 1712) offered sixty-two carefully crafted dialogues between pairs of great men and four trialogues. ("The Prince of Wales and Richard his son" and the *femme forte* Madame de Montpensier stood out as the only figures represented who were not either French or classical men.) The criteria of selection implied an all-but-continuous male intellectual tradition and synthetic debate carried on from ancient Greece to turn-of-the-century France. These dialogues "were subsequently adapted for generations of schoolboys as pedagogical tools to introduce the great figures of history and antiquity and offer a critique of human endeavor in the past" (P. Brown, "Girls Aloud" 204).

Such philosophical dialogues, pared down in the hands of some authors to a schematic conversation between an interlocutor A and an interlocutor B, sometimes mediated by a third arbiter, developed as a characteristically Enlightenment form for revisiting the battle of the Ancients and the Moderns. They facilitated debate about the value of cultural inheritance and received wisdom on the one hand and modernity and enlightened thinking on the other (Prince 13). The *Parallèle des Anciens et des Modernes* (1688–92) set the stage for the *querelle* when its author, Charles Perrault (better known now for his fairy tales) used the form of dialogue to make a case for the greatness of the present age of Louis XIV, with interlocutors representing the Ancients and the Moderns, respectively. George Lyttelton's *Dialogues of the Dead* (1760), written with contributions from Elizabeth Montagu, largely involved pairings between men across time or place (Plato and Fénelon, for example, and Boileau and Alexander Pope), but included a few women from the pantheon (as in the trialogue between Octavia, Portia, and Arria). When Richard Hurd sought to codify the dialogue form in 1764 in his "Preface, On the Manner of Writing Dialogue," he reacted against the liberal tendencies of dialogues by arguing that they should avoid the most serious and sacred religious and philosophic topics (Prince 214). Merely the existence of the voice of a questioning interlocutor—in other words, the very form of the dialogue itself—might succeed in casting doubt on the propositions presented by the voice of tradition and authority. The battle of the Ancients and the Moderns inhered in the dialogue form, which founded intellectual identity on the transfer of knowledge from the past as well as reaction to it among subsequent generations. Moroever, the form bore little connection with immediate oral culture. It depended on stylized elements of rhetoric based on classical antecedents and on church catechism. Adrian Wallbank argues that in Britain even working- and middle-class readers unfamiliar with classical and elite works were familiar with "mentoring" dialogues such as church catechisms; "alongside the classical and philosophical examples of mentoring," he argues, "all sectors of society were permeated by an acute awareness of catechetical/dialogueic mentoring and pedagogy" (13).

Fénelon had advocated for the education of girls in 1687 in a treatise *On the Education of Girls* (*De l'education des filles*), proposing that education would fortify them against vice and allow them to better perform their roles as wives, mothers, and directors of the household "economy."[11] Given their disposition for imitation, children needed to be presented with virtuous models. Fénelon devoted chapters to the special faults of girls: vanity, of course, but also their propensity to speak a lot out of vanity, passion, and a failure to examine their own thoughts. Controlling girls' speech was thus paramount to cultivating their reason. Fénelon proposed in the abstract that girls' curiosity should be channeled toward useful subjects and their wandering imaginations controlled. "A poor girl filled with tenderness [*tendre*] and the marvelous that have charmed her in her reading," he wrote, "is surprized not to find in the world real characters who resemble these heroes; she would like to live like these imaginary Princesses in novels who are always charming always adored, always above need. How distasteful for her to have to descend from Heroism to the lowest detail of housekeeping!" (15). He argued (and here the text comes from Charlotte Lennox's 1760 translation for her women's magazine *The Lady's Museum*) that "the sex is more capable of attention than we imagine: what they chiefly want is a well directed application. There is scarcely a young girl who has not read with eagerness a great number of idle romances, and puerile tales, sufficient to corrupt her imagination and cloud her understanding. If she had devoted the same time to the study of history, she would in those varied scenes which the world offers to view, have found facts more interesting, and instruction which only truth can give" (13).

Departing completely from Fénelon's allegorical mentor-pupil dialogue in *Télémaque* and from the form of dialogues of the dead, Madame de Maintenon built her educational project around modeling girls' speech to develop girls' virtue. She set her model conversations in the present of Saint-Cyr, making four or five female contemporary adolescent girls into interlocutors free of adult supervision or mentorship. This format generated, as Penny Brown writes, "an illusion of informality, autonomy, and learning from each other" ("Girls Aloud" 5). Edifying tales illustrate Maintenon's points about the true nature of virtue; the unnamed lady of the court in "On Privilege" is a veiled self-portrait (Maintenon, *Dialogues* 33). The young women take turns leading the debate through moral reasoning to a firm conclusion. In the dialogue "On Reason," Adelaide points out that "piety can be too emotional. That's never the case with reason." Then her friends put her to the test:

> *Eleanor*: Honestly, I think that you like reason too much. It seems to me you're placing it above all the virtues.
> *Adelaide*: The virtues need reason to act wisely and to avoid all extremes of behavior.
> *Euphrosina*: Just what would reason do against a case of bad luck?
> *Adelaide*: It would make the victim endure it with great firmness. It would make her so attractive and so admirable that she would find people to give her some relief in her troubles.
> *Marcelle*: Miss X has a good bit of reason. Is she happier in her state of retreat from the world?
> *Adelaide*: Don't doubt it for a minute. She finds strength in her reflections. She understands that many face situations more tragic than her own. Every evening she counts the days spent by those who are happier than herself—and she recognizes that nothing will remain from their fleeting pleasures. She is loved by the people with whom she lives, because she only thinks of pleasing them. (Maintenon 85)

In another conversation, a girl proposes that "true eminence" does not consist in receiving recognition for greatness, honor, noble birth, military valor, or civic achievement. Instead, as Madame de Maintenon wrote for her audience of poor daughters of the aristocracy, "True eminence is respecting only virtue. It is knowing how to live without fortune when it passes us by and how to avoid being intoxicated by fortune when it is favorable to us. It is knowing how to bring consolation to the unfortunate and never to hold them in contempt. It is the willingness to be of assistance to everyone without wanting anything disproportionate to what we are" (Maintenon 47).

Madame de Maintenon's conversations modeled the pleasing, clear, and elegant style of speaking for which aristocratic French women became famous in the late seventeenth century and that they molded into a sign of intimate exceptionalism. Yet the conversations also redefined male aristocratic virtues for women, opening their sphere through the idea of a "shared destiny" to women of lower ranks, with an emphasis on neo-Stoic and Christian values of personal merit, struggle, self-knowledge, and resignation. Maintenon crafted her vision for Saint-Cyr around a stoic reworking of salon culture calculated on the late seventeenth-century model of *repos. Repos* involved the active choice to retire from worldly sociability, especially that of the court, as the only means of preserving one's virtue compatible with acceptance of one's place in the world. While Maintenon's sketches could be read by a quiet solitary reader or performed aloud by a group, they presupposed that a girl developed moral reasoning and agency in choosing virtue through familiar conversation within a community of other girls. With a shift in address to middling-rank eighteenth-century readers, the late seventeenth-century aristocratic notion of *repos* would go on to serve as an argument that courageous resignation to one's lot in life (a marriage without love, the death of a dear friend, poverty) demonstrated a feminized natural nobility of the mind.

Maintenon developed her educational model in the period when the question of women's worth at the heart of the *querelle des femmes* became reconfigured into a debate on the proper scope of girls' preparation for productive roles in society. Critics conceded that cases like those of Anna Maria van Schurman and Anne Dacier demonstrated that women were capable of extraordinary intellectual achievement. And, indeed, translating from Greek or Latin into a vernacular continued to set a standard for intellectual exemplarity among women. Yet as nonaristocratic women readers (and writers) became an increasingly identifiable social group, critics also presented women's scholarly endeavor as evidence of failed socialization. The insufferable, vain, sexually jealous, and overeducated spinster or the aging, scribbling widow or wife popped up repeatedly as a stereotype of cultural sterility and wayward modernity. This stereotype went hand in hand with the emergence of female readers as a distinct social category within literary markets. The perception that young women played a crucial role, as agents of physical and cultural reproduction, in guaranteeing social health and the concomitant development of complementary gender roles in families of the middling ranks in the early eighteenth century contributed to broad interest in women's education. In Foucauldian terms, the education of girls constituted an advance front in biopower, since the management of social hygiene necessarily entailed the sanctity of the agents of reproduction. Women could be enlisted to ensure the fitness and virtue of populations through education tailored to their specific role in securing the health of family and nation (McAlpin 1–22).

The resulting discourse on education built on a gendered model of intellectual transmission. It opposed a male transfer of knowledge across generations occurring in a one-to-one mentor to mentee relationship, in the mode of Mentor and Telemachus, to a female education of virtue within a familiar group, in the mode of Saint-Cyr. Theaters of education, as Marie-Emmanuelle Plagnol-Diéval has called printed pedagogical conversations and sketches, presented the female education of virtue textually under the signs of oral culture—or, in mixed collections, of intimate letters remediating unavoidable distance between friends. Plagnol-Diéval calculates that over two hundred familiar conversations in the form of theatrical sketches for children appeared in French, German, and English in the eighteenth century (3). Even the celebrity author Françoise de Graffigny, whom we often associate more with the Enlightenment worldliness of the salon and the theater than with the nursery, wrote a moral play in 1747 entitled *Ziman and Zenise* to be performed in Vienna by the children of Maria Theresa of Austria and Emperor François-Étienne of Lorraine, while her famous and critically successful play *Cénie* (1752) focused on intimate affinity between a governess and the girl who turns out to be her daughter (*Œuvres posthumes*). Graffigny's most famous character, Zilia, became, in turn, the eponymous heroine of Georgina, Duchess of Devonshire's play for children, *Zillia*, modeled after Stéphanie de Genlis's pedagogical theater (Heuer).

In contrast to the one-on-one dialogue between two great men or between mentor and male pupil, the familiar conversation group offered an idealized and frequently reprised picture of intelligent contemporary and often feminized sociability. Scudéry had novelized the catalog of famous women, emphasizing the homologies between them and the contemporary conversationalists in her frame narrative. Insulating the feminized conversation from suspicion of pride, seduction, and pedantry, Maintenon transposed the conversation format away from the worldly context and made it into a private and single-sex vehicle of contemplation about real girls' proper role and behavior in the present. Sarah Fielding then novelized the familiar moral conversation among girls in *The Governess, or the Little Female Academy* (1749).

The Governess is the first cohesive fiction written in English for the entertainment of school-aged children who could read on their own. (John Newbery's *A Little Pretty Pocket-Book* [1744], published five years earlier, had targeted very young children and their parents or nurses with a hodge-podge of short pieces).[12] Educated as a child at Mrs. Mary Rooke's boarding school at the Cathedral Close in Salisbury, Sarah Fielding learned with her sisters "to work and read and write and to talk French and Dance and be brought up as a Gentlewomen."[13] Although she had little independent income, at the time that she wrote *The Governess*, she was already the successful published writer of *The History of David Simple* (1744), a text that made it into translation in German, Dutch, and French and was frequently anthologized.[14] After her brother Henry Fielding lost his wife in 1744, she managed his household and cared for his young children for several years (Bree 59). Both the stoicism of *The Governess* and its emphasis on "characters who were supposed to be real children" within "a distinct contemporary social environment" bore a resemblance to Maintenon's conversations (Grey 78–79). Fielding could have been aware of the experiments at Saint-Cyr and of French pedagogical practices, given the presence of French female educators in England. The most notable of these was Jeanne-Marie Leprince de Beaumont, educated at a teaching convent in Rouen, who began working in London in 1748 for Lady Pomfret, a patron of educated women, including Fielding's friend Elizabeth Carter. And Fielding may well have read Scudéry's works in French or in English and have been sensitive to their formal qualities. Scudéry presented first-person harangues by Cleopatra and Octavia in *Les femmes illustres*; Fielding used the first-person harangue in her own *Lives of Cleopatra and Octavia* (1757). In the preface to the *Lives*, she noted drily that from her presentation of the words of the two heroines "as supposed to have been delivered by themselves in the Shades below," the reader could expect an "impartial, distinct, and exact Narrative of their several Adventures . . . unless he is so inveterately prejudiced in Disfavour of the Sex, as to presume, with the ill-natured Satirist, That a Woman is not to be credited, any more than trusted, tho' dead" (vi).

While Fielding's *The Governess* would enjoy less transnational reach than her *History of David Simple*, it was translated into Dutch in 1750 and into German in 1761.[15] Alessa Johns encapsulates Fielding's project in all of her novels, from the *History of David Simple* to *The Governess,* to *Ophelia*, as that of "creat[ing] learning environments in and of her fictions, schools that would become gardens for tending the growth of benevolent individuals. With such an education, women in particular could turn into self-possessed utopian subjects capable of engaging the interest of others by teaching, writing, and undertaking philanthropic activities" (*Women's Utopias* 69). As in Madame de Maintenon's conversations, in *The Governess*, the entirely female group of pupils discuss questions of virtue in the absence of an adult preceptress. Despite the book's title, the governess, Mrs. Teachum, functions largely as an implied presence in the text; she is sometimes consulted after the fact but never participates directly in the familiar conversations of the girls in her school. After a vicious fight over an apple, the oldest student, Jenny Peace, helps the girls talk over their differences and identify their own moral failings. On their own, the girls discover the device of meeting daily in a shaded arbor to tell their own life histories and to share the histories of other girls and women through stories and letters. Borrowing an earlier episodic narrative structure, in which travelers or friends meet daily to tell tales, *The Governess* dispenses the girls' histories across nine successive days. The storytelling girls inherit the seventeenth-century feminist conversational space of the garden. Each girl's story appears within the context of a veritable multigenre catalog (including biography, letters, conversations, and a fairy tale) of lives of girls and women. As a girl becomes capable of identifying her own fault and the path to virtue through telling her story, so does the young female reader, presumably, become capable of laying her own life history alongside those told in the conversation group in the arbor. When Mrs. Teachum requests that Jenny Peace "get the Lives of her Companions in Writing" (89) she confirms Jenny's status as the exceptional girl in the conversational group. To get a girl's life in writing corresponds in the text with moral exemplarity. The female writer or storyteller collects and examines exemplary female lives, encouraging self-contemplation, comparison, and emulation. After Jenny leaves the little group, the "Name and Story" of Jenny Peace are sufficient to renew friendship and excite emulation among the school girls left behind: "And if any Girl was found to harbour in her Breast a rising Passion, which it was difficult to conquer, the Name and Story of Miss *Jenny Peace* soon gained her Attention, and left her without any other Desire than to emulate Miss *Jenny*'s Virtues" (175–76). Fielding valued emulative reading for its capacity to educate readers and endow them with personal and social virtue. In Fielding's fictions, the utopian community is fostered by the interpretation of female lives under the guidance of an exceptional female figure worthy of emulation and the community has the capacity to reproduce, through emulation, subsequent virtuous generations.[16]

In writing *Millenium Hall* (1762), Sarah Scott not only sketched a women's utopia heavily influenced by her friend Sarah Fielding's ideas, she also anchored what might be called an important node in eighteenth-century women writers' repertoire. This is why, although scholars have already given it extensive attention, I want to rehearse briefly here the well-known story of Scott and her sister Elizabeth Montagu, who played a central role in cultivating bluestocking culture and a network of female patronage. *Millenium Hall* drew specifically on the former practice of women writers—building on ideas taken from Fielding and from Maintenon—and made future practice possible. Scott's novel connects educational fictions from the first half of the century with those of the second. It offers evidence of women's cultural transfer among French, English, and German texts. It links filiations of women writers via personal relationships, relations of patronage, and literary influence across Britain and Western Europe in the long eighteenth century. And through its long histories of unfortunate but exemplary ladies from good but not noble families, it translates aristocratic stoicism and politeness into an elevated and educated virtue toward which women of the middling ranks might aspire.

Fielding directly influenced Scott's utopian feminist fiction. After a disastrous end to her marriage, the impoverished Sarah Scott created a feminized community of friendship at Bath with her companion Lady Bab whose purse, along with that of Scott's sister Elizabeth Montagu, funded ventures in philanthropy that Scott often directed. Scott, Lady Bab, and Elizabeth Montagu helped Sarah Fielding to live independently in Bath, while both sisters welcomed into their intellectual and social circles impoverished and educated women, such as Hester Chapone, who had turned to companionship and writing to make a living. After Lady Bab's death, Sarah Scott would apply the reformist ideas of gentry capitalism that were fostered in Bluestocking milieus to the foundation of a community of friends at the small farm of Hitcham, relying in part on the aging Sarah Fielding's designs for the project.

Sarah Scott's sister Elizabeth had married the wealthy landowner Edward Montagu, grandson of the first Earl of Sandwich. Elizabeth Montagu used her position, including presentation at court, to extend patronage to her family and to women writers and intellectuals. Beginning around 1750, privileged women, such as Montagu, Elizabeth Vesey, and Ann Ord, sought to build social circles around conversations focused on literary and cultural questions as a reform alternative to the upper-class côteries that gathered to play cards and engage in aristocratic social jousting. As Gary Kelly explains, "Bluestocking feminism was formulated in a situation of expanding gentry capitalism. This was the application of capitalist practices of entrepreneurship, investment, and modernization to the agrarian economy of the landed estate" ("Introduction" 16). Kelly characterizes Scott's novel as "the fullest literary expression of the first wave of bluestocking feminism" ("Introduction" 11).

Eve Tavor Bannet situates the novel in relation to Scott's projects at Bath and Montagu's management of her husband Edward's large country estate at Sandleford, where Scott often came to visit. Bannet argues that Scott's *Millenium Hall* is

an amalgam and imaginative extension of the sisters' various philanthropies: an idealized and politicized recreation of a great estate like Sandleford onto which an establishment populated by impoverished gentlewomen was in imagination recreated, along with Sarah's school and manufactory for poor women at Bath, Elizabeth's practice of giving asylum to vagrants and the poor, both sisters' philanthropic visits to cottagers on the estate, and Elizabeth's practice of filling the main house with her female friends (and even perhaps those occasional male visitors, like Edmund Burke, who came to Sandleford not to stay, but to admire, to praise, and to pass on). (38)

In *Millenium Hall*, Scott hued to the familiar structure of conversations studded with the recounting of virtuous female lives, packaging the whole within a letter written by a gentleman to another male friend recounting his recent travels with a young coxcomb named Lamont. The novel's frame narrative implicitly contrasted female and male education. When the gentleman and the coxcomb sustain an accident to their chaise while touring near Cornwall, they happen upon a community of women running a country estate in an idyllic location. There, they encounter the wise Mrs. Maynard who explains how the utopian community came into being and describes its philanthropic arrangements for unfortunate women of all classes. Impoverished gentlewomen live in harmony overseeing the orderly estate, which includes a carpet and tapestry factor that employs poor and fallen women. The estate farm itself is worked by couples enabled to marry by the gentlewomen's timely provision of dowries and cottages. Over a succession of days, Mrs. Maynard provides oral histories of the lives of the founders of the community and their friends: the exemplary pair Miss Mancel and Mrs. Morgan, along with Lady Mary Jones, Miss Selvyn, and Miss Trentham. With financial dependency undergirding her social and sexual vulnerability, each "lady" has, before finding refuge at Millenium Hall, been harrassed, abandoned, taken advantage of, and maltreated by lubricious men and avaricious female relatives. Each has survived through reliance on friendship and the exercise of virtue. Indeed the subtitle of *Millenium Hall* proposes that the "characters of the inhabitants" and "historical anecdotes and reflections" in the volume "May excite in the Reader proper Sentiments of Humanity, and lead the Mind to the Love of VIRTUE" (51). The histories are interwoven with the gentleman's and Lamont's brief conversations on what they have seen and heard, a Mentor-to-Telemachus leitmotif, producing a conclusion in which the gentleman resolves to found a community such as Millenium Hall on his own estate (an idea returned to by Scott in her subsequent novel *The History of Sir George Ellison* (1766), while the young Lamont renounces an attitude that might otherwise have led him to become the male agent of a virtuous woman's ruin.

Banet suggests that Madame de Maintenon's *Memoirs and Letters* divided Elizabeth Montagu and Sarah Scott over the model of powerful female influence and patronage at court that Maintenon represented (and that Scott may have feared her sister would imitate) and that this directly affected the conception of *Millenium Hall*. Elizabeth Montagu read the *Memoirs* in 1756 or 1757, perhaps in French, perhaps in Charlotte Lennox's English translation. Writing to her sister, Montagu exclaimed of Maintenon:

> She is worthy to be admitted to your abode at Bath Easton on many accounts, I think she has no fault but being a Papist. . . . She is full of compassion towards the poor. . . . Her foundation of St. Cyr is wise in the design and in all the rules for the support of it she meant it as a place of education, they were forced to add Nuns of profession for reasons of convenience, she was wise enough to see there was greater merit in educating young Women in such a manner as would qualify them to make good wives and good mothers than in adding to the number of nuns. Indeed I think there is no charity equal to that of imparting the advantages of religious and virtuous education. I should think the Races of the Nobility and Gentry of France must have been improved by the Eleves of St. Cyr. I wish we had such a foundation here.[17]

"She will never be my heroine," Sarah Scott responded, condemning Maintenon's involvement in court politics and her appropriation "sans façon" of other people's children for the Saint-Cyr project.[18] Scott's reaction against aristocratic court intrigue took full flesh in her history of Theodore Agrippa d'Aubigné, Maintenon's grandfather, whom she depicted as a staunch Protestant defender of civic virtue. In Scott's reading, Papist court-intriguer Maintenon betrayed her Protestant grandfather long after his death when she destroyed his legacy by contributing "a great share" to Louis XIV's anti-Protestant policy, the Revocation of the Edict of Nantes.[19] In *Millenium Hall*, Scott adapted Maintenon's model for an ideal school run by philanthropic gentlewomen and organized by an abiding stoic privileging of reason and virtue, but she divorced it from both courtly culture and the privileged bonds of noble blood (Johns, *Women's Utopias* 91). The invocation of life stories of wronged womanhood and engagement in charitable acts for the poor ritually

secured voluntary entry by the women of Millenium Hall into a compassionate contract grounded in friendship, affinity, and shared experience. The
project of regenerating social bonds in *Millenium Hall* and its sequel *Sir
George Ellison* even justified removing girls from families, despite Sarah
Scott's initial attack on Maintenon, so that away from the fathers, uncles,
and stepmothers who were guided by lust, jealousy, and avarice and who
sought profit from their marriage, sale, or banishment, young women could
learn virtue from exemplary, genteel, but not noble, women teachers. Scott's
work adapted Saint-Cyr for the British countryside and transferred its feminized stoic educational project to nonaristocratic women.

Educator and writer Jeanne-Marie Leprince de Beaumont probably
encountered *Millenium Hall* while she was running a school for daughters of
the elite in London. The feminized utopian vision of gentry capitalism that it
provided allowed Leprince de Beaumont to transpose Richardson's *Clarissa,* a
crucial text in women readers' repertoire, by providing a reformist transnational alternative to the heroine's rape and death. With the pedagogical heritage of Maintenon's Saint-Cyr, Leprince de Beaumont used Sarah Scott's
Maintenon- and Fielding-influenced *Millenium Hall* to infiltrate Richardson's work and retool Clarissa. In *The New Clarissa* (*La nouvelle Clarisse,*
1767), Leprince de Beaumont reworks Richardson's and Rousseau's formulas
to create epistolary relationships between four women: the new Clarissa who
flees the circumstances attending Richardson's Clarissa in England and is
welcomed by her mother-in-law the Baroness d'Astie in Bordeaux; Clarissa's
mother, Mrs. Darby, who moves to Paris; and Clarissa's friend Harriet, who
becomes Mrs. Darby's protégé. The affinity among these women and their
trust in each others' accounts of experience and emotion displaces the external realist account of women's mental states. The abiding subjects in the
correspondences are the virtuous survival of women characters and the set of
reforms instituted by the Baroness d'Astie on her Bordeaux lands. These
reforms are modeled on Scott's British gentry capitalism, on the one hand,
and, on the other, on the work of French physiocrats who sought in a return
to agriculture a remedy for a supposed decline in population health. Alessa
Johns deftly describes the response to both Richardson and Scott that
Leprince de Beaumont engineers:

> It is a situation meant to oppose the quandary of Richardson's lonely
> protagonist, vainly seeking shelter and protection and forever unable to
> act on her own behalf, let alone on behalf of others. In their letters, the

women applaud the baroness's innovations; she has studied agricultural methods, livestock diseases, and remedies and has increased the area's productivity by introducing new ways of fertilizing, composting, and irrigating. Every poor family is given a cow, and the baroness ensures that babies can be fed the milk—so mothers are "freed" for agricultural labor—by fashioning ceramic nipples to attach to bottles, which older nurses can then use for feeding the infants. (*Women's Utopias* 135)

The Baroness d'Astie and Clarissa become physiocratic *femmes fortes*, while the novel as a whole, integrated into the repertoire and available in both French and English, became—alongside the English and German versions of *Millenium Hall*[20]—reference and incitement to writing for women working in German and in Dutch: Sophie von La Roche[21] and Elisabeth Bekker-Wolff (Van Dijk and Montoya), discussed in the next chapter. Leprince de Beaumont figured a heroine who flees England for France and contributes to a utopian farm that blends British gentry capitalism and French physiocracy in Bordeaux, a region subject to recurring territorial renegotiation between Britain, France, and the Dutch Republic. As a reader of Leprince de Beaumont (and perhaps also of Fielding in translation), Sophie von La Roche creates a heroine who flees the perversion of the French-influenced German court for England, where she develops and establishes her own philanthropic community for destitute women and families in the countryside through a fusion of British gentry capitalism and German appreciation of the land. As a reader and translator of Leprince de Beaumont and Stéphanie de Genlis, Elisabeth Bekker-Wolff created (along with her cowriter Agatha Deken) a heroine whose salvation from kidnapping, attempted rape, and the decadent luxury of the East India trade is a Dutchified version of gentry capitalism. The improving habitus of the multivocal women's conversation about exemplary lives turns, in their work, into an international feminized philanthropic and pedagogical vision.

Conduct manuals, magazines, and novels for young girls represented and reiterated the habitus of virtuous female conversational sociability as virtual ideal women's communities. Texts for teaching and modeling female virtue provided pathways for new reader-writers to become contributors to the repertoire of women writers through their own recounting and assessment of female lives. Leprince de Beaumont provided an influential print template for a utopian and pedagogical female conversational sociability in her "magazines." After Voltaire, Leprince de Beaumont is the author whose name appears the most frequently in eighteenth-century catalogs for sales of private libraries in the Netherlands, a center of the eighteenth-century book trade (Montoya, "Madame de Beaumont" 33). Leprince de Beaumont's magazines presented model conversations built around the assumption that the capacity to reason and to choose personal virtue could be deliberately developed through age-appropriate exploration of the natural world and of emotional experience. In their diffusion and conception, her magazines were fundamentally transnational and profoundly intertextual; they appeared in French, English, Dutch, Russian, Spanish, Italian, German, Swedish, Bulgarian, Danish, Serbian, Polish, Hungarian, Czech, and Greek (Seth 7–8). Writer Charlotte von Einem remembered receiving the translation of Leprince de Beaumont's *Magasin des enfants* alongside her first Bible when she was six years old.[22]

Born to a family of artisans and musicians and educated by a teaching order of nuns near Rouen, with whom she served as an instructor to younger children, Leprince de Beaumont acquired a position as a singer and music teacher at the court of Stanislaus in Lunéville. She married in 1737 and, over the next dozen years, may or may not have been an actress, had a relationship with another man, sought to have her marriage annulled, and given birth to a daughter (Seth 21). In 1748, she published two works, a response to a misogynist text in which she imagined the felicitous outcome of a year in which gender roles were at least partially reversed and a pedagogical novel expressing the compatibility of faith with reason. In the preface to *Le triomphe de la vérité*, Leprince de Beaumont overtly announced her gendered pedagogical method and her own special suitability as a woman for transmitting religious principles fused with reason to women. Religious and philosophical books by men of "profound erudition" would "frighten" the women for whom Leprince de Beaumont wrote. Such women needed to be "entertained, if one wants to instruct them, told only things within their reach, brought by degrees and imperceptibly to more elevated knowledge." "This is what I flatter myself," wrote Leprince de Beaumont, "to have achieved" (ix).

By 1749, the year that Fielding's *The Governess* was published, Leprince de Beaumont was established as a French governess in London for Sophia Carteret, granddaughter of the patroness Lady Pomfret. Leprince de Beaumont's past and current experience teaching began to form the basis for a series of pedagogical works largely aimed at girls and young women. *Le magasin des enfants*, her most well-known publication, appeared first in a French-language edition in 1756 that was, in fact, published in London with a remarkably international list of subscribers, including Russians and Swedes (Shelfrin, "Governesses" 212n37). It appeared the following year in English under the bilingual title of *Le magasin des enfans, or The Young Misses' Magazine in Four Volumes.*" Like many of her later pedagogical collections, this first magazine can hardly be assessed as belonging to a single national literary field or tradition. It was available in German by 1758, in Polish by 1774, and in Spanish by 1779. The character Mademoiselle Bonne (or, in English, Lady Affable) could easily be associated with Leprince de Beaumont, who advertised her services as a governess on a back page of the magazine (Seth 24). Lady Sensée (or Lady Sensible in the English version) was recognizable as Leprince de Beaumont's famous early pupil, the at-first intractable and later reformed Lady Sophia Carteret, future Countess of Shelburne. Leprince de Beaumont's pupils were the daughters of well-known British peers; they appeared as characters in her magazines and maintained relationships with her throughout their lives, visiting her in a group in France, for example, for her sixtieth birthday. Their correspondence with her suggests that they applied her methods to the education of their own daughters (Shelfrin, "Governesses").

If Leprince de Beaumont's pedagogical works for girls relied on the form of female conversational sociability, tellingly, the first of her works devoted to male education was, like Fénelon's *Télémaque*, a mirror for princes. Resourcefully drawing on the fashion for Oriental tales, *Civan, King of Bungo, A Japanese Tale, or Tableau of the Education of a Prince* (*Civan, roi de Bungo, histoire japonaise, ou tableau de l'éducation d'un prince*, 1758) offered an allegorical account of the education of a prince who must travel away from his own country to Japan to learn wisdom. It was dedicated to the seventeen-year-old Archduke Joseph II, future Holy Roman Emperor. Leprince de Beaumont's second work on boys' education, *Modern Mentor, or Instructions for Boys and Those Who Raise Them* (*Mentor moderne, ou instructions pour les garçons et pour ceux qui les élèvent*, 1772–73), retained the masculine one-to-one transmission structure prized by both Locke and Fénelon; it offered a series of dialogues between "D" and "R" on the lessons to be learned from antiquity.

In contrast, group conversation among contemporary girls frames Leprince de Beaumont's works for girls and women, including her most well-known work today: "The Beauty and the Beast." The story is told by Mademoiselle Bonne to her pupils in "Dialogue V" of the *Magasin des enfants*. In retelling "The Beauty and the Beast," LePrince de Beaumont drew on repertoire, condensing Madame de Villeneuve's detail-filled aristocratic novella of

1740 into a short tale.[23] After Mademoiselle Bonne tells the story, one of the girls extrapolates from Beauty's situation with the Beast to her own life. The girl explains how she herself has overcome her initial fear of the little black servant boy her father has engaged as a servant. She has learned to stop thinking about her horror of the face of her black servant boy and has at last come to feel perfectly safe when he lifts her into a carriage (*Magasin* 84–85). Shortly after this revelation, when the girls catch a butterfly, they learn about metamorphosis. The precocious Lady Spirituelle remarks, "But tell us, my governess, how can that be? I have always seen metamorphoses as tales proper for the amusement of children" (86–87). In response, Mademoiselle Bonne explains that *Metamorphoses* were the Greek way of telling history but that Lady Spirituelle needs to be better educated before she can properly understand this.

From the ugly Beast in the fairy tale, to the black servant boy at home, to the caterpillar turned butterfly in nature, to Ovid, the *Magasin des enfants* displays a premodern world organized by sacred analogies; an Enlightenment world governed by supposedly natural laws and structured by colonial, gender, and class distinctions; and proscription of classical knowledge as off-limits to young girls. The sensible privileged girl reader can learn to decipher and negotiate these with an enlarged moral imagination. Like the girls in Sarah Fielding's *Governess,* the girls in the *Magasin des enfants* are to undergo metamorphosis through parsing lives in conversation with each other and through seizing the key point that the heroine's attempt to find the path to virtue in a complex world is analogous to their own (and to that of any good female reader).[24] The model of reading and self-crafting is replicated throughout the intertwined genres of conduct manual and novel: participating in the virtual community of the book, girls undergo a metamorphosis in virtue by judging the lives of women and imitating and revering the most virtuous ones.

In the hands of women educators in the second half of the eighteenth century, the characteristic horizontal, vernacular, and transnational form inherited from the *querelle des femmes* could communicate a moderate and moral version of the Enlightenment project. Alicia Montoya points out that the popularity of Leprince de Beaumont's writing can be traced in part to her ability to communicate scientific theories and experiments to a popular audience while relying on the "critical vocabularly of the *philosophes.*" Leprince de Beaumont steered a meliorist course reconciling religious faith with reason, Alicia Montoya suggests, in contrast with the positions taken by materialist proponents for a radical Enlightenment ("Madame de Beaumont" 133–34). In other words, Leprince de Beaumont and her successors presented an inclusive version of Enlightenment, one that offered the promise of education and sensibility to children, women, believers, and, in books such as Leprince de Beaumont's *Magazine for the Poor, Artisans, Servants and Country People* (*Magasin des pauvres, artisans, domestiques et gens de la campagne*, 1768), an identity group formed around membership in the lower ranks but with limits: black servant boys were evidently not included.

The form for this reconciliation of Enlightenment and virtue grounded in faith was conversational affinity. In contrast, when radical materialist and philosophical works incorporated a female interlocutor, this was achieved by merging the quest for knowledge with a quest for sexual knowledge (or, more mildly, a suggestion of flirtation) in a one-to-one dialogue between a knowledgeable man and an uninitiated woman. The radical Enlightenment dialogue offered an occasion for suggestive banter and for staging male brilliance via the naïveté of a questioning female interlocuter, as, for example, in Bernard le Bovier de Fontenelle's *Conversations on the Plurality of Worlds* (*Entretiens sur la pluralité des mondes*, 1686) or in Diderot's *D'Alembert's Dream* (*Le rêve de d'Alembert*, 1769). In the introduction to her translation of Fontenelle's work, *Discovery of New Worlds* (1688), Aphra Behn criticized Fontenelle for depicting a marquise whose only role is to elicit clear answers about astronomy from a highly intelligent male narrator. "He makes her say a great many very silly things," Behn noted.[25] In contrast, the moderate Enlightenment conduct book or novel, presented sensible moral reasoning as the product of group conversation among female friends. Clarissa Campbell Orr has argued that the softened and moralized version of Enlightenment imbued with pietism offered women a rampart against seduction and abuse by family and society at large ("La Fite"). Stoic resignation and piety, transferred from aristocratic conversations to middling rank magazines, pervade the moral Enlightenment vision disseminated by women educators and writers of the late eighteenth century.

Pedagogical texts for women and girls served as the vehicle for transferring to middling rank female readers the cosmopolitan identity bred within an international aristocracy that married its daughters to foreign nobles and that also employed multilingual women as "readers" and governesses for its children. Translated into multiple languages but also available as introductions to French, texts relying on the template of the familiar conversation with its transnational extension, the intimate letter, formed a veritable shared curriculum for groups gaining increasing access to literacy across Europe from Britain to Russia. Between 1749 and 1830, the number of pedagogical publications dedicated to girls probably multiplied by a factor of five (Huguet and Havelange 238).

Despite its self-proclaimed radicalism, Jean-Jacques Rousseau's *Émile, ou de l'éducation* (1762), which appeared eight years after *Le magasin des enfants*, relied on the male mentor-pupil structure; it thus confirmed the vertical generational flow of knowledge between men. Émile learns in properly male one-on-one conversations with his tutor or the Savoyard preacher who guide his reflections as they "naturally" arise from experience. Framed with extensive didactic commentary that Leprince de Beaumont did not permit herself, Rousseau's *Émile* nonetheless draws on the conceit of *Le magasin des enfants*, rather than on a classical or an allegorical context. The conversations in *Émile* follow a flow similar to the flow of conversation between Mademoiselle Bonne and her charges. In *Émile*, as in a tradition of women's pedagogy dating back to the beginning of the century, apparently familiar conversations unfold from questions arising in the mind of an ostensibly real child through experience of the surrounding world. *Émile* proved to be a central text in the readerly repertoire with which women writers engaged, yet this was not only because of the maddening portrait that it provided of Émile's future wife, Sophie (who is, like all women according to Rousseau, coquettishly driven by passion and the capacity to gain what she wants through a seduction that needs to be tamed). Nor was it entirely because of the captivating idea of a privileged complementary role for woman as woman encapsulated in Rousseau's prescription that "all the education of women should be relative to men. Pleasing men, being useful to them, making themselves loved and honored by them, raising them when they are young, caring for them when they are old, counseling them, consoling them, making their lives agreeable and sweet: there are the duties of women in all times, and what they should be taught from their childhood" (475). It was also because Rousseau in *Julie, ou la nouvelle Héloïse* and in *Émile* occupied the same space as women educators and, in fact, drew on the same repertoire that they drew on. Rousseau forged a reconciliation between Enlightenment principles and faith and fused the novel with pedagogy so as to create a vehicle for self-transformation, social hygiene and a regenerative social vision based on a country gentry model.

For Rousseau, as for the women educators who preceded him, such as Sarah Fielding and Leprince de Beaumont, and as for the next wave of women writers and educators, such as Stéphanie de Genlis and Mary

Wollstonecraft, personal virtue arose from a reasoned encounter with a natural world and from contemplation of negative and positive models.[26] Such a moral encounter with the natural world testified to the existence of a divine being and could only be cultivated through withdrawal from the seductive dangers of a degenerate worldliness.[27] Rousseau reprises the political refrain of women writers who understand virtue as conditional on a withdrawal from a dangerous *mondanité* and who see the morally regenerated human being—the seed of a community guided by virtue—as the product of this reasoned encounter with the natural world.

The greatest popularizer of the sociable conversation group as a vehicle for a moderate, feminized, and internationalized version of Enlightenment was undoubtedly Stéphanie de Genlis, who engaged in a sustained debate with Rousseauian ideas for much of her career and who, as a French mistress and governess to a prominent member of the royal family, inherited the controversy around Maintenon. Genlis addressed this inheritance head on by drafting a revisionist biography of Maintenon toward the end of her own career. Genlis's *Théâtre à l'usage des jeunes personnes* (1779) stood among the most frequently translated works of moral conversations (Plagnol-Diéval 350). Her epistolary novel of education *Adèle et Théodore*, displaying a model education in the countryside and including the cautionary female life of Madame de C***, became a best-seller across Europe. In *Adèle et Théodore,* Genlis develops a powerful mother-educator the Baronness of Almane who devises, controls, and anticipates every aspect of her daughter's and her son's education and records her pedagogical plans in letters to a friend. The related *Tales of the Castle* (*Veillées du château,* 1784) offered a series of didactic fireside stories presented as having been written by the mother and read to the children in *Adèle et Théodore*. In both texts, Genlis provided the son with a male tutor but gathered both children to listen to and draw conclusions from stories about girls and women faced with moral choices. Genlis's own somewhat notorious use of English girls as props for language teaching in the education of the children of the duc d'Orléans, who was also her lover, modeled multilingualism and conversation as the means for evaluating moral behavior. Among the many parents in the European composite elite who were taken with Genlis's methods, Marie Tolstoy translated the first and last chapters of Genlis's *New Method of Teaching for Early Childhood* (*Nouvelle méthode d'enseignement pour la première enfance,* 1800) into Russian for teaching her five children, including Leo Tolstoy (Polosina and Montoya 133). Genlis's publications constituted a veritable common core of reading for

LES AVENTURES
DE
TÉLÉMAQUE
FILS D'ULYSSE

LIVRE PREMIER

CALYPSO ne pouvoit se consoler du
départ d'Ulysse. Dans sa douleur, elle se
trouvoit malheureuse d'être immortelle. Sa
grotte ne résonnoit plus de son chant. Les

Figure 4. Engraving by Droüet, for Fénelon's *Les aventures de Télémaque, fils d'Ulysse* (Paris: Chez Droüet graveur, 1781). Courtesy of Harvard Library, Harvard University. 715.81.388.

J.M. Moreau le jeune, Inv.   M.me Ponce, Sculp.

Figure 5. "Let's go quickly, astronomy is good for something." Engraving by Noël
Le Mire, after Jean-Michel Moreau le Jeune, for Jean-Jacques Rousseau, *Émile, ou de
l'Éducation*, in *Œuvres complètes de J. J. Rousseau*, vol. 11 (Paris: Poinçot, 1788–1793).
Image opposite p. 60. Courtesy of Harvard Library, Harvard University. 715.88.753a.

Figure 6. Frontispiece. Mary Martha Sherwood's 1827 edition of Sarah Fielding's *The Governess: or, the Young Female Academy* (New York: O. D. Cooke Hartford by J. & J. Harper, 1827). Courtesy of Harvard Library, Harvard University. 17436.18.

several generations of readers across Europe and modeled a trans-European elite female cultural identity.

Genlis functioned as a node for a community of practice, supplying source material, a model for emulation or for self-differentiation, publishing leverage, and a means of entering publication. Elisabeth Bekker-Wolff's entry into writing prose was mediated by her translation of Genlis's writing into Dutch (Dijk, "'Gender' et Traduction"). We know that future novelist and educator Maria Edgeworth cut her teeth on a translation of *Adèle et Théodore* and that Anna Laetitia Barbauld's and her brother John Aikin's *Evenings at Home, or the Juvenile Budget Opened* (1792–96) built from Genlis's popularity. Barbauld and Mary Wollstonecraft, in turn, transmitted a feminized and Anglicized model of Enlightenment education recalculated for a next generation of middle-class readers.[28] As Gillian Dow points out, Genlis deliberately fostered a relationship with international women readers by dedicating one of her works to Madame Bocquet, a *salonnière* who had welcomed her in Berlin during her years of exile from France, and her historical novel *Madame de Maintenon* to Margaret Chinnery, "an English mother known as an educationalist" (Dow, "Genlis").

Reading Genlis's books while she worked as a governess in Ireland, Mary Wollstonecraft developed *Original Stories from Real Life: with Conversations Calculated to Regulate the Affections and Form the Mind to Truth and Goodness* (1788), while excerpts from Genlis's writings and educational theater would appear in Wollstonecraft's *The Female Reader* (1789) (P. Brown, "Tales" 8). In addition, Wollstonecraft rewrote Arnaud Berquin's French translation of Margareta Geertruid van der Werken's *The History of Little Grandison* in 1790, a Dutch-language epistolary novel for children. *Little Grandison* featured a Dutch boy separated from his mother in Amsterdam who exchanges letters with her about his sojourn with the Grandison family in London and receives her wise counsel in reply. Wollstonecraft also translated and reworked Christian Gotthilf Salzmann's *Moralisches Elementarbuch* (1783) as *Elements of Morality for the Use of Children* (1790), partly to improve her German-language skills. Johns notes that in the Salzmann translation, Wollstonecraft introduces "an omniscient, nearly omnipotent female figure," a "mother-instructor, who reflects Wollstonecraft's own view of what ought to be women's new domestic sovereignty, with the home as microcosm of the polis and the mother as unacknowledged legislator" (*Bluestocking* 65). The French, German, Dutch, and English pedagogical texts to which Wollstonecraft had access provided the medium for development of the mother-instructor figure that was so central to her work—a version of Stéphanie de

Genlis's Baronness d'Almane who had undergone, German, Dutch, and English tempering.[29] My point here is not to privilege a Gallic influence on British women's writing or to argue for the lodestone pull of Genlis over Wollstonecraft. Instead, the emphasis is on how women writers entered into print in the second half of the eighteenth century via a habitus of translation and through exploration of a gendered international repertoire.

Comparison of Gender Roles Through Repertoire

A few cases, several of which have been highlighted in recent scholarship on British and European women writers, may be instructive here. Writing in England, before and after a stay in newly British Canada, Frances Brooke interspersed translation of three contemporary French novels, including two by Marie-Jeanne Riccoboni at intervals between the publication of her own novels. Work on these contemporary novels written in French not only allowed her to develop her own style for writing fiction; it also provided her with models of character to import into her writing. Male and female characters in her novels deliberately comment on the contrast between British and French manners; the setting of *The History of Emily Montague* (1769) in Canada just after the Seven Years' War (and the French cession of Quebec to the British) provides extensive opportunity for sketches of national contrasts. On her side, Riccoboni worked on novellas and novels throughout her writing career with a strong penchant for English settings and English miladies and milords for characters, as well as one North American setting. At the same time, she produced collections of contemporary English theater in translation in collaboration with her companion Maria Theresa Biancolelli. Sorting writing according to available stereotypes of national character and language in translations by Brooke and Riccoboni (and Biancolelli) is complicated by the pervasive use of foreign locales. The first novel by Riccoboni that Brooke translated into English and that influenced her own style as a novelist was set in England; it brought a fashionable portrait of English women's manners to a French audience. What then did it mean to "translate" the novel into English, and how did Riccoboni's French picture of an English heroine affect Brooke's subsequent depiction of a heroine in newly British Canada who combined the best of the French and the British female character? What was the effect of Brooke's versions of national gender models on the Dutch readers who read the *Historie van Lady Julia Mandeville: Geschreeven in den smaak van Pamela, Clarissa en Grandison* (*History of Lady Mandeville: Written in the Style of Pamela, Clarissa, and Grandison*) published in Amsterdam in 1764?[30] In the preface to her 1771 translation of Abbé Millot's *Elements of the History of France*, Frances Brooke placed gender above national identity when she wrote that "woman alone can paint with perfect exactness the sentiments of woman." In doing so, as Marijn Kaplan has pointed out, she echoed her acquaintance, Miss Roberts (translator of Graffigny's *Lettres d'une Péruvienne* and of Leprince de Beaumont's *Le triomphe de la vérité*) who justified her choice of a novel by a woman as "suitable to a Translator of the same Sex."[31] For women like Roberts, translation may have been attractive as a means of straddling the line of authorship in public. At the same time, translation choices were organized by the assumption that different national and cultural settings provided alternate tests of virtuous womanhood while women understood the meanings of other women, regardless of linguistic differences. A 1769 Italian edition of Riccoboni's *Lettere di Milady Giulietta Catesby a Milady Henrica Campley sua Amica, Tradotte dal Francese della Signora Riccoboni, per la Signora di Gourge* acknowledged something of this through the place of publication emblazoned on its title page: "in Cosmopoli."

In a second case, Isabelle de Montolieu responded to the "reproach repeatedly made" to her that she "translated instead of composing" in the preface to a reedition of her novel *Caroline de Litchfield*, subtitled *Memoirs of a Prussian Family* and written in French. At the time of the reedition, Montolieu had a career as a prolific translator behind her; she transmitted Jane Austen's novels to the Continent (Cossy) and rendered Johann Rudolph Wyss's *Swiss Family Robinson* (1812) into French in an extended version that, along with the German original, informed William and Mary Godwin's translation (Sánchez Eppler 437). Montolieu explained in her preface that she "lacked the gift of genius" necessary for composition of a good novel. In general, she needed something to "seize" or "electrify" her: at that point she could "develop the impetus" and "take advantage of it." This was how she proceeded with her translations, and even her own novel *Caroline de Litchfield* was drawn from "a little German story" (Montolieu 9). The preface is certainly a meditation on Montolieu's own process of composition and on the origins of a novel about a young woman who asserts unusual authority over her marriage as she gradually accommodates herself to the physical monstrosity of her husband. (Caroline overcomes her revulsion at her husband's disfigurement when she discovers it is due to a wound incurred when he saved a young peasant woman from ravishing.) Yet Montolieu's preface also communicated a lifelong practice of moving across an international range of texts to find inspiration while invoking a textual tradition of shying away from claims of female originality and genius.

In one last case, Marie Elisabeth le Boué de La Fite—the host of the tea party with which this book began and the woman who begged for a lock of Frances Burney's hair on La Roche's behalf—used the international repertoire of a women writers' community of practice and deployed the international network of that community to establish an identity as a woman writer. In *Eugénie et ses élèves*, we see the major turning points in La Fite's own life—her husband's death, her emigration, the intimate work of being a governess to a royal family, translation projects, and her daughter Elise's death two years before the publication of *Eugénie*—refracted into a loose narrative inciting female moral reasoning. The narrative emerges through a series of fictional letters, dialogues, personal histories, tales, and plays that connect the lives of women and girls in a sentimental network. The characters in La Fite's *Eugénie* have all become geographically separated by life circumstances despite their intimacy: young Julie (identifiable as Louisa Frederica of Orange, *stadtholder* William V's daughter) writes letters to her governess Eugénie who has departed to educate a princess named Ernestine (George III's daughter Princess Elizabeth). Princess Ernestine learns from the example of governess Eugénie's friend Madame Boloni, who supports the dual loss of her husband and fortune with Christian fortitude and plans to earn her living as an "educator." The governess Eugénie and her princess-pupil read letters by yet another young girl, Lady Cecilia B*, about providing hospitality in her château to the dying Irish girl Sophie Belton. Sophie's mother supports the death of her daughter with Christian fortitude.

The volume contains a gloss on why a girl should learn languages: "The advantage of knowing several languages," governess Eugénie explains to the princess, "puts you in the position of being able to translate; and I am revealing here a new way for you to do good. By providing a knowledge of useful works, you will render an essential service to people who are less educated than you" (134). The girls bear given names drawn from international French, British, and German sentimental works, chiefly by women: Riccoboni's *Histoire d'Ernestine* (1765), Burney's *Cecilia, Memoirs of an Heiress* (1782), as well as the infinite number of Julies and Sophies deriving from Jean-Jacques Rousseau's work, including Sophie von La Roche's heroine Sophia in *History of Sophia von Sternheim* (*Geschichte des Fräuleins von Sternheim*, 1771). Eugénie's students are linked across space by shared reading and ascription to the moral principles inculcated by Governess Eugénie and materialized in their exchange of letters and stories and through their apprenticeship in translation. Governess Eugénie is the primary link among the girls and women, but in the text she is certainly not the only preceptor to generate material for reflection or the only person to facilitate relationships, nor does she have a direct relationship with all of the women and girls whose life stories or correspondence are shared in the text. The girls reason on their own or together, but they base their reflections on the stories of girls' and women's lives that they read and hear. Their idealized international friendship secured by the recounting of lives reprises the structure of cosmopolitan affinity of the city of ladies.

"Marie-Elisabeth de la Fite is an obscure figure now," Clarissa Campbell Orr writes, "but her cosmopolitanism and mediating role as a translator helps us glimpse an international culture of pietism and sensibility that continued to enjoin a life of moral and social responsibility on both men and women in high places, and to defend women against sexual and family exploitation" ("Aristocratic" 316). A striking pattern in La Fite's life is the gendering of her professional relationships and publishing opportunities, with much of her work before 1781 being devoted to translation and compilation as a hardworking companion supporting her husband's intellectual ventures (see Chapter 1). After her husband's death in 1781, her work benefited from both the pragmatic leverage of relationships with women writers and an imaginative cultivation of the idea of literary and virtuous affinity among exceptional literate women.

Campbell Orr explains that La Fite's careers in education "were based upon patronage from the interlinked dynasties of Hohernzollern (Prussia), Orange (the Netherlands), and Brunswick (Hanover and Great Britain), which, as well as employing members of the Huguenot diaspora, also gave opportunities to German Swiss savants as educators and academicians" ("La Fite"). She broke into print independently of her husband the same year as the birth of her third child, who died in infancy; her French translation of Sophie von La Roche's *History of Sophia von Sternheim* appeared with Gosse in 1773. It was dedicated to her patron "Madam, her Royal Highness Princess of Orange and of Nassau, born Princess of Prussia." She then published some critical essays of her own and translated into French a biography of Christian Fürchtegott Gellert along with his model letters, in which he extolled the natural epistolary style of women and urged his female readers to write in German rather than in French (an enjoinder that Sophie von La Roche took seriously).[32] La Fite also became a translator and production editor for the French edition of German-Swiss Johann Caspar Lavater's multivolume illustrated *Essay on Physiognomy*. And she established herself as an educator of girls in the mold of Leprince de Beaumont with her most well-known book, *Entretiens, drames et contes moraux*, a work employing the format of a familiar conversation between a maternal preceptress and a group of girls. The book ran to six French editions between 1778 and 1821 and was translated into German and Russian.[33] Within a minimal frame narrative involving a mother's education of her daughter and niece in the countryside, La Fite inserted translations of tales and short didactic plays pulled from the writings of two male German pedagogues, Johann Gottlieb Schummel and Christian Felix Weisse. Weisse's magazine for children, *Der Kinderfreund* (1775–82) was inspired by Jeanne-Marie Leprince de Beaumont's *Magasin des enfants* (1757) (Plagnol-Diéval 324).

After the deaths of her husband and father in 1781, La Fite consolidated her profile as an educator of girls and a moralist for women. Taking advantage of her connections in the Huguenot diaspora, she profited from an introduction by the Genevan Jean-André de Luc, who was the French reader to Queen Charlotte of Great Britain. La Fite was appointed to the position of reader to the queen and instructress in German and French to the three eldest princesses who were, as La Fite explained in a letter to her uncle, "of an age to reap fruit from the conversation of an educated person" (Janse, *éducatrice* 311).[34] La Fite's French-speaking daughter Elise, who was eleven at the time they moved to England, served as a teaching prop in the education of Princess Elizabeth of Great Britain, resuming the role of companion that she had played in the Hague to Louisa Frederica of Orange, with whom Elise continued to correspond from England. La Fite would owe her publications from 1781 on, when she was based in England in Queen Charlotte's household, to active female networking but also to a *mentalité* of affinity among exceptional women.

La Fite can be considered as both a handmaiden of cultural transfer within the Huguenot intellectual diaspora and as a fundamentally transnational woman whose engagement with writing by other women and advantageous placement in royal households with formidable German female cultural patrons yielded the basis for a successful intellectual career as a single working mother. Campbell Orr situates her within a network of women governesses or educators in the service of the international European aristocracy—from Madame de Maintenon, to Jeanne-Marie Leprince de

Beaumont, to Stéphanie de Genlis, who as spokespeople for the moral education of girls and women became at the same time reformers in educational methods. La Fite's publication history provides a picture of establishing a position within an international women's literary field achieved through leverage of connections between women, underwritten by multilingualism and the exploitation of gendered genres. Altogether, La Fite's writing and translations appeared in French, German, English, Dutch, and Russian with publishers in the Hague, Lausanne, Paris, Leipzig, London, and St. Petersburg. After her death in the central London neighborhood of Pimlico in 1794, her educational work continued to be reedited for another quarter century.[35]

The introductions to La Fite's works employ intertwined pretexts for legitimating her role as translator and writer: construction of a virtuous affinity with the heroine on the part of the author, the reader, and even the translator, on the one hand, and an insertion of the woman writer into a larger ahistorical collectivity of women writers and their books, on the other. In her 1773 preface to her French version of Sophie von La Roche's *The History of Sophie von Sternheim*, La Fite reprinted the letters in which she had asked permission to undertake the translation. The letters were addressed to Christoph-Martin Wieland, who had edited and facilitated publication of La Roche's novel (iv).[36] La Fite explained that she had already been seeking works for her young daughter when her husband put *The History of Sophie von Sternheim* into her hands: "I have always thought that the best means for inspiring [virtue] was not to teach morals by chapter but to present virtue put into action, and to provide examples of it" (vi). Skipping over the preface ("for it is fairly rare that a woman begins with the preface") and weeping over the story as she read it, she imagined her daughter as reader: "She must, I said to myself, read this writing some day, and if it can be, may she think and may she act like *Sophie Sternheim!* You see, sir, that my heart translated a point in your preface [to the novel] before I had even read it. I went to find my husband and told him that I thought it my duty in good conscience to translate a work so suited to doing good and that one special reason had made me determined to do it, it was that our child would know French long before learning German" (vii). Moreover, Wilhelmina of Prussia, Princess of Orange, had read La Fite's copy of the original German first volume of the novel and was eager to find out the ending. She had pressed La Fite to translate the work into French and to request the author to finish the next installments (vii). Writing and translation served to present virtue put into action and to provide examples of it so that female readers could, in their turn, become examples of virtue put into action. In this discourse, the idea that the reader would and should act like the heroine was "translated" by the "heart" before the reading experience itself, while the translator performed useful work in transmitting models of female virtue between languages.

La Fite's *Eugénie et ses élèves* (1787) was presented as being *by* a woman writer *within* an international field of women writers. Genlis used writing the preface for La Fite's work as the opportunity to present herself as the node in a network of women writers, referring first to Isabelle de Montolieu and then to La Fite: "The ingenious author of *Caroline* [*de Litchfield* by Isabelle de Montolieu] charged me last year with distributing in Paris the first copies of this charming Novel, which had such a brilliant success; and this year, another woman [La Fite] was good enough to trust me with her manuscript and to rely on me completely for the care in getting it printed." Finally, Genlis explained that the bond drawing women writers together was senti-mental: "Men repeat that Women can't love each other, because *jealousy, envy, self-interest, (their dominant passions) always divide them.* I will not reject this odious accusation with arguments that could be contested; but I will answer with facts that it is impossible to deny. I have seen men of genius lost by these shameful passions, and I have never seen envy torment and debase a woman of distinguished merit" (*Eugénie* xvi). Putting the lie to her conten-tion about the mutual trust and regard among women writers, Genlis would elsewhere recycle a misogynist stereotype, attacking her young rival Germaine de Staël for having "learned to speak quickly and say a lot without thinking," in her mother's salon, only to conclude uncharitably, "and this is how she writes" (Broglie 3). Yet in the preface to La Fite's *Eugénie,* Genlis elides com-petition so as to construct relations between women writers "of distinguished merit" in affective and intimate terms, even as she presents herself as a power-broker. She proceeds very much as did La Fite in her request for a lock of Burney's hair by collecting women "of merit" into a sentimental, conversa-tional affinity group.

When she built an idealized international friendship among girls and women in *Eugénie et ses élèves* based on the recounting of lives, La Fite reprised the structure of intellectual and virtuous affinity that La Roche relied on in her account of the tea party at Windsor and that Genlis invoked in her preface. This structure was not simply a textual corollary to the exchanges of letters that we know to have traversed Britain, Western Europe, and the Atlantic or a mirror of life in a school for privileged girls, such as the one run by Jeanne-Marie Leprince de Beaumont in London. Nor was it wholly the product of eighteenth-century salon sociability since, however international the guest list and however much it featured some women prominently as celebrity visitors and hosts, the salon functioned as a mixed institution for mediating literary rivalry and cultural value and for facilitating cultural transfer from one national literary field to another. The ideal cosmopolitan community of exceptional women reprised in *Eugénie* had a textual genealogy anchored in a repertoire and in a habitus of movement across modern European languages. "The ladies here speak perfect French" (*Sophie* 180), Sophie von La Roche wrote in her travel diary of the tea party La Fite hosted in her honor.

That repertoire enabled practice: it invited women writers into the field through an emulative structure. And it limited practice: it required that the work of fiction by a woman advertise its utility for the model of female virtue it provided rather than through a claim a culturally transformative aesthetic originality. The repertoire also exploited a structural opening in the European Republic of Letters. Where discourses of aesthetic capital engaged an idea of modern male national genius in contention with the burden of the classical past, the feminized discourse of the capital of virtue was fundamentally international, contemporary, and comparative. Providing the groundwork for Germaine de Staël's method in *On Literature,* it explored recurring tropes of female existence within different national gender contexts.

Chapter 5

Heroines and Local Girls

Contrast the mid-century movement of Richardson's Clarissa in Britain
or of Rousseau's Julie from her father's Swiss home to her husband's Swiss
home (to the boat excursion on Lake Geneva that leads to her death) with
the displacement of other eighteenth-century heroines and of heroes. Early
in the century, Daniel Defoe's Roxana and the Abbé Prevost's Manon
travel throughout their countries of birth to national capitals and to the
New World. Their attraction to cities as well as their Atlantic transit signify a dangerous, exciting, and unvirtuous worldliness—even their willing
participation in becoming and profiting from becoming traded sexual
commodities. In fiction by men, male protagonists may travel a great deal,
with travel registering progress toward knowledge and maturity. After
drugging and raping Clarissa, Lovelace departs for the continent and, in
Munich, recognizes that even his death may not expiate his crime. After
seducing Julie, Rousseau's hero Saint-Preux travels a grand tour that
includes Paris and the Pacific. In Paris, Saint-Preux notes that women's
participation in public life contributes to French intellectual liveliness and
stimulates the rise of the arts and sciences—until it leads to artifice and
corruption. By the end of his travels, Saint-Preux grasps the cornerstone
of Enlightenment political economy: relations between the sexes, as mea-
sured by the treatment of women and their relative participation in public
life, correlate with the progress of nations (Cheek, *Sexual Antipodes* 31,
120). This insight then supports the vision of gender complementarity
arrayed across masculine public and feminine private spheres put forth in
the section of the novel in which Saint-Preux returns to find Julie in her
Swiss home and garden regulating the moral and physical hygiene of her
family and friends.

Generally speaking, in novels by male authors, virtuous women stay within one or two days' journey from home. Men may travel. This distribution of characters supported what Michèle Cohen and Susan Dever call a gendered "novel-nation homology" (9). In *Imagined Communities,* Benedict Anderson sketched how the novelistic representation of characters' daily experiences as simultaneous communicates shared habitation of and belonging to an otherwise difficult-to-imagine national space. Building on this work, critics have identified how the happy marriage and procreation of a couple within their homeland anchors national space, as it is imagined in the novel.[1] A mental map for readers coalesced through the novel's representation of the national marriage market and establishment of tranquil family life (Moretti, *Atlas* 14–17).

Where, in a period in which novels linked national character to gender roles, a heroine in a novel by a woman writer might feel "at home" was a complicated question. For many women writers, home was not coterminous with national borders, as the flight of Leprince de Beaumont's new Clarissa from abuse and predation in England to a safe utopian estate in Bordeaux made abundantly clear. Women writers relied on the devices of the novel of sympathy and sentiment to highlight the gender roles supposed to be typical of particular nations or regions, even as they created heroines whose very mobility or hybrid origins signified their transcendence of local conditions of gendered oppression. Susan Staves notes that after the Seven Years' War, women writers in Britain demonstrated "heightened interest in the representation of place" and "repeated efforts to articulate what was distinctive about British places" (Staves, *Literary History* 24). Similar trends appear in Continental writing with respect to Dutch, French, Swiss, and German locales, a phenomenon that correlates with the urgency in the rising genre of travel writing to depict the particularity of foreign places. This chapter argues that it was implication in a network of women's writing (the consumption of, practice in, and innovation upon a women's repertoire) that provided individual writers with the impetus and analytic power to diagnose and describe culture- and place-specific gender roles *and* to situate these with respect to an emerging universal idea of the condition of woman as devolving from social and educational practices. John Tomlinson observes that globalization "involves the reach of global connectivity into localities. This involves the simultaneous penetration of local worlds by distant forces and the dislodging of everyday cultural meanings from their 'anchors' in local cultural contexts." Attaching to a trans-European network entailed using codes from elsewhere to depict and evaluate local cultural contexts. Through that process, in turn, women writers "dislodged" women's experiences from their local anchors and developed a shared notion of the (transnational) condition of woman.

The Novel as Vehicle for Comparing National Gender Roles

The 1782 preface to the first edition of *The History of Miss Sara Burgerhart* (*Historie van Mejuffrouw Sara Burgerhart*) by Elisabeth Bekker-Wolff and Agatha Deken announced that it was the very first national Dutch novel.[2] Appraising the state of writing in the Dutch Republic in a period when war with Great Britain had elicited an eruption of nationalist sentiment,[3] its authors expressed the opinion that the Dutch reputation for being too clumsy and thick-witted to write would soon be shattered. Since the English and then the Germans had shown that they could contest the French pretention to an empire over good taste and over the art of literary "depiction," the Dutch too would prove that their taste and language were increasingly refined instruments for displaying their own character and values: "Do not conclude . . . that we believe that the work of an Englishman will be as agreeable to an Italian as it would be for one of his compatriots," the authors wrote. "Each nation must have its own writers, as well as its heroes and men of state. . . . Convinced of these truths, we hope finally to see the glow of this happy day. While we await it, we have ventured to publish an original and national novel, calculated on the meridian of ordinary bourgeois life. We have wanted to depict Dutch characters, men such as one encounters at every step in our country" (10–11).[4] The preface bluntly placed the reader in the territory of rival national literatures vying for greatness and for a distinctive national literary character. It claimed "ordinary bourgeois life" as the Dutch national terrain through a depiction of characters who, like the eponymous Sara, had the heart of the burger or true Dutch citizen.

The preface to the second edition of *The History of Miss Sara Burgerhart*, written in 1783, emphasized gender as much as nation: "It is possible that it is to curiosity that we owe the great début of this novel. A national novel, composed by two women, is really a singular production, suited to awakening the attention of the public" (23). The two women authors of *Sara Burgerhart* already enjoyed recognition in the Dutch Republic for their appeals for religious tolerance and moderation as well as for their celebration of a Dutch work ethic and a virtuous, patriotic womanhood. Bekker-Wolff (1738–1804) played the leading role in the collaboration. The talented and well-educated daughter of a prominent businessman in Vlissingen, Zeeland, she studied Latin, English, French, German, and English and wrote poetry as a girl and young woman. When she was seventeen, she was officially censured by the Vlissingen Council of the Dutch Reformed Church and attacked by family and community after she spent one night away from her father's home in 1755 with an officer named Mathijs Gargon. The officer subsequently departed for the Dutch East Indies. In 1759, Bekker-Wolff married the fifty-two-year-old Reverend Adriaan Wolff and retired with him to his country parish in De Beemster, in the northern part of Holland. Reflecting on her life in a 1770 letter, Bekker-Wolff wrote,

> With a heart torn to the roots whose wound does not refrain from bleed-ing occasionally, even after ten years, I have paid for the ectasy of a young love! I have never been what you would call a beautiful woman, but I was given *l'irrésistible* and a *charmant air de plaire* to make up for that lack. My sister is a *beauté*, yet I managed to snatch away from her anything with taste and good looks that had the heart to come to "Altijd Wel" [All is well]. You may say, however, that my fortune turned out very meager: an old country minister. You are correct, but wait until I publish *mes mémoires* before judging whether I did something foolish when, at the age of twenty I said good-bye to my family and *ma très chère patrie* in order to be tied to an old stately man. . . . There is only one disadvantage to the non-fulfillment of my wish: the learned world would not have had to put up with my poetic trivia. I would have done nothing else in God's world than love my dear young man and rack my brains night and day to hold on to his whole heart; I would not have wanted to forego even the tiniest pin-head particle of it.[5]

In satire-laden retrospect, at least, marriage to a pastor was a move calculated to provide the respectable position from which to write. She developed an extensive correspondence and started publishing essays and poetry critical of religious fanaticism and of women who aped French fashion. Elisabeth Bekker-Wolff translated into Dutch key books in the repertoire used to edu-cate generations of European girls, including Stéphanie de Genlis's *Adèle et Théodore* in 1782, Louise d'Epinay's *Conversations d'Émilie*, and writing by Sophie von La Roche and by Jeanne-Marie Leprince de Beaumont (Dijk,

"Early Historiography" 81–94).[6] Bekker-Wolff's correspondence with Agatha Deken, a moral poet in Amsterdam, turned into a long-lasting relationship after the death of Bekker-Wolff's husband in 1777. The pair wrote two novels together, *The History of Miss Sara Burgerhart* and *Willem Leevand,* along with an epistolary continuation of the first. After a long companionship, the two died in the Hague, ten days apart, as was their professed wish (Van Betten 107). Bekker-Wolff's 1804 obituary in the *Algemeene Konst- en Letterbode* remarked on the relationship between the two writers and duly distinguished her for contributing to the country's reputation for "erudite" women, such as Anna Maria van Schurman, who brought fame to the nation: "She never was without her delightfully cheerful spirit or the consolation of the friendship of Agatha Deken, who, uninterrupted, for more than twenty-eight years, shared the good and the bad with her. . . . How much are we Netherlanders indebted to her? How many hours of entertainment and edification do we owe to her imagination and intellect? How much has the literary renown of our country increased through her, a renown which, as far as *erudite women* are concerned, certainly surpasses the fame of all other peoples."[7]

"Entertainment and edification" almost surely referred to Bekker-Wolff and Deken's most famous work, *The History of Miss Sara Burgerhart.* (The novel was translated into French in 1787 by Henri Rieu. Like many European readers of the period, I rely on Rieu's translation.) As the two authors advertised in their preface to the first edition, in the novel they sought to "depict Dutch characters such as one encounters at every step in our country": the "good, honest, Patriot" Abraham Blankaart who is the benevolent guardian of the eponymous heroine, Sara, the best friend Anna Willis who "numbers among that ancient class of Dutchwomen whose impassiveness is not easily altered" (3:287), honest young men "to whom the two Indies are available" as "resources" for their industry, the housewife resigned over her tablecloth blackened by soot from the stinking gin distillery town of Schiedam (2:76), and the hospitable people of Rotterdam who enjoy their tidy white linens, their good tea, and their copious doses of sugar (1:312). Bekker-Wolff and Deken build from a long tradition of writing on and by the Dutch that held that Batavian men were lazy and the women were subsequently hardworking, and that this resulted in relative equality between the sexes. Women's attention to cleanliness was, in this stereotype, related to their direct involvement in shopkeeping and other enterprises (Heuvel 41). Despite the focus on scenes from Dutch life across the republic, the novel's xenophobia is always curbed. This is not surprising, perhaps, in a work calculated to represent a nation whose positive male characters, from Sara's guardian Abraham Blankhart to her future husband Henry Eberling, are all merchants working abroad and profiting from global trade.

Within Bekker-Wolff and Deken's Dutch landscape, painting a Dutch woman who might rival in sentimental appeal contemporary French and British heroines was a challenging proposition. The story is explicitly situated as different from the British Richardsonian universe. As the authors remind us, the hero Henry Eberling is "not a Grandison" (Werken's *De kleine Grandisson* appeared in 1782). And Sara is not a "Clarissa Harlove [*sic*]" (1:21 and 266). By name, Sara Burgerhart bears the heart of a citizen, yet her tastes are cosmopolitan. When her superstitious and zealously pious aunt gives three-year-old Sara a doll "dressed in a humble and proper manner as should be all those who believe in God," Sara reveals her predilection for pretty things by choosing instead the doll given her by the French servant Pernette—a doll described by the aunt as "ornamented like a veritable Jezebel, covered with ribbons and pompoms, . . . who had curled hair and no bonnet, who had large paniers and who completely resembled a streetwalker" (1:72–73). Sara's guardian Abraham Blankhart, the generous counterweight to her strict aunt, delights her with an English dollhouse (2:202). By the time Sara is twenty, the period at which the novel is set, her childhood cosmopolitan consumption has developed into a refined taste supported by a French shop, a *marchande de mode,* where she receives letters and books and meets her friends. As a young woman profiting from her education by a French schoolmistress, Sara writes letters sprinkled with French phrases and elegant and topical French, English, and German cultural references for women. She sees a copy of Abbé Raynal's *Histoire des deux indes* and treasures Christian Fürchtegott Gellert's model letters for women. She possesses a copy of Frances Brooke's *History of Lady Julia Mandeville,* which is confiscated by her aunt (1:67). The villainous seducer Mr. R– loans her a copy of Alexander Pope's *Essay on Man,* translated into four languages. Visiting the Comédie Française for a performance in Amsterdam, Sara laughs at the depiction of intellectual women in Molière's *Les femmes savantes* and savors a line making fun of women who pretend to know classical languages (1:346).

The presentation of Sara as both a cosmopolitan and a Dutch sentimental heroine pivots around the question of the female savant and the problem of a woman's proper cultural repertoire. To construct their "national novel," Bekker-Wolff and Deken weave in references to many Dutch writers, including seventeenth-century Dutch poet Joseph Cats (2:330–31) and eighteenth-century poet Lucretia Wilhelmine van Merken (1:55), who had influenced

Bekker-Wolff's own early poetry (Van Betten 110). Still, in an impressive act of cultural amnesia, the authors make no reference to Cats's contemporary and protegée Anna Maria van Schurman, the most famous Dutch woman and the most famous European female intellectual and writer of the early modern period. Schurman's absence from the sprawling *History of Miss Sara Burgerhart* is noteworthy given that Bekker-Wolff was her direct successor in published advocacy of women's education. Bekker-Wolff's *Bespiegelingen over der Staat den Regheit* (*Reflections on the State of Justice*, 1765) argued for the importance of education as an instrument for instilling morality and virtue in women, an argument itself influenced by Pietism. Like many women writers of the second half of the eighteenth century, Bekker-Wolff and Deken used the novel as a forum for arguing that better education would preserve women from the very frivolity and levity of which they were constantly accused. They dismissed the idea that women might be public actors, and they rejected as well the position advanced by Schurman a century before that women might be scholars and had "the right to interiority" (Schurman, *Anna Maria van Schurman* 269). Instead, as the verse epigram to the novel moralized, the education of girls should find a "just middle" between too much severity and too much freedom. The orphan Sara becomes the mouthpiece and object lesson for this proposition.

Sara Burgerhart comes into definition as a Dutch sentimental heroine through contrasts with older women who embody the two negative stereotypes often attributed to Schurman: the fanatically pious spinster and the unmarried female savant who violates proper gender boundaries. Sara's censorious aunt Suzanne Hofsland, with whom she lives after the deaths of her parents, has been seduced into Calvinist extremism by the hypocritical preacher Brother Benjamin and Sister Slimpslamp. Benjamin is a former butcher, from the "dregs of the population" (4:10) whom Sara, fluent in the works of Molière, dubs a "Tartuffe" (1:89). Under Benjamin's and Slimpslamp's pressure and the influence of sectarian Dutch religious publications, Sara's aunt commits the first act of "Dutch" gendered oppression in the novel. She imprisons Sara under the guise of improving her. Sanctimoniously criticizing the vanity of the world, she forces Sara to wear punitively dowdy dresses, to give up her favorite books and entertainment, and to serve pancakes to the lower-class Benjamin and Slimpslamp. It is the pancakes that are finally too much. Sara informs her guardian Abraham Blankaart by letter that she is removing to a respectable young ladies' boardinghouse in Amsterdam and bolts.

In the boardinghouse, where a circle of well-bred young women live under the nominal supervision of the proprietress, Sara encounters the second negative avatar of Anna Maria van Schurman, the thirty-year-old boarder Miss Hartog, who "passes for a savant." "Tall, thin, dry," "mannish" and with "brazen" eyes, Hartog is perpetually "unclean" and overdressed. "She goes out often, frequents the churches, and knows many people of the first rank, to whose houses she is sometimes invited." Most important, she reads "profound works in four or five languages" and maintains a correspondence with several "gens de lettres" (1:201). Jealous of hero Henry Eberling's interest in Sara, Miss Hartog circulates damaging rumors about Sara's behavior. As severe and dogmatic in her way as Sara's aunt Hofsland, the francophilic Hartog takes as her maxim "no Dutch books" (1:183). In a frenzy of antinational sentiment tying together the Dutch East India trade and Dutch horticulture, she derisively compares Dutch verse to fashionable pineapples cultivated in hothouses (2:178). Lest the point about cultural imports, national self-loathing, and the remedy to be provided by Dutch writing be lost on the reader, the first preface caustically satirizes precisely the sort of young woman who might live in the boardinghouse alongside Sara: "We seem to hear some of our young ladies, who have no other merit than a respectable name and who have conserved of their country only the treasures amassed in commerce by their fathers, raising their voice and crying out in a disdainful tone while wrinkling their brow: 'what! A Dutch novel! Good God, my dear, what do you know?—I never read anything in that language, which I don't even believe that I understand, but I am curious to give it a try'" (1:18). The pedantic Hartog, then, merges with the fashionable Dutch female reader in rejecting homegrown culture. It is Hartog's censure of things Dutch as well as the aunt's xenophobic bigotry that teach Sara, in reaction, to be overly trusting and fun-loving, thus exposing her to the villain, Mr. R–.

The scene of Sara's seduction is the Hortus Medicus—the renowned Amsterdam botanical garden established in 1638 with plants imported by the Dutch East India Company (3:36). She agrees to visit the gardens to see "a foreign plant" with Mr. R– (3:208). He delays her there all day and then succeeds in abducting her by drawing her into a carriage with the promise of showing her "flowers from all over the world" at a country house (3:336). The life story of Widow Spilgoud, the proprietor of the young ladies' boardinghouse in Amsterdam where Sara lives, provides a context for measuring the risks run by women in a world in which men can tempt them to forget themselves with the lure of imports. Spilgoud had endured a loveless marriage of convenience to an older merchant who had acquired Asiatic habits of debauchery along with a vast fortune from the "Oriental Indies" and who sought to satisfy the "gross pleasures of the senses" (1:325–27) with his wife and with his mistress. The debauched merchant demonstrates his retrograde autocracy by refusing to allow his wife to nurse their child. When he dies, he leaves his wife penniless. Within this framework, the Hortus serves as both the sine qua non of Dutchness and as a national cautionary site, a potential if unrealized scene of seduction because it features an enchanting collection imported from elsewhere and cultivated through Dutch genius.

Sara manages a gutsy escape from the villain with her virtue miraculously intact, her reputation is cleared and marriages for her and her friends ensue. Yet the novel closes by returning to the problem of the female spinster and savant. The final line assures the reader that Charlotte Nothing-At-All, a feather-headed girl from the boardinghouse, is "more useful to the world in knitting thick socks than Miss Hartog in her learned dissertations on corpuscules" (4:287). The negative definition of the Dutch heroine, in which Sara is not only not a "Clarissa Harlove" but not an Anna Maria van Schurman, helps negotiate the problem crystallized in the chronotope of the Hortus: how to characterize the essence of a country whose economic character and international reputation devolve from profits importing luxury items and raw materials and trading them in Europe. Avowing that trade might be an honorable basis for a national identity was a vexed proposition. Trade could transmit foreign passions. It required that the lucre-driven merchant be endowed, somehow, with greater honor than the disinterested hereditary noble. And it demanded that novelistic discourse be reframed so that the vulgar idea of trade did not invoke dependency on import and consumption of foreign commodities and culture. How, as Miss Hartog alerted the reader, were things Dutch, from the novel to the heroine herself, to amount to anything other than pineapples cultivated in the Hortus at great bother and expense? The answer lay in providing depictions of specifically Dutch trials for the heroine and travelogue descriptions of Dutch places and people while, at the same time, identifying the heroine and the novel with cultural cosmopolitanism. Bekker-Wolff and Deken employed the gendered concrete universal; they created a transnational heroine whose subjection to specifically local experiences tries her character. In Sara's case, these local experiences include the refusal to serve pancakes to the pious aunt and her friends and the almost utopian existence at the Amsterdam boardinghouse of living a community of fashionable and polite young women who can mingle with young men with some freedom. They coalesce in the stereotypes of female pedantry and piety, on the one hand, and in an image of somewhat balanced gender relations, on the other. Even Dutch seduction is, relative to British seduction, somewhat mild, as the authors stress. Sara nonetheless shares attributes with many late eighteenth-century heroines: a French-influenced education, survival of sexual assault, the world's misapprehensions about her virtue, and, finally, marriage.

Even as they evicted Schurman, the most famous Dutch woman, from their national novel, Bekker-Wolff and Deken adapted the portraits of a devout Aunt Hofsland seduced by a Tartuffe and of the *femme savante* Miss Hartog directly from the French playwright Molière. The portraits serve in the novel as cautions against women whose spinsterhood and financial ease has permitted them too much freedom in forming their own ideas, too great a sense of entitlement to the "right to interiority" (Schurman, *Anna Maria van Schurman* 269). The displacement of Schurman onto negative models of excessive piety and excessive francophilia, both associated with problematic female reading practices, amounts to a refusal to construct Dutch female identity in terms of an intellectual filiation based on national intellectual inheritance. Instead, the positive model of Dutch female identity is built around practices of female sociability that include transnational cultural tastes and consumption and discrimination about women's virtue based on assessment of their lives.

Schurman's absence from the novel also registers a shift in writing about European women away from the idealized city of exceptional ladies and its literary grouping of extraordinary women in catalogues and utopian or Elysian imagined communities. Like Sappho, Schurman was a prominent and obligatory reference in these catalogues and, correlatively, in prefaces to works by women writers in the late seventeenth and early eighteenth centuries. Bekker-Wolff and Deken crafted exceptional female identity not through endowing their heroine with membership in an essentially a-geographic and ahistoric city, palace, garden, or roll call of extraordinary women, and not by situating her as an inheritor in a national Dutch tradition of exceptional women (drawing a line from Schurman to their fictional heroine), but by inserting their protagonist novelistically into a specific time and place while, at the same time, giving her a supranational affinity. The ideal qualities supporting this affinity were transnational reading habits, cultural interests and tastes, and the privileging of reason as the support of virtue—all belonging to intelligent, sensitive, and articulate women. Bekker-Wolff had full command of the necessary repertoire for positioning Sara Burgerhart as a heroine endowed with supranational virtue owing to her experiences as a translator. At the same time, Bekker-Wolff and Deken could insist on local detail and anti-French sentiment to muster Dutch national cultural and literary pride. Sara's moderate transnationalism is paired with her successful passage through specifically Dutch trials in her aunt's bigoted household and in the Hortus Medicus. Like its heroine, the novel itself oscillates between the cosmopolitan and the Dutch, alternating satiric and affection-ate pastiches of the habits and people of the Netherlands with the sentimen-tal codes characteristic of contemporary French, English, and German fiction. These sentimental codes provided a conduit for offering a mild critique of the treatment of women in the Dutch Republic. The structure of pairing trials of local girls with the *je ne sais quoi* of virtuous heroines was infinitely reproduceable.

For example, *Caroline de Litchfield, ou mémoires d'une famille prussienne* published in French in 1786 did for Prussians (but also for the readers across Britain and Europe who read it) what the *History of Miss Sara Burgerhart* had done for the Dutch. Writing from the canton of Vaud, in the region of Lausanne, Isabelle de Montolieu, future translator into French of Jane Aus-ten's novels and of *The Swiss Family Robinson*, assembled recognizable types and topoi: an affectionate aunt whose judgment is clouded by excessive read-ing of romances; a feminine sanctum for music, reading, and drawing trans-formed into a scene of seduction; an ambitious father who marries the heroine to a hideous man for the sake of advancement; and the educated independent heroine herself. Caroline resists paternal and spousal tyranny by crafting a letter requesting that she be allowed to withdraw to the countryside without having to perform the duties of a wife to the disfigured count to whom she is fatally unattracted. Caroline's specifically Prussian trial is the simultaneously fractious and fraternal, mimetic relationship between the two Prussian officers who are both in love with her. A complex prediegetic plot, inserted into the text via a journal, reveals how the one officer has shot and disfigured the other, mistaking him for a rival ravisher of the Prussian country maid he is trying to seduce. This disclosure of the smoking gun, as it were, and discovery that her husband was disfigured by his rival in an attempt to save the country maid, allows Caroline, in a "Beauty and the Beast" story, to overcome her horror of her husband and recognize his interior worth. The almost seduced Prussian country maid functions as a local type setting off the exceptionalism of Caroline in a culture in which female virtue and happiness are hostage to Prussian military brotherhood, honor, dishonor, and rivalry.

In part, Bekker-Wolff and Deken's declaration that they had written the first national Dutch novel amounted to a power grab—an attempt to define Dutch sentimental existence on the contemporary terms of a Sara Burgerhart, or of the woman reader who has and is the heart of the bourgeois nation, itself the heart of a network of commercial import. At the same time, the authors presented set features of women's lives—education, housing, rape, marriage, courtship, pregnancy, nursing, abandonment, motherhood, and widowhood—as culturally contingent rites, as rites of national power and violence that an exceptional woman might survive and/or manage to describe because of her supranational affinities.

Similar depictions of gender roles (as both the essence of a place and the problem with which an exceptional woman had to contend) appeared in novels by women throughout the last third of the eighteenth century. The supranational affiliations allowing a heroine somehow to triumph over local conditions of gendered oppression began, in some fiction, with birth or early childhood. Although it is possible to have entirely domestic orphans, of course, Marie-Jeanne Riccoboni's *Histoire d'Ernestine* (1765) opens with the intriguing information that the little four-year-old Ernestine, whom female neighbors discover beside her deceased mother Christine, is foreign: "The little stranger was named Ernestine. She was German and did not appear to have been born to a lowly station. She expressed herself in French with difficulty. Through questioning her, it became understood from what she said, that a mean husband had forced the unfortunate Christine to leave her home and country, and never did anyone learn anything more about it" (5). While the narrator holds true to this last clause and Ernestine's foreignness never comes up again, the mystery of her origins facilitates the character's elevation over the course of the novella even when, to all appearances, she seems to be a courtesan maintained in a country house by a French nobleman as if she were a *femme entretenue*. The unexceptional women around Ernestine, who suffer from impoverishment owing to widowhood or spinsterhood, contrast with her pure virtue. Her ultimate marriage to the French nobleman who had appeared to "keep" her exonerates her honor and rewards her purity. Her mysterious foreign birth defers any determinate answer to the question of whether she is or is not actually a blue blood, but it is a detail facilitating exceptionalism. The equally extraordinary (untold) story of the mother Christine, who has died away from the home of her German husband, leaving behind the beautiful orphan, anticipates the tension between prosaic female fates associated with local conditions of oppression and the supranational exceptionalism at work in Ernestine's story.

The History of Ernestine traces the heroine's brush with a specific cultural world, the Parisian demimonde in which the theater functioned as a milieu for the prostitution of adolescent girls to aristocratic men through contracts arranged by more experienced women for maintaining them in posh houses. This was a distinct world with which Marie-Jeanne de Heurles Laboras de Mézières Riccoboni was intimately familiar (Cheek, "*Demi*-Monde" 123). As a young woman of illegitimate birth with few prospects, she had married the son of the famous theatrical Riccoboni family. Her husband proved to be an abusive drinker, gambler, and womanizer. The marriage introduced her to the stage, where she formed a friendship with Marie-Thérèse Biancolelli, the daughter of another prominent theatrical family in the Comédie-Italienne. During her career as an actress, Biancolelli "was supported by a series of high-paying patrons," notably the marquis d'Hauteville, who maintained her for seven years ending in 1744 (Kushner 155, 176–77). Beginning in 1755, Riccoboni and Biancolelli shared an apartment, ultimately retiring from the theater and turning their joint efforts to collaboration on translations of British plays. In a letter to English singer and musician Ann Forde Thicknesse, Riccoboni would claim that, owing to Biancolelli's sweetness and even temper, the word "no" was never spoken between them (Thomas 103). *The History of Ernestine* recounts the victimization of Ernestine by an older theater-loving woman who negotiates a contract for her to be maintained in a country house by a marquis who respects her virtue but shows an utter disregard for the public appearance of the arrangement. When the narrator signs off at the end of the novella with the phrase "and I who have nothing more to say of this sweet and sensitive Ernestine, I will perhaps occupy myself with the worries and troubles of another woman," she reminds the reader of the specificity to Paris of Ernestine's trial to virtue and of the relationship of this trial with the condition of women beyond Paris (81).

In the place of mixed parentage, displacement could produce a superior sort of blended heroine in a novelistic landscape that began to mix the codes of travel writing with those of the sentimental novel. This mixture produced a means for highlighting the difference between exceptional women and local girls. In *The History of Emily Montague* (1769), Frances Brooke took advantage of her experience living in Canada to sketch gender roles among the British newly installed after the Seven Years' War, the French Quebecois, and indigenous women, whom the lively Arabella Fermor terms "my good sisters, the squaws" (Wyett 53). Before rejecting the lives led by indigenous women in North America on the grounds of the hard labor and absence of love they endure, Arabella Fermor offers primitivist approval of the peripatetic lives of indigenous North American women: "I will marry a savage, and turn squaw. . . . Never was anything so delightful as their lives; they talk of French husbands, but commend me to an Indian one, who lets his wife ramble five hundred miles, without asking where she is going" (52). The perfect senti- mental heroine Emily, Arabella's friend, stands out against the landscape of other culturally typed women as a hybrid, as her lover remarks in a letter to a friend: "With as much beauty, good sense, sensibility and softness, at least, as any women on earth, no women please so little as the English. . . . There is a lady here [in Quebec], whom I wish you to see, as the shortest way of explaining to you all I mean; she is the most pleasing woman I ever beheld, independently of her being one of the handsomest; her manner is irresistible: she has all the smiling graces of France, all the blushing delicacy and native softness of England" (118–19).

Mixed parentage and displacement could be combined. In the first novel written in German by a woman, *The History of Miss Sophia von Sternheim* (*Geschichte des Fraüleins von Sternheim*, 1771), Sophie von La Roche created an orphan heroine of mixed English and German parentage and decidedly supranational qualities. Sophia von Sternheim's trials devolve from the with- drawal or failure of paternal protection and family support but also from a specifically German cultural problem: excessive emulation by German courts of the Louis XIV and Louis XV models. A socially ambitious and financially strapped aunt and uncle plan to force their beautiful orphaned niece Sophia von Sternheim to become the prince's mistress at a francophilic German court governed by intrigue and worldly vice. To preserve her virtue, Sophia flees the court with an aristocratic Englishman who marries her, imprisons her, and rapes her. It is the corruption of the German court, minutely de- scribed and compared with the simple virtues of local peasants, its aping of "French" artifice and vice, and its disregard for solid German pietistic virtues and agrarian utopianism that allow the seducer to accomplish his plan. After Sophie escapes from the English mine where the villain has confined her, she marries the Englishman she has always loved and founds a charitable commu- nity for orphan girls in England, one that is heavily influenced by both Ger- man pietism and by Leprince de Beaumont's reinterpretation of the gentry capitalism of *Millenium Hall.*

Frances Burney's *Evelina, or the History of a Young Lady's Entrance into the World* (1778) featured the unacknowledged daughter of an English lord who undergoes a series of social-sexual mortifications while under the thumb of an outrageously improper French grandmother. She must wend her way through the unsolicited sexual attentions of a Frenchman, several English men of different social rank, and a man from Scotland who turns out to be her half-brother. Evelina's peculiarly British problem, beyond her philandering father's failure to acknowledge her and her inappropriate French family, resides in her polite inability to say no in social situations in which British distinctions in social class are muddied or illegible to her. This leads to Evelina's unrelenting shaming and embarrassment. Her trials take place in the mixed social spaces of the Vauxhalls and drawing rooms of the era. In these very British modern public spaces, the absence of a trustworthy male family member and the financial blurring of clear measures of class membership inevitably lead her to compromise herself despite her virtuous intentions. Her ultimate capacity to triumph is owed, like that of so many heroines of the late eighteenth century, to a vaguely supranational exceptionalism. Her conversational politeness and her virtue are a birthright identifiable to her future husband and a powerful noblewoman despite the external attempt to construe her meanings for her. These nostalgic and symbolic legacies of elite feminized French culture war with the caricature of French vulgarity and sexual excess embodied by Evelina's grandmother. Evelina's exceptionalism is set off at the end of the novel when the British nursemaid's daughter with whom she was switched at birth and who has been raised in France as a British nobleman's daughter is revealed to be petty, mean, and unscrupulous, while Evelina combines the French exceptionalism of her lost mother with solid British virtue and innocence.

In Charlotte Smith's *Celestina* (1791), an ostensibly orphaned girl discovered in a French convent and raised as an adoptive sister to the hero Willoughby, must wander across Britain to the sublime wilds of the Isle of Man and back before her true identity is discovered by Willoughby in a ruined castle in the Pyrenees. (*Celestina* was one of the nine novels by Smith translated into French and the only one verifiably translated by a woman, "Mme de Rome née Marnée de Morville" [1795]).[8] Celestina avoids the fates of the other British women in the novel who recount their stories to her: the gambling coquette, the unfortunate mistress, the exhausted mother of a large family with an impecunious husband, the ill-treated and overworked farmer's daughter, the affected heiress. Subject to the same public embarrassment as

Evelina, Celestina speaks perfectly accented French and Italian and is capable of writing sonnets when a landscape conjures a particular melancholy. By the end of the novel, all of Celestina's gifts tally with her hybrid parentage: she is discovered to be the offspring of a British officer who has died in the American Revolutionary War of sorrow over lost love and the deceased daughter of an abusive French count, a caricature of *ancien régime* tyranny. English with a touch of French, Celestina improves the lives of those around her through dissemination of her natural gifts.

Why all of these hybrids? Where Richardson and Rousseau kept their variables simple by confining Clarissa and Julie within Britain and the Swiss canton of Geneva, respectively, women writers made their not-Clarissas and not-Julies into figures of mixed parentage or education, with complex tastes and sometimes direct experience of places, people, things, and even social models from elsewhere. Women writers' couplings of the stories of local girls with the story of heroines staked the claim that culturally specific rites of subjection informed but did not circumscribe the exceptional woman. The women's novel invested in collective curiosity about the national or cultural form taken by rites of subjection—a morbidly anthropological comparison of practices that participated in an Enlightenment discourse on the treatment of women as an index of the greatness of nations. It cultivated affinity among readers on the basis of a demonstration that the most exceptional woman might triumph above, or at least record in writing, like the unnamed narrator of *The History of Ernestine* or Arabella Fermor in *The History of Emily Montague*, the cultural rites of womanhood. Fiction by women evaluated a prime problem in contemporary natural philosophy: how to relate the treatment of women to cultural character. By laying different gendered cultural contexts side by side in different fictions, they developed a comparative picture.

At the same time, these fictions focused on the virtuous heroine's struggle to rise above a normative fate by controlling the way that the story of her gendered trials is received. They display through epistolarity or narrative shuttling between interiority and exteriority the difference between a person's experience and cultural reception of that experience. They built supranational affinity around recognition of how the cultural rites of womanhood constrain exceptionalism. (It is perhaps no surprise, at this juncture, to learn that Bekker-Wolff translated Sophie von La Roche, Isabelle de Montolieu translated Charlotte Smith, and Charlotte Smith translated the almost archetypal story of a traveling woman whose interiority remains indecipherable, Prevost's *Manon Lescaut*.)

Heroines and Local Girls

The year of her death, Isabelle de Charrière wrote a retrospective letter explaining her return to writing fiction in the 1780s and 1790s: "Sadness and the desire to distract myself made me write the *Neuchâtel Letters*. I had just seen in *Sara Burgerhart* (a Dutch novel) that in painting places and habits with which one is very familiar, one can give fictive characters a precious reality. . . . In painting no one, one paints everyone. That must be so, and I hadn't thought of it. When one paints a herd of sheep from fantasy, but with truth, every sheep can find his own portrait in it, or at least the portrait of his neighbor" (*Œuvres* 6:558–59). Charrière's letter registers her first discovery of the literary concrete universal ("in painting no one, one paints everyone") and of the realist impulse ("painting places and habits with which one is very familiar"). The "concrete universal," as Jonathan Culler succinctly puts it, is "that special combination of particularity and generality that enables Hamlet, for instance, to be more than a merely actual person: Hamlet is embodied in particular details yet nevertheless open and general in ways that actual persons are not" (281).

It was peculiar that, as late as 1805, Charrière credited "a Dutch novel" with her return to fiction and not the vast array of French, British, and German writing with which she was intimately familiar. Yet Clarissa, Julie, and Werther, of course, were hardly the sheep next door. Despite the differences between the sprawling, uneven epistolary novel *The History of Miss Sara Burgerhart*, written in Dutch, and the laconic, polished *Neuchâtel Letters* (*Lettres neuchâteloises*, 1784), written in French, both novels did provide portraits of the herd. More specifically, they explored how Clarissa and Julie fared in the herd by asking what happened to exceptional women when they were subjected to distinctive cultural forms of gendered oppression. In *Neuchâtel Letters* (*Œuvres* 8:45–89), written after her discovery of how to paint a herd of sheep, Charrière addressed the Swiss canton's legal practice of exiling women who became pregnant out of wedlock and publicizing an infant's status as a bastard child. At the same time, Charrière built readerly identifications with a transnational heroine, using the heroine's sensibility and French education as marks of the extraordinary, while gesturing toward a universal condition of women. Both *Sara Burgerhart* and *Neuchâtel Letters* presented women's disenfranchisement as determined by specific local conditions and, simultaneously, as the basis for transnational readerly affinity among women. These novels rely on a new device: a gendered concrete universal that privileged heroines as hybrid or supranational figures by contrasting them with local girls unable to rise above a particular set of local gender tribulations. For Charrière, writing *Neuchâtel Letters* might have involved offering a corrective to the charmed existence led by the independently wealthy Sara Burgerhart who happily escapes assault with her reputation intact and lives unsupervised in Amsterdam, amusing herself as she chooses. Charrière's insistence on local detail involves emphasizing how the restricted circumstances of a woman shape the way she is treated (Pelckmans 35).

Isabelle de Charrière read the Dutch original of *The History of Miss Sara Burgerhart* from her home near the Swiss town of Neuchâtel where she lived with her Swiss husband, the former tutor to her brother.[9] Born Isabella Agneta Elisabeth van Tuyll van Serooskerken to a prominent family in the Dutch Republic, she published a novella in French when she still lived with her parents in a castle near Utrecht and was courted by a number of international suitors who knew her as Belle de Zuylen. Entitled *The Noble* (*Le noble, conte moral*, 1764), this first novella satirized the stodgy blue-blood genealogical prejudice of old noble families (*Œuvres* 8:13–34). In the story, nominally set in France but without any culturally specific detail, a clever noble heroine elopes with her lover by using the portraits of ancestors to break her fall as she leaps from the window of her family's castle. The story caused a scandal which Belle's parents sought to stifle by buying up copies of the magazine and of the separate volume in which it had appeared and, subsequently, by sending her abroad to London where she waited for things to cool down. Throughout Charrière's life, she maintained an extensive international correspondence, and she wrote political commentary on the Dutch and French Revolutions. Beginning in 1784, after reading *The History of Miss Sara Burgerhart*, she published novels and plays in French as well as in English and German translations. None of her fiction ever featured Dutch "places and habits." Nor did her writing appear in Dutch until her novella *Caliste* (*Œuvres*, vol. 8) was translated in 1942.[10]

Armed with the gendered concrete universal, Charrière proceeded in her fiction to strand a series of thoughtful, cultivated, French-speaking heroines across Western Europe, always in moderate yet highly gendered and culturally specific situations of subordination. High-stakes sexual assault and involuntary marriage scenarios had served as vehicles for dramatizing the clash between aristocratic libertinism and bourgeois cultural values in *The History of Miss Sara Burgerhart*, *The History of Sophia von Sternheim*, and *Caroline de Litchfield*. These texts emphasized the difference between a heroine's account of her own story and construal of motivations from the outside. Taking

Bekker-Wolff and Deken's cue in avoiding the Richardsonian extreme of a rape, Charrière developed moderate quotidian scenes that nonetheless displayed how the treatment of women specific to a culture might define that culture and its class relationships while also setting off the exceptionalism of a woman. Thus, in her novel set in Neuchâtel and written after 1784, the heroine Marianne de la Prise is not raped by a young foreign nobleman, the Alsacian Count Max, passing through Switzerland on the Grand Tour. She is simply forced to acknowledge economic realities; Max is destined for marriage with a wealthy women, while, as the daughter of a bon vivant from Neuchâtel who had made his career in the French army, Marianne is hardly marriageable. For all the charms she has inherited from her French mother, the cultivated heroine merely serves as one of the town's fleeting tourist attractions.

The story of *Neuchâtel Letters* unfolds from a chance encounter in the streets. Henry Meyer, an attractive German merchant's son newly arrived in Lausanne and working as a clerk, bumps into Julianne, a seamstress's apprentice who drops the dress she is carrying in a puddle. Henry vouches for her before the head seamstress. Later, he sees Julianne eyeing a gold cross in a shop window and buys it for her. The dress belongs to Marianne de la Prise; Henry recognizes the dress on her at a public concert and falls in love with her. During a dress fitting, Julianne tells Marianne that she has become pregnant by Henry. Using Count Max as a social cover for an intimate conversation at a polite social gathering, Marianne tells Henry that he is responsible for Julianne's pregnancy. Along with its rainy and icy streets, its tiny world in which most inhabitants bear one of a handful of family names, and a wealth of other social detail, Neuchâtel is distinguished for its rules governing births outside of wedlock. The status of children as illegitimate is published at their baptism, and their mothers are exiled from the town.[11] Indeed, in 1795, against Charrière's will, her beloved maid Henriette Monachon was found guilty of moral depravity and expelled by the Council of State of the Principality of Neuchâtel when she had a second illegitimate child and refused to marry the father (*Œuvres* 5:9).[12] In *Neuchâtel Letters*, Marianne will serve as a go-between in arranging for Julianne to give birth in secrecy, to give up her child so that it can be placed somewhere by Henry's uncle with eventual financial support from Henry, all so that Julianne will not be exiled from Neuchâtel and lose her job.

Remarkably, Julianne is given voice as one of the letter writers in the short epistolary novel, yet narrative sympathies follow class lines and lie more with the well-bred and well-born Marianne de la Prise than with the pregnant apprentice seamstress. The heightening sexual tension between Henry and Marianne is displaced in the story onto the bearer of Marianne's dress; when Julianne has sex with Henry, she strengthens his desire for Marianne while allowing Marianne to remain virtuous. Julianne's pregnancy magnifies the qualities that make Marianne, not Julianne, an exceptional woman. These are qualities that Henry perceives in Marianne at an assembly after their conversation:

> All the polite company of Neuchâtel was there. Mlle. de la Prise served as the hostess and the ornament of the assembly. Her countenance and behavior appeared changed to me: she is no less natural, but she is no longer so happy, I find her imposing, there is a noble assurance in her bearing, sometimes I think I see sadness in her eyes, yet she is tranquil, she is assured: her movements are more serious, like her air. It seems as though freedom from cares and vivacity had made room for a gentler and more serious feeling of her own merit and importance . . . ah! I hope that I'm not wrong. This sentiment is correct! Let her enjoy it! Let her enjoy it! Let it be her reward! She preserved a woman from horrible poverty, from vice, perhaps from death and a child from opprobrium and maybe death as well, or extended misery, and a young man, who thought himself honest, whom nothing should have as yet corrupted, she saved him from doing the same wrongs as a scoundrel. (8:85)

Pregnancy out of wedlock subordinates Julianne; it makes her victim to the local rites of gender. Yet knowledge, not sexual knowledge but knowledge of the condition of women, elevates Marianne. The letter form of the novel, in which the reader gains the same secondhand knowledge of Julianne's pregnancy that Marianne does, reproduces the internal structure of female enlightenment. Like Marianne, sympathetic readers become aware of how powerless women are seduced and of how women who have sex out of wedlock and bear illegitimate children may be treated in Lausanne. Henry's description of Marianne as less lively and more noble than before the conversation about Julianne's illegitimate child echoes the idealized description of Sara Burgerhart and of Sophia von Sternheim after their own coming to knowledge.

Marianne, like so many of Charrière's heroines, has an inconclusive fate at the end of *Neuchâtel Letters*; the story subscribes to what Germaine de

Staël described as Charrière's "annoying habit" of not coming to a resolution in a conclusion (Stewart, "Designing" 557). This may have something to do with Charrière's complex characterization of transnational female exceptionalism, according to which however superior a female character she will nonetheless be caught and rendered tragic by the way men perceive her according to their own national gender expectations and construe her meanings for her. Charrière's tragic sentimental realism entails representing the contrast between a heroine's understanding of herself and external insistence on constraining or reinterpreting her meanings for her. The most striking example of this is the French-educated Mistress Henley in Charrière's *Letters of Mistress Henley* (*Lettres de Mistress Henley*, 1784) who chooses with apparent virtue to forego the worldly glory of marriage to a rich nabob by marrying a highly rational member of the English gentry and living with him in virtuous retirement at his country estate (*Œuvres* 8:91–122). Satirizing the euphoric embrace of the country gentry model in novels of the preceding decade, including Samuel Constant's *The Sentimental Husband* (*Le mari sentimental*, 1781), Charrière creates a character whose every attempt to exhibit taste and virtue is greeted as the height of irrationalism by her husband. The novella explores minutely the contrast between a female character's (French-formed) desires and her English husband's exterior construal of her wishes and meanings. At the conclusion of the novella, a pregnant Mistress Henley communicates her inability to determine whether her strong desire to breastfeed her future infant is reasonable or whether, as her husband claims, it is a dangerous infatuation; her desire to nurse is, from Mr. Henley's point of view, the evidence proving that she is too unstable to take on the rigors of nursing. *Millenium Hall, The New Clarissa,* and *The History of Sophia von Sternheim* recuperated the landed estate by transforming it into a feminocentric site for disbursing charity and patronage. The *Letters of Mistress Henley* present the estate as the essence of rational virtue—a perfect embodiment of the imagined British national community when viewed from the perspective of the husband. Yet the estate becomes the nightmare site of psychological and physical entrapment only escapable by death when viewed from the perspective of the transnational woman.

Charrière organizes women into those who become representative of place through subordination to local oppression, those who transcend it, and culturally mixed characters, who become exquisite tragic victims superior to the fates assigned by national gender expectations. Social class contributes directly to this distribution; the sacrifice of Julianne makes possible the elevation of Marianne. Yet elevation of bourgeois women within the context of local and class distinctions is not the only factor at stake for Charrière or her contemporaries, as the multiplication of the life stories of bourgeois female friends and acquaintances in late eighteenth-century novels by women makes clear. Figures such as Bekker-Wolff and Deken's Widow Spilgoud, who is subjected via her Dutch merchant husband to the vices of the Oriental Indies or Sara Burgerhart's and Marianne de la Prise's female correspondents, whose own life stories become part of the knowledge the heroine and the reader acquire, function as the bourgeois representatives of national female identity. In contrast with all of the women who constitute a circle of friendship around the heroine and who share with her what the novels construe as a female condition, the heroine displays an extraordinary sensibility which, as April Alliston has suggested, correlates with "a hybridization of national character" (137).

The code pairing hybrid heroines with local girls conjured and reified a series of set moments in women's lives: loss of a parent, subordination to an unfeeling relative, female friendship, courtship, sexual harassment or assault, marriage, separation from female friends, pregnancy, loss of a child, motherhood. It also denoted the culturally specific form of subordination configuring these set moments in local contexts. The code replaced the medieval transnationalism and ahistoricity of the city of women with the hybrid heroine and the production of the wrongs of woman as a function of history and place. It organized the distribution of fiction into the transnational category of women's fiction in contradistinction to the categories of national literatures with their discursively affiliated qualities of national genius and heritage. *The History of Miss Sara Burgerhart* and *Neuchâtel Letters* sit at the crossroads of the division of women's fiction and national literatures, never completely a first and second national Dutch novel because they encouraged affinity with a supranational heroine. The power of the code of heroines and local girls inheres in its capacity to yoke together female exceptionalism, local women's experience, and a universal women's biography. On the one hand, it focuses attention on local conditions subordinating women. On the other, it depoliticizes these by defining the exceptional woman in terms of her transcendence of local conditions of subordination. The hybrid heroine, and the reader, leave their sister behind at home, taking with them the grace and nobility that only knowledge of fellow female suffering can bring.

Charrière's work in the late 1780s and 1790s registers both a progressive flight from French and a continuing attraction to the power of French language, French taste, and French femininity as a locus for an exceptional female literary identity. In the second half of *Letters Written from Lausanne* (*Lettres écrites de Lausanne*, 1785–87), French talents distinguish Caliste, a poor English girl sold by her mother to a Pygmalion-like libertine who has her exquisitely educated on the Continent (*Œuvres* 8:123–248). Caliste's Continental education and sexual past make her an internal exile when she returns to England—a perfect model of virtue, accomplishments, and taste save for her unfortunate past as a mistress, which renders her unmarriageable. She is possessed of all of the qualities that, could her lover bring himself to marry a fallen woman, might fix him on his estate and revitalize his lineage. Despite the antipathy between Charrière and Germaine de Staël, the tragic portrait of the tainted and exquisite Caliste served as the prototype for Staël's monumental character Corinne (Trousson). In the grand tradition of Madame de Maintenon, Caliste concludes her life by teaching and providing charity to unfortunate girls—a practice that Staël's Corinne imitates as well.

By the time that Charrière wrote *Three Women* (which would be published in German as *Drei Weiber* [1795] and then in French as *Trois femmes* in London [1796] and in Paris [1797]), Charrière had concluded from the violent and autocratic turn of the French Revolution that France had to be given up altogether and that Britain was no easy substitute. She created an exceptionally wise and charming French-speaking global traveler, perhaps also a precursor to Corinne, who goes by the adopted name of Constance de Vaucourt. Constance has no real home and, as the inheritor of an uncle, father, and husband who have amassed fortunes in the East and West Indies through exploitation, including slave ownership in Martinique, she has assigned herself the task of finding some place in the world where she can do good *incognita* with her family's ill-gotten wealth. She alights by accident in Altendorf when her carriage breaks down. There, she uses her money to create a happy society—a cross between the garden cultivated at the end of Voltaire's *Candide* (invoked throughout *Three Women* in pastiche) and Sarah Scott's *Millenium Hall*. Constance tells the young and orphaned French émigré Emilie, whom she befriends,

"We should quash our desires to establish a little France here in Germany, or to treat the people who tolerate our presence in this country as if they were the foreigners and we the ones tolerating them."

"Whatever do you mean!" exclaimed Emilie. "When I have been exiled from the most wonderful country in the world, may I not at least retain its manners and customs, which have been sanctioned by good taste?"

"No," said Madame de Vaucourt, "no, that is forbidden." (47)

Early in *Three Women,* Emilie serves as the transnational heroine, forced by the French Revolution to join the flood of aristocratic émigrés who have been "exiled from the most wonderful country in the world." Emilie's romance with the young noble Théodore in Altendorf begins to bring the elegance of France to the German countryside, with Emilie demonstrating exceptionalism chiefly in her capacity to learn flexibility by abandoning aristocratic and national prejudice. Later in *Three Women,* however, Charrière rewrites Emilie into the position of the local girl who elopes with the German noble against the wishes of his family. Like Julianne in *Neuchâtel Letters,* Emilie requires the intervention of a truly exceptional heroine, Constance de Vaucourt, to save her reputation. After the marriage of Emilie and Théodore, it is Constance's vigorous insistence on creating a happy community that results in a new avatar of the ideal landed estate in the novel—one in which the merger of utopian philanthropy with a late Enlightenment pedagogy is calculated to wreak dramatic social change without revolution. On his estate, Théodore sponsors a school for peasants with a Dutch atheist mathmetician as headmaster, while Constance insists on switching a girl and a boy baby at birth as well as on having an aristocrat's child and a servant's child raised in exactly the same way so as to observe the outcomes. Constance incarnates a new radically rootless transnational heroine. Her belonging to noplace is confirmed textually by her having no living father, husband, or lover. Her melancholia manifests as a kind of *mal-de-pays* with no actual country a place she might call home.

Exile

The personal and literary relationship between Frances Burney and Germaine de Staël illustrates the complexity of a national identity for major women writers, as well as the melancholic flight after the French Revolution from identification with French as a prodigious literary language for female affinity. Germaine de Staël had narrowly escaped French Revolutionary violence when the two met in England in 1793 and had taken up residence with a party of fellow constitutionalists in Surrey, near the home of two of Burney's friends. Through these intermediaries Burney met her future husband, Alexandre d'Arblay, as well as the twenty-eight-year-old Germaine de Staël. Known since adolescence for her striking conversation in her mother's Parisian salon, Staël had circulated some critical works, published a novella, and was working on her first major piece of criticism, *De l'influence des passions* (*On the Influence of the Passions*). At the time of their meeting, Burney enjoyed an international reputation. Her first novel, *Evelina*, had appeared in 1778 when she was Staël's age; her second novel, *Cecilia* (1782), and her third, *Camilla* (1796), were both well received. All three of Burney's early novels were quickly translated and received internationally as models of sentimental fiction. Despite the two women's affinities, Burney followed her father's cue to break off the friendship with Staël—whose extramarital relationship was as notorious in England as her politics—just as she had avoided forming a relationship with Genlis.

In 1802, the year that her first novel, *Delphine*, was published, Germaine de Staël was forced out of France for a second time, this time by Napoleon's hostility to her political influence. She took up residence along with her children in her father's Swiss home in Coppet and, unable to return to Paris until 1814, traveled throughout Europe and Russia, using Coppet as a base. The novel *Corinne* partially reproduces Staël's peregrinations skirting the borders of France and traveling into Italy. The same year that Staël went into exile, Frances Burney hurriedly crossed the Channel with her young son to join her French husband, Alexandre d'Arblay, who had renewed his pre-Revolutionary military commission to become a general under Napoleon. The family became trapped in France by both the Napoleonic blockade and the need to show loyalty until 1812, when Burney and her son were finally able to return to England. Burney had to display careful diplomacy on the voyage home, negotiating in English with a British captain who refused to transport her son because he appeared to be French. She also negotiated in French for permission to emigrate with the hefty English manuscript of her final novel, *The Wanderer*, which she had probably begun writing in 1798 (Burney, *Journals and Letters* 460–61).

In addition to their experiences wandering, two other biographical similarities contributed to the parallel concerns evinced in the authors' later fiction. First, Burney and Staël had strong relationships with their fathers, both well-known public figures, and devoted considerable energy to commemorating their fathers' lives in print and to negotiating a precarious balance between filial devotion and intellectual and personal independence.[13] Second, both writers disconnected themselves from filiation with earlier women writers. Burney presented herself as a distinct phenomenon, unlike Mary Hays who registered a relationship with a tradition. Staël payed proportionately little attention to writing by women in her criticism, unlike Genlis who repeatedly invoked it. Third, neither writer could have considered herself as having a single, clear nationality by the time she wrote her final novel. Burney, who was born and raised in England, married the French *ancien régime* count and Napoleonic general Alexandre d'Arblay. Frances Burney d'Arblay's nationality seems not to have been at issue during her stay in France but only because she was careful not to draw any attention to herself (*Journals and Letters* 484–85). Moreover, Burney's maternal grandparents were French immigrants and Roman Catholics (she had learned French from her grandmother), while her father's family was originally Scottish. This complex parentage informed her depiction of Evelina's family in her first novel. On both sides, Burney's social position was decidedly common, although her own fame and her father's carefully crafted cultural prominence as a professional musicologist had helped her secure a position as second keeper of the robes to Queen Charlotte. Germaine Necker de Staël was Swedish, according to a ruling of Napoleonic jurisprudence, since she had been united in an arranged marriage with Eric-Magnus, Baron de Staël-Holstein, the Swedish ambassador to France (Hesse 65). Staël's father was a Swiss Protestant from Geneva; her mother, Suzanne Curchod Necker, was the daughter of a pastor in Lausanne from a Provençal family. Necker's service as finance minister to the king elevated him to a position of nobility, and his wife's salon guaranteed the family impressive social and intellectual credentials. As Margaret Doody puts it, Burney and Staël were on the "cusp of national and class identities" and religious identities as well ("Missing les Muses" 84).

After Burney submitted to paternal injunction and guiltily abandoned the friendship with Staël, the two writers kept track of each other's subsequent published work and produced clearly intersecting reflections on women's exile in their final novels. In her journals and letters, Burney records anxiety about her relationship with Staël but also her impressions of Staël's works, including *On Germany, Reflections on Suicide*, and *On the Influence of the Passions upon the Happiness of Individuals and of Nations* (*Journals* 357, 468). Staël gave her father a copy of Burney's *Cecilia* to provide him with solace after he lost power in the fall of the French monarchy, and she probed the possibility of a renewed acquaintance after Burney arrived in France (*Journals and Letters* 358n7, 416–17). Burney's publisher later sent Staël an advance copy of *The Wanderer.* Retaining the heroine's Continental accent, *The Wanderer* is in some sense an English translation (by way of Charlotte Smith's *Celestina*) of *Corinne* (conceived by way of Isabelle de Charrière's *Caliste*). Long after the pre-Revolutionary and early Revolutionary promotion of international sociability had faded, and despite the material impediment of the Napoleonic blockade, the two writers' continuing engagement with each other's ideas kept to a practice of transnationalism that they mourned in their novels.

Corinne ou l'Italie, published in 1807 by Germaine de Staël, and *The Wanderer, or Female Difficulties,* published in 1814 by Frances Burney, explore the idea of the woman who has no home nation with particular attention to the contingency of women's nationality on fathers and husbands. Critical studies to date have highlighted the cultural hybridity of the heroines of these novels, while discussions of Staël have noted her central preoccupation with exile. Both novels reflect a transformation in discourse about woman's cultural identity by dismissing the French model of femininity for its decadence and redefining women's non-nationality as a melancholic exile. Both writers reworked the existing spatial codes of the novel to invent the fleeting figure of the woman exile. Katie Trumpener has written that "to explore the ways in which the romantic novel takes up and reworks the nationalist debates of the late eighteenth century is to watch a process through which ideology takes on generic flesh" (xv). To explore how Staël and Burney sound the national meanings that different forms ascribe to space is to watch an attempt to resist nineteenth-century nationalist ideology and, most particularly, the role it assigned to women.

For Staël's protagonist, Corinne, and for Burney's wanderer, Britain is the primary site of exile to which the heroine returns as a stranger in her own land. Such a displacement of the site of exile defied both recent history and the current of writing on either side of the Channel. From the beginning of the French Revolution, France loomed large as a homeland unwillingly left behind by unfortunate émigrés. Over the course of the 1790s, a hundred thousand people emigrated from France to England, with perhaps as many as twenty-five thousand fleeing at the height of the Terror (Curran 642). Among officially classified French émigrés, only 15 percent were women, although the actual numbers may have been higher (Greer 91). The French clergy emigrated to England in such large numbers that they became a particular object of charity. Burney herself wrote a plea to the women of England on behalf of "these destitute wanderers," pitching her claims in unusually non-nationalist terms. She called on women readers to recognize that "we are too apt to consider ourselves rather as a distinct race of beings, than as merely the emulous inhabitants of rival states. . . . O let us be brethren with the good, wheresoever they may arise! and let us resist the culpable, whether abroad or at home" ("Brief Reflections" 12–13).[14] After Britain declared war on France in 1793, the British were displaced as well, but it was chiefly men who traveled when they were marshaled to fight in large numbers; perhaps a fifth of the male population was involved in the war by 1803. To the classes of "displaced persons" in the 1790s can be added convicts forced to emigrate to British penal colonies in or near Australia, of whom some 20 percent were women (Curran 641–42). Napoleonic campaigns subsequently made migrants of Central European men, women, and children on both sides of the political divide, with those resisting Napolean moving away from areas of occupation and with German Jacobins being forced from unoccupied areas.

In the émigré fiction of the 1790s, the focus fell on exile from France, allowing authors to capitalize on the extraordinary material, as author Sénac de Meilhan described it in his novel *L'Émigré* (1797), offered by the Revolution and the Terror: "All presents the semblance of truth and all is *romanesque* in the revolution of France. . . . The most extraordinary encounters, the most surprising circumstances, the most deplorable situations become common events and surpass even what the authors of novels can imagine."[15] As Adriana Craciun points out, "While conservatives in the tradition of Burke used the *émigré* theme to idealize Britain as a refuge from French atheism and anarchy, the true home of liberty and justice, progressive writers used the *émigrés* to critique everything from homegrown British xenophobia, to Britain's injustices against its own subjects, to Britain's role in fomenting war and thus contributing to the Terror" (141).

Despite appearing over a decade later than the emergence of the émigré novel in 1793–94, Staël's and Burney's productions are émigré novels worth considering here for the way that they hold on to the code of heroines and local girls while melancholically abandoning identification with French as a language of female exceptionalism. The repeated spectacle in their novels of the heroines' modest withdrawal from exemplary performances in cultural spaces where men and women mix freely registers a traumatic post-Revolutionary disengagement from the celebrated *ancien régime* cultural model of gender.

Although they were written by novelists at opposite ends of the political spectrum, *Corinne* and *The Wanderer* converge in reversing the terms of emigration. In the two novels, the protagonists are not young men who have come to England fleeing France, but young women, exiled from Britain at birth, who later return *incognita*, only to suffer an exile from within. Their internal exile fits within bookends of women's literary history. Their perspective of "estrangement from one's own culture" (Gilroy 67), one that enables the progressive criticism of home outlined by Craciun, had been inaugurated in women's writing by Françoise de Graffigny's *Lettres d'une Péruvienne*, which both Burney and Staël had read and referred to in their work (Doody, "Missing les Muses" 101, 103). Their hybrid origins, exquisite skills on the harp and as poets, their fluency in English, French, and Italian all fall within the molds set by the public personality of Stéphanie de Genlis, Isabelle de Charrière's Caliste, and Charlotte Smith's Celestina. The heroines' victimization by families that have disavowed them—made manifest in a succession of scenes in which the heroine peers into interiors she would rightfully inhabit were she not an outcast—anticipates nothing so much as the exile of Frankenstein's monster and the concealment of a somehow monstrous parentage in Mary Shelley's Romantic, global, and Gothic novel of 1818 (Lynch, "[Dis]locations" 205). Staël's and Burney's emigré novels about women exiled from Britain rather than men exiled from France cycle through the novelistic forms and related spatial codes that were available between 1747 and 1818. Staël's work was received by male critics, as Madelyn Gutwirth has shown, as evidence that, like the "spider-eating" Anna Maria van Schurman, she was poorly inserted into her gender (26). With the publication of *The Wanderer*, Burney was criticized both for being a traitor to the sentimental form, which she had previously been hailed as having mastered, and for being too antiquated in her style to address the realities of a post-Revolutionary age (Justice 160–61). Yet the novelists' meditations on woman's non-nationality, which proceed through a reworking of existing novelistic spatial codes, reveal not a betrayal of form or of gender but a prescient sense that the two have become linked. Staël and Burney blend the spatial conventions of the sentimental novel, the historical novel, and the Gothic novel, choosing formal hybridity in a melancholic reaction to the nationalist implications of the gendering of form in the nineteenth century.

Pre-Revolutionary sentimental fiction juxtaposed national characters, presenting them as intriguing features of the present age. In contrast, *Corinne* and *The Wanderer* yoke the viability of national types to moments in history through chronotopes for the three possible national romantic choices available to the male protagonist. The nationality of the two heroines remains a mystery for much of each novel. Staël withholds an account of the family and national origins of her heroine until the fourteenth book of a twenty-book novel, while Burney virtuosically reveals nothing directly until the ninth book of ten. To shield innocent people, the heroines of *Corinne* and *The Wanderer* must hide their true identities. Thus, the reader, along with the other characters, especially the male lovers, can only judge the heroines on the basis of their behavior and in comparison with other female characters. Each novel sets up a nationally marked triad of women: more mature women who possess qualities associated with French femininity, adolescent incarnations of British identity or local girls, and the *incognita* heroines—Staël's Corinne and Burney's wanderer, whom the reader comes to know by her accidental alias, Ellis, and later her first name, Juliet.

The stories of the female characters who personify the French national type, Madame d'Arbigny and Elinor Joddrel, are narrated more or less retrospectively. Staël's Madame d'Arbigny mixes "calculation with passion" and displays "that art of forging the truth that is so frequently encountered in countries where the desire to produce an effect by one's sentiments is more powerful than the sentiments themselves" (*Corinne* 322). Burney's Elinor Joddrel, an Englishwoman who travels to France seduced by the Revolutionary chimera of liberty for women and humanity, is equally given to a feminine "Machiavellian policy" and serves as a vehicle for collecting a variety of stereotypes about the stridency of women in public (*Wanderer* 161). Like Madame d'Arbigny, who feigns illness, pregnancy, and Revolutionary attacks on her fortune, Elinor parades her emotions, using illness, histrionic scenes, and a public suicide attempt in an unsuccessful scheme to keep the hero of the novel in her thrall (Burney's portrayal of Elinor's overly dramatic espousal of suicide doubtless satirizes Staël's espousal of suicide in *Reflections on Suicide* and in the novel *Delphine*). These women who perform French femininity are potential love objects only in France during the early years of the French Revolution (before 1793) and during a period that precedes the time of the story. While Burney creates a milder French version of French femininity in the character of Gabrielle, the friend with whom Ellis (Juliet) has been raised in France, Gabrielle shares with Elinor and Madame d'Arbigny the central quality of having no imaginable future. In Gabrielle's case, the aristocratic despotism of her French husband and his inability to recognize that he can no longer rely on *ancien régime* privilege lock her in the past, an imprisonment conjured forcefully in the novel by Gabrielle's perpetual mourning for her young son (a noble French heir) who has died prematurely.

Commentators throughout the eighteenth century, including Germaine de Staël in *On Literature*, often pointed to the active participation of privileged women in public cultural life when they sought to explain the politeness, sociability, wit, and cultural radiance of France. Exaggerating the sentimental novel's conventions for tracing national character, both Staël and Burney obviate the eighteenth-century model of "French" femininity and locate the possibility of successful romance and positive sexual attraction to a woman with wholly French qualities in the historical and narrative past. France is something sensuous, frivolous, artificial, and addictive that, as Charrière's Constance tells Emilie, must be given up.

Staël's and Burney's heroines each have younger half-sisters who fulfill the function of local girls. These daughters of their father's second marriages to British women from aristocratic families fully incarnate British femininity and serve as potential erotic rivals for the male protagonists' affections. Staël's Lucile Edgermond in *Corinne* has been raised by her strict and retiring mother near the border with Scotland in Northumberland. When Corinne sees Lucile, she compares herself with the young girl who is utterly artless, in both senses of the word: "[Corinne] found herself so inferior, she exaggerated to herself so deeply, if it were possible to exaggerate it, the charm of this youth, this whiteness, this blonde hair, this innocent picture of the spring of life, that she felt it almost humiliating to do battle with her talent and intelligence, with gifts that she had acquired, or at least perfected, against graces provided by nature itself" (481).

Like Staël's Lucile, Burney's Lady Aurora Granville in *The Wanderer* is hemmed in by a prejudiced older female relative and incarnates innocence and inexperience: "Lady Aurora, who had just reached her sixteenth year, was now budding into life, with equal loveliness of mind and person. She was fair, but pale, with elegant features, a face perfectly oval, and soft expressive blue eyes, of which the "liquid lustre" spoke a heart that was the seat of sensibility . . . of compassionate feeling for woes which she did not suffer" (117).

Based in the discourse of British and French national contestation, the women embodying the polar erotic choices in the novels have self-evident identities with clear geographic and temporal coding. Whether *ancien régime* or Jacobin in their politics, Madame d'Arbigny and Elinor Joddrel share the French vice of manufacturing passions for public effect. The time for their space is over, as the heroes' ultimate erotic choices, the time of the story, and their own comparatively advanced ages make clear. The profoundly British and extremely young Lucile Edgermond and Aurora Granville are the daughters by a second marriage of English peers; aristocratic and English on the maternal and paternal sides, they have been raised by severe and powerful older women to operate only in private, domestic circles. While they are frequently rendered powerless by their sensibility, they exert little genuine attraction because they are without art. In *De la littérature*, Staël sketched the English social model into which she would insert Lucile in the novel *Corinne*: "The English live retired in their families or gathered in public assemblies for national discussions. The intermediary that is called society hardly exists among them; and [yet] it is in this frivolous space of life that wit and taste are nonetheless formed" (234–35). For all that the English model entails giving up "society," the perfect incarnations of British femininity, Lucile and Aurora Granville, represent a confined and artless women's future as their youth and the incomplete narration of their stories imply.

The heroines that Staël and Burney devise are possessed of an extraordinary sensibility that in sentimental novels "can be passed on by birth," as April Alliston has suggested, "as if it were a racial characteristic, but when it is so inherited, it tends to mark a hybridization of national character" (137). National hybridity allows the sentimental heroine into the 1790s like Charrière's Emilie in Westphalia or Charlotte Smith's Celestina at Willoughby's estate of Alvestone to enjoy marriage with a foreign man and to use her exceptional talents to foster an ideal community based on philanthropy and education at a remove from corrupting society. In contrast, over the course of *Corinne* and *The Wanderer*, the hybridity of the heroine veers toward abjection.

Both *Corinne* and *The Wanderer* rely on extradiegetic prehistories revolving around the fathers' erotic choices in a first marriage—choices that jeopardize the aristocratic and Protestant lineages of their families and overdetermine the heroines' fates. This was a formula for sentimental fiction that Burney had, in fact, helped to establish with her first novel, *Evelina*, almost thirty years before. The first marriage of Corinne's Scottish father, Lord Edgermond, is to an Italian Catholic woman, and Corinne is raised at first in Italy, where she acquires the talents that allow her to become a gifted improvisational performer who accompanies herself on the lyre. Nonetheless, in Staël's schema of national character, Corinne is not Italian by nature, despite the identification of the heroine with the country in the title *Corinne or Italy*, since she refuses an "Italian" feminization of men, recognizes the importance of subordinating individual talent to the larger good of civic virtue, and has a cosmopolitan appreciation of the varied cultural contributions of European nations. As an adolescent, she goes to England to live with her father and her rigid stepmother, but after her father's death she flees the restrictive gender role imposed on her in Northumberland and returns to Italy, promising her stepmother to pass for dead and not to reveal her family name so as not to dishonor her younger half-sister, Lucile. When she performs, she is described not as acting but as communicating something that emanates from her natural sensibility. Lord Oswald Nelvil, Corinne's lover, describes her to her rigid British stepmother as having "those talents that come from the soul, and cannot exist without the most elevated character, without the most feeling heart, those talents that are tied to the most touching goodness to the most generous heart" (458). Corinne follows Lord Nelvil back to England in disguise so as not to violate her vow to her stepmother, where she finds that his guilt over his father's death has drawn him to Lucile, his father's choice for him.

In the extradiegetic prehistory of *The Wanderer*, Ellis/Juliet's father, Lord Granville, marries a commoner and hides this from his father by sending his young family to France, where his daughter is placed in a French convent and benefits from the guardianship of an aristocratic French bishop and his sister. In France, Ellis/Juliet acquires the talents that are surprised out of her once she returns, *incognita*, to England. She plays the harp and sings beautifully, and like Corinne too, she draws. Ellis/Juliet's remarkable performances, like Corinne's, are represented as deriving from nature. When she spontaneously fills leading roles in some private theatricals, for example, the spectators speculate about the source of her exceptional performance: "Whether this excellence were the result of practice and instruction, or a sudden emanation of general genius, accidentally directed to a particular point, was disputed by the critics among the audience. . . . This, however, was nature, which would not be repressed; not art, that strove to be displayed" (95).

The heroines' performances emanate naturally; Corinne and Ellis/Juliet produce art without being artful. For Burney, the natural performance marks anxiety about the impropriety of a woman's appearance in public (Salih 48). For Staël, it registers modest feminine subscription to the cult of sensibility. For both writers, it reconciles femininity with genius. Female genius derives from the heroines' cultural hybridity, evident in their capacity to speak both English and French perfectly. Corinne's French is accented with English in a reminder of her British origin and as an indication of how her incarnation of the female artist is distinct from the French artfulness of a Madame d'Arbigny, while her delivery of Italian is entirely unaccented (Batsaki 35). Ellis/Juliet's English is accented with French as a reminder of her childhood exile from her homeland, of her distinctive taste and talent, and as an indication that she cannot be fully assimilated to English society as an adult. The hybrid heroines straddle cultures in a way that should represent an ideal.

Yet when they cross into England, they return home to a place where they are not acknowledged as rightful daughters and heirs. For their border crossings into England, Corinne and Ellis/Juliet each adopt costumes of mourning for a self that fails to fit acceptable categories, choosing not to disappear into the crowd with their disguises but to stand out as culturally exotic, wounded apparitions. Their blackness and evident suffering contrast with the appearances of their local girl half-sisters: Lucile's "whiteness" or "fairness" (*blancheur*) and Lady Aurora Granville's "fair" and "pale" complexion, as well as her "feeling for woes which she did not suffer." Aware of her own "black hair, her complexion somewhat darkened by the sun of Italy and her pronounced features," and languishing with an unnamed illness, Corinne decides to wear a "black dress in the Venetian style" and covers "her face and her waist with the mantua worn in that country" (488). For her Channel crossing, Ellis/Juliet deliberately paints her "hands and arms of so dark a colour, that they might rather be styled black than brown." She gives her "muffled up face" an "equally dusky hue," while "a large black patch" covers half of her left cheek and a "broad black ribbon" binds a "bandage of cloth over the right side of her forehead" (20). Sara Salih has read Ellis/Juliet's disguise as indicative of how in *The Wanderer*, "Burney problematically and opportunistically equates slavery with the oppression of white middle-class women" (50). This is an apt observation, equally applicable to Staël's fiction, particularly her exoticist stories "Pauline" and "Zulma." The choice made by both heroines to don blackness, the blackness of southern Catholicism and the blackness of the slave, on their return to the land from which they have been exiled also points to acknowledgment of their own abjection—an inability to belong to a homeland.

Reading *Corinne* and *The Wanderer* first as sentimental novels— examining how they map gender roles onto national space by relying on conventional eighteenth-century sentimental codes—brings the two novels' attempts at cosmopolitanism into focus. In *The Literary Channel: The International Invention of the Novel*, Margaret Cohen has argued that the sentimental novel "served as a privileged site for the exchange of literary codes and observations concerning national character and difference, along with reflection on the process of exchange and translation itself" ("Sentimental Communities" 107). Both *Corinne* and *The Wanderer* certainly fill this brief, but they do so through negation. They construct French space as a no-longer-viable option. They make British space exilic. And they turn the "process of exchange and translation itself," of crossing the Channel, into an experience of hybrid abjection. In a sense, then, these are antisentimental novels in that they mourn the end of the age of the hybrid heroine. The use of chronotopes to distribute national models of femininity along a timeline involves the over-lay of a new "historical" strategy onto an older "sentimental" strategy.

When *Corinne* and *The Wanderer* are examined in relation to the spatial coordinates of the historical novel, their ambivalence toward a national model of femininity becomes readily apparent. In *Atlas of the European Novel,* Franco Moretti suggests that external borders between states offer sites of adventure. They "easily generate narrative—but in an elementary way: they take two opposite fields, and make them collide." In contrast, internal borders "work differently, and focus on a theme which is far less flamboyant than adventure, but much more disturbing: *treason*" (37). The "veritable phenomenology of the border" offered by adventurous collision and treason arose in the era of Napoleon, when, Perry Anderson has written, "The sense of national community, systematically orchestrated by the State . . . may well have been a greater reality . . . than at any time in the previous century."[16] Read according to this schema, *Corinne* and *The Wanderer* offer narratives of external borders in their double layers of prehistory. The fathers' decisions to marry outside of the Protestant British nobility and then to hide their daughters abroad generates conflict and action, just as do Lord Nelvil's and Elinor Joddrel's prolonged stays in France and their attraction to the ways of French women. In contrast, the experience of the daughters-heroines in England occurs chiefly in outlying areas along internal borders. Corinne wanders along a northern border region between Northumberland and Scotland, while Ellis/Juliet wanders along a southern triangle of coastline and an interior of forests, cathedrals, and ruins between Brighton, Salisbury, and Torquay. Wandering along internal borders corresponds to the heroines' treason against the British gender model of retiring domesticity that their half-sisters embody. In the fateful letter that becomes a postmortem paternal injunction to Lord Oswald Nelvil not to marry the woman he loves, Nelvil's father asks his friend Lord Edgermond to marry Lucile Edgermond to his son. Corinne (Lucile's older half-sister) is the wrong match because, as the one father explains to the other, "Our life in the countryside, our domestic habits would, of necessity, thwart all her tastes. A man born in our happy country must be English before everything else. He must fulfill his duties as a citizen since he has the happiness to be one. And in the countries where political institutions give men honorable opportunities to act and to prove themselves, women must remain in the shadow. How can you expect someone as distinguished as your daughter to content herself with such a fate?" (*Corinne* 467).

By presenting two heroines whose treasonous behavior consists in being too talented to remain in the shadows, Staël and Burney reluctantly concede that an emerging model of male national citizenship traced in the father's letter requires women to efface themselves in domestic space. Staël and Burney offer a phenomenology of the border, registering the death of the appreciation for and discrimination among different cultural gender models that had been the hallmark of sentimental novels like Graffigny's *Lettres d'une Péruvienne*. Their historical novels argue that the nation is founded on the sacrifice of the heroine's hybridity.

Sentimental novels, historical novels—*Corinne* and *The Wanderer* also deploy the spatial codes of the Gothic novel, a form, as Jerrold Hogle writes, that "rehearses the death of an old order" and expresses anxiety "on the birth of a new order" (2). In exile, the heroines are drawn into "gothic machinery" (Doody, "Burney and Politics")—the tomb of the father, a drawn carriage, a roadside ditch, and the castle of the father in *Corinne;* a seaside grave, a tomb, Salisbury Cathedral, Stonehenge, and the bloody attic of a poacher's cottage in *The Wanderer;* and, in both, the storm-tossed Channel. Yet these spaces are nothing compared to the representative Gothic and British spaces of the novels, the domestic interior ruled by ill, prejudiced, and sadistic older women. These older women, or "furies," as they are called in *The Wanderer*, torture the heroines because they cannot submit to the living death of the tea room that their local girl half-sisters inhabit. The Gothic *Corinne* and *The Wanderer* paradoxically express both a longing for the return of *ancien régime* authority through the characters' absorption in seeking to fulfill the wishes of the dead fathers and a longing for a new order of Protestant and bourgeois civic virtue and national identity through their privileging of the complementary gender roles enforced by the "furies" that should underwrite this order. The impossibility of embracing either the old or the new order is registered by the way that the heroines always exceed the space of the tea room, bursting out to become exiles once again.

The Gothic *Corinne* and *The Wanderer* indict the fathers for not having displayed the courage to challenge the old order and to honor openly their attraction to other cultures and other social classes. Because the fathers consign romantic choices of foreign women to the level of covert and transitory personal liaisons rather than elevating them to substantive, visible social ties, Corinne must pass for dead in England and Ellis/Juliet must pass for never having been born. In other words, the hybrid, neither-nor status of both heroines is a function of their fathers' inability to legitimate the positive value of alterity or to argue for the recognition of alterity as a civil responsibility incumbent on the individual living in the world. Because of the fathers' failure to sanction the potential of their own cross-class and cross-cultural relationships, the hybridity of the heroines amounts to a condition of non-nationality. Their non-nationality registers as a repressed cosmopolitanism, evident in their extraordinary social talents, and as an expressed abjection in exile. Harriet Guest explains that in Gothic novels revelation of the secret of the past liberates the heroine from her martyrdom and allows her to be redeemed as an exemplary figure of chaste British femininity (Guest, "Wanton Muse" 128). As such, *Corinne* and *The Wanderer* are Gothic novels but in reverse, for the secret of the heroines' births—the very cultural hybridity that has yielded their excellence—has made them monstrously unfit to inhabit the space of perfected British femininity. The Gothic culmination of each novel, the revelation of the heroine's secret hybrid national identity, expresses longing for the hybrid identity of the eighteenth-century heroine and surrender to the narrow national gender models ushered in by the Napoleonic era.[17]

The impoverished reaction of Staël and Burney to the triumph of the national model is to displace exile onto Britain. They make the country that was discursively privileged in Enlightenment thought for its model of civic virtue and political liberty into the only available space for a woman of virtue. In doing so, the place the seal on the transfer of female literary affinity away from French and France and to English and England. Yet Britain is also a space where exceptional women are condemned to wander or to sacrifice their hybridity since they cannot pretend to citizenship. The two authors retreat into a melancholic mourning for the international community of sentiment supported by the sentimental novel before 1789 rather than proposing a gendered cosmopolitanism or a fully politicized stance of exile for a new age. On the one hand, the reversal of sentimental, historical, and Gothic spatial codes in *Corinne* and *The Wanderer*, as well as the novels' formal hybridity, betray what Paul Gilroy, in a discussion of the limits of contemporary planetary thinking, has called "a failure of political imagination" (5). On the other hand, the transformation of spatial codes involves resistance to the gendering of form in the nineteenth-century novel.

Franco Moretti argues in *Atlas of the European Novel* that different novelistic forms effectively construct the space of the nation in the nineteenth century: "Think of Austen's world: everything within a circle centering on London (a day, a day-and-a-half away). Well, historical novels show the opposite pattern: a weak centripetal pull, with the story running immediately away from the national capital. . . . And that [Walter] Scott's world should end exactly where Austen's begins . . . such a perfect fit, of course, is only a (beautiful) coincidence. But behind the coincidence lies a solid reality: namely, that different forms inhabit different spaces" (34). And, as Moretti indirectly acknowledges through his choice of authors, in the nineteenth century different genders inhabit different forms in different spaces. While the sentimental novel was not a purely female or male form in the eighteenth century, it would, as Margaret Cohen has argued in *The Sentimental Education of the Novel*, become lastingly associated with women writers and readers in the nineteenth. A truly nineteenth-century genre, the historical novel would increasingly be written and peopled by men. Moretti confirms this in the list of novels he chooses to illustrate his argument. Published at the cusp of the transition from sentimental to historical to romantic fiction and at the tail end of a period in which women and men wrote sentimental historical fiction about French Revolutionary émigrés, *Corinne* and *The Wanderer* anticipate and resist the gendering and nationalization of form in fiction. Staël and Burney reworked the spatial codes of available novelistic forms to claim the melancholic transnational space of exile—not for all women but for exceptional women like themselves. When *Corinne, or Italy* and *The Wanderer, or Female Difficulties* hover over the "or" in their titles, when a single form cannot describe the heroine's experience and a single space cannot encompass her, when home is equivalent to exile, this reflects an intuition of gendered deterritorialization. Gilles Deleuze and Félix Guattari remind us that a minor literature is "that which a minority constructs within a major language" and that it is generated by "the impossibility of not writing because national consciousness, uncertain or oppressed, necessarily exists by means of literature."[18] The six hundred pages of *Corinne* and the nine hundred pages of *The Wanderer*, urgent with the impossibility of not writing, do not constitute a minor literature exactly in the sense offered by Deleuze and Guattari. The novels negate existing forms for imagining national identity. And they do not secure consciousness of the oppression of women through a single "major language." Rather, they transform the fashionable practice of learning modern languages into a vehicle for imagining a powerful female voice speaking lyrically and being heard in a foreign language. For women writers and readers, the novel could offer a melancholic site for affinity beyond the nation state by demonstrating the discomforts of home for women as a class.

Within a nation as narration form of criticism, the "or" in *Corinne, or Italy* seems to mean that the heroine holding the lyre incarnates a subordinated national culture. M. Ione Crummy makes a strong case that Germaine de Staël derived her travelogue approach to representing woman as national "bard" and metaphor for a subordinated nation from Sydney Owenson's *The Wild Irish Girl* (1806). Owenson's heroine Glorvina takes to her harp to sing the wealth of Irish culture (Crummy 95–110). The replicability of *Corinne*, what Deirdre Lynch calls "the bardic" as "currency of transcultural exchange" ("[Dis]locations" 202) involves an equation of the status of the woman bard with that of a peripheral, subordinated, or colonized culture—a nation in the making. In each novel, however, the tenor and the vehicle of the metaphor are interchangeable; Italy and Ireland are also figures for Corinne and for Glorvina. The conversible quality of the equation between woman writer and subordinated nation, between colonized nation and woman bard, captures the peripheral *and* overlapping placement of "women's writing" with respect to privileged national literary fields and national aesthetics.

Eighteenth-century novels developed a magnificent apparatus for imagining national space. Women writers built that apparatus alongside men. Yet women's novels incorporated the alternate architecture of heroines and local girls. Since this novelistic architecture demonstrated that women's behavior varied according to assigned cultural roles, these novels' national and geographic stereotypes about women could be pressed into service to prove that women were educable. Culture and education, not nature, made women weak, ignorant, verbose, manipulative, passionate, and vain or, on the other hand, virtuous. The comparison of gender roles in different cultures combined with the insistent figure of a displaced heroine with a foreign accent allowed imaginative engagement, anchored to the novel, with an idealized virtuous womanhood belonging to a non-national elsewhere. Novelistic description of the wrongs endured by women in local spaces supported an idea of woman, not as a national type, but as she could be.

One can see Frances Burney d'Arblay, still living in France, reaching for a fuller vision of post-Revolutionary cosmopolitanism, based in the sentimental convention of an international marriage, in a letter sent to her father in

1810. Hoping for an end to the war after Napoleon's marriage to the Archduchess of Austria and an end to enforced separation from her English family and friends, she wrote:

> Could you but send me a little food for the Hope now in private circulation that the new alliance of the Emperor may perhaps extend to a general alliance of all Europe—ah Heaven! How would that brighten my faculties of enjoyment! I should run about to see all I have hitherto omitted to seek with the ardent curiosity of a traveler newly arrived and I should hasten to re-view and consider all I have already beheld with an alertness of vivacity that would draw information from every object I have as yet looked at with undiscerning tameness.—Oh such a gleam of light would new-model—or re-model me, and I should make you present to all my sights, and partake of all the wonders that surround me. (*Journals and Letters* 430)

The idea that "a general alliance of all Europe" would allow her to "re-view" her world as a "newly arrived" traveler appears in the letter as an improbable dream of cosmopolitanism, penned from France in British exile.

Faith Beasley writes that "in the seventeenth century, Frenchness was associated in part with the particular freedom accorded women in the social and cultural arenas. It is indeed this quality of Frenchness, or association with it . . . that later led to the process of re-memorization of France's *Grand Siècle*" (13). Renewing Molière's attack on *préciosité,* writers such as Rousseau in the eighteenth century condemned the artifice and publicity of French women—connecting these with a French social disease. They hacked inroads into the imagined space of female literary affinity that French represented for women writers through its association with the illustrious network surrounding Scudéry and Sévigné, as well as with the pedagogical community of practice emanating from Leprince de Beaumont and Genlis. The Terror completed the job by providing commentators with a field for yoking to mass violence tropes of disparate social classes who were all female and French: decadent *aristocrates,* voluble market women marching in public with severed heads displayed on pikes, and strident writers deluded into violence in their advocacy for liberty. Charrière's Émilie and Constance, Staël's Corinne, and Burney's Ellis all melancholically acknowledged that French and France had to be abandoned. "O France," wrote Charrière late in life, "O tired and exhausted land, can you not be left in peace! Perhaps after four or five centuries, with a rejuvenated spirit and a new language, something satisfying and agreeable may be reborn in you" (*Œuvres* 9:504). Yet, as Charlotte Lennox's Arabella already knew by 1752, solitary musing about virtue in internal exile within the manor house of a British landed estate was poor fare compared with the French literary chimera of a feminized community of interlocutors who served, in the lost Scudérian world, as the cultural legislators of virtue.

Chapter 6

Heroines in the World

The 1766 marriage contract letter written in French by Scottish writer James Boswell, 9th laird of Auchinleck, to the Dutch father of Belle de Zuylen provides a glimpse of how marriage could cut a woman off from country, language, beliefs, and literature: "I should marry her, no doubt, by the forms of the church. But that would not be enough for me. I should require a clear and express agreement," Boswell began. Perhaps with the controversy surrounding Belle de Zuylen's short story "The Noble" in mind, he continued: "I should require an oath, taken in your presence, Sir, and before two of her brothers, that she would always remain faithful, that she would never design to see, or have any exchange of letters with, any one of whom her husband and her brothers disapproved; and that without their approbation she would neither publish nor cause to be acted any of her literary compositions; and in conclusion she must promise never to speak against the established religion or customs of the country she might find herself in" (Boswell, *Holland* 346). "I don't know your Scotland," Belle de Zuylen had written to Boswell, "on the map it seems to be somewhat away from the world. You call it a *sober country*, I have seen fairly despotic husbands come from there and modest good wives who blushed and looked at their husbands before opening their mouths" (397). In another letter, she closed off the possibility of marriage, noting, "I have no talent for subordination."[1]

Following her marriage to the Swiss Charles-Emmanuel de Charrière de Penthaz in 1771, Belle de Zuylen became Madame de Charrière and lived at her husband's home at Le Pontet in Colombier near Neuchâtel for thirty-four years—with an eighteen-month visit to Paris in 1785–86—until she died in 1805. She wrote pointed critiques of all of the countries where she had been. Was Belle de Zuylen/Isabelle de Charrière Dutch, like her father and brothers, or, like her husband, a member of the principality of Neuchâtel and therefore, in a sense, German, since Neuchâtel was under the protection of Frederick I of Prussia? Legally, she shared the civil status of her husband Charrière. Should we trust her voice in her personal letters where she wrote as a young woman before her marriage, "I would like the whole world to be my country"? (*There Are No Letters* 395). In a 1788 essay written in the voice of an Amsterdam merchant and thus nominally suggesting a Dutch identity, Charrière exclaimed that France had become "a second country for most of us, a country chosen out of personal taste and elegance" (*Œuvres* 10:79). Would we now call Charrière French or Francophone because French was her first language of publication in the 1780s, as well as her preferred language of composition throughout her life?[2] Did Charrière become German by choice in the 1790s when she responded to the Terror and European conflict with a painful reaction against her former Francophilia and began to experiment with publishing her work in German?

Charrière represents an exceptional case of transnationalism among eighteenth-century women writers for her careful oversight and orchestration of publication in three different languages, none of which was the language of her country of birth, and for her active mentorship of women in three languages. Yet sifting through different cultural gender models, as she did in her fictions and in her collaborations, was a generalized practice derived, in part, from elite women writers' habitus. Many women writers like Belle de Zuylen/Charrière lived for considerable periods outside of the countries in which they were born, a decade or more in some cases.

Displacement was due, for some, to professional or political reasons mixed with personal ones. Gathering political intelligence sent Behn and Aulnoy abroad at the beginning of the eighteenth century. Teaching put Leprince de Beaumont and La Fite into circulation in the middle of the century. Acting and training in elocution drew Elizabeth Inchbald for several months to France. As a rich feminist scholarship on women's travelogues has shown, narratives composed on the road offered a means of supplementing income or of enhancing intellectual viability at home while sometimes enabling a reimagining of self through contact with a new locale and culture.[3] Mary Wortley Montagu's *Turkish Embassy Letters*, published posthumously, set something of a template for subsequent women writers with their account of culturally representative relations among the sexes to which only a woman might bear witness. After her husband's death, Sophie von La Roche turned to travel writing about Switzerland, Holland, France, and England to make ends meet in 1787–88. Wollstonecraft penned *Letters Written During a Short Residence in Sweden, Norway and Denmark* (1796). Germaine de Staël's extended exile from Napoleonic France yielded *Of Germany* (*De l'Allemagne,* 1813). And so on.

Relationships with parents, lovers, or husbands catalyzed women's movement. Françoise de Graffigny's disastrous marriage to a man who beat her and dissipated their fortune led to a rare court decision in favor of legal separation. This made her chronically dependent on patronage and hospitality, early on at the Court of Lunéville and later, famously, in the home of Voltaire and Émilie du Châtelet at the Château de Cirey before she finally established herself in Paris (*Lettres d'une Péruvienne* x). Marie-Joséphine de Lescun de Monbart left France to elope to Prussia with her first husband. From there she participated in the international conversation on the education of girls with her rebuttal to Rousseau in *Sophie, ou de l'éducation* (1771). In her *Lettres tahitiennes* (1784), Monbart engaged with Françoise de Graffigny's meditation in *Lettres d'une Péruvienne* on being torn from one's own culture.[4] Julianne Vietinghof von Krüdener, born in Riga, then part of the Russian Empire, circulated throughout Europe with her Russian aristocratic parents in 1776 and, after her marriage to a Russian ambassador, drew from successive travels to write the epistolary novel cum travelogue, *Valérie* (1803) (Herman).[5] She then leveraged the novel into fashion in Parisian and German literary circles, manufacturing a marketing phenomenon for blue shawls and tea cups "à la Valérie" and encouraging readers to associate her own biography with the depiction of her heroine's inspiration of a chaste and impossible love (Hilger).

The colonial peregrinations of male family members stimulated interest in or contributed knowledge of the foreign. As a young girl, Françoise d'Aubigné, future Madame de Maintenon, traveled to Martinique; newly released from prison, her father mistakenly believed that he had been appointed colonial governor. He abandoned his family there after only a few months. On their return to France two years later in 1647, Françoise was forced by her mother to beg in the streets (Conley 2). An enduring stoicism is doubtless the primary mark left in her work by her travels. Charlotte Ramsay Lennox probably spent a portion of her childhood in a fort in Albany, New York, where her father was a junior officer; the idea of the passage to North America, military life, and kidnapping by Native Americans contributed to two of her novels (Facer).[6] Frances Brooke brought her son and sister to live with her in Quebec for several years, where she joined her husband, a British

Army chaplain, and gathered details for *The History of Emily Montague* (1764) (Garwood). Letters written to Sophie von La Roche by her son Fritz and his wife, Elsina, who lived in the United States between 1792 and 1797, inspired her long utopian idyll, *Phenomena at Lake Oneida* (*Erscheinungen am See Oneida*, 1798) about a French émigré couple living in edenic tranquility with the Oneida in the wilds of New York (Dietrich 16–29).

At the end of the century, political stances in revolutionary politics displaced writers. Mary Wollstonecraft left for Paris in December 1792, attracted by the revolutionary promise of rights, and lived there and in Le Havre until April 1795. She passed for an American citizen (when her American lover Gilbert Imlay falsely vouched before the American Embassy in Paris that the two were married so as to protect her from anti-British reprisals), gave birth to her first daughter, and wrote two treatises on the French Revolution (Furniss 67). Helen Maria Williams documented her travels through France in published letters that fed British curiosity about the Revolution; in Paris she was arrested by the Committee on Public Safety as a foreigner. She also harbored the personal papers of Stéphanie de Genlis, who was forced to flee the city in 1793 because of her connections to the royal family and her moderate Girondin politics (Kennedy 212). Genlis's husband, the marquis de Sillery (from whom she had been separated for over a decade), was guillotined that same year. After actively supporting the Patriot position in the revolt against the ruling House of Orange in 1787, Elisabeth Bekker-Wolff and Agatha Deken lived together for nine years in the French town of Trévoux. Bekker-Wolff's composition of the innocuous sounding *Walks in Burgundy* (*Wandelingen in Bourgogne*, 1789) belies the fact that she continued her Patriot writing. She probably translated into Dutch a tract on the abolition of the slave trade, and she demonstrated sufficient support of the French Revolution to receive a financial subvention and to survive charges brought against her before the Committee on Public Safety for hoarding a scarce commodity—sugar. When Bekker-Wolff visited Paris in 1789, she may well have met Williams and Genlis and certainly knew people in their Girondin circle (Everard 147–67).[7]

In earlier chapters, I have argued that conversational sociability and conversancy with modern European languages were features of the educated eighteenth-century woman's habitus that contributed to women writers' position in the literary field. A third feature of this habitus was extended displacement from place or country of birth. Displacement further stripped away clear lines of national political affiliation, since the nationality or civil status of a woman was generally contingent on that of her male family members. Widowhood represented a partial exception, although in actuality the widowed Bekker-Wolff was forced to rely on men of variable dependability to negotiate questions about property, publication, and civil status (Everard). The contingency of status on father, brother, or husband and the difficulty of controlling intellectual property complicated national belonging. Displacement produced a practical opportunity to observe more than one culture and learn more than one language. From their full habitus, which included displacement, women writers secured an idea of shared female exceptionalism across borders through the reproduceable code of heroines and local girls. By examining texts that sought to build an ethic of hospitality across borders through fiction written in response to the global violence and displacement of people produced by the Terror and the Revolutionary Wars, this chapter examines the promise and cost of this code.

Heroic Transport on a Global Stage

Family, politics, profession, and Pacific travel intertwined in the work of novelist, translator, and later newspaper editor Therese Heine Forster Huber. The travels of her first husband Georg Forster as a young naturalist on Captain James Cook's voyages to Australia and New Zealand provided fodder for her earliest novella. Georg Forster's dire experience representing German Jacobins in Paris also informed *The Seldorf Family* (*Die Familie Seldorf,* 1795–96), the novel for which Huber is best known.[8] Her pro-Revolutionary stance forced her to move her family from Mainz, after it came under control of allied forces, and to become a refugee in Neuchâtel along with her lover (and soon to be second husband) L. F. Huber.

While working on translations, Huber developed *Adventures on a Journey to New Holland* (*Abenthuer auf einer Reise nach Neu-Holland*), the story of a woman sent to Norfolk Island, the British penal colony located between Australia, New Caledonia, and New Zealand.[9] The novella was published in the women's journal *Flora* in December 1793. Written well before Staël's *Corinne* and Burney's *The Wanderer,* Therese Huber's *Adventures on a Journey to New Holland* places three exiles in parallel: the narrator Rudolph, a German Jacobin fleeing Revolutionary Paris after the failure of his dreams; Henry Bolton, the Welsh leader of a failed mining strike; and, most important,

Frances Belton, a heroine with an unknown identity discovered by the narrator Rudolph aboard a convict ship. "Enveloped in a deep hood," as well as a shawl (25), Frances Belton first appears in the narrative as a condemned thief acquitted of murder who, along with her small daughter, is confined in the prostitutes' quarters below deck. In that underworld, the fascinating Frances Belton delivers the baby of a terrified young prostitute who dies in childbirth. She brings the baby to the narrator, Rudolph, saying, "There, Sir, my dear Sir, you must make this unfortunate creature a present of one of your shirts or sheets or what you will. I have nothing, absolutely nothing but this apron that I am wearing" (32). Frances Belton's quality is made manifest when she addresses the suffering of another human being and overcomes her sense of the barrier between herself and the other woman to provide care. She delivers the baby and, ultimately, becomes a mother to the orphan. On seeing Frances holding the prostitute's baby, the narrator Rudolph interprets the vision in relation to his own experience working on behalf of the French Republic and then fleeing its descent into violence: "[I] had thought to put my virtue to best use amongst those who sought by their actions to obtain the greatest good for a nation and to teach it to mount the highest step that man can reach below God. But I found the workshop of Freedom built in the very abyss of Vice. Exhausted by the frightful illusions with which Fate had ensnared me, I took refuge with the last dregs of mankind, with people in whom judges and laws had blotted out the image of the Deity. And it is here that I find—a living creature!" (33).

Within the moral universe of the *Adventures,* Frances qualifies as a heroine, particularly in comparison with the prostitute whose baby she delivers. Not only does Frances deliver the baby aboard a convict ship and subsequently adopt it; the embedded story of her past discloses many wrongs sustained and many instances of moral virtue. Her parents, Mr. and Mrs. Watson, abandon her as a child. For organizing a miners' strike, her husband is shipped to a penal colony where he is reputed to have died. While working as a housemaid to support her daughter, Frances kills the steward who tries to rape her and is acquitted of murder only to find that she has been framed by the steward for the theft of household silver. And this is only part of a plot that ends with Frances recovering her husband and discovering that he works on an idyllic farm on Norfolk Island run by two reformed convicts who turn out to be her lost parents. (In a just-deserts ending, the hardhearted mother who had abandoned Frances to lead a life of pleasure dies shortly after the family is reunited when she is bitten by a rabid dog.)

Melodrama notwithstanding, as a whole, the narrative focuses on people—Rudolph, Henry Belton, Frances Belton, her parents, her daughter, and the prostitute's orphaned baby—who have been divested of civil status and abused by law. Frances becomes the center of moral regeneration on Norfolk Island. Her sense that she has become "a true citizen of the world" (90) liberates her to show her hybridity by singing and speaking in the Scottish accent that her rigid English aunt had forced her to hide. To those around her, the adopted infant Clara "looks as if she felt that Love and Humanity are the only bonds that join her to society" (98). As Rudolph registers in his exclamation at her birth, "And it is here that I find—a living creature!" all that matters morally is immediate human existence and human need. Frances Belton recognizes this and provides care in spaces (the hold of a convict ship and Norfolk Island) abandoned by law and God.

Moments in fiction when female protagonists provide care may quickly register as the manifestation of a gender imperative in a private domain of intimacy, precisely because the person offering care is female. Yet when Huber sets Frances Belton's delivery and adoption of the prostitute's baby on the high seas of traumatic revolutionary history, she points to the public and cosmopolitan character of the act of providing care and refuge. The stakes of Huber's setting come into focus if it is contextualized within the debates in which Huber took part when she was writing the *Adventures*.

L. F. Huber was the primary translator of Immanuel Kant's essays into French and transmitter of these to a French public. Carla Hesse has shown in a remarkable reading of *Three Women* that Charrière developed the novel in specific response to Kant's essay "On the Old Saw: *That May Be Right in Theory but It Won't Work in Practice*" (1793), which L. F. Huber translated and which was published in Paris in 1795. Hesse is primarily concerned with the way that Charrière parries Kantian provisions for "a moral compact of universal law or general precept" by holding "on to the separate and contingent relation of women to both moral and judicial law" (128). As an active translator and intellectual engaged directly with her husband's and Charrière's projects, Therese Huber doubtless also read and discussed Kant's "Theory and Practice." Therese Huber's representation of Frances Belton's virtue, on the one hand, gives an affirmative answer to the old question—posed by Pierre Le Moyne in his seventeenth-century catalog—of "whether heroic transport is necessary to perfection of the chastity of women?" (334). On the other, it counters the Kantian claim that only the civil state secured by law and developed from sound theory offers the individual the field for realizing his destiny, whether as a person or as a member of the human race. Law has failed all of the characters in the *Adventures,* whether in England, where Frances and her husband have been wrongfully convicted, or in France, where Rudolph had sought to put Kantian principles into action and from which he has fled as a refugee, or even in Hamburg, where the unscrupulous Mr. and Mrs. Watson had begun to behave virtuously only to be pushed back into criminality by an excessive stringency of the law. For Therese Huber, addressing fundamental need through hospitality, which Frances Belton is uniquely equipped to do, is both the primary principle for action and the basis for forming a moral society outside of law. Frances Belton's cold mother, indeed, illustrates the maxim and vindicates herself when she throws herself in front of the rabid dog at the end of the *Adventures* in order to save the lives of Frances's legitimate and adopted daughters. The welcome provided by Frances's dying father to Rudolph and Henry Belton, both refugees from European laws, at the cottage on Norfolk Island consecrates it.

Kant's idea of a cosmopolitan right to hospitality was already embryonic in "On the Old Saw" and took on more form in "Perpetual Peace," which many German, French, and English intellectuals read and discussed after 1795, and in *Idea of a Universal History with a Cosmopolitan Purpose.* As Garrett Wallace Brown neatly summarizes it, Kant's cosmopolitanism insists that "first, individuals represent the unit of ultimate moral concern equally and that our human capacities can only be fully developed within a condition of universal justice. Second, the attainment of universal justice requires the broader cultivation of a cosmopolitan civil society, one based solely on our humanity alone, without reference to nationality, localized political affiliation or place of birth. Third, the sole concern of cosmopolitan law is with establishing this matrix of universal justice and with formulating the necessary fundamental normative principles that underwrite a cosmopolitan constitution" (46).

For Kant, hospitality must be extended to any human being regardless of origin since we are all equal sharers in the planet and are part of a larger human community. Kant's further position was that humans have the obligation to understand each others' ways of thinking; fulfilling that obligation aligns with being a "citizen of the world" (M. Nussbaum 33). Yet the guarantor of human beings' capacity to arrive at their fullest potential, including the adoption of universal justice, is not recognition, perception, or experience but cosmopolitan law.

Developed within the context of a fiction, since fiction was the only space in which women could practice philosophy (Hesse 111), Therese

Huber's cosmopolitanism utterly rejects law and normative principles in favor of the capacity of the personal story to link feeling heart to feeling heart. In *Adventures,* awareness of one's status as citizen of the world is contingent on having been expelled from a society of laws unjustly applied to benefit the powerful. The human capacity for virtue is hindered by civil society. Recognition of shared humanity occurs among refugees from laws rather than from the foundation of law.

Elizabeth Inchbald arrives at similar findings within a comparable global frame in *Nature and Art* (1796).[10] Henry, an impoverished noble savage of sorts, has grown up among Africans near Sierra Leone with care from his fiddle-playing father who has been shipwrecked on Zocotora Island.[11] Henry's sanctimonious cousin William has benefited from all the privilege of being born to a bishop in England and raised with every advantage. Out for a walk in a "thick wood" not far from the English home of his uncle, the bishop, and his cousin William, the kind-hearted Henry makes a discovery:

> As he advanced, in spite of the thick fog, he discerned the appearance of a female stealing away on his approach. His eye was fixed on this object; and regardless of where he placed his feet, soon he shrunk back with horror, on perceiving they had nearly trod upon a new-born infant, lying on the ground!—a lovely male child, entered on a world where not one preparation had been made to receive him. "Ah!" cried Henry, forgetting the person who had fled, and with a smile of compassion on the helpless infant, "I am glad I have found you—you give more joy to me, than you have done to your hapless parents." (93–94)

The infant has been left there by the desperate country girl Hannah Primrose, who has been carelessly seduced and abandoned by William. Wrapping the baby in his coat and filled with the urgent sense that the baby needs care, Henry takes the infant directly to his beloved Rebecca. Rebecca instantly takes charge of the baby, hiding it and devoting herself to the infant until it is at last discovered and she is falsely charged with being its mother and is, as a consequence, cut off from Henry. When, later, the baby is restored to his birth mother, Hannah struggles to feed and care for him, losing job after job until she finally turns to prostitution and becomes innocently embroiled in a forgery scheme. Meanwhile, bearing no consequences for his actions, her seducer William rises to become a judge in London and harshly condemns Hannah to execution without taking the time to read her plea or recognize her. This leads not only to her own death but that of their child. Henry embarks on a search for his lost father, and, after many years, the two return, impoverished, and form a happy rural family with Rebecca: "Exempt both from patronage and from controul—healthy—alive to every fruition with which nature blesses the world; dead to all out of their power to attain, the works of art—susceptible of those passions which endear human creatures one to another, insensible to those which separate man from man—they found themselves the thankful inhabitants of a small house or hut, placed on the borders of the sea" (153).

Elizabeth Inchbald makes the same moves as Therese Huber. The broader frame of focusing on people from Great Britain as they are tossed around the globe provides the setting for addressing inequality and need. From radical poverty and statelessness come the capacity to see suffering. "Susceptible of those passions which endear human creatures one to another," the refugee family finds happiness by moving away from laws to the "borders of the sea" (153).

As Isabelle de Charrière had also done a decade before in *Neuchâtel Letters* (within the smaller compass of European displacement due to trade and leisure), Huber and Inchbald elevate the heroine by having her provide for the illegitimate child of the local girl from whom she is separated by a slim social class margin. Charrière, Huber, and Inchbald shift heroinism from being defined, as it was in the previous generation of women's writing, as surviving seduction with virtue intact, to addressing the consequences of seduction (experienced by another) through providing care. Huber covers her bets by having her heroine resist seduction *and* provide care. The shift carries with it a movement away from the indirect critique of a society of ranks inherent in scenarios in which a chaste woman resists a villainous, generally aristocratic seducer. Huber, Inchbald, and Charrière put sociopolitical critique front and center: laws calculated to protect the powerful result in systemic inequality exemplified in seduction and in the abandonment of mothers and newborns.

In addition to acknowledging the consequences of seduction, all three scenes indicate a gendered division of labor for managing the destruction engendered by movement: birth and infant care, wherever they occur, are women's work. And, from the heroine's capacity to engage intimately with the problem of abandonment and illegitimate birth faced by the local girl, all three scenes generate through those births an evanescent promise of social regeneration—one that is based on recognition of shared humanity among women across class. The admiration and erotic attraction that the male protagonists—Rudolph and Henry Belton (Huber), Henry Norwynne (Inchbald), and Henry Meier (Charrière)—feel for the heroine reinforce the message of promise.

That Huber, Inchbald, and Charrière assign their heroines the capacity to recognize human need and provide care in a violent world in movement, "abandoned by law and God," has two implications. First, it makes visible a gendered division of labor in eighteenth-century cosmopolitanism: because birth, hunger, illness, death, and the need for shelter occur in relation to intimacy, close involvement in addressing these needs of others, the *work* of hospitality (as opposed to the intellectual benefits from it), appears to falls naturally to women. Sophie von La Roche makes much the same point in *Phenomena at Lake Oneida* but in reverse by giving her heroine Emilie the opportunity to articulate a gendered principle of hospitality based on the work that she and Oneida women in northern New York perform together when she delivers her baby. La Roche's French émigré heroine Emilie convinces her husband to swim with her across Lake Oneida so that she can give birth with the help of indigenous Oneida women, "for Nature makes no distinction in anything that is part of physical life, and women know only too well that when we are in this condition, we need help."[12] Emilie exclaims, "Oh, in the hut of my Indian women I was convinced that Nature makes no distinction, that my pains, my needs during the birth of my son, and his helplessness, are the situation of every woman giving birth and every newborn child." She then extrapolates from this to philosophize on the conditions that have brought her to the point of living on an island in Lake Oneida: "Only in the feelings and needs of Nature is to be found the one true equality," which "the new philosophers of France" tried and failed to instill through revolution and revolutionary government.[13] The Kantian cosmopolitan right to hospitality underpinning the right to be enlightened and to facilitate human perfectibility through the development of law is transformed, in these scenes of birth, into an identity of shared humanity among women based in intimate life events. This ethic of hospitality stands outside of law. These scenes of birth invite the reader to see the intimate as a privileged space for testing sentimental hypotheses: of humanity as a shared condition across nations, of seeking and providing refuge rather than merely travel as the experiences that yield knowledge, of intimate hospitality as the foundation for community. As Sheldon Pollock and colleagues put it in an attempt to welcome a feminist politics into cosmopolitan thought, such a "perspective would allow us to recognize that domesticity itself is a vital interlocutor and not just an interloper in law, politics, and public ethics" (8). Huber, Inchbald, and La Roche all seize on the separatist utopian logic of the 1760s and early 1770s proposed by the development of woman-directed and philanthropic landed estates in Sarah Scott's *Millenium Hall,* Leprince de Beaumont's *The New Clarissa,* and La Roche's own *History of Lady Sophia Sternheim.* Yet they reduce the scope of beneficence to the family of refugees from global injustice and move them away from the estate in the heart of the nation to the precarious water's edge.

The development of nascent feminist cosmopolitanism through the depiction of heroines who save the babies of local girls comes at a cost. First, the elevation of heroines is achieved on the backs, as it were, of local girls whose suffering disappears as it catalyzes elevation of heroines into a transnational pantheon. Representation of the heroine's chastity and brave securing of care in lawless spaces (the convict ship, the farthest abandoned reaches of a Gothic parish house, Norfolk Island, the cottage by the sea, an island in the middle of Lake Oneida) promises domesticized spaces of intimacy isolated from global upheaval as an antidote to unjust laws. Such a representation presents heroism as the antidote's guarantor rather than transforming law and politics to make them just. Heroic transport is, indeed, necessary to perfection of the chastity of women and to the constitution of fragile virtuous communities—or not communities but homes—bound by passion and in exile from a world of laws.

Where philosophy may propose law as the principle governing social relations, Huber proffers the spectacle of social bonds cemented through the revelation of a woman's story. Here, again, context matters. The narrative and political stakes of tales of seduction written by women revolve around the tension between a woman's experience of her own wishes and the external attempt to construe her meanings for her, to dispose of her by controlling the narrative of her story in her stead. In Huber's *Adventures* and in Inchbald's *Nature and Art,* the law comes in to ratify the narrative that the woman is criminal by piling on condemnation for crimes ostensibly unrelated to seduction. The law determines that Frances Belton is a thief and sends her to a penal colony, while the judge who seduced Hannah Primrose rules that she is a forger and sentences her to death.

In contrast to the way that Charrière keeps Marianne's negotiations around Julianne's pregnancy hidden from public view in *Neuchâtel Letters,* Huber and Inchbald create opportunities for external affirmation of a woman's version of her story of injustice that clarify the relationship between seduction and the appearance of other crimes that have been heaped upon her. Huber's Frances Belton, after laboring under the "poisonous breath of dishonor" (81) in England and on the convict ship, recounts her story on Norfolk Island. "I always felt," Frances Belton explains to the narrator Rudolph, "that if I told you my story you could only take it on trust" (81). On hearing her story, the circle of friends on Norfolk Island respond with overwhelming feeling, confirming the truth of her story and exonerating her. Inchbald goes even further. A printed broadside disseminates "the last dying words, speech, and confession; birth, parentage, and education; life, character, and behaviour, of Hannah Primrose who was executed this morning between the hours of ten and twelve, pursuant to the sentence passed upon her by the Honorouble Justice Norwynne" (139). The broadside concludes with a scene of passionate and public exoneration: "A crowd of spectators followed her to the fatal spot, most of whom returned weeping at the recollection of the fervency with which she prayed, and the impression which her dreadful state seemed to make upon her" (140). The scenes imbricate feeling into a literary technology of passionate "virtual witnessing"[14] reminiscent of Rousseauian invocations of transparent community gatherings. Huber's depiction of the gathering of friends on Norfolk Island displays an audience whose overflowing collective emotion validates the truth of Frances Belton's story, exonerates her, and provides a textual spectacle of the generation of social bonds. The broader claim is that fiction provides a space of intimacy generating recognition of shared humanity through the outpouring of emotion. Stories offer the condition for superior readers to join in validation of the heroine's story, to travel by way of female hospitality and heroism away from a political discourse of rights toward a depoliticized domestic discourse of emotional recognition based in human need.

Colonial Spectacles of Virtue

Conservative reaction across Europe to the Terror as well as Thermidorean French cultural policy after the 1794 turning point of the fall of Robespierre and the Committee on Public Safety constituted a check on novelists' claims to inculcating virtue through their work. Revising her initial endorsement of the Revolution, Mary Wollstonecraft joined a chorus of pundits when, in *An Historical and Moral View of the French Revolution; and the Effect It Has*

Produced in Europe (1794), she blamed the Terror on a media- and spectacle-fueled "frivolity of the French character."[15] When Inchbald, heavily engaged in British Jacobin debates, opposed a humane "nature" to an inhumane "art" in both her title and in the conclusion to her novel, she invoked the powerful terms of European cultural rivalry that came to a head in response to the Revolution. A century's worth of attacks on the degenerative influence of French artifice on Europe seemed to have found their proof in the Terror. Carla Hesse indicates that Thermidorean French cultural policy was driven by "the desire to temper public passions inflamed by market-driven literary culture." With the idea of public virtue delegitimated by its use to sanction state violence and mass purging under Robespierre, "moral duty became the order of the day, and moral philosophy the *lingua franca* of Thermidorian cultural life" (105). Philosophy could counter the socially degenerative incitement of the passions and satisfaction of the senses characteristic of *ancien régime* culture. Hesse points out that a Thermidorean embrace of philosophy and official academic culture barred women and novels from participation. "Thermidorian cultural and educational policies," she writes, "specifically excluded women from the new arenas where serious philosophical discourse was to take place. At the same time, they devalued the genre in which women might find an alternative venue for philosophical reflection" (111).

Germaine de Staël's response was to publish a story entitled "Zulma" and to follow it with a defense of fictions. In "Zulma," passionate virtual witnessing of the heroine's tale of seduction and abandonment goes primitive. Staël revises Rousseau's social contract to create a tragic social bond among a group of "savages" on the banks of the Orinoco who witness Zulma's confession and exonerate her before she takes her own life for having killed her faithless lover.[16] She subsequently republished the story along with several others, introducing the collection with an "Essay on Fictions," in *Collection of Detached Pieces* (*Recueil de morceaux détachés,* 1795). In "Essay on Fictions," Staël argued for the unique moral efficacy of a certain kind of "natural" fiction, "where everything is both invented and imitated, where nothing is true, but everything resembles the truth."[17] (35). She discounted all other literary forms, from tragedies to novels of gallantry for their lack of interest, excessive didacticism, selection of characters and events that rarely appear in life, and corrupting influence. Even history comes under attack: "It is not to individuals, but to peoples that its lessons are regularly applicable. The examples history offers apply always to nations" (46). In contrast, "the

morality of novels pertains more to the development of the interior move-
ments of the soul" (47). In working directly on moving the passions of readers
through depictions of the workings of the human heart, fictions have the
capacity to instill the individual virtue and feeling that may transform a people. Staël cites the familiar repertoire of novels offering delicate principles on
women's conduct as evidence, adding as well other examples of useful fictions
that display a "spectacle of virtue" (55): William Godwin's *Caleb Williams*,
Henry Fielding's *Adventures of Tom Jones*, and "many other French, English,
and German works" (50–55).[18] "There are men," she writes in direct reference
to Thermidorian cultural reform and Kantian ethics, "over whom duty will
hold no empire, and who could be guaranteed from criminality through
development in them of the possibility of being moved to emotion" (57).
Fiction serves this purpose while also providing exceptional souls a tether to
the world through the reminder that these souls are not alone in what they
feel.

Staël's "Essay on Fictions" legitimates the spectacle of the passionate
hybrid heroine in a circum-Atlantic theater. To illustrate her principles, Staël
proffered three colonial tales. "Zulma," republished with the "Essay,"
recounts the heroine's betrayal by Fernand who turns from her to a more
prosaic woman. Notably, Fernand has traveled among Europeans and teaches
Zulma to read: "He succeeded in making me understand the books of Europeans, and it is to this very study that I owe the talent of painting for you
the horrid picture of my misfortunes" (14). Against the background of French
establishment of a sugar plantation in Gorée off the coast of Senegal where
"happy" (45) Africans may work, "Mirza" tells the story of a French-educated
Jolof woman who sacrifices herself for the man she loves, even after he has
married the subservient Ourika, by taking his place in a slave coffle headed
for Caribbean-bound slave ships. A Jolof prefiguration of Corinne, Mirza
recites the cultural history of her people in perfect French alone on a moun-
taintop (49–50). "Pauline" is the story of a Caribbean creole, reeducated in
France, who spends her life expiating the childhood crime of letting herself
be seduced. The passionate tragic heroines Zulma, Mirza, and Pauline are all
highly literate cultural hybrids. As Staël explains of "Zulma," to exhibit the
limits of passion fully, it was necessary to bring together "all imaginable
energy in a savage soul and cultivated mind, for the faculty of judgment adds
considerably to pain even if this same faculty removes nothing from the
power to feeling" (2). The conquest of Peru in "Zulma" and the slave trade

in "Mirza" and "Pauline" provide the atmospherics of passion. Staël's "fictions" ask readers to be moved by these colonial heroines' exceptional displays of feeling in a French accent. Their "heroic transport" is made possible by a colonial *mise en scène*. Yet when the protagonists rise to heroine status by displaying the extreme passion of women who have loved and lost, local identity and colonial history disappear. The code of heroines and local girls, which Staël's early fictions deploy in the circum-Atlantic, bears the signature of an emerging global virus.

Forces of Fictions

Giving up fiction, as a woman writer, meant giving up a forum for engaging in political thought. Giving up the French gender model, both celebrated and reviled over the course of the second half of the eighteenth century, meant giving up a cultural model as well. In *A Vindication of the Rights of Woman*, Mary Wollstonecraft encapsulated a recurring Enlightenment argument: "In France, there is undoubtedly a more general diffusion of knowledge than in any part of the European world, and I attribute it, in a great measure, to the social intercourse which has long subsisted between the sexes" (85–86). Wollstonecraft drew on intertwining threads in Enlightenment natural philosophy. One thread wound through the works of writers from Montesquieu to John Millar to Rousseau and linked the progress of nations with the role and treatment of women in private and public life. A more culture-specific thread, pursued in a philosophically oriented travel literature of the second half of the century, connected the quality and character of different cultures with the status of women in given societies.

Germaine de Staël built this last in 1799 into a primary thesis of the first work of comparative literature, *De la littérature,* where she sought to explain why literature had distinct characters in different nations. One approach Staël takes in *De la littérature* is to compare contemporary nations and to correlate the retirement or publicity of women with national character and literary production. Yet Staël went further by leaping directly into the quarrel of the Ancients and Moderns. She wrote that "in reading books composed since the renaissance of letters, one can note on every page the ideas that we didn't have before women were accorded a sort of civil equality" (254). More generally, Staël argued, the relative absence of women from civil life in antiquity, as well as the rejection of intimate relationships with women, explained why classical literature revolved around a masculine love of the nation. If Latin literature was somewhat more open to comedy than Greek literature, this correlated with a Roman attribution of a respected role above servility to women in marriage. It followed that in modern societies, the place of women influenced the kind and quality of literature. In a key passage, Staël proposed that "the moderns, influenced by women" have "easily ceded to the ties of philanthropy; and the mind has become more philosophically free, in devoting itself less to the empire of exclusive associations." In other words, the presence and influence of nonservile women in society made it possible to think and write about humanity beyond nation and tribe. "The only advantage of writers of recent centuries over the ancients, in works of the imagination," Staël continued, "is the talent for expressing a more delicate sensibility, and for varying the situations and the characters through knowledge of the human heart" (261–62). Anti-French and anti-Bourbon writers could explain the vices of the French monarchy as having resulted from too great a presence of women in public life. Still, women writers such as Wollstonecraft and Staël had a vested interest in proclaiming the prime tenet of their community of practice's regime of competence: the idea that women who had been accorded "a sort of civil equality" could bring to modern thought and literature a virtuous concern with humanity as a whole rather than "the virtue of the ancients founded on love of country." Stael's contention that the nonservility of women elevated modern writing by producing a literature for humanity rather than a literature for nations was a master stroke. It positioned women indirectly but deftly as the agents bringing to the modern world literary field a concern for humanity.

Goethe translated Staël's *Essay on Fictions* for *Horen* in 1796, while Staël, in a certain sense, translated the intellectual network of Goethe for a European audience in *De l'Allemagne* (1813). At least one commentator has linked Goethe's development of the idea of autonomous aesthetics to his reaction to the *Essay* (Voisine). Staël maintains her grip in the *Essay* on the idea of the socially redemptive power of fictions. Deriving her claims from the transnational women's writing of the long eighteenth century, she argues for the unique power of fictions to gather humanity together through the "spectacle of virtue." Goethe's approach to world literature, in contrast, was one of traffic. In *What Is World Literature?* David Damrosch writes, the "world of world literature as Goethe practices it: less a set of works than a network. As Fritz Strich has observed, this network had a fundamentally economic character, serving to promote 'a traffic in ideas between peoples, a literary market to which the nations bring their intellectual treasures for exchange'" (3).[19] Participating in women writers' networks, in the networks of male writers, including the one in which Goethe was the hub, and situated as the hub of her own network at Coppet, Staël approached literature less through the lens of economic traffic in virtuosic national texts and more through comparison of the cultural conditions for producing human virtue developed by the transnational projects of women's writing in the preceding century. Yet, of course, Stael's project and Goëthe's project are also the interdependent products of cultural transfer; whether through spectacle or traffic, each vests in cosmopolitan conditions within literature rather than in law the capacity for humans to meet their highest potential.

On a personal level, Staël's contrast between a tribal nationalist literature and a "sensible" literature of the human heart, between societies subordinating and societies granting civil equality to women, reclaimed her displacement. In her major work of cultural transfer, "Of Germany," as well as in "Ten Years of Exile," she figured her own biography of ejection from Paris as an exile from conversation toward the novel.[20] The substance of her audacious argument about national literature and a human literature derived from a thick repertoire of women's writing. Because of her simultaneous participation in a French national literary tradition, in an international community of women's writing, and in German intellectual and philosophical circles, she could establish a stark opposition between the national literatures dividing Europe and what she saw as the literature of modernity: a feminized transnational literature of the human heart.

Networks and European Women Writers

To describe her collaborations, Isabelle de Charrière drew on the metaphor of the Dutch Old Masters' workshop in which different painters were responsible for filling in landscape, faces, animals, plants, and other details of design (Letzter 185). Collaborations with the Swiss Isabelle Morel de Gélieu were mediated by a shared interest in testing British models of femininity. In 1797, Charrière and Gélieu collaborated on a French translation of Elizabeth Inchbald's *Nature and Art* (1796). In *Sainte-Anne* (Leipzig, 1799), Charrière would lift an important device from Inchbald's novel—a hardly literate country woman struggling with letters that seal her fate.[21] The novel Isabelle

Morel de Gélieu wrote with Charrière's support unfolded in direct response to Frances Burney's fiction. The narrator of *Louise and Albert, or the Danger of Being Too Exacting* (*Louise et Albert ou le danger d'être trop exigeant*, 1803) opined that the censorious character Edgar in *Camilla* by 'Madame d'Arblay' would have had "a hard time succeeding with any woman" (1–2). Charrière facilitated Therese Huber's career by acceding to her request to write a continuation of the *Letters Found in Wallets of Emigrés* (*Lettres trouvées dans des porte-feuilles d'émigrés*, 1793) and supplying her with works to translate (Astbury, "Adapting" 99–110).[22] To test a German model of femininity, Charrière wrote a play, *Elise, or the University* (*Elise, oder die Universität*, 1794), based on Therese Huber's experience as one of the renowned highly educated daughters of professors in the university town of Göttingen. *Elise, or the University* (*Œuvres* 7:407–60) explored the nascent German female literary type through a dilemma that Charrière often revisited as her acrimonious personal and generational rivalry with Germaine de Staël developed[23]: how to be a highly educated woman without becoming someone whose main goal was to draw admiration. Writers of the first half of the eighteenth century had argued that a proper education would contain young women's penchant for vanity. The distinctively German scenario of a young woman endowed with passionate sensibility *and* a modern education was overlaid in *Elise, or the University* onto a critique of an emerging Romantic style that Charrière associated with both Huber and Staël. Charrière triangulated her dislike of Staël through a competing representation of a slave woman. To Staël's passionate characters Zulma, Mirza, and Pauline, Charrière opposed her global heroine Constance who, in a continuation of *Three Women* (*Œuvres* 9:127–68), reveals the intertwining of her own story with that of the seduced Martiniquan slave Bianca and Bianca's biracial daughter Biondina.[24] Biondina is none other than Constance's cousin. The local or colonial girl, it turns out, is the heroine's immediate relative, ready to become a heroine in her own right the moment she learns to tell her story. In the teleological structure of "women's writing," the local girl's transport to telling her story transforms her into a heroine. In feminist literary history, the rediscovered woman writer, Isabelle Morel de Gélieu, say, becomes a heroine through having come to writing. And for readers attached to a repertoire, the lives of heroines and the lives of women who write merge into a powerful incitement. Such is the recursive structure that eighteenth-century European women's writing put into play as it became a category in the world literary field.

Another scholar with a different area of national and linguistic literary expertise might have entered the Charrière-Staël-Huber-Inchbald-Burney-Gélieu network by pulling on a different thread than Charrière. Teasing out both Huber's connections to other women writers and intellectuals, including the Göttingen daughters whom she knew as a girl, opens a window on the significant increase in the number of women writing in German in the late eighteenth and early nineteenth century. A German early nineteenth-century Romantic network composed of Therese Forster Huber, Caroline Michaelis Böhmer Schlegel-Schelling, Dorothea von Schlegel (and on and on) parallels in *belles lettres* the seventeenth-century French network around Scudéry, La Fayette, and Sévigné. The lives, letters, memoirs, and writings of major women writers in early nineteenth-century Germany mingled in early literary histories and then were domesticated into fictional fodder. In earlier generations of criticism, their work was transformed into binary secret histories of an era, either as the bedroom stories of the great Romantic male writers or as parables of the wrongs of woman.

Many women entered the expanding German literary field at the turn of the century through the tried-and-true path of apprenticeships as translators of French and English works. Following Therese Huber's connection with her childhood friend Meta Forkel Liebeskind suggests incidentally that Inchbald's *Nature and Art* may well have ended up in Charrière's hands because of this relationship.[25] More important, it shows, as Alessa Johns highlights, that a significant portion of English Jacobin writing, including the works of Charlotte Smith, Inchbald, and Thomas Paine entered German through Forkel's translation work (56–57). From Therese Huber a link runs directly to a childhood friend of sorts and adult rival, the prolific letter writer Caroline Michaelis Böhmer Schlegel-Schelling, and from her runs a correspondence and family relationship with novelist, critic, and *salonnière* Dorothea von Schlegel. The women writing in German to whom Huber was connected were engaged in consolidating women's position in German literary and intellectual life, with Goethe serving as "the most proximate locus of the new vernacular tradition in German letters" (Hirsch, Perry, and Swain viii). Yet threads also ran out to other nations and other tongues. When Dorothea von Schlegel translated into German in 1807 the famously French novel *Corinne* about an exile from England, what sense did her readers make of the subtitle to the publication *Corinna: oder Italien?*[26]

Pulling on the Elizabeth Inchbald thread or the Frances Burney thread or the Gélieu thread would expose more connections stitching under and over and across but also always in a pattern. When women "came to writing" across Europe in increasingly large numbers from the late eighteenth and early nineteenth century on as their national literary fields expanded, they asserted national aesthetics in their fictions, and they subscribed to the rules for entry into literary production that national literary fields enforced. Yet they entered a world literary field too in which women's writing occupied a space—not quite akin to that of a nation—established by an eighteenth-century history of women writers' transnationalism. Under certain conditions and by adhering to certain codes, by drawing on a repertoire, and by citing a differential experience of intimate moments of violation, care, birth, abandonment, love, displacement, every local girl could deploy the capital of virtue. At the risk of having to remain there, she could enter the city of women and share her history.

Notes

1. Burney, *Court Journals*, December 1787. Burney believed that La Roche was seeking a position at court and hoped that Burney would be an intermediary or ally (I:165).

2. Sophie von La Roche, *Pomona für Teutschlands Töchter*, vol. 1 (Speier: Enderes, 1783–84), 248–49. Quoted in Dawson 14.

3. Orr, "La Fite, Marie Elisabeth de."

4. Janse, "Madame de La Fite." I am grateful to Ineke Janse for sharing her thoughtful and thorough thesis with me as well as to James ter Beek, Information Services Department, Leiden University Libraries, who went out of his way to help me contact Ms. Janse.

5. La Fite, "Lettre de la traductrice," 7.

6. See also Dawson, 27–29.

7. Dijk, " 'Les femmes me sont toujours de quelque chose.' "

8. See Kaplan, "Introduction," in *Translations*.

9. On Gottsched and cultural transfer, see Hilary Brown, *Luise Gottsched*.

10. *Eugénie* is a pedagogy *à clef.* "Miss Amélie B*** corresponded to Burney: "A few days later I had the pleasure of becoming acquainted with Miss Amélie B***, the author of two moral fictions, deservedly admired, & which have acquired a reputation that is quite rare to obtain and to merit at her age. . . . Fame, youth, and modesty, such a combination I had not yet seen. . . . Despite the difference in our ages, we felt the spell of mutual attraction." In a footnote, La Fite wrote, "One will recognize easily, even in France this portrait, so charming and so like the orginal, which depicts so faithfully the celebrated author of *Evelina* & *Cecilia*." *Eugénie* (100–1). Quoted and translated in *Court Journals* II:139n376.

11. "Préface," *Eugénie*, unnumbered ninth page.

12. Elizabeth and Florence Anson, *Mary Hamilton*, 107. Quoted in Orr, "Aristocratic Feminism," 319.

13. See also van Dijk, "I Have Heard About You."

14. "Women Writers in History."

15. The naming convention here is to provide the full name and title of French women nobles and to follow with the name associated with their publications. Thus, Marie-Catherine Le Jumel de Barneville, baronesse d'Aulnoy, is referred to subsequently as "Aulnoy." DeJean discusses the politics of women writers' names in French in *Tender Geographies* (2). For women writers known by their maiden and married names, I will, on occasion, use last names to emphasize differences in reception or positioning as well as "Madame," which was a period convention; for example, Frances Burney was received for much of her lifetime as Frances Burney but was generally referred to as Madame d'Arblay after her marriage.

16. Benedict Anderson; Franco Moretti.

17. In *Novels in the Time of Democratic Writing*, Nancy Armstrong and Leonard Tennenhouse provide a clue to understanding why critics as different as Ian Watt and Pascale Casanova rely on Jane Austen as the touchstone for explaining the national novel. "No one, not even Flaubert," Armstrong and Tennenhouse explain, displays greater "proficiency" than Jane Austen in using the novel to "dispose us to imagine managing" a world "made of property," where property and the array of characters within its boundaries form the basis for imagining the community of the nation. Critics from E. M. Forster to Ian Watt defined the novel as "self-contained" and reliant on a "formal machinery that at once detached it from the larger field of prose and set it in relation to other novels that redistributed property to provide the basis of a restored or reformed community." In doing so, they assumed without acknowledging it the novelistic imagining of property ownership "whether inherited or acquired" as the basis for community (8–10).

18. Carla Hesse makes a related point that scholars have been eager to read the textual and visual record of the French eighteenth century as an accurate representation of women's enjoyment of participation in public life rather than as a representation (31–32).

19. For the notion of "semiperipheral cultural transmitters," see Broomans and van Voorst, 10.

20. Manuela Rossini and Michael Toggweiler write that "culture itself may be read *as* transfer . . . and, more specifically, as an ongoing negotiation and differentiation. . . . Despite the transferring nature of objects and environments, demarcations of borders are not only very real, but there are also strict limits and often unsurpassable obstacles and barriers to the mobility of things. Discourses of 'culture' and 'text' prove highly effective in terms of inclusion or exclusion, and 'imaginary communities' are potent political agents" (5).

21. Johns, in *Bluestocking Feminism*, refers to Anthony Kwame Appiah's "Cosmopolitan Patriots," *Critical Inquiry* 23, no. 3 (Spring 1997): 617–39.

22. Dorothea Schlegel, "Gespräch über die neuesten Romane der Französinnen," in *Europa: Eine Zeitschrift*, ed. Friedrich Schlegel, 1803 (reprint, Stuttgart, 1963), 2 vols., ed. Ernst Behler; vol. 1, 89. Quoted and translated by J. Martin, 42.

23. See Warner, *Reading Clarissa*; Castle; Ferguson; and Eagleton.

24. On these, see Dawson, 142, and Alison Martin.

25. Sophie von La Roche, letter to Julie Bondeli, August 1778, reprinted in Renate Feyl, "Das mühselige Amt der Poeterey: Sophie la Roche an Julie Bondeli," *Querelles: Jahrbuch für Frauenforschung* 3 (1998): 313–14. Quoted in Fronius, 90.

26. Charlotte Finch, *The Gamut and Time-Table in Verse: For the Instruction of Children* (London: Printed and sold by Dean and Munday, 1820s). On Finch, see Shelfrin, *Such Constant Affectionate Care*.

27. Judith E. Martin, 52–53. Martin quotes *Ich bin mehr Herz als Kopf: Sophie von La Roche—Ein Lebensbild in Briefen*, ed. Michael Maurer (Munich: Beck, 1983), 385; and, for Staël's impressions of La Roche, see Alfred Götze, *Ein fremder Gast: Frau von Staël in Deutschland, 1803–04*, 18–19 (Jena, Germany: Walter Biedermann, 1922).

28. Dow, "Introduction," *Adèle and Theodore*, xx.

29. *Mein Schreibtisch*, 103. Quoted and translated by J. Martin, 53.

30. For arguments about the colonial products supporting metropolitan identity, including gender identity, as well as the pivotal role played by these imports in literary texts, see both Said and McClintock. Madeleine Dobie discusses muslin, china, and marquetry wood specifically in *Trading Places*.

31. On Reeve, see Kelly, "Clara Reeve: Provincial Bluestocking."

32. *Europa: Eine Zeitschrift*, ed. Friedrich Schlegel, 1803. Quoted and discussed in Judith Martin, 40–43. I rely on Martin's discussion here.

33. See Goldsmith and Goodman, *Going Public.*

34. Scholarship on German translation is particularly rich, see, for example, Freedman; and Johns, *Bluestocking*, 39–87.

35. See Simon, "Gender in Translation," 27; Hayes; and McMurran.

36. See Cheek, *Sexual Antipodes*, 2–4; and Tomaselli.

37. The scholarship on this is vast. See especially Barker-Benfield and Vila.

38. Immanuel Kant, *Grounding for a Metaphysics of Morals*, trans. J. Ellington (Cambridge: Hackett, 1981), 30. Quoted in Garrett Wallace Brown, 56.

CHAPTER 2

1. The famous women listed under S are "Sade, Laura. Sappho. Scala, Alexandra. Schurman, Anna Maria. Scudery, Madeline de. Seguier, Anne de. Semiramis. Seturman, Madame. Sevigne, Marchioness de. Seymour, Lady Arabella. Seymour, Ladies Ann, Margaret, and Jane. Sforza, Catherine. Sforza, Isabella. Sheridan, Mrs. Frances. Sophronia. Sulpicia, or Sulpitia. Sunderland, Countess of. Suze, Countess de la. Sydney, Mary, Countess of Pembroke" (Hays, *Female Biography*, vol. 3, contents).

2. Since Joan Kelly's article, the *querelle* has drawn significant scholarly attention, notably the collaborative project organized by SIEFAR, Société Internationale pour l'Étude des Femmes de l'Ancien Régime, leading to three volumes edited by Éliane Viennot and colleagues. SIEFAR has also digitized many works related to the *querelle* and to catalogs of women and has created alphabetized hyperlinks to entries in some cases. See http://siefar.org/dictionnaire-des-femmes -de-l-ancienne-france/dictionnaires-anciens/.

3. Quoted in Bate, 6.

4. Quoted in Casanova, *The World Republic of Letters*, 9.

5. Melton notes that "the ability to sign one's name did not always mean an individual could read, nor can illiteracy always be inferred from an inability to sign. Because women, for example, often learned to read without ever knowing how to write, counting signatures will necessrily yield a lower rate of female literacy. But for all their methodological shortcomings, signatures are the only universal standard of literacy historians have at their disposal" (82).

6. See also Gemert et al., *Women's Writing from the Low Countries.*

7. See Howatt and Widdowson, 56; Michèle Cohen, "Sexualizing and Gendering the French Tongue."

8. Spink, "Teaching of French Pronunciation in England in the Eighteenth Century," 155, as quoted in Michèle Cohen, "Sexualizing and Gendering," 73.

9. On references to Sappho, see DeJean, *Fictions of Sappho*; and Greene, *Re-reading Sappho.*

10. Dijk, "Foreword," *Writing the History*, xiii.

11. For example, Symphorien Champier, *La nef des dames vertueuses* (1503); François de Billon, *Le fort inexpugnable de l'honneur du sexe féminin* (1555); Pierre Le Moyne, *Gallerie des femmes fortes* (1647); Francesco Pona, *Galeria delle donne celebre* (1641); Puget de la Serre, *Le temple de la gloire, contenant les éloges historiques de treize Annes royales et princesses de France* (1645) and *L'histoire et les portraits des impératrices, des reynes et des illustres princesses de l'auguste*

maison d'Autriche, qui ont porté le nom d'Anne (1648). On the spatial metaphors of the genre, see Dunn-Lardeau, 37; Pascal; and Bolzoni.

12. On the rhetorical stakes of the catalog genre, see McLeod, *Virtue and Venom.*

13. A search of WorldCat, EEBO, the catalogs of the Bibliothèque Nationale and the British Library, and consultation of Erdmann, *My Gracious Silence,* reveal that Domenichi's *Rime* was not translated and the poetry of the other most notable Italian women writers of the sixteenth century—Laura Terracina, Gaspara Stampa, Tullia d'Aragona, and Vittoria Colonna—is not identifiable by translation of author in the sixteenth, seventeenth, and eighteenth centuries. Their lyric could, of course, have been published in collections and also without attribution. WorldCat contains a reference to an untitled volume of selected poems by Vittoria Colonna published in 1558, cites it as being in English, and references a similar volume as being published three times in the eighteenth century. The first WorldCat reference to a translation of Colonna is an English translation in 1818. Moderata Fonte's work remained untranslated until the twentieth century. Isabella Sforza's *Della vera tranquillità dell'animo* was translated into French (1549) and Spanish (1568). See Erdmann, *My Gracious Silence,* 126.

14. Pohl writes, "However, in opposition to Boccaccio, the 'contemporary community of good women' is based on the meritocratic *imitatio* (not *admiratio*)—Lanyer implies that through patronage, good example and learning, women readers are able to participate in this virtual community of women" (29).

15. Pohl has shown how "pastoral separatist communities" of women appear in reactions against idyllic depictions of the "'traffic in women' in a patriarchal world that [Sir Philip] Sydney so eloquently wove into his text" on Arcadia (24).

16. Broad relies on Mary Astell, *A Serious Proposal to the Ladies, Parts I and II.* Quotations are from *Proposal* I: 37, 20, 36.

17. "conversation, n.," OED Online, June 2018, Oxford University Press. http://www .oed.com.libproxy.unm.edu/view/Entry/40748?rskey=JM6d3&isAdvanced;eqfalse (accessed June 23, 2018).

18. Dacier's lines are translated and quoted by Fabienne Moore, 94.

19. McDowell, "Consuming Women," 219–52. She quotes Barash, 415–16. No translations of George Coleman and Bonnell Thornton's *Poems by Eminent Ladies* (1755), the anonymous *Biographium Faemineum—The Female Worthies: or Memoirs of the Most Illustrious Ladies, of All Ages and Nations* (1766), or of George Ballard's *Memoirs of Several Ladies of Great Britain* (1775), for example, appear in WorldCat. Chantel Lavoie does a nice job in *Collecting Women* of describing the differences between anthologies, miscellanies, and biographical catalogs while also acknowledging the shared tendencies and impulse toward "investing women poets with authority, and the claim to have authority over them" (12).

20. Lavoie mentions, for example, that the poet Mary Monck appeared as "Mrs. Molesworth" in Giles Jacob's 1720 *Lives and Writings of Our Most Considerable English Poets* (29).

21. [Author] "Madame Dacier," *Femmes savantes, savoirs des femmes,* ed. Colette Nativel (Geneva: Librairie Droz, 1999), 209.

22. Equally, the fictional character Elise in a story by Sophie von La Roche wishes to become "die teutsche Laura Bassi" after the famous Italian physicist. La Roche, *Pomona, für Teutschlands Töchter,* bd. 4 (Stuttgart: Speyer, 1783–84; Munich: K. G. Saur, 1987), 254. As quoted in Strauss Sotiropoulos, 230.

23. As Peruga writes in a discussion of women in eighteenth-century Spain, the emphasis on women's uniqueness or exceptionalism became a "powerful reference for real early modern

women of letters, one that they incorporated into their works and reshaped to fit their needs of self-assertion and cultural authority" (18).

24. Jean Pierre Nicéron, *Mémoires pour servir à l'histoire des hommes illustres dans la république des letters: Avec un catalogue raisonné des leurs ouvrages* XXXIII (Farnborough: Gregg, 1968), 22. Cited in Pal, 56.

25. The application of Spacks's notion of spiritual autobiography (302) to *Eukleria* is made by Mirjam de Baar, 148.

26. Letter to Princess Elizabeth of the Palatinate in Anna Maria van Schurman, *Opuscula* (1650), 158–60. In Schurman, *Anna Maria van Schurman*, 58.

27. On relations among clusters of women in this period, see Campbell and Larsen, *Early Modern Women.*

28. Barthélémy and Kervilier, *Un tournoi de trois pucelles*, 44. Quoted in Larsen, "Anne Marie de Schurman," 274. I rely on Larsen's analysis here.

29. Madeleine de Scudéry "recuperates Sappho's voice for women writers" in, as Joan DeJean writes, "the first indication of the feminization of prose fiction for which she would eventually be responsible, a telling shift in the early development of the French novel away from tales of 'arms and the man' that won for her an enormous readership and that may well have been the key factor in the articulation of what we now recognize as the modern novel." *Fictions of Sappho*, 103.

30. On literary portraits, see Plantié, *La mode du portrait littéraire en France.*

31. See description, "Acceuil," on landing page of artamène.org.

32. Mary Pendarves (later Delany) to Ann Granville (later Dewes), June 28, 1732, in Pendarves, *Autobiography and Correspondence of Mary Granville*, I:362. Quoted in Doody, introduction to Lennox, *Female Quixote*, xv.

33. Parts of the text were translated into German by Sybille Ursula von Braunschweig-Lüneburg, who "was immersed in Latin studies at the age of nine and was able to amass an extensive private library of classical, French and German literature (nearly half of the 809 volumes were in French)." Brown, *Luise Gottsched the Translator*, 23, citing Spahr, "Sibylla Ursula."

34. On Ménage, see Maber, "Re-gendering Intellectual Life: Gilles Ménage and His *Histoire des femmes philosophes.*"

35. From Molière, *Les précieuses ridicules*, scene 17, lines 9–12. Quoted in Beasley 45.

36. Janet Letts traces the circulation of stories about famous sixteenth-century figures and their appearance in *Legendary Lives in "La princesse de Clèves."*

37. On Sévigné's influence on women readers, see Constant, *Un monde*; and Goldsmith, "Authority, Authenticity."

38. The index compiled under the direction of Jennie Batchelor to the *Lady's Magazine* identifies three entries on Maintenon, probably all from Lennox's translation of Angliviel de la Beaumelle's *Mémoires*: Oct. 1778, p. 533; Nov. 1778, p. 582; "Striking Instances," Dec. 1778, p. 645. Batchelor, *Lady's Magazine.*

39. McDowell, *Women of Grub Street*, 263n84.

40. *Oroonoko* appeared in German as early as 1709 and then in what was probably a different translation in 1759, while Antoine de la Place's French translation was published in 1745 in Amsterdam and The Hague and would be reissued in French editions several times over the course of the century. Behn's *Agnès de Castro* appeared in French in 1761. A Russian translation of *Oroonoko* appeared in Saint Petersburg in 1796. Manley's work was quickly translated into French and German. Manley's scandalous history of the Duchess of Marlborough,

The Secret History of Queen Zara and the Zarazians (1705), appeared in at least three French editions between 1708 and 1712 and a German edition published at The Hague in 1712.

41. Manley, *New Atalantis*, 161. Ballaster associates the Caball with Phillips's coterie on p. xviii.

42. See Felicity Nussbaum's discussion "The Better Women: The Amazon Myth and *Hudibras"* in her book *The Brink of All We Hate*, 43–56.

43. This is on the first page of two sets of prefatory pages, both numbered in Roman numerals.

CHAPTER 3

1. The first of these was in usage at least through 1793 and the second through 1758, according to the *OED* sample usages.

2. On the rape of Philomela and literary genre, see Klindienst.

3. See "consent, n." and "consent, v." *Oxford English Dictionary*. http://www.oed.com/view/Entry/39517?rskey=nm1hoN&ampRsult=1.

4. The "Turkish Embassy Letters" would not be published until 1763, when a rogue copy of Lady Mary Wortley Montagu's letters appeared as *Letters of the Right Honourable Lady M[ar]y W[ortle]y M[ontagu]e, Written, During Her Travels in Europe, Asia, and Africa to Persons of Distinction*. Mary Wortley Montagu Montagu, *The Turkish Embassy Letters*, ed. Theresa Heffernin and Daniel O'Quinn (Ontario: Broadview Press, 2012).

5. See Staves, "Don Quixote in Eighteenth-Century England"; Paulsen, *Don Quixote in England*; and Marshall, *The Frame of Art*.

6. See Doody, "Introduction," xxii; Looser, 107.

7. On the double entendre around "adventures," see also Gallagher, 182.

8. On the print and continuation history, see Kaplan, ix; Mallinson, "Reconquering Peru," 291–310; and Showalter, "*Les lettres.*"

9. David Smith, 5.

10. *The Early Journals and Letters of Fanny Burney*, ed. Lars Troide (Kingston: McGill-Queen's University Press; Oxford: Clarendon, 1988–), vol. 1, 304. Quoted in D. Smith, 5.

11. "The first was an anonymous seven-letter *Suite* which went through four editions in 1747 alone. In late 1748, but under the date 1749, Hugary de Lamarche-Courmont brought out a second sequel, the *Lettres d'Aza*, in thirty-five letters, in which the voice of the absent Aza is heard at last. Publishers started routinely including them in editions of the *Péruvienne*, so that Graffigny, to her annoyance, was often thought to be the author. . . . She tried to outflank these sequels in 1752 by rewriting the last part of her novel, increasing the number of letters from thirty-eight to forty-one. . . . The last three sequels were in English (1774, nine letters), by R. Roberts . . . , in Spanish (1792, one letter), by Maria Romero Masegosa y Cancelada . . . and in French (1797, fifteen letters), by Mme Morel-Vindé." D. Smith, 7.

12. "Il faut ici tuer quelqu'un . . . C'est Zilia, la seule personne à laquelle vous vous intéressiez véritablement; il faut la tuer, afin qu'elle vous intéresse encore davantage." *Cinq années littéraires* 1 (1748): 21. Quoted in Kaplan, xiii.

13. The literary histories of writing by women that refer to "writing back" are too numerous to cite here. For one recent intervention that explores connections among European women writers, see Gilleir and Montoya, *Women Writing Back*.

14. For insights on *L'espion du grand seigneur/The Turkish Spy,* I am grateful to Alain Antoine and to the analysis he provides in his unpublished University of New Mexico doctoral dissertation, *The Turkish Spy: A Peripatetic Novel.*

15. On Zilia's status as a foreigner, see Vanpée.

16. On the role played by Graffigny's idea of the *quipu* in *Encyclopédie* definitions of language, see Piroux.

17. In "Lettre sur les spectacles," Rousseau responds to d'Alembert's *Encyclopédie* article "Genève" with an attack on the artifice of the French theater. *Jean-Jacques Rousseau, Citoyen de Genève à M. d'Alembert . . . sur son article Genève, dans le VIIe volume de l'Encyclopedie, et particulièrement sur le projet d'établir un théâtre de comédie en cette ville* (Amsterdam: Marc-Michel Rey, 1758).

18. I owe the recognition of the parallelism between the scenes in *Zaïre* and the scenes in *Lettres d'une Péruvienne* to Mallinson, " 'Cela ne vaud pas Zaide,' " 121.

19. See Brooks.

20. The contestation between sentimental and realist codes is nicely explored in Margaret Cohen's *Sentimental Education of the Novel* where she argues that Balzac and Stendhal

> forged fundamental features of realist poetics in a hostile takeover of the sentimental form. Thus, such an important code as the bildungsroman plot placing the individual in insolubly fractured relation to the collective turns out to derive from sentimentality. But when works like *Le rouge et le noir* and *Le père Goriot* appropriated sentimental codes, they transvalued those codes' significance. In the sentimental novel, the plot of fracture, for example, paves the way for a tragic struggle of principles. In realist novels, principles are discredited as sentimental illusions and the plot of fracture opens the door to realist compromise, to the protagonist's amoral struggle to succeed. (12–13)

21. On the engravings by J. B. Patas, after Le Barbier l'aíné, in the Paris Migneret edition of 1797, see Ionescu.

22. Jeanne-Marie Leprince de Beaumont, *The Triumph of Truth* (London: Cadell, 1775), x. Quoted in Kaplan, xvii.

23. The title phrase includes this. Theresa Ann Smith points out that in 1794 the *Correo literario de Murcia* recorded María Josefa de Rivadeneyra's accusation that Romero plagiarized her own translation (which scholars have been unable to locate), along with Romero's published letter of refutation. Smith, "Writing out of the Margins," 179n5.

24. I would like to thank translator Theodore Walker for providing this polished translation of Romero's introduction.

25. G. L. Deodati's French-Italian parallel edition (Paris: Migneret, 1792); R. L. Whitehead's English edition (London: T. Jones, 1805); C. Cooke's English edition (London, 1794); etc. On Graffigny's life, see Showalter, English. *Françoise de Graffigny.*

26. Sophy Elphinstone's calamities begin when she is sixteen and an older man seduces her "still younger and more thoughtless" sister (261) and encourages her to run away with him.

Chapter 4

1. I am grateful to Margaretmary Daley for sharing her paper "German Julies? Rousseauvian Protagonists in the Female Bildungsroman," presented at the annual meeting of the American Society for Eighteenth-Century Studies, San Antonio, TX, March 23, 2012.

2. See also, Beebee, *Clarissa on the Continent*.

3. Cf. Felicity Nussbaum, *The Autobiographical Subject*.

4. See Goldsmith, *Exclusive Conversations*.

5. See on this, for example, Parfitt, "Far from the Whirlwind"; and Pohl, *Women, Space and Utopia*.

6. This chapter is heavily indebted to the work of Michèle Cohen and of Alessa Johns.

7. See Carla Hesse on the transition from orality to writing. Paule Constant describes the transition experienced by eighteenth-century women and girls as a movement from "une civilisation orale, avec tout ce que cela comporte de traditions et de savoir-faire dont les femmes tiennent le dernier bastion, à une civilisation de l'écrit proprement masculine" (16).

8. See also Cravera, *L'âge de la conversation*.

9. On eighteenth-century rhetoric surrounding the role of women in French public life, see Landes, *Women and the Public Sphere*.

10. French Jesuit schools relied abundantly on theatrical performances in the seventeenth century.

11. Mary Astell likely learned about Saint-Cyr through reading Fénelon's essay and may well have been influenced by it in her *Serious Proposal to the Ladies*. Astell was acquainted with Fénelon's English translator, George Hickes. See Springborg, introduction to Mary Astell, *A Serious Proposal to the Ladies*; and Perry, *The Celebrated Mary Astell*, 118–19; cited in Bannet, "Bluestocking Sisters," 54n51.

12. M. O. Grenby points out in "Delightful Instruction? Assessing Children's Use of Educational Books in the Long Eighteenth Century" that *Telemachus* was available for child readers in English within a year of its appearance in French in 1699 and that Robert Wharton's *Historiae pueriles* was published in 1734 as a collection of little histories for amusement and "to stir up Boys to a love of books" (181–82).

13. Statement of Frances Barber, servant at East Stour, PRO C24.1396.Pt1. No29. As quoted in Bree, *Sarah Fielding*, 3.

14. In Dutch by 1745 (Amsterdam: Steeve van Esveldt); in German by 1746 (Breslau: Pietsch); in French by 1749, in a translation by Pierre Antoine de la Place (Amsterdam: La Compagnie, 1749); anthologized in Spanish in 1795 (Madrid: En la Imprenta de la Viuda de Ibarra); in Russian in 1796 (St. Petersburg: Pri Imperatorskoi Akademii Nauk).

15. Sarah Fielding, *De verstandige Engelsche leermeestres, of Kweekschool van jonge jufferen: naer 't begrip der teedere jaren, tot vermaek en onderwys der jeugt van goeden huize, en ter bevordering eener deftige opvoeding, beschreven*, ed. P. A. Verwer and Pieter Adriaen (Haerlem: Izaak en Johann Enschede; Haarlem: Jan Bosch, 1750); and *Die Hofmeisterinn, oder die kleine Akademie für das Frauenzimmer: Zum Vergnügen und Unterrichte junger Personen dieses Geschlechtes bey ihrer Erziehung* (Leipzig: Weidmann, 1761).

16. Alessa Johns identifies the passage quoted above to explain how the "'Name and Story' of Jenny Peace create a presence sufficient to construct the ideal atmosphere of friendship and calm" and goes on to connect this to emulatory figures in Fielding's other fictions. Johns, *Feminist Utopias*, 71–74.

17. Elizabeth Montagu to Sarah Scott, May 28, [1756], MO 5754. As quoted in Bannet, "Bluestocking Sisters," 40.

18. Sarah Scott to Elizabeth Montagu, [September 7, 1756], MO 5264. As quoted in Bannet, "Bluestocking Sisters," 40.

19. Johns, *Women's Utopias*, 96; Bannet, "Bluestocking Sisters," 42.

20. Scott, *Beschreibung von Millenium-Hall*.

21. Johns discusses Sophie von La Roche's two novels *Die Geschichte des Fräuleins von Sternheim* (1771) and *Erscheinungen am See Oneida* (1798) and establishes thematic links with *Millenium Hall* without addressing whether or not La Roche had read the work or had read Leprince de Beaumont's *La nouvelle Clarisse* (*Women's Utopias*, 141–55).

22. Charlotte von Einem, "Jugendgeschichte," in *Ich wünschte so gar gelehrt zu warden: drei autobiographien von frauen des 18. Jahrhunderts*, ed. Magdalena Heuser et al. (Gottingen: Wallstein, 1994), 30. Translated and quoted in Dawson, *Contested Quill*, 49.

23. Shortened to a dozen pages from Gabrielle Suzanne Barbot de Villeneuve's hundred-page version published in *La jeune américaine et les contes marins* (1740).

24. As the English translator of another well-read conduct book for girls, Madame d'Épinay's *Conversations d'Emilie* (1774), put it in 1787: "My dear Girls, Your parents having intrusted [*sic*] me with the direction of your first studies, I thought it a duty incumbent on me, to discharge it in a manner that might both instruct and amuse you. Such is the plan of the Conversations which I have translated, and now dedicate to you. That you may, one day, imitate the virtues of the mother, and walk in the steps of the daughter, is the sincere wish of, Ladies, Your affectionate friend, The Translator." *The Conversations of Emily: Translated from the French of Madame la Comtesse d'Epigny. In Two Volumes*, vol. 1 (London: John Marshall, 1787), ix. Quoted in Dow, "Introduction: Women Readers in Europe," 1.

25. Aphra Behn, *Works*, ed. Janet Todd, 7 vols. (Columbus: Ohio State University Press, 1992–96), 4:77. Quoted in Sarah Annes Brown, "Women Translators," 115.

26. For a comparison of the positions taken by Genlis and Staël, see Poortere, *The Philosophical and Literary Ideas of Mme de Staël and Mme de Genlis*.

27. As Isabelle Tremblay points out, "A filiation can be traced between the spiritual thought of Pascal, the fiction of Lafayette, who 'affirms the capacity of women to exercise reason and to make moral choices,' Rousseau's writings, which defend the importance of introspection for knowing happiness, and the novels of Mme de Genlis in which heroines are rewarded for being faithful to themselves" (20).

28. On translators and children's literature, see Lathey, *The Role of Translators in Children's Literature: Invisible Storytellers*.

29. Rebecca Davies has associated this literature with the creation of a new kind of moral authority for mothers, especially in texts such as Genlis's that idealize the maternal role (*Written Maternal Authority*).

30. "History of Lady Mandeville: Written in the Style of Pamela, Clarissa, and Grandison," (Amsterdam, 1764). Mentioned in Van Betten, 81n49.

31. Brooke's preface to *Elements of the History of France, Translated from the Abbé Millot . . . by the Translator of Select Tales from Marmontel, and Author of Sermons by a Lady* (London: Dodsley and Cadell, 1771), vi; cited in Kaplan, xvi. Kaplan traces the relationship between Brooke and Roberts and their prefatory remarks on translation in her excellent introduction.

32. See Fronius on the influence on women of Christian Fürchtegott Gellert's *Briefe, nebst einer praktischen Abhandlung von dem guten Geschmacke in Briefen* (1751) (*Women and Literature*, 156).

33. La Fite's *Entretiens, drames et contes moraux, destinés à l'éducation de la jeunesse* went into six editions (1778, 1784, 1791, 1801, 1809, 1821) and was translated into German and Russian.

34. See also Janse, "Traveller, Pedagogue and Cultural Mediator."

35. WorldCat records are the basis for this.

36. In her prefatory letter, La Fite mistakes Wieland for the author and only realizes that the real author is La Roche when he writes back and corrects her error.

CHAPTER 5

1. See also Niklas Luhmann's *Love as Passion*, which explores how the novelistic idea of passionate love supported the emerging unit of the couple as a fundamental social structure in a complex modernity.

2. The novel was translated into French in 1787 by Henri Rieu and published in Lausanne. This translation has sometimes been mistakenly attributed to Isabelle de Charrière.

3. See van Saas, "Varieties of Dutchness," 11; and Dekker and Vega, "Women and the Dutch Revolutions," 195.

4. Translation mine, from the 1787 French translation of Henri Rieu.

5. Vieu-Kuik, *Keur uit het Werk*, 7–8. Translated and quoted in Van Betten, 103n6.

6. Stéphanie-Félicité du Crest, comtesse de Genlis, *Adele en Theodoor, of Brieven over de Opvoeding door Mevrouw de Gravin de Genlis* (Gravenhage [The Hague]: I. Van Cleef, 1782–1783).

7. "Korte Levensschets van Elisabeth Bekker-Wolff, Weduwe van Adrianus Wolff," death notice in *Algemeene Konst- en Letterbode* 49 (Nov. 16, 1804): 310. Translated and quoted in Van Betten, 107n11.

8. *Célestine, ou la victime des préjugés, par Charlotte Smith: Traduit de l'anglais sur la seconde édition par la citoyenne R . . . ,* 4 vols. [Mme de Rome née Marné de Morville] (Paris: Buisson, An III [1795]). Cited in Astbury, "Charlotte Smith's *The Banished Man*,"133. For more on Smith, see Labbe, *Charlotte Smith in British Romanticism.*

9. See the French translation of *The History of Miss Sara Burgerhart* by Henri Rieu.

10. On Charrière's use of Dutch in writing, see Courtney, *Isabelle de Charrière*, 32.

11. See Caspard, "Conceptions prénuptiales et développement du capitalisme"; and Jeffrey Watt, *Making of Modern Marriage.*

12. Carla Hesse notes this in her discussion of the pregnant servant Josephine in *Trois femmes*, 122.

13. On their relationships with their fathers, see Doody's *Frances Burney*, 10–11, 18–21; and Gutwirth, *Madame de Staël*, 35–45. After her father's death in 1804, Germaine de Staël published *Manuscrits de M. Necker*, preceded by her own "Du caractère de M. Necker, et de sa vie privée." Frances Burney published the three-volume *Memoirs of Doctor Burney* in 1832.

14. See also Rennhak, "Tropes of Exile in the 1790s."

15. Sénac de Meilhan, *L'Émigré* (1797), quoted in Genand, *Romans de l'émigration*, 13.

16. Perry Anderson, *Arguments Within British Marxism*, 37–38, quoted in Moretti, *Atlas of the European Novel*, 29.

17. Cf. Massé, *In the Name of Love.*

18. Translation from Gilles Deleuze and Félix Guattari, "Kafka: Toward a Minor Literature, " in *The Norton Anthology of Theory and Criticism*, ed. Vincent Leitch, 2nd ed. (New York: W.W. Norton, 2010), 1598.

CHAPTER 6

1. Letter in Boswell Papers, Yale University Library, L1249, reproduced and quoted in Courtney, *Isabelle de Charrière*, 211.

2. Carla Hesse includes Charrière in her list of French women writers on "cultural, rather than juridical grounds," and she also makes the point that I make here that "a woman's legal nationality was determined by the citizenship of her father or husband" and indicates that in juridical terms, Madame de Staël was Swiss and then Swedish (35).

3. This scholarship is too extensive to be cited here, but see especially Linda Colley, *The Ordeal of Elizabeth Marsh: A Woman in World History* (New York: Random House, 2007).

4. On Monbart, see Douthwaite, *Exotic Women*; and Monbart, *Lettres tahitiennes*, 36.

5. Elena Gretchanaia, "Varvara-Juliana de Krüdener, Russian author, 1764–1824," Women Writers' Networks, http://www.womenwriters.nl/index.php/Varvara-Juliana_de_Krüdener.

6. *The Life of Harriot Stuart* (1750) and *Euphemia* (1790).

7. On eighteenth-century women travelers from the Netherlands, see Strien-Chardonneau, "Belle, Betje."

8. Therese Huber's tumultuous *The Family Seldorf*, about a German woman of the middling ranks who is seduced and betrayed by a French aristocrat in Revolutionary Paris. See Kontje's reading in *Women, the Novel, and the German Nation*; Hilfiger's in *Gender and Genre*; and Astbury's in *Narrative Responses*.

9. On Huber's short stories, see Gokhale, *Walking the Tightrope*.

10. For discussion of an ethics of hospitality in Inchbald's play *The Massacre*, see Grinnell, "Timely Responses."

11. For notes on the connection of the novel to Sierra Leone, see Shawn Lisa Maurer's excellent appendix to the 2005 Broadview edition of Inchbald, *Nature and Art* (207).

12. Sophie von La Roche, *Erscheinungen am See Oneida*, 3 vols. (Leipzig, 1798); repr. *Sophie: Literatur,* http://sophie.byu.edu/, 2:81–82. Cited by Dietrich, who identifies this passage as noteworthy and provides the translation in "Schwimme mit mir," 17.

13. La Roche, *Erscheinungen*, 2:146 (see previous note). As cited and translated by Dietrich, 23.

14. This is Shapin and Schaffer's term for one of the "technologies" that produces scientific and experimental validation. *Leviathan and the Air-Pump*, 22–79.

15. Mary Wollstonecraft, *Historical and Moral View of the French Revolution*, in *Works of Mary Wollstonecraft*, 7 vols., ed. Marilyn Butler and Janet Todd (London: Pickering and Chatto/New York: New York University Press, 1989), 6:230. Quoted in and discussed by Furniss, 70.

16. Through publication of "Zulma," Staël sought, as she claimed in a letter to her husband, to vindicate herself from Dumouriez's charges of inappropriate interference in politics by placing herself before the public as the author of a fiction, in a way that was completely independent from politics. Accused by General Dumouriez of joining "other women on the trestles of the Revolution," Staël was charged with playing the "common role of a female intriguer like the women of the court, or of a fanatic, like the *poissardes* [voluble market women]." *Mémoire du Général Dumouriez écrit par lui-même* (Hamburg, 1794), 118. Germaine de Staël, *Correspondance générale,* ed. B. W. Jasinski (Paris : J.-J. Pauvert, 1965), 2:604–5. Quoted and discussed in Broccardo, "Penser aux frontières du politique," 409–10.

17. This quotation and the following from *Essai sur les fictions* published in Staël, *Zulma, et Trois nouvelles.*

18. Richardson's *Clarissa*, La Fayette's *Princesse de Clèves*, Claudine Alexandrine Guérin de Tencin's *Mémoires du comte de Comminge*, Bernardin de Saint-Pierre's *Paul et Virginie*, "most of the writings of madame Riccoboni," Isabelle de Montolieu's *Caroline de Litchfield*, Charrière's "Caliste," Frances Burney's *Camilla, A Picture of Youth*, and Rousseau's *Julie, ou La Nouvelle Héloïse* (50–51).

19. Fritz Strich, *Goethe and World Literature* (London: Routledge, 1949), 13. Quoted in Damrosch, 3.

20. See the opening pages of Germaine de Staël's "Dix années d'exil."

21. Charrière, *Sainte-Anne et les Ruines de Yedburg*, in *L'Abbé de la Tour ou recueil de nouvelles et autres écrits divers*, tome III (Leipzig, 1799).

22. Championing women who developed a dedicated skill, whether writing, sewing, or laundering, and perhaps not reluctant to take on the role of Dutch Old Master, Charrière also extended opportunities for translation to Therese Huber's daughter. Astbury, "Adapting the Revolution," 101. For the Charrière and Thérèse Huber relationship, Astbury refers readers to Courtney, *Isabelle de Charrière*, 543. For *Lettres trouvées dans des porte-feuilles d'émigrés*, see *Œuvres 8:* 766–79.

23. On the animosity and rivalry between Charrière and Staël, see Trousson, *Mme de Charrière et Mme de Staël.*

24. Trousson also notes that Charrière writes the continuation in response to Staël's tales.

25. Therese's childhood friend from Göttingen, Meta Forkel-Liebeskind, translated as a subcontractor for Therese Heyne's first husband, Georg Forster, and went on to translate alongside Heyne's second husband, Ludwig Ferdinand Huber. Johns, *Bluestocking,* 57.

26. On Dorothea von Schlegel's personal response to Staël and the translation, see J. Martin, 55, 60.

Works Cited

Alighieri, Dante. *Dante's Inferno, A New Translation in Terza Rima*. Trans. Robert M. Torrance. Bloomington, IN: Xlibris, 2011.

Alliston, April. "Transnational Sympathies, Imaginary Communities." In *The Literary Channel: The Inter-National Invention of the Novel*, ed. Margaret Cohen and Carolyn Dever, 133–48. Princeton: Princeton University Press, 2002.

Anderson, Benedict. *Imagined Communities: Reflections on the Origin and Spread of Nationalism*. London: Verso, 2006.

Anderson, Perry. *Arguments Within British Marxism*. London: Verso, 1980.

Angliviel de la Beaumelle, Laurent. *Mémoires pour servir à l'histoire de Mme de Maintenon et à celle du siècle passé*. 2 vols. The Hague: Chez Pierre Gosse; Leiden: Chez Elie Luzac, 1757. Google Books.

Anson, Elizabeth, and Florence Anson, editors. *Mary Hamilton, . . . from Letters and Diaries, 1756–1816*. London: John Murray, 1925.

Apter, Emily. *Against World Literature: On the Politics of Untranslatability*. London: Verso, 2013.

Armstrong, Nancy. *Desire and Domestic Fiction: A Political History of the Novel*. New York: Oxford University Press, 1987.

Armstrong, Nancy, and Leonard Tennenhouse. *Novels in the Time of Democratic Writing: The American Example*. Philadelphia: University of Pennsylvania Press, 2018.

Astbury, Katherine. "Adapting the Revolution: Therese Huber and Isabelle de Charrière's *Lettres trouvées dans les porte-feuilles d'émigrés*." In *Translators, Interpreters, Mediators: Women Writers 1700–1900*, ed. Gillian E. Dow, 99–110. Oxford: Peter Lang, 2007. European Connections 25.

———. "Charlotte Smith's *The Banished Man* in French Translation: Or the Politics of Novel-Writing During the Revolution." In *Charlotte Smith in British Romanticism*, ed. Jacqueline Labbe, 129–44. London: Pickering and Chatto, 2008.

———. *Narrative Responses to the Trauma of the French Revolution*. London: Legenda, 2012.

Astell, Mary. *A Serious Proposal to the Ladies, Parts I and II*. Ed. Patricia Springborg. London: Pickering & Chatto, 1997.

Auger, L. S. *Lettres de Mmes. de Villars, de La Fayette, de Tencin, de Coulanges, de Ninon de l'Enclos et de Mademoiselle Aïssé: Accompagnées de notices biographiques, de notes explicatives, et de "La coquette vengée."* Paris: Chez Léopold Collin, 1806. Google Books.

Aulnoy, Marie-Catherine Le Jumel de Barneville, comtesse d'. *Mémoires de la cour d'Espagne*. The Hague: Chez Adrien Moetjens, 1691.

———. *Nouvelles d'Elisabeth Reyne d'Angleterre*. Paris: Chez Claude Barbin, 1674.

Ballard, George. *Memoirs of Several Ladies of Great Britain, Who Have Been Celebrated for Their Writings or Skill in the Learned Languages, Arts and Sciences.* Oxford: W. Jackson, 1752. https://archive.org/details/memoirsofseveralooball.

Ballaster, Ros. *Seductive Forms: Women's Amatory Fiction from 1684 to 1740.* Oxford: Oxford University Press, 1992.

Bannet, Eve Tavor. "The Bluestocking Sisters: Women's Patronage, Millenium Hall, and 'The Visible Providence of a Country'." *Eighteenth-Century Life* 30, no. 1 (December 2006): 25–55.

Batchelor, Jennie, and Gillian Dow. "Introduction: Feminisms and Futures: Women's Writing 1660–1830." In *Women's Writing, 1660–1830: Feminisms and Futures*, ed. Jennie Batchelor and G. Dow, 11–20. London: Palgrave Macmillan, 2016.

Batchelor, Jennie. "The Lady's Magazine (1770–1818): Understanding the Emergence of a Genre." https://www.kent.ac.uk/english/ladys-magazine/about/index.html.

Barash, Carol. *English Women's Poetry, 1649–1714: Politics, Community, and Linguistic Authority.* Oxford: Oxford University Press, 1996.

Barbapiccola, Giuseppa Eleonora. "The Translator to the Reader." In *The Contest for Knowledge: Debates over Women's Learning in Eighteenth-Century Italy*, ed. and trans. Paula Findlen and Rebecca Messbarger, 52–55. Chicago: University of Chicago Press, 2005.

Barbauld, Anna Laetitia, and John Aikin. *Evenings at Home, or the Juvenile Budget Opened.* 6 vols. London: Baldwin, Cradock, and Joy, 1819. babel.hathitrust.org.

Barker-Benfield, G. J. *The Culture of Sensibility: Sex and Society in Eighteenth-Century Britain.* Chicago: University of Chicago Press, 1992.

Barthélémy, Édouard de, and René Kervilier. *Un tournoi de trois pucelles en l'honneur de Jeanne d'Arc: Lettres inédites de Conrart, de Mlle de Scudéry et de Mlle du Moulin.* Paris: Picard, 1878.

Bate, Walter Jackson. *The Burden of the Past and the English Poet.* New York: Norton, 1970.

Batsaki, Yota. "Exile as the Inaudible Accent in Germaine de Staël's *Corinne, ou l'Italie*." *Comparative Literature* 61, no. 1 (Winter 2009): 26–42.

Beasley, Faith. *Salons, History and the Creation of Seventeenth-Century France: Mastering Memory.* Burlington, VT: Ashgate, 2006.

Beebee, Thomas O. *Clarissa on the Continent: Translation and Seduction.* University Park: Pennsylvania State University Press, 1990.

Bekker-Wolff, Elisabeth, and Aagke Deken. *Histoire de Mademoiselle Sara Burgerhart; publiée en forme de lettres . . . Traduite du Hollandois d'après la seconde édition.* Trans. Henri Rieu. Lausanne: Chez François Grasset, 1787.

Béringuier, Nadine. *Conduct Books for Girls in Enlightenment France.* Farnham, UK: Ashgate, 2011.

Binhammer, Katherine. "Later Fiction." In *The Cambridge Companion to Women's Writing in Britain, 1660–1789*, ed. Catherine Ingrassia, 180–95. Cambridge: Cambridge University Press, 2015.

Birberick, Anne L. "Behind Closed Doors: Theater, Pedagogy and the 'Crisis' of *Esther*." In *The Art of Instruction: Essays on Pedagogy and Literature in Seventeenth-Century France*, ed. Birberick, 179–99. Amsterdam: Rodopi, 2008.

Boccaccio, Giovanni. *Concerning Famous Women.* Trans. Guido Guarino. New Brunswick, NJ: Rutgers University Press, 1963.

———. *De preclaris mulieribus, that is to say in Englyshe, of the ryghte renoumyde ladyes.* London: Egerton, Whitehall, 1789. Eighteenth-Century Collections Online. Gale. 2 Feb. 2019.

Bolufer, Mónica. "Expression of Interest. CIRGEN: Circulating Gender in the Global Enlightenment: Ideas, Networks, Agencies." ESHORIZONTE 2020. https://eshorizonte2020.es/expressions-of-interests/monica-bolufer.

Bolzoni, Lina. *The Gallery of Memory: Literary and Iconographic Models in the Age of the Printing Press*, trans. Jeremy Parzen. Toronto: University of Toronto Press, 2001.

Boswell, James. *Boswell in Holland, 1763–1764*. Ed. Frederick A. Pottle. New York: McGraw-Hill, 1952.

———. *The Life of Samuel Johnson*. 6 vols. Ed. George Birkbeck Hill. Oxford: Clarendon Press, 1897.

Bourdieu, Pierre. *The Field of Cultural Production: Essays on Art and Literature*. New York: Columbia University Press, 1994.

———. *The Rules of Art: Genesis and Structure in the Literary Field*. Cambridge: Polity, 2016.

Boureau, Alain. "Franciscan Piety and Voracity: Uses and Strategies in the Hagiographic Pamphlet." In *The Culture of Print: Power and the Uses of Print in Early Modern Europe*, ed. Roger Chartier, 15–58. Princeton: Princeton University Press, 1989.

Bowers, Toni. *Force or Fraud: British Seduction Stories and the Problem of Resistance, 1660–1760*. Oxford: Oxford University Press, 2011.

Bree, Linda. *Sarah Fielding*. New York: Twayne, 1996.

Briquet, Fortunée. *Dictionnaire historique, littéraire et bibliographique des Françaises et des étrangères naturalisées en France*. Paris: Treuttel et Würtz, 1804. http://siefar.org/dictionnaire/fr/Cat%C3%A9gorie:Dictionnaire_Fortun%C3%A9e_Briquet.

Broad, Jacqueline. "Mary Astell on Virtuous Friendship." *Parergon* 26, no. 2 (2009): 65–86.

Broccardo, Laura. "'Penser aux frontières du politique' le 'cas' *Zulma* de Germaine de Staël." *Dix-huitième siècle* 47 (2015): 409–28.

Broglie, Gabriel de. *Madame de Genlis*. Paris: Libraire Académique Perrin, 1985.

Brooke, Frances. *The History of Emily Montague*. 1769. Reprint, Toronto: McClelland and Stewart, 1995.

Brooks, Peter. *The Novel of Worldliness: Crébillon, Marivaux, Laclos, Stendhal*. Princeton: Princeton University Press, 1969.

Broomans, Petra, and Sandra van Voorst. *Rethinking Cultural Transfer and Transmission: Reflections and New Perspectives*. Groningen, Netherlands: Barkhuis, 2012.

Brouard-Arends, Isabelle. "Introduction." In *Lectrices d'ancien régime*, ed. Brouard-Arends. Rennes, France: Presses Universitaires de Rennes, 2003.

Brown, Garrett Wallace. "Kant's Cosmopolitanism." In *The Cosmopolitanism Reader*, ed. Garrett Wallace Brown and David Held, 45–60. Cambridge: Polity, 2010.

Brown, Hilary. *Luise Gottsched the Translator*. Rochester, NY: Boydell and Brewer, 2012.

Brown, Penny. *A Critical History of French Children's Literature: The Beginnings, 1600–1830*. Vol. 1. London: Routledge, 2008.

———. "'Girls Aloud': Dialogue as Pedagogical Tool in Eighteenth-Century French Children's Literature." *The Lion and the Unicorn* 33, no. 2 (April 2009): 202–18.

———. "Tales of Castle and Cottage: Mme de Genlis and Women Writers for Children in the Romantic Period." Corvey Women Writers on the Web, *CW3 Journal*, Sheffield Hallam University. https://www2.shu.ac.uk/corvey/cw3journal/issuethree/brown.html. Accessed March 9, 2017.

Brown, Sarah Annes. "Women Translators." In *The Oxford History of Literary Translation in English*, Vol. 3: 1660–1790, ed. Stuart Gillespie and David Hopkins, 111–20. New York: Oxford University Press, 2005.

Brown, Susan, Patricia Clements, and Isobel Grundy, eds. *Orlando: Women's Writing in the British Isles from the Beginnings to the Present.* Cambridge: Cambridge University Press Online, 2006–. http://orlando.cambridge.org.

Brown, Virginia. "Introduction." In Giovanni Boccaccio, *Concerning Famous Women*, trans. Virginia Brown, i–xxv. Cambridge, MA: Harvard University Press, 2003.

Burney, Frances. "Brief Reflexions Relative to the Emigrant French Clergy." 1793. Project Gutenberg (Ebook #29125). http://www.gutenberg.org/cache/epub/29125/pg29125.txt.

———. *The Court Journals and Letters of Frances Burney, Vol. 1: 1786.* Ed. Peter Sabor. Oxford: Clarendon, 2011.

———. *The Court Journals and Letters of Frances Burney, Vol. 2: 1787.* Ed. Stewart Cooke. Oxford: Clarendon, 2011.

———. *Evelina.* Ed. Edward A. Bloom. Oxford: Oxford University Press, 2008.

———. *Journals and Letters.* Ed. Peter Sabor and Lars E. Troide. London: Penguin, 2001.

———. *The Wanderer; or, Female Difficulties.* Ed. Margaret Anne Doody et al. Oxford: Oxford University Press, 2001.

Campbell, Julie D., and Anne R. Larsen, editors. *Early Modern Women and Transnational Communities of Letters.* London: Routledge, 2009.

Casanova, Pascale. *The World Republic of Letters.* Cambridge, MA: Harvard University Press, 2004.

Caspard, Pierre. "Conceptions prénuptiales et développement du capitalisme dans la principauté de Neuchâtel (1678–1820)." *Annales: Économies, Sociétés, Civilisations* 29, no. 4 (July–August 1974): 989–1008.

Castle, Terry. *Clarissa's Ciphers: Meaning and Disruption in Richardson's* Clarissa. Ithaca, NY: Cornell University Press, 1982.

Chambers, Ephraim. *Cyclopedia, or an Universal Dictionary of Arts and Sciences.* The ARTFL Project I, no. 309. http://digicoll.library.wisc.edu/cgi-bin/HistSciTech/HistSciTechidx?type = turn&entity = HistSciTech.Cyclopaedia01.p0464&isize = M&id = HistSci Tech.Cyclo paedia01.

Charrière, Isabelle de. *Œuvres complètes.* 10 vols. Amsterdam: G. A. van Oorschot, 1979–84.

———. *Lettres de Mistress Henley.* Ed. Joan Hinde Stewart and Philip Stewart. New York: MLA Texts and Translations Series, 1993.

———. *There Are No Letters Like Yours: The Correspondence of Isabelle de Charrière and Constant d'Hermenches.* Ed. and trans. Janet Whatley. Lincoln: University of Nebraska Press, 2000.

———. *Three Women.* Trans. Emma Rooksby. New York: MLA Texts and Translation Series, 2007.

Cheek, Pamela. " 'Demi-Monde'—Review Essay: Nina Kushner, *Erotic Exchanges: The World of Elite Prostitution in Eighteenth-Century Paris.*" *Eighteenth-Century Life* 40, no. 1 (January 2016): 119–21.

———. *Sexual Antipodes: Enlightenment Globalization and the Placing of Sex.* Stanford: Stanford University Press, 2003.

Clark Schaneman, Judith. "Rewriting *Adèle et Théodore:* Intertextual Connections Between Madame de Genlis and Ann Radcliffe." *Comparative Literature Studies* 38, no. 1 (2001): 31–45.

Cohen, Margaret. "Sentimental Communities." In *The Literary Channel: The Inter-National Invention of the Novel*, ed. Margaret Cohen and Carolyn Dever, 106–32. Princeton: Princeton University Press, 2002.

———. *The Sentimental Education of the Novel.* Princeton: Princeton University Press, 1999.

Cohen, Margaret, and Susan Dever. "Introduction." In *The Literary Channel: The International Invention of the Novel,* ed. Margaret Cohen and Carolyn Dever, 1–34. Princeton: Princeton University Press, 2009.

Cohen, Michèle. "Sexualizing and Gendering the French Tongue in Eighteenth-Century England." *French Studies Bulletin* 31:4, no. 117 (December 2010): 73–76.

Conley, John. "Madeleine de Scudéry." In *The Stanford Encyclopedia of Philosophy,* ed. Edward N. Zalta, Spring 2016 edition. http://plato.stanford.edu/archives/spr2016/entries/madeleine-scudery/.

Constant, Paule. *Un monde à l'usage des demoiselles.* Paris: Gallimard, 1987.

Cossy, Valérie. *Jane Austen in Switzerland.* Geneva: Slatkine, 2006.

Courtney, C. P. *Isabelle de Charrière (Belle de Zuylen): A Biography.* Oxford: Voltaire Foundation, 1993.

Cox, Virginia. *Lyric Poetry by Women of the Italian Renaissance.* Baltimore: Johns Hopkins University Press, 2013.

———. *Prodigious Muse: Women's Writing in Counter-Reformation Italy.* Baltimore: Johns Hopkins University Press, 2011.

Craciun, Adriana. *British Women Writers and the French Revolution: Citizens of the World.* New York: Palgrave MacMillan, 2005.

Cravera, Benedetta. *L'Âge de la conversation.* Paris: Gallimard, 2002.

Crummy, M. Ione. "The Peripheral Heroine Takes Center Stage: From Owenson's National Tale to Staël's European Genre." In *Staël's Philosophy of the Passions: Sensibility, Society, and the Sister Arts,* ed. Tili Boon Cuillé and Karyna Szmurlo, 95–116. Lewisburg, PA: Bucknell University Press, 2013.

Culler, Jonathan. "The Literary in Theory." In *What's Left of Theory: New Work on the Politics of Literary Theory,* ed. Judith Butler, John Guillory, and Kendall Thomas, 273–293. New York: Routledge, 2002.

Curran, Stuart. "Romanticism Displaced and Placeless." *European Romantic Review* 20, no. 5 (December 2009): 637–50.

Dacier, Anne Le Fèvre. *L'Iliade d'Homère, traduite en françois, avec des remarques.* 4 vols. Paris: Gabriel Martin, Jean-Baptiste Coignard et les Frères Guerin, 1741. https://scholarworks.umass.edu/cgi/viewcontent.cgi?article = 1016&content + french_translators.

———. *Les poésies d'Anacreon et de Sapho.* Amsterdam: Chez la Veuve de Paul Marret, 1716. Google Books.

Damrosch, David. *What Is World Literature?* Princeton: Princeton University Press, 2003.

Darnton, Robert. *The Corpus of Clandestine Literature in France, 1769–1789.* New York: W.W. Norton, 1995.

Davies, Rebecca. *Written Maternal Authority and Eighteenth-Century Education in Britain: Educating by the Book.* Burlington, VT: Ashgate, 2014.

Dawson, Ruth P. *The Contested Quill: Literature by Women in Germany, 1770–1800.* Newark: University of Delaware Press, 2002.

De Baar, Mirjam. "Transgressing Gender Codes: Anna Maria van Schurman and Antoinette Bourignon as Contrasting Examples." In *Women of the Golden Age: An International Debate on Women in Seventeenth-Century Holland, England and Italy,* ed. Els Kloek et al., 143–52. Hilversum, Netherlands: Verlorun, 1998.

DeJean, Joan. *Fictions of Sappho, 1546–1937.* Chicago: University of Chicago Press, 1989.

————. *Tender Geographies: Women and the Origins of the Novel in France.* New York: Columbia University Press, 1991.

DeJean, Joan, and Nancy K. Miller. "Introduction." In Françoise de Graffigny, *Lettres d'une Péruvienne.* New York: Modern Language Association of America, 1993.

Dekker, Rudolf M., and Judith A. Vega, "Women and the Dutch Revolutions of the Late Eighteenth Century." In *Political and Historical Encyclopedia of Women,* ed. Christine Fauré et al., 195–213. London: Routledge, 2003. ProQuest Ebook Central. https://ebook central.proquest.com/lib/unm/detail.action?docID = 183243.

Deleuze, Gilles, and Félix Guattari. *Kafka: Pour une littérature mineure.* Paris: Éditions de minuit, 1975.

Diaconoff, Suellen. *Through the Reading Glass: Women, Books and Sex in the French Enlightenment.* Albany: State University of New York Press, 2005.

Dictionnaire de l'Académie française, 1st ed. (1694). In *Dictionnaires d'autrefois.* University of Chicago, ARTFL Encyclopédie Project, Spring 2016 edition. Ed. Robert Morrissey and Glenn Roe. http://encyclopedie.uchicago.edu/.

Dietrich, Linda. "Schwimme mit mir hinüber zu den Hütten unserer Nachbarn": Colonial Islands in Sophie von La Roche's *Erscheinungen am See Oneida* (1798) and Jacques-Henri Bernardin de Saint-Pierre's *Paul et Virginie* (1788)." In *Sophie Discovers Amerika: German-Speaking Women Write the New World,* ed. Robert B. McFarland and Michelle Stott James, 16–29. Rochester, NY: Camden House, 2014.

Dijk, Suzan van. "Early Historiography of Dutch and French Women's Literature." In *Writing the History of Women's Writing: Toward an International Approach,* ed. Suzan van Dijk, Lia van Gemert, and Sheila Ottway, 81–94. Amsterdam: KNAW, 2001.

————. " 'Les femmes me sont toujours de quelque chose': Isabelle de Charrière rencontre Elizabeth Inchbald." In *Topographie de la rencontre dans le roman européen,* ed. Jean-Pierre Dubost, 399–411. Clermont-Ferrand, France: Presses universitaires Blaise Pascal, Maison des sciences de l'homme, 2008.

————. " 'Gender' et traduction: Madame de Genlis traduite par une romancière hollandaise, Elisabeth Bekker (Betje Wolff)." In *La traduction des genres non romanesques au XVIIIème siècle,* ed. Annie Cointre and Annie Rivara, 299–314. Metz, France: Presses Universitaires de Metz, 2003.

————. "La lecture féminine: les correspondantes d'Isabelle de Charrière comme témoins." In *Le second triomphe de roman de XVIIIè siècle,* ed. Philip Stewart and Michel Delon, 85–104. Oxford: Voltaire Foundation, 2009.

————, editor. *Writing the History of Women's Writing: Toward an International Approach.* Amsterdam: KNAW, 2001.

Dijk, Suzan van, and Alicia C. Montoya. "Madame Leprince de Beaumont, Mademoiselle Bonne en hun Nederlandse lezers." *De achttiende eeuw* 34 (2002): 5–32.

Dijk, Suzan van, and Jo Nesbit et al., editors. " 'I Have Heard About You'—Foreign Women's Writing Crossing the Dutch Border: From Sappho to Selma Lagerlöf." Hilversum, Netherlands: Verloren, 2004.

Dobie, Madeleine. *Trading Places: Colonization and Slavery in Eighteenth-Century French Culture.* Ithaca, NY: Cornell University Press, 2010.

Doody, Margaret Anne. "Burney and Politics." In *The Cambridge Companion to Frances Burney,* ed. Peter Sabor, 93–110. Cambridge: Cambridge University Press, 2007.

————. *Frances Burney: The Life in the Works.* New Brunswick, NJ: Rutgers University Press, 1988.

———. "Introduction." Charlotte Lennox, *The Female Quixote, or the Adventures of Arabella*, ed. Margaret Dalziel, xi–xxxii. Oxford: Oxford University Press, 2008.

———. "Missing les Muses: Madame de Staël and Frances Burney." *Colloquium Helveticum: Cahiers Suisses de Littérature Générale et Comparée* 25 (1997): 81–117.

Douthwaite, Julia V. *Exotic Women: Literary Heroines and Cultural Strategies in Ancien Régime France.* Philadelphia: University of Pennsylvania Press, 1992

Douxménil. *The Memoirs of Ninon de l'Enclos, with her Letters to Monsr de St. Evremond and to the Marquise de Sévigné: Collected and Translated from the French, by a Lady*, vol. 1. Trans. Elizabeth Griffith. London: R. and J. Dodsley, 1761.

Dow, Gillian, editor. *Adelaide and Theodore.* London: Pickering and Chatto, 2014.

———. "Introduction—Women Readers in Europe: Readers, Writers, Salonnières, 1750–1900." *Women's Writing* 18, no. 1 (February 2011), ix–xx.

———. "'The Biographical Impulse' and Pan-European Women's Writing." In *Women's Writing, 1660–1830: Feminisms and Futures*, eds. Jennie Batchelor and G. Dow, 203–23. London: Palgrave Macmillan, 2016.

———. "Stéphanie-Félicité de Genlis and the French Historical Novel in Romantic Britain." *Women's Writing* 19, no. 3 (August 2012): 273–92.

———, ed. "Introduction." In *Translators, Interpreters, Mediators: Women Writers 1700–1900*, ed. Dow, 9–20. Oxford: Peter Lang, 2007.

Dubois-Nayt, Armel, Nicole Dufournaud, and Anne Paupert, editors. *Revisiter la "querelle des femmes": Discours sur l'égalité/inégalité des sexes, de 1400 à 1600*, 3. Saint-Étienne, France: Publications de l'Université de Saint-Étienne, 2013.

Dufrénoy, Adélaïde Gillette Billet. *La femme auteur, ou les inconvéniens de la célébrité*, vol. 1. Paris: Chez Bichet, 1812. http://gallica.bnf.fr/ark:/12148/bpt6k113937q/f10.image.

Dunn-Lardeau, Brenda. "The Mnemonic Architecture of the *Palais des Nobles Dames* (Lyons, 1534): In Defence of Famous Women." In *Ars Reminiscendi: Mind and Memory in Renaissance Culture*, ed. Donald Beecher and Grant Williams, 32–33. Toronto: Center for Reformation and Rennaissance Studies, 2009.

Eagleton, Terry. *The Rape of Clarissa: Writing, Sexuality, and Class Struggle in Samuel Richardson.* Minneapolis: University of Minnesota Press, 1982.

Edgeworth, Maria. *The Life and Letters of Maria Edgeworth*, vols. 1–2. London: Houghton Mifflin, 1894.

Encyclopédie, ou dictionnaire raisonné des sciences, des arts et des métiers, etc., ed. Denis Diderot and Jean le Rond d'Alembert. Chicago: University of Chicago, ARTFL Encyclopédie Project, Autumn 2017 edition, ed. Robert Morrissey and Glenn Roe. http://encyclopedie.uchicago.edu.libproxy.unm.edu/.

Épinay, Madame d'. *The Conversations of Emily: Translated from the French of Madame la Comtesse d'Epigny. In Two Volumes*, vol. 1. London: John Marshall, 1787. Google Books.

Erdmann, Axel. *My Gracious Silence: Women in the Mirror of 16th Century Printing in Western Europe.* Lucerne: Gilhofer & Ranschburg, 1999.

Espagne, Michel. "La notion de transfert culturel." *Revues Sciences/Lettres* 1 (2013): 1–21. https://journals.openedition.org/rsl/219.

Everard, Myriam, "Twee 'dames hollandoises' in Trévoux." *De Achttiende Eeuw. Jaargang* 38 (2006): 147–67.

Ezell, Margaret J. M. *Writing Women's Literary History.* Baltimore: Johns Hopkins University Press, 1993.

Facer, Ruth. "Charlotte (Ramsay) Lennox (c. 1729–1804)." Women Writer Biographies, Chawton House. https://chawtonhouse.org/_www/wp-content/uploads/2012/06/Charlotte-Lennox.pdf.

Fénelon, François de Salignac de la Mothe. *De l'éducation des filles*. Paris: P. Auboin, 1687. Bibliothèque Nationale de France, Gallica. ark:/12148/btv1b86233115h.

———. *Dialogue des morts*. Ed. B. Julien. Paris: L. Hachette, 1889. Bibliothèque Nationale de France, Gallica. ark:/12148/bpt6k9691708s.

———. *Télémaque*. Paris: Garnier-Flammarion, 1968.

Ferguson, Frances. "Rape and the Rise of the Novel." *Representations* 20 (1987): 88–112.

Fielding, Henry. *Joseph Andrews and Shamela*. Ed. and intro. Judith Hawley. London: Penguin Book, 1999.

Floyd, Ann, trans. *Fatal Gallantry: or, the Secret History of Henrietta Princess of England, Daughter of K. Charles the I. and Wife of Phillip of France, Duke of Orleans. With the Manner of Her Death, Illustrated by Letters from the Ministers of State, Then Employed Both at the Courts of France and England, and the Characters of the Principal Quality in the French Court. Writ by the Countess de la Fayette Who Had the Honour of Being Very Intimate with the Princess.* London, 1722.

Fielding, Sarah. *The Governess; or, the Little Female Academy*. Ed. and intro. Candace Ward. Peterborough, Ontario: Broadview, 2005.

———. *The Lives of Cleopatra and Octavia*. London: A. Millar, 1758. Google books.

Freedman, Jeffrey. *Books Without Borders: French Cosmopolitanism and German Literary Markets*. Philadelphia: University of Pennsylvania Press, 2012.

Fronius, Helen. *Women and Literature in the Goethe Era, 1770–1820: Determined Dilettantes*. Oxford: Clarendon, 2007.

Furniss, Tom, "Mary Wollstonecraft's French Revolution." In *Cambridge Companion to Mary Wollstonecraft*, ed. Claudia Johnson, 59–81. Cambridge: Cambridge University Press, 2002.

Gallagher, Catherine. *Nobody's Story: The Vanishing Acts of Women Authors in the Marketplace, 1670–1820*. Berkeley: University of California Press, 1995.

Garwood, Rebecca. "Frances Brooke (1724–1789)." Women Writer Biographies, Chawton House. https://chawtonhouse.org/_www/wp-content/uploads/2012/06/Frances-Brooke.pdf.

Gélieu, Isabelle de. *Louise et Albert ou le danger d'être trop exigeant*. Lausanne: Chez Hignou, 1803. Google Books.

Gemert, Lia van, Hermina Joldersma, Olga Van Marion, Dieuwke Van der Poel, and Riet Schenkeveld-van der Dussen, eds. *Women's Writing from the Low Countries 1200–1875: A Bilingual Anthology*. Amsterdam: Amsterdam University Press, 2010.

Genand, Stéphanie. *Romans de l'émigration, 1797–1803*. Paris: Honoré Champion, 2008.

Genlis, Stéphanie-Félicité Du Crest, comtesse de. *Adèle et Théodore, ou lettres sur l'éducation*. 3 vols. Paris: M. Lambert & F.J. Baudouin, 1782. Bibliothèque nationale de France. ark:/12148/bpt6k5478136b.

———. *De l'influence des femmes sur la littérature française, comme protectrices des lettres et comme auteurs, ou précis de l'histoire des femmes françaises les plus célèbres*. Paris: Maradan, 1811. Bibliothèque Nationale de France, Gallica. ark:/12148/cb304956583.

———. *Dictionnaire critique et raisonné des étiquettes de la cour*, vol. 1. Paris: P. Mongie aîné, 1818.

———. *Histoire de la duchesse de C****. Ed. Mary Trouille. Modern Humanities Research Association, Critical Texts 21. London: Modern Humanities Research Association, 2010.

———. *Théâtre à l'usage des jeunes personnes.* 4 vols. Paris: Chez Panckoucke, 1779. Bibliothèque nationale de France. ark:/12148/cb304955982.

———. *Veillées du château, ou cours de morale à l'usage des enfans.* 2 vols. Paris: Lambert and Baudouin, 1784. Bibliothèque nationale de France. ark:/12148/bpt6k62607816.

———. *Zélie, ou l'ingénue, comédie en cinq actes.* In *Théâtre de Société,* vol. 2, 167–368. Paris: M. Lambert & F. J. Baudouin. Google books.

Gilleir, Anke, and Alicia Celina Montoya. "Introduction: Toward a New Conception of Women's Literary History." In *Women Writing Back/Writing Women Back: Transnational Perspectives from the Late Middle Ages to the Dawn of the Modern Era,* ed. Gilleir et al., 1–20. Leiden: Brill, 2010.

Gilroy, Paul. *Postcolonial Melancholia.* New York: Columbia University Press, 2005.

Goethe, Johann Wolfgang von. *The Autobiography of Goethe: Truth and Poetry, from My Own Life,* 13 vols. Trans. John Oxenford. London: Henry G. Bohn, 1848. https://archive.org/stream/autogoetheoogoetuoft/autogoetheoogoetuoft_djvu.txt.

Gokhale, Vibha Bakshi. *Walking the Tightrope: A Feminist Reading of Therese Huber's Stories.* Columbia, SC: Camden House, 1996.

Goldsmith, Elizabeth C. "Authority, Authenticity, and the Publication of Letters by Women." In *Writing the Female Voice: Essays on Epistolary Literature,* ed. Goldsmith, 46–59. Boston: Northeastern University Press, 1989.

———. *"Exclusive Conversations": The Art of Interaction in Seventeenth-Century France.* Philadelphia: University of Pennsylvania Press, 1988.

Goldsmith, Elizabeth C., and Dena Goodman, eds. *Going Public: Women and Publishing in Early Modern France.* Ithaca, NY: Cornell University Press, 1995.

Goodman, Dena. *"L'Ortografe des Dames: Gender and Language in the Old Regime."* In *Women, Gender, and Enlightenment,* ed. Sarah Knott and Barbara Taylor, 195–223. New York: Palgrave MacMillan, 2007.

Graffigny, Françoise de. *Lettres d'une Péruvienne.* Intro. Joan DeJean and Nancy K. Miller. New York: Modern Language Association of America, 1993.

———. *Œuvres posthumes de Madame de Grafigny; contenant Ziman & Zenise, suivi de Phaza, Comédies en un Acte en Prose.* Amsterdam, 1770. Google books.

Greene, Ellen, editor. *Re-Reading Sappho: Reception and Transmission.* Berkeley: University of California Press, 1999.

Greer, Donald. *The Incidence of Emigration During the French Revolution.* Cambridge, MA: Harvard University Press, 1951.

Grenby, M. O. "Delightful Instruction? Assessing Children's Use of Educational Books in the Long Eighteenth Century." In *Educating the Child in Enlightenment Britain: Beliefs, Cultures, Practices,* ed. Mary Hilton and Jill Shefrin, 181–98. Farnham, UK: Ashgate, 2009.

Gretchanaia, Elena. "Varvara-Juliana de Krüdener, Russian author, 1764–1824." Women Writers' Networks. http://www.womenwriters.nl/index.php/Varvara-Juliana_de_Krüdener.

Grey, Jill E. "Introduction." In Sarah Fielding, *The Governess, or Little Female Academy,* 78–79. Facsimile ed. London: Oxford University Press, 1968.

Griffiths, Elystan. "Cosmopolitanism, Nationalism and Women's Education: The European Dimension of Sophie von La Roche's Journal *Pomona für Teutschlands Töchter* (1783–84." *Oxford German Studies* 4, no. 2 (2013): 139–57.

Grinnell, George C. "Timely Responses: Violence and Immediacy in Inchbald's *The Massacre.*" *European Romantic Review* 24, no. 6 (2013): 645–63.

Guest, Harriet. *Empire, Barbarism, and Civilisation: Captain Cook, Wiliam Hodges and the Return to the Pacific.* Cambridge: Cambridge University Press, 2007.

―――. "The Wanton Muse: Politics and Gender in Gothic Theory After 1760." In *Beyond Romanticism: New Approaches to Texts and Contexts, 1780–1832,* ed. Stephen Copley, 118–39. London: Routledge, 1992.

Gutwirth, Madelyn. *Madame de Staël, Novelist: The Emergence of the Artist as Woman.* Urbana: University of Illinois Press, 1978.

Hampsten, Elizabeth. "Petticoat Authors: 1660–1721." *Women's Studies* 7, no. 1–2 (1980): 21–38.

Havelange, Isabelle de. "Des livres pour les demoiselles du XVII siècle–1ère moitié du XIXe siècle." In *Lectrices d'ancien régime,* ed. Isabelle Brouard-Arends, 575–84. Rennes, France: Presses Universitaires de Rennes, 2003.

Hayes, Julie Candler. *Translation, Subjectivity and Culture in France and England, 1600–1800.* Stanford: Stanford University Press, 2009.

Hays, Mary. *Female Biography, or Memoirs of Illustrious and Celebrated Women, of All Ages and Countries.* 3 vols. Philadelphia: Byrch and Small, 1807.

Hazlitt, William. *Lectures on the Comic Writer.* London: John Templeman, 1841.

Herman, Jan. "Les années de pélerinage de Mme de Krüdener: *Valérie* et l'Italie." In *Dupaty et l'Italie des voyageurs sensibles,* ed. Jan Herman, Kris Peeters, and Paul Pelckmans, 171–88. New York: Rodopi, 2012.

Hesse, Carla. *The Other Enlightenment: How French Women Became Modern.* Princeton: Princeton University Press, 2003.

Heuer, Imke. " 'Something in Mme de Genlis Stile': Georgiana, Duchess of Devonshire's 'Zillia,' Playwriting and Female Aristocratic Authorship." Special Issue: Women Readers in Europe, Readers, Writers and Salonnières, 1750–1900. *Women's Writing* 18, no. 1 (February 2011): 68–85.

Heuvel, Danielle van den. *Women and Entrepreneurship: Female Traders in the Northern Netherlands, c. 1580–1815.* PhD dissertation, University of Utrecht, 2007. https://dspace.library .uu.nl/bitstream/handle/1874/24010/index.htm?sequence = 14.

Hilfiger, Stephanie M. *Gender and Genre: German Women Write the French Revolution.* Newark: University of Delaware Press, 2015.

Hilger, Stephanie M. "Epistolarity, Publicity, and Painful Sensibility: Julie de Krüdener's Valérie." *French Review* 79, no. 4 (2006): 737–47.

Hirsch, Marianne, Ruth Perry, and Virginia Swain. "Foreword." In *In the Shadow of Olympus: German Women Writers Around 1800,* ed. Katherine R. Goodman and Edith Waldstein, vi–xi. Albany: State University of New York Press, 1992.

Hogle, Jerrold E., editor. *The Cambridge Companion to Gothic Fiction.* Cambridge: Cambridge University Press, 2002.

Howatt, A. P. R., with H. G. Widdowson. *A History of English Language Teaching.* Oxford: Oxford University Press, 2004.

Huber, Therese. *Adventures on a Voyage to New Holland and The Lonely Deathbed.* Ed. Leslie Bodi, trans. Rodney Livingstone. Melbourne: Landsdowne, 1966.

Huguet, Françoise, and Isabelle de Havelange. *Les livres pour l'enfance et la jeunesse de Gutenberg à Guizot.* Paris: Klincksieck, 1997.

Hurd, Richard. "Preface, on the Manner of Writing Dialogues." In *Moral and Political Dialogues.* London: T. Cadell, 1771. Google books.

Inchbald, Elizabeth. *The Child of Nature, A Dramatic Piece in Four Acts: From the French of Madame the Marchioness of Sillery, formerly countess of Genlis.* Dublin: Messrs. Byrne, Collis Jones et al., 1789.

———. *Nature and Art*. Ed. Shawn Lisa Maurer. Peterborough, Ontario: Broadview, 2005.

Ingrassia, Catherine. *Authorship, Commerce and Gender in Early Eighteenth-Century England: A Culture of Paper Credit*. Cambridge: Cambridge University Press, 1998.

Ionescu, Christina. "La série illustrative dessinée par le Barbier l'aîné pour les *Les lettres d'une Péruvienne* de Mme de Graffigny." In *Françoise de Graffigny: Femme de lettres*, ed. Jonathan Mallinson, 229–45. Studies on Voltaire and the Eighteenth Century 12: Voltaire Foundation, 2004.

Jacob, Margaret C. *Strangers Nowhere in the World: The Rise of Cosmopolitanism in Early Modern Europe*. Philadelphia: University of Pennsylvania Press, 2006.

Janse, Ineke. *Madame de La Fite: Une éducatrice et un intermédiaire culturel du XVIIIe siècle*. Master's thesis, Université de Leiden, 2008.

———. "Traveller, Pedagogue and Cultural Mediator: Marie-Elisabeth de La Fite and Her Female Context." In *Women Writing Back/ Writing Women Back: Transnational Perspectives from the Late Middle Ages to the Dawn of the Modern Era*, ed. Anke Gilleir et al., 309–26. Leiden: Brill, 2010.

Jenkins, Annabel. *I'll Tell You What: The Life of Elizabeth Inchbald*. Lexington: University of Kentucky Press, 2003.

Johns, Alessa. *Bluestocking Feminism and British-German Cultural Transfer, 1750–1837*. Ann Arbor: University of Michigan Press, 2014.

———. *Women's Utopias of the Eighteenth Century*. Chicago: University of Illinois Press, 2003.

Johnson, Samuel. *A Dictionary of the English Language*, vol. 1. London: J. F. and C. Rivington, 1785.

Jordan, Constance. "Boccaccio's In-Famous Women: Gender and Civic Virtue in the *De mulieribus claris*." In *Ambiguous Realities: Women in the Middle Ages and Renaissance*, ed. Carole Levin and Jeanie Watson, 25–47. Detroit: Wayne State University Press, 1987.

Judovitz, Dalia. "Implausibility: La Princesse de Clèves." *Modern Language Notes* 99, no. 5 (1984): 1037–56.

Justice, George. "Burney and the Literary Marketplace." In *The Cambridge Companion to Frances Burney*, ed. Peter Sabor, 160–61. Cambridge: Cambridge University Press, 2007.

Kaltz, Barbara. "Introduction." In Jeanne Marie Leprince de Beaumont, *Contes et autres écrits*, ed. Kaltz, 37–51. Oxford: Voltaire Foundation, 2000.

Kant, Immanuel. "Idea of a Universal History with a Cosmopolitan Purpose." In *The Cosmopolitanism Reader,* ed. Garrett W. Brown and David Held, 17–27. Cambridge, UK: Polity Press, 2010.

———. *On the Old Saw: That May Be Right in Theory but It Won't Work in Practice*. Trans. E. B. Aston. Philadelphia: University of Pennsylvania Press, 2013.

Kaplan, Marijn S. *Translations and Continuations: Riccoboni and Brooke, Graffigny and Roberts*. London: Pickering and Chatto, 2011.

Kelly, Gary. "Clara Reeve, Provincial Bluestocking: From the Old Whigs to the Modern Liberal State." *Huntington Library Quarterly* 65, no. 1/2 (2002): 105–25.

———. "Introduction: Sarah Scott, Bluestocking Feminism, and Millenium Hall." In Sarah Scott, *Millenium Hall*, ed. Kelly, 11–46. Peterborough, Ontario: Broadview, 2004.

———. "Women's Provi(d)ence: Religion and Bluestocking Feminism in Sarah Scott's *Millenium Hall* (1762)." In *Female Communities, 1600–1800: Literary Visions and Cultural Realities*, ed. Rebecca D'Monte and Nicole Pohl, 166–83. New York: St. Martin's, 2000.

Kelly, Joan. "Early Feminist Theory and the 'Querelle des femmes,' 1400–1789." *Signs* 8, no.1 (Fall 1982): 4–28.

Kennedy, Deborah. *Helen Maria Williams and the Age of Revolution.* Lewisburg, PA: Bucknell University Press, 2002.

King, Margaret L., and Albert Rabil. "Series Editors' Introduction." In *The Contest for Knowledge: Debates over Women's Learning in Eighteenth-Century Italy*, ed. and trans. Paula Findlen and Rebecca Messbarger, xi–l. Chicago: University of Chicago Press, 2005.

Klindienst, Patricia. "The Voice of the Shuttle Is Ours." In *Rape and Representation*, ed. Lynn A. Higgins and Brenda A. Silver, 35–64. New York: Columbia University Press, 1991.

Kontje, Todd. *Women, the Novel, and the German Nation, 1771–1871: Domestic Fiction in the Fatherland.* Cambridge: Cambridge University Press, 1998.

Kopsch, Barbara Helena. *Kluge Unterredungen der in Frankreich berühmten Mademoiselle de Scudery worinnen uber unterschiedliche Sachen sehr nachdenkliche Gedanken/und lehrrichtige Gespräche enthalten; erster Theil; aus dem Französischen in das Teutsche gebracht/und mit beygesetzten Figuren und Gedichten erweitert.* Nuremberg: Zieger, 1685. Universitäts Bibliothek Erlangen-Nürnberg. urn:nbn:de:bvb:29-bv040316335–4.

Kord, Susanne. *Little Detours: The Letters and Plays of Luise Gottsched (1713–1762).* Rochester, NY: Camden House, 2000.

Kulessa, Rotraud von. "Françoise de Graffigny et la genèse des *Lettres d'une Péruvienne*: L'écriture comme auto-réflexion." In *Françoise de Graffigny: Femme de lettres*, ed. Jonathan Mallinson, 63–73. Studies on Voltaire and the Eighteenth Century, vol. 12. Oxford: Voltaire Foundation, 2004.

Kushner, Nina. *Erotic Exchanges: The World of Elite Prostitution in Eighteenth-Century Paris.* Ithaca, NY: Cornell University Press, 2013.

Labbe, Jacqueline, ed. *Charlotte Smith in British Romanticism.* London: Pickering and Chatto, 2008.

La Fayette, Marie-Madeleine de la Pioche de la Vergne, comtesse de. *Histoire de Madame Henriette d'Angleterre premiere femme de Philippe de France, duc d'Orléans: Par Dame Marie de la Vergne comtesse de La Fayette.* Amsterdam: Jean-Frederic Bernard, 1742. Google Books.

———. *La princesse de Clèves.* Ed. Antoine Adam. Paris: Garnier-Flammarion, 1966.

———. "Zaïde, histoire espagnole." In *Oeuvres de Mesdames de la Fayette, de Tencin et de Fontaines*, vol. 1, ed. M. Auger, 113–381. Paris: Chez Mme. V. Lepetit, 1820.

La Fite, Marie Elisabeth de. *Entretiens, drames et contes moraux, à l'usage des enfans.* 2 vols. n.p. 1791. Bibliothèque nationale de France. ark:/12148/cb444777719.

———. *Eugénie et ses élèves; ou, lettres et dialogues à l'usage des jeunes personnes.* Preface by Stéphanie Félicité de Genlis. Paris: Onfroy et Née de la Rochelle, 1787. Google Books.

———. "Lettre de la traductrice, à monsieur Wieland." In *Mémoires de mademoiselle de Sternheim, publiés par Mr Wieland et traduits de l'allemand par Madame ***.* The Hague: Pierre Frédéric Gosse, 1775. Google Books.

Landes, Joan B. *Women and the Public Sphere in the Age of the French Revolution.* Ithaca, NY: Cornell University Press, 1988.

Laqueur, Thomas. *Making Sex: Body and Gender from the Greeks to Freud.* Cambridge, MA: Harvard University Press, 1990.

La Roche, Sophie von. *Erscheinungen am See Oneida.* 3 vols. Leipzig, 1798. Sophie: Literatur. http://sophie.byu.edu.

———. *Geschichte des Fräuleins von Sternheim.* Ed. Barbara Becker-Cantarino. Stuttgart: P. Reclam. 1983. babel.hathitrust.org.

————. *Mémoires de Mademoiselle de Sternheim.* 2 vols. Trans. Marie-Elisabeth de LaFite. The Hague: Pierre-Frédéric Gosse, 1774. Google Books.

————. *Mein Schreibtisch.* 2 vols. Leipzig: Graff, 1799. Google Books.

————. *Sophie in London, 1786.* Trans. Clare Williams. London: J. Cape, 1933.

Larsen, Anne R. "Anne Marie de Schurman, Madeleine de Scudéry et les lettres sur la pucelle." In *Lectrices d'ancien régime,* ed. Isabelle Brouard-Arends, 269–79. Rennes, France: Presses Universitaires de Rennes, 2003.

Lathey, Gillian. *The Role of Translators in Children's Literature: Invisible Storytellers.* New York: Routledge, 2012.

Lauriol, Claude. "Le premier biographe de Maintenon réévalué: La Beaumelle." *Albineana, Cahiers d'Aubigne'* 10, no. 1 (1999): 91–106.

Lavoie, Chantel. *Collecting Women: Poetry and Lives, 1700–1780.* Lewisburg, PA: Bucknell University Press, 2009.

Le Moyne, Pierre. *La gallerie des femmes fortes.* Paris: Antoine de Sommaville, 1647. openlibrary.org.

Lennox, Charlotte. *Donquichotte femelle: Traduction libre de l'Anglois,* vol. 1. Trans. J. M. Crommelen. Lyon: Chez les Libraires Associés, 1773. Google Books.

————. *The Female Quixote.* Ed. Margaret Dalziel. Oxford: Oxford University Press, 2008.

————. *The Lady's Museum: By the Author of* The Female Quixote, vol. 1. London, [1760–1761].

Leprince de Beaumont, Jeanne Marie. *Civan, roi de Bungo, Histoire japonnoise, ou tableau de l'éducation d'un prince.* London: Jean Nourse, 1758. Google books.

————. *La nouvelle Clarisse, histoire véritable.* 2 vols. Lyon: Pierre Bruyset-Ponthis, 1767. Bibliothèque nationale de France. ark12148/bpt6k655021p.

————. *Le magasin des enfants, ou dialogues entre une sage gouvernante et plusieurs de ses élèves de la premiere distinction, . . . Par Mad. Le Prince de Beaumont.* 2 vols. in 1. The Hague: Pierre Gosse, 1768.

————. *Magasin des pauvres, artisans, domestiques et gens de la campagne.* Lyon: Pierre Bruyset-Ponthus, 1768. Google Books.

————. *Le mentor moderne, ou instructions pour les garçons et pour ceux qui les élèvent.* 12 vols. Paris: Claude Herissant, 1772–1773. Google books.

————. *Le triomphe de la vérité, ou mémoires de Mr. de la Villete,* vol 1. Liège, Belgium: J. F. Bassompière, 1774. Google Books.

Letts, Janet. *Legendary Lives in "La princesse de Clèves."* Charlottesville, VA: Rookwood, 1998.

Letzter, Jacqueline. *Intellectual Tacking: Questions of Education in the Works of Isabelle de Charrière.* Amsterdam: Rodopi, 1998.

Locke, John. *Some Thoughts Concerning Education.* Ed. John W. and Jean S. Yolton. Oxford: Oxford University Press, 1989.

Long, Mary Beth. "A Medieval French Book in an Early Modern English World: Christine de Pisan's *Livre de la Cité des Dames* and Women Readers in the Age of Print." *Literature Compass* 9, no. 8 (August 2012): 521–37.

Looser, Devoney. *British Women Writers and the Writing of History, 1670–1820.* Baltimore: Johns Hopkins University Press, 2005.

Lorenzo-Modia, María Jesús. "Charlotte Lennox's 'The Female Quixote' into Spanish: A Gender-Biased Translation." *Yearbook of English Studies* 36, no. 1 (2006): 103–14.

Luhmann, Nicklas. *Love as Passion: The Codification of Intimacy.* Trans. Jeremy Gaines and Doris L. Jones. Stanford: Stanford University Press, 1998.

Lynch, Dierdre Shauna. "The (Dis)locations of Romantic Nationalism: Shelley, Staël and the Home-Schooling of Monsters." In *The Literary Channel: The Inter-National Invention of the Novel*, ed. Margaret Cohen and Carolyn Dever, 194–224. Princeton: Princeton University Press, 2002.

———. *The Economy of Character: Novels, Market Culture and the Business of Inner Meaning.* Chicago: Chicago University Press, 1998.

Lyons, John D., editor and translator. *The Princess of Clèves: Contemporary Reactions, Criticism.* New York: Norton, 1994.

Maber, Richard. "Re-gendering Intellectual Life: Gilles Ménage and His *Histoire des femmes philosophes.*" *Seventeenth-Century French Studies* 32, no. 1 (July 1, 2010): 45–60.

Mack, Ruth. "Quixotic Ethnography: Charlotte Lennox and the Dilemma of Cultural Observation." *Novel: A Forum on Fiction* 38, no. 2/3 (New Work on 18th-Century Fiction) (Spring–Summer 2005): 193–213.

Maintenon, Françoise d'Aubigné, madame de. *Dialogues and Addresses.* Ed. and trans. John J. Conley. Chicago: University of Chicago Press, 2004.

———[attrib.]. *Les loisirs de Madame de Maintenon.* London: Chez Duchesne, 1757. Google Books.

Mallinson, Jonathan. " 'Cela ne vaud pas Zaide': Graffigny, lectrice de Mme de La Fayette." In *Françoise de Graffigny—Femme de lettres: Écriture et réception*, ed. Mallinson, 118–28. Oxford: Voltaire Foundation, 2004.

———, editor. "Introduction." In Françoise de Graffigny, *Lettres d'une Péruvienne*, vii–xxix. Oxford: Oxford University Press, 2002.

———. "Reconquering Peru: Eighteenth-Century Translations of Graffigny's *Lettres d'une Péruvienne.*" *Studies on Voltaire and the Eighteenth Century* 6 (2007): 291–310.

Mandell, Laura. *Misogynous Economies: The Business of Literature in Eighteenth-Century Britain.* Lexington: University of Kentucky Press, 1999.

Manley, Delarivier. *Adventures of Rivella, or, a History of the Author of the Four Volumes of* The New Atalantis, 2nd ed. London, 1715. Google Books.

———. *The New Atalantis.* Ed. Ros Ballaster. London: Pickering and Chatto, 1991.

———. *Secret Memoirs and Manners of Several Persons of Quality, of Both Sexes: From the New Atalantis, an Island in the Mediteranean—Written Originally In Italian . . .* 2 vols. London: Printed for J. Morphew and J. Woodward, 1709. Hathi Trust Digital Library. https://catalog.hathitrust.org/Record/010943989.

Marshall, David. *The Frame of Art: Fictions of Aesthetic Experience, 1750–1815.* Baltimore: Johns Hopkins University Press, 2005.

Martin, Alison E. "Travel, Sensibility and Gender: The Rhetoric of Female Travel Writing in Sophie von La Roche's *Tagebuch einer Reise durch Holland und England.*" *German Life and Letters* 57, no. 2 (2004): 127–42.

Martin, Judith E. *Germaine de Staël in Germany: Gender and Literary Authority, 1800–1850.* Madison, NJ: Fairleigh Dickinson University Press, 2011.

Massé, Michelle. *In the Name of Love: Women, Masochism, and the Gothic.* Ithaca, NY: Cornell University Press, 1992.

McAlpin, Mary. *Female Sexuality and Cultural Degradation in Enlightenment France.* Burlington, VT: Ashgate, 2012.

McClintock, Anne. *Imperial Leather: Race, Gender and Sexuality in the Colonial Contest.* New York: Routledge, 1995.

McDowell, Paula. "Consuming Women: The Life of the 'Literary Lady' as Popular Culture in Eighteenth-Century England." *Genre* 26, no. 2–3 (1993): 219–52.

———. *The Women of Grub Street: Press, Politics, and Gender in the London Literary Market-place, 1678–1730*. Oxford: Oxford University Press, 1998.

McLeod, Glenda. *Virtue and Venom: Catalogs of Women from Antiquity to the Renaissance*. Ann Arbor: University of Michigan Press, 1991.

McMurran, Mary Helen. *The Spread of Novels: Translation and Prose Fiction in the Eighteenth Century*. Princeton, NJ: Princeton University Press, 2009.

Melehy, Hassan. *The Poetics of Literary Transfer in Early Modern France and England*. Burlington, VT: Ashgate, 2010.

Melton, James van Horn. *The Rise of the Public in Enlightenment Europe*. Cambridge: Cambridge University Press, 2001.

Millar, John. *The Origin of the Distinction of Ranks*. Indianapolis: The Liberty Fund, 2012.

Monbart, Joséphine de. *Lettres tahitiennes*. Ed. Laure Marcellesi. Modern Humanities Research Association Critical Texts 36. London: Modern Humanities Research Association, 2012.

Montesquieu, Charles-Louis de Secondat, baron de. *Œuvres complètes*. Paris: Bibliothèque de la Pléiade; Éditions Gallimard, 1951.

Montolieu, Isabelle de. *Caroline de Litchfield, ou mémoires d'une famille prussienne*. Paris: Arthus Bertrand, 1843. Google Books.

Montoya, Alicia. "Madame de Beaumont et les lumières religieuses." In *Marie Leprince de Beaumont: De l'éducation des filles à 'La Belle et la Bête,'* ed. Jeanne Chiron and Catriona Seth, 131–43. Paris: Classiques Garnier, 2014.

Moore, Fabienne. "Homer Revisited: Anne Le Fèvre Dacier's Preface to Her Prose Translation of the *Iliad* in Early Eighteenth-Century France." *Studies in the Literary Imagination* 33, no. 2 (Fall 2000): 87–107.

More, Hannah. *Pensées sur les mœurs des grands*. Trans. Marie-Elisabeth de La Fite. The Hague: Gosse, 1790. http://www.mdz-nbn-resolving.de/urn/rTheFemesolver.pl?urn = urn:nbn:de :bvb:12-bsb10041381–6.

Moretti, Franco. *Atlas of the European Novel, 1800–1900*. London: Verso, 1998.

———. *The Way of the World*. London: Verso, 2000.

Naudin, Marie. "Stéphanie-Félicité, Comtesse de Genlis (1746–1830)." In *French Women Writers*, ed. Eva Martin Sartori and Dorothy Wynne Zimmerman, 178–97. Lincoln: University of Nebraska Press, 1994.

NEWW Women Writers: A Network and Tool, Huygens Ing. resources.huygens.knaw.nl/womenwriters.

Norton, Bonnie. *Identity and Language Learning: Extending the Conversation*. 2nd ed. Bristol, UK: Multilingual Matters, 2013.

Nussbaum, Emily. "Graphic, Novel: 'Marvel's Jessica Jones' and the Superhero Survivor." *New Yorker* (December 21 and 28, 2015). http://www.newyorker.com/magazine/2015/12/21/graphic-novel-on-television-emily-nussbaum.

Nussbaum, Felicity. *The Autobiographical Subject: Gender and Ideology in Eighteenth-Century England*. Baltimore: Johns Hopkins University Press, 1989.

———. *The Brink of All We Hate: English Satires on Women, 1660–1750*. Lexington: University Press of Kentucky, 1994.

Nussbaum, Martha C. "Kant and Cosmopolitanism." In *The Cosmopolitanism Reader*, ed. Garrett Wallace Brown and David Held, 27–44. Cambridge: Polity, 2010.

Orr, Clarissa Campbell. "Aristocratic Feminism, the Learned Governess, and the Republic of Letters." In *Women, Gender and Enlightenment*, ed. Sarah Knott and Barbara Taylor, 306–25. New York: Palgrave MacMillan, 2007.

———. "La Fite, Marie Elisabeth de." In Colin Matthew and Brian Harrison, eds.,. *Oxford Dictionary of National Biography*. Oxford: Oxford University Press, 2004. http://www.ox forddnb.com/.

Paige, Nicholas D. *Before Fiction: The Ancien Régime of the Novel*. Philadelphia: University of Pennsylvania Press, 2011.

Pal, Carol. *The Republic of Women: Rethinking the Republic of Letters in the Seventeenth Century*. Cambridge: Cambridge University Press, 2012.

Parfitt, Alexandra. "Far From the Whirlwind: Christian Ethics and the Classical Tradition in Genlis' Pedagogy." *Relief* 7, no. 1 (September 2013): 4–18.

Pascal, Catherine. "Les recueils de femmes illustres au XVIIe siécle." Communication donnée lors des premières Rencontres de la SIEFAR, "Connaître les femmes de l'Ancien Régime: La question des recuils et dictionnaires." Paris, June 20, 2003. http://www.siefar.org/wp -content/uploads/2015/09/Pascal-dicos.pdf.

Paulsen, Ronald. *Don Quixote in England: The Aesthetics of Laughter*. Baltimore: Johns Hopkins University Press, 1998.

Paulson, Sara. "La Roche, Sophie von (1730–1807)." In *The Feminist Encyclopedia of German Literature*, ed. Friederike Eigler and Susanne Kord, 275–76. Westport, CT: Greenwood, 1997.

Pelckmans, Paul. "Les lettres neuchâteloises et Sara Burgerhart: Eléments pour une mise au point. *Cahiers Isabelle de Charrière* 5 (2010): 35–46.

Pendarves, Mary. *The Autobiography and Correspondence of Mary Granville, Mrs. Delany*. 3 vols. Ed. Lady Augusta Hall Llanover. London: R. Bentley, 1861.

Perry, Ruth. *The Celebrated Mary Astell: An Early English Feminist*. Chicago: University of Chicago, 1986.

———. "Clarissa's Daughters, or the History of Innocence Betrayed: How Women Writers Rewrote Richardson." *Women's Writing* 1, no. 1 (1994): 5–24.

Peruga, Mónica Bolufer. "Expression of Interest: CIRGEN: Circulating Gender in the Global Enlightenment: Ideas, Networks, Agencies." https://eshorizonte2020.es/expressions-of-in terests/monica-bolufer.

———. "Women of Letters in Eighteenth-Century Spain: Between Tradition and Modernity." In *Eve's Enlightenment: Women's Experience in Spain and Spanish America, 1726–1839*, ed. Catherine M. Jaffe and Elizabeth Franklin Lewis, 17–32. Baton Rouge: Louisiana State University Press, 2009.

Piper, Andrew. "The Making of Transnational Textual Communities: German Women Translators, 1800–1850." *Women in German Yearbook* 22 (2006): 119–44.

Piroux, Lorraine. "The Encyclopedist and the Peruvian Princess: The Poetics of Illegibility in French Enlightenment Book Culture." *PMLA* 121, no. 1 (January 2006): 107–23.

Pizan, Christine de. *The Book of the City of Ladies*. Trans. Earl Jeffrey Richards. New York: Persea, 1982.

Plagnol-Diéval, Marie-Emmanuelle. *Madame de Genlis et le théâtre de l'éducation au dix-huitième siècle*. Studies on Voltaire and the Eighteenth Century 350. Oxford: Voltaire Foundation, 1997.

Plantié, Jacqueline. *La mode du portrait littéraire en France (1641–1681)*. Paris: Honoré Champion, 1994.

Pohl, Nicole. *Women, Space, and Utopia, 1600–1800.* Aldershot, UK: Ashgate, 2006.

Pollock, Sheldon. "Cosmopolitan and Vernacular in History." In *Cosmopolitanism,* ed. Carol Breckenridge et al., 15–53. Durham, NC: Duke University Press, 2002.

Pollock, Sheldon, et al. "Introduction." In *Cosmopolitanism,* ed. Carol Breckenridge et al., 1–14. Durham: Duke University Press, 2002.

Polosina, Alla, and Alicia C. Montoya. "Madame de Genlis dans la littérature russe du XIXe siècle: Pouchkine, Léon Tolstoï et autres." *Relief* 7, no. 1 (2013): 123–40. http://www .revue-relief.org.

Poortere, Machteld de. *The Philosophical and Literary Ideas of Mme de Staël and Mme de Genlis.* Trans. John Lavash. New York: Peter Lang, 2007.

Prince, Michael. *Philosophical Dialogue in the British Enlightenment: Theology, Aesthetics, and the Novel.* Cambridge: Cambridge University Press, 1996.

Reeve, Clara. *The Progress of Romance: And the History of Charoba, Queen of Aegypt.* New York: Facsimile Text Society, 1930.

Rennhak, Katharina. "Tropes of Exile in the 1790s: English Women Writers and French Emigrants." *European Romantic Review* 17, no. 5 (December 2006): 575–92.

Riccoboni, Marie Jeanne. *Histoire d'Ernestine.* Eds. Joan Hinde Stewart and Philip Stewart. New York: Modern Languages Association of America, 1998.

———. *Lettere di Milady Giulietta Catesby a Milady Henrica Campley sua Amica.* Trans. Signora di Gourgue. Cosmopoli, 1769. Google Books.

Richardson, Samuel. *Clarissa, or the History of a Young Lady.* Ed. Andrew Ross. London: Penguin, 2004.

———. *Pamela, or Virtue Rewarded.* Oxford: Oxford University Press, 2001.

Robin, Diana Maury. *Publishing Women: Salons, the Presses, and the Counter-Reformation in Sixteenth-Century Italy.* Chicago: University of Chicago Press, 2007.

Romero, María Masegosa y Cancelada. *Cartas de una peruana escritas en frances por Mad. de Graffigni y traducidas al castellano con algunas correcciones, y augmentada con notas, y una carta para su mayor complemento . . .* Valladolid, Spain: Officina de la Viuda de Santander, é Hijos, 1792. Google Books.

Rossini, Manuela, and Michael Toggweiler. "Cultural Transfer: An Introduction." *Word and Text: A Journal of Literary Studies and Linguistics* 4, no. 2 (December 2014): 5–9.

Rousseau, Jean-Jacques. *Confessions,* vol. 1. Paris: Gallimard, 1963.

———. *Émile, ou de l'éducation.* Paris: Garnier-Flammarion, 1966.

———. *Julie, ou la nouvelle Héloïse.* Paris: Garnier-Flammarion, 1966.

Saas, Nicolaas van. "Varieties of Dutchness." In *Images of the Nation: Different Meanings of Dutchness, 1870–1940,* ed. Annemieke Galema, Barbara Henkes, and Henk te Velde, 5–16. Amsterdam: Rodopi, 1993.

Said, Edward. *Culture and Imperialism.* New York: Alfred J. Knopf, 1993.

Salih, Sara. "*Camilla* and *The Wanderer.*" In *The Cambridge Companion to Frances Burney,* ed. Peter Sabor, 39–54. Cambridge: Cambridge University Press, 2007.

Sánchez-Eppler, Karen. "Castaways: *The Swiss Family Robinson,* Child Bookmakers, and the Possibilities of Literary Flotsam." In *The Oxford Handbook of Children's Literature,* ed. Julia L. Mickenberg and Lynne Vallone, 433–54. Oxford: Oxford University Press, 2011.

Schabert, Ina. " 'To Make Frequent Assemblies, Associations, and Combinations Amongst Our Sex': Nascent Ideas of Female Bonding in Seventeenth-Century England." In *Women Writing Back/Writing Women Back: Transnational Perspectives from the Late Middles Ages to the Dawn of the Modern Era*, ed. Anke Gilleir, Alicia Montoya, and Suzanna van Dijk, 73–92. Leiden: Brill, 2010.

Schellenberg, Betty A. *The Professionalization of Women Writers in Eighteenth-Century Britain.* Cambridge: Cambridge University Press, 2005.

Schenkeveld-van der Dussen, Riet. "Women's Writing from the Low Countries, 1575–1875." In *Women's Writing from the Low Countries, 1200–1875: A Bilingual Anthology*, ed. Lia van Gemert et al., 39–64. Amsterdam: Amsterdam University Press, 2010.

Schurman, Anna Maria van. *Anna Maria van Schurman: Whether a Christian Woman Should Be Educated and Other Writings from Her Intellectual Circle.* Trans. and ed. Joyce Irwin. Chicago: University of Chicago Press, 1998.

———. *The Learned Maid; or, Whether a Maid May Be a Scholar? A Logick Exercise.* London: John Redmayne, 1659. Early English Books Online.

Scott, Sarah. *Beschreibung von Millenium-Hall, und der benachbarten Gegend . . . Von einem Herrn auf Reisen [or rather, by Sarah Scott].* Aus der neueren englischen Ausgabe. Hamburg: Bey Hertels Witwe & Gleditschen, 1768.

———. *Millenium Hall.* Ed. Gary Kelly. Peterborough, Ontario: Broadview, 2004.

———. *The Story of Sapho.* Trans. Karen Newman. Chicago: University of Chicago Press, 2003.

Scudéry, Madeleine de, and Georges de Scudéry. *Artamène, ou le Grand Cyrus.* Corpus électroniques de la première modernité, Université Paris-Sorbonne. www.artamene.org.

———. *Clélie, histoire romaine.* Ed. Chantal Morlet-Chantalat. Paris: Honoré Champion, 2001.

———. *Les Femmes illustres ou les harangues héroïques.* 1642. Google Books.

Seth, Catriona. "Introduction—Marie Leprince de Beaumont: Lumières et ombres." In *Marie Leprince de Beaumont: De l'éducation des filles à La Belle et la Bête*, ed. Jeanne Chiron and Catriona Seth, 7–42. Paris: Classiques Garnier, 2013.

Shapin, Steven, and Simon Schaffer. *Leviathan and the Air-Pump: Hobbes, Boyle and the Experimental Life.* Princeton: Princeton University Press, 1985.

Shelfrin, Jill. "Governesses to Their Children: Royal and Aristocratic Mothers Educating Daughters in the Reign of George III." In *Childhood and Children's Books in Early Modern Europe*, ed. Andrea Immel and Michael Wittmore, 181–212. London: Routledge, 2013.

———. *Such Constant Affectionate Care: Lady Charlotte Finch, Royal Governess, and the Children of George III.* Los Angeles: Cotsen Occasional Press, 2003.

Showalter, English. *Françoise de Graffigny: Her Life and Works.* Oxford: Voltaire Foundation, 2004.

———. "*Les lettres d'une Péruvienne*: Composition, Publication, Suites." *Archives et Bibliothèques de Belgique* 54, no. 1–4 (1983): 14–28.

Simon, Sherry. "Gender in Translation." In *The Oxford Guide to Literature in Translation*, ed. Peter France, 26–33. Oxford: Oxford University Press, 2000.

———. *Gender in Translation: Cultural Identity and the Politics of Transmission.* London: Routledge, 1996.

Smith, Charlotte Turner. *Celestina.* Ed. and intro. Loraine Fletcher. Peterboro, Ontario: Broadview, 2004.

Smith, David. "The Popularity of Mme de Graffigny's *Lettres d'une Péruvienne*: The Biographical Evidence." *Eighteenth-Century Fiction* 3 (1990): 1–20.

Smith, Theresa Ann. "Writing out of the Margins: Women, Translation, and the Spanish Enlightenment." *Journal of Women's History* 15, no. 1 (Spring 2003):116–43.

Société internationale pour l'étude des femmes de l'ancien régime. siefar.org.

Spacks, Patricia Meyer. *Imagining a Self: Autobiography and Novel in Eighteenth-Century England.* Cambridge: Cambridge University Press, 1976.

Spahr, Blake Lee. "Sibylla Ursula and Her Books." In *Problems and Perspectives: A Collection of Essays on German Baroque Literature,* 85–110 Frankfurt: Peter Lang, 1981.

Spink, J. S. "The Teaching of French Pronunciation in England in the Eighteenth Century, with Particular Reference to the Diphthong oi." *Modern Language Review* 16, no. 2 (April 1946): 155–63.

Springborg, Patricia. "Introduction." Mary Astell, *A Serious Proposal to the Ladies* [1694]. Peterborough, Ontario: Broadview, 2002.

Staël, Germaine de. *Corinne, ou l'Italie.* Ed. Simone Balayé. Paris: Gallimard, 1985.

———. *De la littérature, considérée dans ses rapports avec les institutions sociales.* Paris: Chez Maradan, 1800. Bibliothèque Nationale de France, Gallica. http://catalogue.bnf.fr/ark:/12148/cb31397249g.

———. "Dix années d'exil." In *Mémoires de Madame de Staël.* Paris: Charpentier, 1861. Bibliothèque Nationale de France. ark:/12148/cb313972333.

———. *De l'Allemagne.* Paris: Firmin Didot Frères, 1852.

———. *Recueil de morceaux détachés.* Lausanne, Switzerland: Chez Durand, Ravanel et Compagnie; Paris: Chez Fuchs Libraire, 1795. Google books.

———. *Zulma, et Trois nouvelles: précédé d'un Essai sur les fictions.* London: Colburn, 1813. Google books.

Stanton, Judith. "Statistical Profile of Women Writing in English from 1660 to 1800." In *Eighteenth-Century Women and the Arts,* ed. Frederick Keener and Susan Lorsch, 247–54. New York: Greenwood, 1988.

Staves, Susan. "Don Quixote in Eighteenth-Century England." *Comparative Literature* 24 (1972): 193–215.

———. *A Literary History of Women's Writing in Britain, 1660–1789.* Cambridge: Cambridge University Press, 2006.

Stewart, Joan Hinde. *Gynographs: French Novels by Women of the Late Eighteenth Century.* Lincoln: University of Nebraska Press, 1993.

———. "1787: Isabelle de Charrière Publishes *Caliste*. Designing Women." In *A New History of French Literature,* ed. Denis Hollier et al., 553–58. Cambridge: Harvard University Press, 1994.

Stoler, Ann Laura. *Race and the Education of Desire: Foucault's History of Sexuality and the Colonial Order of Things.* Durham, NC: Duke University Press, 1995.

Strauss Sotiropoulos, Carol. "Pomona, für Teutschlands Töchter": Sophie von La Roche as Editor, Educator, and Narrator." *Colloquia Germanica* 33, no. 3 (2000): 213–38.

Strien, Kies van. "Jean Daniel La Fite (1719–81)." In *Dictionnaire des journalistes (1600–1789).* Voltaire Foundation. http://dictionnairejournalistes.gazettes18e.fr/journaliste/441a-jean-daniel-la-fite.

Strien-Chardonneau, Madeleine van. "Belle, Betje, Antje . . . et les autres: Néerlandaises en voyage au XVIIIe siècle." *Cahiers Isabelle de Charrière/Belle de Zuylen Papers* 9 (2014): 115–34.

Subligny, Adrien Thomas Perdou de. *The Mock-Clelia: Being a Comical History of French Gallantries and Novels, in Imitation of Dom Quixote.* London: Printed by L.C. and are to be sold by Simon Neale and Charles Blount, 1678. Early English Books Online.

————. *La fausse Clélie: Histoire françoise, galante et comique.* Amsterdam: Jaques Wagenaar, 1671. Bibliothèque nationale de France. ark:/12148/bpt6k6553447h.

Tautz, Birgit. "Moral Weeklies." In *The Feminist Encyclopedia of German Literature*, ed. Friederike Ursula Eigler and Susanne Kord, 328–30. Westport, CT: Greenwood Publishing, 1997.

Thicknesse, Ann. *Sketches of the Lives and Writings of the Ladies of France: Addressed to Mrs. Elizabeth Carter*, vol. 1. London, 1778.

Thomas, Ruth P. "Marie-Jeanne Riccoboni (Marie-Jeanne de Heurles Laboras de Mézières Riccoboni) (1713–1792)." In *Dictionary of Literary Biography*, vol. 4, 102–3. New York: Thomson Gale, 2005.

Todd, Janet. *The Sign of Angellica: Women, Writing and Fiction, 1600–1800.* London: Virago, 1989.

Tomaselli, Sylvana. "The Enlightenment Debate on Women." *History Workshop Journal* 20, no. 1 (January 1985): 101–24.

Tomlinson, John. "Deterritorialization." In *The Wiley Blackwell Encyclopedia of Globalization*, ed. George Ritzer. Malden, MA: Wiley-Blackwell, 2012. https://doi.org/10.1002/9780470 670590.wbeog143.

Tremblay, Isabelle. "La fiction de Madame de Genlis espace d'interrogation sur la vertu." *Relief* 7, no. 1 (2013): 19–32.

Trousson, Raymond. *Mme de Charrière et Mme de Staël ou le conflit des générations.* Brussels: Académie Royale de Langue et de Littérature Françaises de Belgique, 2000. http://www .arllfb.be/ebibliotheque/communications/trousson130500.pdf.

Trumpener, Katie. *Bardic Nationalism: The Romantic Novel and the British Empire.* Princeton: Princeton University Press, 1997.

Turner, Cheryl. *Living by the Pen: Women Writers in the Eighteenth Century.* London: Routledge, 1994.

Turner, James Grantham. *Schooling Sex: Libertine Literature and Erotic Education in Italy, France, and England, 1534–1685.* Oxford: Oxford University Press, 2003.

Turnovsky, Geoffrey. *The Literary Market: Authorship and Modernity in the Old Regime.* Philadelphia: University of Pennsylvania Press, 2010.

Van Betten, Herman. "*Richardson in Holland and His Influence on Wolff and Deken's* Sara Burgerhart." PhD dissertation, University of Southern California, Language and Literature, 1971. University Microfilms, Ann Arbor, Michigan.

Vanpée, Janie. "Etre(s) sans papier et sans domicile fixe: La femme comme figure de l'étranger chez Graffigny." In *Françoise de Graffigny: Femme de lettres*, ed. Jonathan Mallinson, 328–36. Studies on Voltaire and the Eighteenth Century 12. Oxford: Voltaire Foundation, 2004.

Vasselin, Martine. "Histoires déformées, miroirs déformants: L'imaginaire artistique des héroïnes au XVIe siècle." *Nouvelle Revue de XVIe siècle* 12, no. 1 (1994): 33–42.

Viala, Alain. "The Theory of the Literary Field and the Situation of the First Modernity." *Paragraph* 29, no. 1 (March 2006): 80–93.

Viennot, Éliane et al. *Revisiter la "querelle des femmes."* 3 vols. Saint-Étienne, France: Publications de l'Université de Saint-Etienne, 2012–13.

Vieu-Kuik, H. J. *Keur uit het Werk van Betje Wolff en Aagje Deken.* Zutphen, Netherlands: W. J. Thieme, 1980.

Vila, Anne C. *Enlightenment and Pathology: Sensibility in the Literature and Medicine of Eighteenth-Century France.* Baltimore: Johns Hopkins University Press, 1998.

Voisine, Jacques. "Goethe traducteur de l' 'Essai sur les fictions' de Madame de Staël." *Etudes germaniques* 50, no. 1 (1995): 73–82.

Vries, Jan de, and Ad van der Woude. *The First Modern Economy: Success, Failure, and Perseverance of the Dutch Economy, 1500–1815.* Cambridge: Cambridge University Press, 1997.

Wacquant, Loic. "Habitus." In *International Encyclopedia of Economic Sociology,* ed. Jens Becket and Milan Zafirovski, 317–21. London: Routledge, 2005.

Wallbank, Adrian J. *Dialogue, Didacticism and the Genres of Dispute: Literary Dialogue in an Age of Revolution.* London: Pickering and Chatto, 2012.

Warner, William Beatty. *Licensing Entertainment: The Elevation of Novel Reading in Britain, 1684–1750.* Berkeley: University of California Press, 1998.

———. "Novels on the Market." In *The Cambridge History of English Literature, 1660–1780,* ed. John Richetti, 87–105. Cambridge: Cambridge University Press, 2005.

———. *Reading Clarissa: The Struggles of Interpretation.* New Haven: Yale University Press, 1979.

Watt, Helga Schutte. "Sophie La Roche as a German Patriot." In *Gender and Germanness: Cultural Productions of a Nation,* ed. Patricia Herminghouse and Magda Mueller, 36–50. Modern German Studies, vol. 4. Oxford: Berhahn, 1997.

Watt, Jeffrey. *The Making of Modern Marriage: Matrimonial Control and the Rise of Sentiment in Neuchâtel, 1550–1800.* Ithaca, NY: Cornell University Press, 1992.

Watts, J. *A Select Collection of Novels and Histories.* 2 vols. London, 1729. Dedication, unnumbered page. Google Books.

Wenger, Étienne. "Communities of Practice and Social Learning Systems: The Career of a Concept." In *Social Learning Systems and Communities of Practice,* ed. Chris Blackmore, 179–98. London: Springer-Verlag London, 2010.

———. *Communities of Practice: Learning, Meaning and Identity.* Cambridge: Cambridge University Press, 1998.

Werken, Margareta Geertruid van der (Madame de Cambon) [attributed to Arnaud Berquin]. *The History of Litle Grandison by M. Berquin.* [Trans. by Mary Wollstonecraft of Van der Werken. *De kleine Grandisson, of de gehoorzame zoon* (The Hague, 1782)]. London: John Stockdale, 1797. Google Books.

Williams, Helen Maria. *Letters Written in France.* Ed. Neil Fraistat and Susan S. Lanser. Peterborough, Ontario: Broadview, 2001.

Wollstonecraft, Mary. *The Female Reader. A Facsimile Reproduction.* Ed. Moira Ferguson. New York: Scholars' Facsimiles & Reprints, 1980.

———. *Original Stories from Real Life: With Conversations Calculated to Regulate the Affections and Form the Mind to Truth and Goodness.* London: J. Johnson, 1796. Google books.

———. *Vindication of the Rights of Woman: With Strictures on Political and Moral Subjects.* Floating Press, 2010. ProQuest Ebook Central. https://ebookcentral.proquest.com/lib/unm/detail.action?docID = 563875.

Women Writers in History: Toward a New Understanding of European Literary Culture. www.womenwriters.nl/index.php/COST_Action.

The Women Writers Project. www.wwp.northeastern.edu.

Wyett, Jodi L. " 'No Place Where Women Are of Such Importance': Female Friendship, Empire and Utopia in *The History of Emily Montague*." *Eighteenth-Century Fiction* 16, no. 1 (2003): 33–57.

Index

aesthetic capital, 17, 20, 30, 38, 45–46, 86, 161. *See also* literariness

affinity: female, 11, 22–23, 26, 37–38, 70, 86–87, 100, 114–16, 142, 157–59, 171, 177–78, 183, 185; group, ix, 19, 39, 41; literary, language of, 18, 28, 36, 49, 198, 201; in translation, 38, 116

Africans: depictions of, 211, 217

Aikin, John, 153

Alliston, April, 183, 193

amatory fiction, 33

Amazons, 53; Amazonian, 69, 72; "Amazons of the pen," 5, 80

Amsterdam, 46, 66, 75, 153, 155, 166–70, 179, 204, 229n40

ancients and moderns, quarrel of the, 14, 43–44, 47, 50, 52, 63, 86, 132, 218

Anderson, Benedict, 16, 34, 38, 85, 163

Anderson, Perry, 196

Angliviel de la Beaumelle, Laurent, 34, 75, 129

anthology, 6, 12, 46, 51, 61, 73, 84, 136, 228n19. *See also* poetry

Apter, Emily, 2–3

aristocratic versus plebian women, 14, 22, 80, 84, 176, 182, 185, 212

Armstrong, Nancy, 15, 22, 121, 226n17

Astbury, Katherine, 221, 234n8, 235n8, 236n22

Astell, Mary, 59, 232n11

Aulnoy, Marie-Catherine Le Jumel de Barneville, 14, 76–78, 80–81, 204, 225n15

Austen, Jane, 17–18, 26–27, 47, 155, 172, 199, 226n17

authorship: public, 30, 35, 55. *See also* publishing

autobiography, 8, 14, 66, 81, 116–17, 119, 229n25, 229n32

Ballard, George, 64, 228n19

Ballaster, Ros, 33, 79–81

Bannet, Eve Tavor, 139

Barbapiccola, Giuseppa Eleonora, 65

Barbauld, Anna Laetitia, 153

Batchelor, Jennie, 13, 229n38

battle of the books. *See* ancients and moderns

Beasley, Faith, 201

Behn, Aphra, 4, 14, 33, 79–82, 84, 147, 204

Bekker-Wolff, Elisabeth, 16, 143, 153, 164–73, 177, 180, 183, 206–7

Béringuier, Nadine, 126

Bildungsroman, 110–11, 231n20, 321n1

Binhammer, Katherine, 22

Birberick, Anne L., 130

birth outside of wedlock, 22, 53, 174, 178, 180–81, 211

blackness, 146–47, 195

bluestocking feminism, 19, 83, 138–39

Boccaccio, Giovanni, 52–53, 228n14

Bolufer, Mónica, 13

Boswell, James, 4, 203

Bourdieu, Pierre, 17, 19, 30–31, 33, 38, 124

Bowers, Toni, 94

breastfeeding, 22, 170, 182

Bree, Linda, 137

Briquet, Fortunée, 83

Broad, Jacqueline, 59

Broglie, Gabriel de, 160

Brooke, Frances, 5, 7, 16, 154–55, 205; *The History of Emily Montague*, 154, 174, 177, 206

Brouard-Arends, Isabelle, 11

Brown, Garrett Wallace, 210

Brown, Hilary, 48, 72, 74–75, 103, 129, 225n9

Brown, Penny, 132–33, 153

Brown, Virginia, 52

Burgerhart, Sara, 164, 166–68, 172–73, 178–79, 181, 183, 234n9. *See also* translators

Burney, Frances (Madame d'Arblay) 1–4, 7,

French women writers, 7–8, 16–17, 45, 84–85, 103
friendship, 18, 68, 115, 136, 162, 166–67, 170, 174, 183, 201, 215, 232n16; between writers, 3, 9, 10, 61, 166–67, 170, 174, 183; community of, 66, 71, 80, 138–42; ending, 186–87; female, 22, 29, 51, 57–59, 66, 74, 183; group, 147, 215; international, 51, 157, 160, 201; language and, 117; marriage and, 89, 107, 109; satire of women's learning and, 58, 134; "virtuous" 59, 68
Fronius, Helen, 3, 45, 233n32
Furniss, Tom, 206

Gallagher, Catherine, 4, 82
Gambara, Veronica, 56–57
garden, 22, 55, 162, 184; botanical, 169; "city or garden of ladies," 86, 171; women's conversational space, as 57–58, 138. See also city of ladies
Garrick, David, 5–7
Garwood, Rebecca, 206
Gélieu, Isabelle de, 6, 220–22
gendered oppression, 163, 168, 173, 178
genius, 2; female, 17, 83, 194; female demurral of 155–56; male, 3, 160; male/individual model of, 3, 15, 126, 161; national, 43, 183; theory of, 39. See also exceptionalism
Genlis, Stéphanie-Félicité de, 5, 6, 8–10, 24–27, 29–30, 36, 76, 79, 85–86, 115, 136, 143, 148–49, 153–54, 159–60, 165, 186–87, 190, 201, 206, 233n26
genre, 6, 31, 44, 84, 91, 101, 146; bias, 13; classical and minor, 32, 50; educational, 131; epistolary, 75; fiction, 31; gender and, 32, 50, 159, 216; of historical novel, 199; literary history and, 28; of psychological novel, 89, 103; split, 96; of travel writing, 163
German women writers, 8–9, 42, 45, 207–11, 220–23
Gilleir, Anke, 12
Gilroy, Paul, 190, 198
Goethe, Johann Wolfgang von, 3–4, 43–44, 219–20, 222
Goodman, Dena, 75
Gosse, Pierre (publisher) 3, 157
Gothic, 12, 25, 190, 197–98, 214
Gottsched, Luise, 6, 64, 74–75, 103, 129
Graffigny, Françoise de, 15, 87–88, 94, 103–12, 115–17, 123, 136, 155, 190, 197, 205, 230n11, 231n16

Gray, Lady Jane, 55, 67
Greer, Donald, 188
Grey, Jill E. 137
Griffiths, Elystan, 9, 46
Guattari, Félix, 38, 199
Guest, Harriet, 37, 198
Gutwirth, Madelyn, 190, 234n13

habitus, 28; and emergence of women's writing, 13; male, 32; women's, 40, 127–28, 161, 143, 204, 206–7; writer's, 31, 124
hair, 1, 3, 9, 23, 156, 160, 167, 192, 195
Hamilton, Mary, 10
Hampsten, Elizabeth, 60
Havelange, Isabelle de, 49, 148,
Hays, Mary, 42, 48, 52, 56, 58, 61–62, 68, 75, 79, 82, 86, 187
Haywood, Eliza, 4, 33–34, 79–80
Hazlitt, William, 100
Henrietta, Princess of England, 76, 78
Herman, Jan, 205
heroine: colonial 16, 217–18; connection to women writers' biography, 18, 47, 221; exceptionalism and, 18, 29, 38; heroine's story, 21–22, 87, 113, 215; hybrid, 16, 183, 195–96, 217; and local girls, 4, 16, 18–9, 38–39, 183, 189, 200, 207, 218; sentimental, 167–68, 175, 193, 213; supranational, 115, 171–78, 183; and translation 111, 196; transnational, 170, 178, 185; and travel, 77, 114, 177
herstory, 14, 23
Hesse, Carla, 45, 127, 187, 209–10, 216, 226n18, 232n7, 234n12, 235n2
Heuer, Imke, 136
Heuvel, Danielle van den, 166
Hirsch, Marianne, 222
Hogle, Jerrold, 197
home, 2, 25–26, 162, 203, 205; discomfort of, 190, 200; as environment for schooling girls, 126, 131; as exile, 190, 199; lack of, 184–85, 188; leaving, 173, 162, 165, 173, 183; as microcosm, 153; question of, 163; returning, 111, 186, 195; text-based, 117; travel and, 105, 163, 204; of women's writing, 16, 18. See also exile
Hoobius, Johanna, 65
hospitality, 156, 205, 207, 215, 235n10; cosmopolitanism and, 209–10, 213
Huber, Therese, 16, 207, 209–15, 221–22, 235n8, 236n22. See also translators

Watt, Helga, 28
Watts, J., 78
Wenger, Étienne, 16, 35, 40, 123
Werken, Margareta Geertruid van der
  (Madame de Cambon), 153, 167
widowhood, 22
William V., 3, 156
Williams, Helen Maria, 20, 206, 217
Wollstonecraft, Mary, 15, 21, 37–38, 120, 124,
  149, 153–54, 205–6, 215, 218–19
woman question, the, 46–47, 52, 59, 63. *See
  also* querelle des femmes
women readers, 1, 11–12, 19, 21, 23, 28, 67, 142,

188; international community, 9, 125, 135,
153, 228n14; languages, and, 15, 85; loyal
group of, 39; market sector of, ix, 28, 55;
repetition and, 119, 122–23; translation,
and, 36, 37, 117
women's literary circle, 31, 37, 77, 68, 205. *See
also* conversation circle
world literature, 39, 43, 45; Goethe, and 43,
219; language/capital of, 17, 45; translation
and, 2; women's writing and, ix, 2, 3, 13–14,
19, 39, 219, 221
writing back, 14, 104
Wyett, Jodi, 175

Acknowledgments

In developing *Heroines and Local Girls,* I have benefited from generations of feminist scholarship on writing by women, not all of which is explicitly acknowledged here but which forms the warp and weft of my work. The discussion of Germaine de Staël and Frances Burney in Chapter 5 first appeared as the fifth chapter of "The Space of British Exile in Frances Burney's *The Wanderer* and Germaine de Staël's *Corinne*" (pages 85–99) in *Gender and Space in British Literature* published in 2014. I appreciate the opportunity granted by the Taylor and Francis Group to present it here. The editors of that volume, especially Mona Narain, provided insights that have helped shape my understanding of the global eighteenth century. Margaretmary Daley kindly shared her then unpublished work, "German Julies? Rousseauvian Protagonists in the Female Bildungsroman." Margaret Waller offered generous encouragement. At conferences and in her books, Alessa Johns's knowledge of British and German women's writing and cultural transfer has helped shape my research, as is evident. Not surprisingly, given that they are part of a network around John Bender, the extended American Society for Eighteenth-Century Studies Stanford lunch crew represents the best combination of reason and conviviality.

Theobald Walker kindly provided a more polished English version of Maria Romero's Spanish translation of *Lettres d'une Péruvienne* than I would have mustered. I am grateful to Ineke Janse for allowing me to dive into her thoughtful thesis *Madame de La Fite: Une éducatrice et un intermédiaire culturel du XVIIIe siècle,* as well as to James ter Beek, Information Services Department, Leiden University Libraries, who went out of his way to help me contact Ms. Janse. My colleague Emma Trentman pointed me to the work of Bonnie Norton at a key time. Anita Obermeier and the Feminist Research Institute at the University of New Mexico (UNM) provided a timely audience and support. Brynn Shaw created order in my herd of citations. Allegra Caldera provided excellent assistance in the final stages. Lastly,

I am grateful to the anonymous readers for the University of Pennsylvania Press and to editor Jerome Singerman, production editor Lily Palladino, and copy editor Pat Wieland, who each in their own ways deftly introduced corrections and calls for precision.

My current and former students, graduate and undergraduate, have stimulated thoughts that have found their way into this book in myriad ways. My thanks to Alain Antoine's careful excavation of the layers of Marana's *Turkish Spy*, Susmitha Udayan's rare ethical commitment to understanding contemporary refugee narratives, Marijn Kaplan's energetic flair for tracing the archival record of texts by Marie-Jeanne Riccoboni and Françoise de Graffigny, and Marie Chantal Mofin Noussi's focused reading with me of the sexual violence subtext in *Lettres d'une Péruvienne*. From different angles, Fu-Ying Chuang and Andrea Mays helped me think about literary practices of attachment.

Several of my delightful colleagues at UNM have somehow known how to offer the right words of intellectual help at just the right moment. Susanne Baackmann, Katja Schroeter, Marina Peters-Newell, Stephen Bishop, and Carmen Nocentelli have shown kindness inside and outside of the halls of Ortega. Pim Higginson helped push this to the finish line with warmth and wit. It is hard to know how to show enough appreciation to Evelyn Harris, Elvine Bologa, and Eva Sanchez for their spirited support of departmental life.

During the evolution of this book, I have been blessed with friends and family beyond compare. I thank Linda Garber for reading early chapters. Linda Garber, Barbara Blinick, Erin Carlston, Carisa Showden, Margot Keener, Anne Keener, and Elizabeth Wahl have given me the best lessons in feminism and fellowship to be had on the planet. Dorsy Baumgartner, Lynn Hicks, and Jane Epstein demonstrate their mastery of the art of friendship morning, noon, and night. The extended circle of Lost Valley around the Strohls has provided magical companionship. The generosity and kindness of Aimee Lee Cheek and William Cheek, scholars' scholars, leave me wordless. Eliza Ennis and Quinn Ennis have shown an inexplicable faith in this project while pursuing their own with an ambition that is my model. This book is dedicated to Matthew Shields Ennis who built a pathway for me by the sweat of his brow. May I do the same for him.